Praise for *Managing the Unmanageable: Rules, Tools, and Insights for Managing Software People and Teams*

"Lichty and Mantle have assembled a guide that will help you hire, motivate, and mentor a software development team that functions at the highest level. Their rules of thumb and coaching advice form a great blueprint for new and experienced software engineering managers alike."

—TOM CONRAD, CTO, *Pandora*

"I wish I'd had this material available years ago. I see lots and lots of 'meat' in here that I'll use over and over again as I try to become a better manager. The writing style is right on, and I love the personal anecdotes."

—STEVE JOHNSON, VP, *Custom Solutions, DigitalFish*

"Managing the Unmanageable is a well-written, must-have reference book for anyone serious about building sustainable software teams that consistently deliver high-quality solutions that meet expectations. It is loaded with incredibly useful and practical tips and tricks to deal with real-life situations commonly encountered by software managers anywhere in the world. It tearlessly peels back the onion layers of the process of managing software developers—whether a handful of co-located programmers or thousands dispersed across the world—through a balance of battle-tested approaches and keen understanding of the various personalities and backgrounds of software team members. Finally, a book on software engineering that focuses on the manager's dilemma of making a team of programmers work efficiently together. Every single software manager should have it on their bookshelf."

—PHAC LE TUAN, CTO, *Reepeet, and CEO, PaceWorks*

"Becoming a great engineering leader requires more than technical know-how; Ron and Mickey's book provides a practical cookbook for the important softer side of engineering leadership, which can be applied to any software development organization."

—PAUL MELMON, VP of Engineering, *NICE Systems*

"EXCELLENT. Well-structured, logical, filled with great personal color and many little gems. You guys have done a great job here. Terrific balance between theory and practice, rich with info."

—JOE KLEINSCHMIDT, CTO and cofounder, *Leverage Software*

"I started reading the nuggets section and it took fewer than four pages to improve my thinking. What struck me about the nuggets was that I could sense the genesis of this book: two masters of their craft learning from each other. Most books feel like a teacher describing a sterile version of what 'ought to be done' that leaves you wondering, 'Will this work in the "real world"?' Reading the nuggets felt like the sort of guidance that I would get from a trusted mentor. A mentor who I not only trusted, but one who trusted me to take the wisdom, understand its limits, and apply it correctly. It's concentrated like a Reader's Digest for technical management wisdom."

—MIKE FAUZY, President and CTO, 1stMediCall LLC

"Managing the Unmanageable is a great collection of sometimes-obvious and sometimes-not-obvious guidance for software managers. I wish that I had had this book when I first started managing teams, and it still is illuminating. For programmers who step into management, the hardest thing is to learn the soft skills. Ron and Mickey do a great job of illustrating not just the why but also the how."

—BILL HOFMANN, Vice President of Engineering, Klamr.to

"Unique dialogue around the human aspects of software development that is very much overdue."

—MARK FRIEDMAN, CEO and founder, GreenAxle Solutions

". . . [W]hat to do on the new employee's first day of work seems unique and very helpful!"

—STEVEN FLANNES, PH.D., Principal, Flannes & Associates

"The book provides insight to a unique group of people: programmers. Companies around the planet have and are still struggling with how to best develop software products. Managing programmers is at the heart of developing software products successfully. Many project and organization leaders are ill-equipped to deal with programmers and software development in general. I think this book can bring insight to leaders of software organizations and help them understand and even get inside the head of programmers and therefore be more effective leaders."

—MICHAEL MAITLAND, CEO (geek-in-charge), WhereTheGeeksRoam

Managing the Unmanageable

Managing the Unmanageable

Rules, Tools, and Insights for Managing Software People and Teams

MICKEY W. MANTLE

RON LICHTY

✦✦Addison-Wesley

Upper Saddle River, NJ • Boston • Indianapolis • San Francisco
New York • Toronto • Montreal • London • Munich • Paris • Madrid
Capetown • Sydney • Tokyo • Singapore • Mexico City

Many of the designations used by manufacturers and sellers to distinguish their products are claimed as trademarks. Where those designations appear in this book, and the publisher was aware of a trademark claim, the designations have been printed with initial capital letters or in all capitals.

The authors and publisher have taken care in the preparation of this book, but make no expressed or implied warranty of any kind and assume no responsibility for errors or omissions. No liability is assumed for incidental or consequential damages in connection with or arising out of the use of the information or programs contained herein.

For information about buying this title in bulk quantities, or for special sales opportunities (which may include electronic versions; custom cover designs; and content particular to your business, training goals, marketing focus, or branding interests), please contact our corporate sales department at corpsales@pearsoned.com or (800) 382-3419.

For government sales inquiries, please contact governmentsales@pearsoned.com.

For questions about sales outside the U.S., please contact intlcs@pearson.com.

Visit us on the Web: informit.com/aw

Library of Congress Cataloging-in-Publication Data

Mantle, Mickey W.
  Managing the unmanageable : rules, tools, and insights for managing software people and teams / Mickey W. Mantle, Ron Lichty.
     p.   cm.
  Includes index.
  ISBN 978-0-321-82203-1 (pbk. : alk. paper)
  1. Computer programmers—Supervision of. 2. Computer software developers—Supervision of. 3. Electronic data processing personnel—Supervision of. 4. Information technology projects—Management. I. Lichty, Ron. II. Title.
  HD8039.D37M36 2013
  005.068'3—dc23

                                                                                            2012023731

ISBN-13: 978-0-321-82203-1
ISBN-10:   0-321-82203-X

4   17

*To programmers everywhere, and particularly those
I've managed, who really make things happen
but rarely wind up in the limelight*

—Mickey

*To my children, Jean and Mike, who provided
my best management training, and who remain
a source of insight, inspiration, and delight*

—Ron

Contents

Preface

ALL TOO OFTEN, SOFTWARE DEVELOPMENT IS DEEMED UNMANAGEABLE. The news abounds with stories of software projects that have run ridiculously over schedule and budget. While strides made in formalizing the practice of software development have improved the situation, they have not solved the problem. Given that our craft has amassed over 60 years of experience and our industry has spent enormous numbers of hours and dollars/yen/rupees/euros trying to bring this discipline under control, how can it be that software development remains so unmanageable?

In this book we answer that persistent question with a simple observation: You first must learn the craft of managing programmers and software teams. That is, you must learn to understand your people—how to hire them, motivate them, and lead them to develop and deliver great products. Based on our own experience, and that of effective managers we have known in virtually every type of software business, we aim here to show you how. Combined, we have spent over 70 years working on and delivering a wide spectrum of software programs and projects, over 55 of those years managing the programmers and teams that delivered them. We hope that this book will help you to avoid many of the mistakes we have made, as well as to leverage for your own success the insights and skills we have learned.

Early in our careers as programmers, we both read Fred Brooks's 1975 book *The Mythical Man-Month*. An instant classic among programmers, it is full of wisdom still relevant today and is widely regarded as a definitive work in the art of software management. Like many others who read it, we found the most memorable parts to be Brooks's one-line nuggets of wisdom such as, *"Adding manpower to a late software project makes it later."* We can't recall the number of times we've used this quote when managing software projects. The desire to find other such memorable rules of thumb was the inspiration and driving force behind the writing of this book.

We were already seasoned managers when, as friends, we began meeting regularly to compare notes on our current work and software development challenges. We found ourselves getting help from each other and sharing an occasional nugget of wisdom or rule of thumb, which we would then take back to our jobs, integrate into our management approach, and share with our teams. We gleaned rules and nuggets from the books we read and the Web sites we surfed, but we never found a collection of them specific to managing programmers and teams developing software. Eventually our own desire to have such a collection led to our decision to write this book.

A broader perspective emerged as we began writing and talked to managers, directors, and CTOs. It became clear that we could draw from the breadth of our industry experience to offer considerably more than the rules of thumb we'd collected. We could also share the tools we'd developed and the insights we'd gleaned from working in start-ups and in organizations of every size.

There are certainly areas we haven't touched in our careers—domains like large-scale government contracting and defense systems. But our experience is relevant to most companies developing software today, including those companies whose managers are working on the edge of innovation. That latter group tends to be young and is seldom offered any formal management training or organizational support—or has time for it anyway. Unfortunately, that's how all too many managers learn today—on the job.

We wanted to write a book that could be a mentor of sorts for programming managers—a book filled with insights, stories, and guidance gained from years of learning the hard way how to do it successfully.

We realized we could also share the tools we have developed over the years that make managing easier—tools such as job descriptions, rankings spreadsheets, project workbooks, team technology inventories, programmer first-day schedule templates, and hiring checklists. They can save managers many hours developing tools from scratch when they find themselves working in organizations that are too immature to provide their people with the tools they need (all too common, unfortunately, in the fast-moving world of software development). These are the tools we wished we'd had when we first started managing.

We wondered if there needed to be another book about software development. Surely—with no end of books, articles, and Web sites about engineering software, managing process, and managing projects—some number of gifted engineering managers must have shared their secrets. Yet we found scant more examples focused on managing programmers and software development teams than we had when we began our careers.

There is no methodology for the newly anointed development manager charged with managing, leading, guiding, and reviewing the performance of a team of programmers—often, the team he[1] was on just days before. There are no off-the-shelf approaches. Unlike project managers, who devote hours and hours of study toward certification in their chosen career path, development managers often win their management roles primarily from having been stellar coders while displaying a modicum of people skills.

Among the books we did find, there were none that contained the kinds of behind-the-scenes stories and anecdotes we have incorporated into this book—stories and anecdotes that speak directly to how to handle specific situations that managers face.

Organization of the Book

In the chapters of this book we share our hard-won experience gained from programming, managing, and delivering software spanning two managerial lifetimes of companies and situations. We have distilled our insights into nine chapters sprinkled with anecdotes from our experience as well as rules of thumb and nuggets of wisdom.

Chapter 1 reviews why programmers are special when it comes to managing them as individuals and managing them as teams. It's thinking about the qualities that characterize programmers that makes it obvious why you can't just pick up any book on management to start managing a team of programmers.

Chapter 2 provides a number of lenses through which to view the programmers on your teams that will help you see the individuality each of them brings—and inform your managing each of them uniquely.

Chapter 3 is a step-by-step guide to finding, recruiting, and hiring great programmers. Early readers of this chapter found themselves tearing it out of the manuscript to use separately. You may, too, but you'll leverage it best

---

1. When we began writing this book, we tried to make our references to people gender neutral; that is, we tried "s/he" instead of "he," we tried substituting "he and she," and then we tried alternating between "he" and "she." In the end we decided that the prose read better if we stuck to the masculine pronoun "he" throughout. We recognize and rejoice that there are many talented women who manage programmers. We have worked with and for them ourselves. If anyone has a more inclusive solution for this challenge, please let us know and we will seriously consider all creative possibilities in our future writing.

from the context of the prior two chapters—knowing just who it is you're hiring—and from incorporating culture and motivation from Chapters 7 and 8.

Chapter 4 counsels how to keep candidates' enthusiasm between "yes" and start; prevent "buyer's remorse"; and, when they do arrive, integrate them quickly, effectively, and productively into your processes and practices. New managers tend to think their recruiting role is finished when a candidate accepts an offer, but too many have learned otherwise when a candidate failed to show up for their first day, floundered in fusing with the team, or never became productive.

Chapter 5 walks through the core of management—managing down. These are the mechanics and how-to of the day-to-day with your team, the tasks and interactions to successfully manage programmers.

In an interlude inserted between Chapters 5 and 6 we've collected hundreds of rules of thumb and nuggets of wisdom that have proven valuable to us over the years, denoted by lightly shaded pages for ease of access. We collected them from a broad cross section of programmers, development managers, and software luminaries.[2] The wisdom drawn from these adages, used judiciously, can help you make a point, win an argument, reframe a conversation, or defuse a tense discussion with a bit of humor that still drives your position home.

Chapter 6 addresses the fact that success as a programming manager also demands that you become skillful at managing up—managing your boss (and possibly his boss); managing out—managing your relationships with your peers, leveraging other departments or folks within your company, and marshaling external resources and relationships; and finally managing yourself—your priorities, your style, your time, your growth, your life.

Chapter 7 turns the focus back to the team and the critical task of motivating programmers to accomplish great feats and deliver difficult projects. The chapter opens with grounding in the motivational theories of Maslow, McGregor, and Herzberg. The differentiation of motivators from demotivators—they are very different, contrary to popular thinking—was essential to our own managerial growth. Given that each programmer is unique, there's no motivational silver bullet, but our framework can help

---

2. If we have misattributed a rule of thumb or quote, we apologize in advance (and please let us know). Some of them are available only through word of mouth or indirect sources, making completely accurate attribution almost impossible. The titles given in the attributions are those for which the person is best known or, in many cases, their title when we knew them and heard their insights directly.

you think about ways to motivate—and how to recognize and avoid the potholes that demotivate—your team.

Chapter 8 provides context to think about your corporate culture and about how you can create the development subculture you need for success within even the most toxic of corporate cultures. Too few managers realize their critical role in creating a team culture that supports success. Chapters 5 and 6 cover the mechanics basic to managing, but Chapters 7 and 8 cover the two subtle sets of soft skills that can differentiate your management and help pave your way to success.

Chapter 9 returns to basics. The eight preceding chapters ultimately point to this objective: delivering software successfully. This chapter is not about project management but about the role seldom addressed: the team manager's essential role in delivery. Success depends on synthesizing all the skills and efforts outlined in the previous chapters, as well as a mindset that is all its own.

The *Tools* section provides a collection of useful tools, among them checklists, forms, reports, and so on, that we devised to aid our efforts to recruit, hire, and effectively manage and motivate programmers to deliver quality software successfully. We're certain they will aid your efforts as well and save you the time of having to create them anew. These tools are available online at www.managingtheunmanageable.net.

Lessons Learned

Programmers and software teams need not be unmanageable, but it takes talented managers who are dedicated to doing the hard work of managing seemingly unmanageable personalities to do it successfully. We can certainly affirm that writing this—and the rules, tools, and conversations we shared as we transformed our thinking into words—made both of us better managers, made our jobs easier, made our teams happier, and made our projects more successful. We hope the rules, tools, and insights we have provided in this book will make your jobs easier, as well.

Acknowledgments

There are many people to thank who have helped us to write this book. First and foremost, we want to thank our wives for encouraging us in our efforts to draft, redraft, and craft this book. Without their patience, help, and advice this book would not have been possible. Second, we want to thank Peter Gordon and Kim Boedigheimer of Addison-Wesley for their continued support and advice over the years and having faith that the work we would create was worth their time and energy to help make it happen. Peter's advice on organizing the book was especially helpful in the late stages. Next, we must thank the many originators of the rules of thumb that we have included in this work. The sage wisdom that they repeatedly imparted was the primary motivation for this book, and we marvel at the depth of insight that can be conveyed in so few words.

We must also thank the many reviewers who spent considerable time and effort to provide detailed feedback that helped guide us to revise and improve our writing over the years. Among them were Brad Appleton, Carol Hoover, Carrie Butler, Clark Dodsworth, Daniel J. Paulish, David Vydra, Dr. Dinesh Kulkarni, George Ludwig, Harinath V. Thummalapalli, Jean Doyle, Joe Kleinschmidt, Kinnar Vora, Margo Kannenberg, Mark Friedman, Michael Maitland, Patrick Bailey, Rama Chetlapalli, Stefano Pacifico, Steve Johnson, Steven Flannes, and others who remained anonymous to us. This work is definitely better because of their thoughtful feedback.

Finally, we would like to thank the legions of programmers, managers, and executives with whom we have worked in all the various companies throughout our careers. It is because of them, and the experiences we gained working with them, that this book is possible.

Mickey W. Mantle
Ron Lichty
July 2012

About the Authors

MICKEY AND RON'S SOFTWARE CAREERS HAVE SPANNED system software, multimedia, interface development, shrink-wrapped products, software-as-a-service, embedded devices, IT, Internet applications, professional services, and data warehousing and analytics, but they have seldom found the problems that plague software development to be domain or channel specific.

While roadblocks have much in common, they also always seem to be unique—a uniqueness that more often than not derives from the challenges, pressures, and organic development of the organizations they're part of, rather than from any differences in technology or industry.

Mickey W. Mantle

Mickey has been developing software for over 40 years, creating hardware and software products and managing development teams. After graduating from the University of Utah (where he was contemporary with computer industry notables such as the founders of WordPerfect, Silicon Graphics, Netscape, Adobe Systems, and Pixar), Mickey had his first job in 1971 developing the overall control software and real-time robotic controls for a six-acre aircraft rework facility for the U.S. Navy at Kenway Engineering (later Eaton-Kenway). He thereafter joined 3-D computer graphics pioneer Evans & Sutherland (E&S) where he coauthored the original 3-D graphics library that paved the way for Silicon Graphics's GL, which has since become OpenGL. At E&S he was a contributor to many notable computer graphics products and first started managing programmers and programming teams.

After leaving E&S in 1984, Mickey joined Formative Technologies, a spin-off from Carnegie Mellon University, where he worked with the industry's first workstations (PERQ and Sun Microsystems) dealing with large-scale bit-mapped graphics for mapping and CAD applications. But his heart was in 3-D graphics, and he was hired by Pixar shortly after it was bought by Steve Jobs and spun out of Lucasfilm Ltd. in 1986. At Pixar, Mickey managed the development of all of the software for their external products, including the Pixar Image Computer, the Pixar Medical Imaging System, and RenderMan. RenderMan is the gold standard of 3-D photorealistic rendering software and by 2010 had been used on every Visual Effects Academy Award Winner for the past 15 years; 47 out of the last 50 nominees for Visual Effects had chosen Pixar's RenderMan.

Mickey left Pixar in 1991, as their focus shifted to making feature-length 3-D animated films and away from external software products, and was recruited to Brøderbund Software as Vice President of Engineering/CTO. At Brøderbund he managed a vast development organization including applications and system programming, art and animation, sound design and music composition, and quality assurance that produced numerous award-winning PC/Mac games such as *Where in the World Is Carmen Sandiego?*, *Kid Pix*, *Myst*, and *Living Books*.

In late 1997 Mickey joined International Microcomputer Software, Inc., as Vice President of R&D/CTO, where he managed on-site and offshore development and support for numerous Windows/Mac applications such as MasterClips and professional-level products such as TurboCAD.

In 1999 Mickey joined Gracenote where he was Senior Vice President of Development (since 2008 Gracenote has been a wholly owned subsidiary of Sony). At Gracenote he managed all development, operations, and professional services associated with the pioneering Web-based CDDB music information service that enables digital music player applications such as iTunes, WinAmp, Sonic Stage, and hundreds of others. Gracenote's products utilize technology ranging from Web services and relational databases to embedded systems and mobile applications, giving him a unique perspective on the wide-ranging needs of the various types of software developed today. He retired from Gracenote in early 2011 to finish this book, develop mobile/tablet applications, and consult with a variety of companies and organizations regarding the management of software people and teams.

His experience includes directing R&D teams around the world and managing multidisciplinary teams working 24/7 to deliver successful products. With experience in selecting, establishing, and managing offshore development organizations in India, Russia, Canada, and Japan, he brings insight into the challenges of managing software development using diverse staff and teams that are hours and oceans apart.

Ron Lichty

Ron has been developing software for 30 years, over 20 of them as a Development Manager, Director of Engineering, and Vice President of Engineering. This followed his first career as a writer in New York, Wyoming, and California, during which he wrote hundreds of articles, published scores of photographs, and authored two books. His software development career began at Softwest in the heart of California's Silicon Valley, coding word-processing products, programming compiler code generators, crafting embedded microcontroller devices like SmartCard-based postage meters and magnetic-keycard hotel locking systems, and designing and developing the computer animation demo that Apple used to launch and promote a new line of personal computers. He was awarded software patents for compression algorithms and wrote two widely used programming texts.

Recruited to Apple in 1988, Ron product-managed Apple's development tools, then led the Finder and Applications groups for the Apple II and Macintosh product lines, managing delivery of Apple's "special sauce," its user interface.

In 1994 Berkeley Systems recruited Ron to direct development of the then most widely used consumer software in the world, the *After Dark* screen saver line, to make engineering predictable and repeatable for the seven development teams creating its entertainment products. Brought into Fujitsu to make sense of its long-overdue *WorldsAway* entertainment product, he lopped off six months of overengineering to take it live in just 11 weeks.

Ron then led software development of the first investor tools on Schwab .com, part of remaking a bricks-and-mortar discount brokerage into the premier name in online financial services. He was promoted to Schwab Vice President while leading his CIO's three-year technology initiative to migrate software development across all business units from any-language-goes to a single, cost-effective platform company-wide.

Since Schwab, he has been a Vice President of Engineering and Vice President of Products both as an employee and as a consultant, and he has continued to focus on making software development "hum." He headed technology for the California offices of Avenue A | Razorfish, the largest Internet professional services organization in the world; products and development for Forensic Logic, the crime detection and prevention company; engineering for Socialtext, the first commercial wiki company; engineering of the consumer ZoneAlarm line for Check Point; and publisher services for HighWire, the largest Internet provider for scholarly publishing. In consulting engagements in America and Europe, he has helped development groups overcome roadblocks, untangle organizational knots, and become more productive.

Ron's developer conference and professional group talks and webinars include implementing Agile and Scrum; the importance of user groups, teamwork, and community; and transforming software development from chaos to clarity. He has been an adviser to a half-dozen start-ups. He cochairs SVForum's Emerging Technology SIG; founded its Software Architecture SIG; chaired East Bay Innovation Group's Software Management Best Practices SIG; and was a member of the board of SVForum, Silicon Valley's largest and oldest developer organization.

1

Why Programmers Seem Unmanageable

PROGRAMMING HAS BEEN A SERIOUS PROFESSION for well over 60 years. The number of people now employed as programmers is in the millions in the United States and in the many millions throughout the world. And those numbers do not include the legions of students and hobbyists who program computers seriously but are not employed or paid to do so.

In spite of the history and the magnitude of the numbers, "software engineering" has a reputation for being unmanageable. There are several reasons for this.

Programming as a serious profession is different from related engineering professions, such as electrical or civil engineering. Since 1968[1] attempts have been made to apply the term *software engineering* to the art of programming. But writing a new program from scratch is much more akin to writing a novel than to the established practices of civil or electrical engineering. New programs frequently begin with the equivalent of a blank sheet of paper, whereas engineering projects are typically assembled from libraries of components and rigorous codes of acceptability. We shall refer to "software engineering" as programming in this book because it continues to be much more a craft than a rigidly defined engineering discipline.

....

Writing a new program from scratch is akin to writing a novel.

---

1. It was in 1968 that the term was coined to describe "the application of a systematic, disciplined, quantifiable approach to the development, operation, and maintenance of software." See "Software's Chronic Crisis," *Scientific American*, September 1994.

Second, anyone can be a programmer. You do not need a formal education to be a programmer, and there are no required certification standards or tests.[2] All you need is a job as a programmer.[3]

Third, and in part as a result of the first two reasons, though many steps have been taken to formalize the process of software engineering (e.g., CMMI[4] Levels 1–5), these steps have had minimal impact. Much of the software that continues to be developed by the legions of programmers does not follow such formalized frameworks. And even when it does, the result has improved the process but not transformed programming into an engineering discipline. Plus, the formalized frameworks address only the process of making software, not how to manage programmers. Following processes only minimally makes the job of managing programmers easier. Programming managers are still left to their own devices to manage their staff of programmers effectively.

The fact is that while there are lots of books, articles, and Web sites about software engineering and managing the software development process, there are scant examples of how to manage programmers effectively. As any manager of a baseball team will tell you, managing the mechanics of baseball is easy compared to managing the personalities. So it also is with managing programmers.

Managing programmers has been a challenge since the early days of computers, as illustrated by this 1961 quote from Grace Hopper, who became one of the world's first programmers during WWII:

> *Programmers are a very curious group . . . They arose very quickly, became a profession very rapidly, and were all too soon infected with a certain amount of resistance to change. The very programmers whom I have heard almost castigate*

---

2. The Association for Computing Machinery (ACM) had a professional certification program in the early 1980s, which was discontinued. The ACM examined the possibility of professional certification of software engineers in the late 1990s but decided that such certification was inappropriate for the professional industrial practice of software engineering. See "A Summary of the ACM Position on Software Engineering as a Licensed Engineering Profession," www.acm.org/public-policy.

3. Many organizations such as Microsoft, Apple, Cisco, and others provide certification courses and tests that are widely used throughout the industry, but these apply to specific technologies or domains of expertise. They may be required for a specific job but are not required throughout the industry.

4. Capability Maturity Model Integration (CMMI) is a process improvement approach developed by the Software Engineering Institute (SEI) that provides organizations with essential elements of effective processes that ultimately improve their performance. See www.sei.cmu.edu/cmmi.

a customer because he would not change his system of doing business are the same people who at times walk into my office and say, "But we have always done it this way." It is for this reason that I now have a counterclockwise clock hanging in my office.[5]

A first step in managing programmers is to better understand them. What is it that attracts these millions of people to the "art of computer programming"? The answer is sometimes quite simple—it's a job that pays pretty well and lets you work indoors all day. However, as many programmers can tell you, the answer is usually not quite that simple. The people who would give that simple answer often don't last as programmers.

In fact, it takes a certain kind of person to be a programmer, and a very special kind of person to be a great programmer. Understanding what it takes to be a great programmer begins with understanding what programmers do.

What Do Programmers Do?

First and perhaps foremost, programmers have fun! Fred Brooks, in one of the classics of software engineering, *The Mythical Man-Month*,[6] wrote brilliantly of why programming is fun:

- "First is the sheer joy of making things . . ."
- "Second is the pleasure of making things that are useful to other people . . ."
- "Third is the fascination of fashioning complex puzzle-like objects of interlocking moving parts and watching them work in subtle cycles . . ."
- "Fourth is the joy of always learning, which springs from the non-repeating nature of the task . . ."
- "Finally, there is the delight of working in such a tractable medium. The programmer, like the poet, works only slightly removed from pure thought-stuff."

---

5. Quoted in G. Pascal Zachary, *Show-Stopper!: The Breakneck Race to Create Windows NT and the Next Generation at Microsoft* (The Free Press/Simon & Schuster, 1994).

6. Frederick P. Brooks Jr., *The Mythical Man-Month, Anniversary Edition* (Addison-Wesley, 1995; originally published in 1975). This classic book on software development is a must-read for anyone who is managing programmers and/or software development projects.

If having fun is what most programmers do, you may begin to understand why managing programmers is so challenging. If you are being paid to have fun, why would you want to be managed? Being managed takes part of the fun out of the work!

This also explains why it is often so hard to work with programmers. Before there were computers, many programmers would have been engineers, accountants, or educators. About 50 percent of the programmers we have hired over the years have fit into this category. However, the other 50 percent are harder to categorize. Many would have been artists, musicians, writers, or other "right-brained" people and are essentially more free-spirited. And more surprisingly, this "right-brained" group often produces the more talented programmers.[7]

Additionally, the fact that programmers work in a medium that is only "slightly removed from pure thought-stuff" encourages a free-spirited, undisciplined approach to programming that makes managing such programmers almost impossible. There are no widely used tools that impose a rigid, disciplined, comprehensive approach to designing and implementing a program. Rather, all too often programmers are allowed to start designing or even coding a program with a blank slate.

It is the necessity to blend these two disparate groups of programmers into a cohesive, effective software development team that creates many of the challenges in managing. Managing engineers is relatively straightforward compared to managing a bunch of artists, musicians, and writers. Without externally imposed processes or procedures, when left to their own devices, many programmers will jump in and just start writing code, designing as they go. Managers must cultivate a software development culture built upon solid development practices, or programming projects will likely fail.

Though programmers can be divided into groups, the key to managing them successfully is to recognize that they are individuals. Programmers truly are quite different from one another, and you must endeavor to play to the strengths of each while striving to improve, or at least neutralize, each individual's weaknesses. While this is a sound management principle in any field, it seems to be much more important when managing programmers.

---

7. Several industry leaders have openly expressed their opinion that musicians make terrific programmers. As a musician himself, Mickey heartily concurs with that opinion.

Even with good software practices and development processes, how do you know progress is being made when the work product is intangible? In almost all software the actual tangible results of a program (i.e., the printed reports, the data output, or even the user interface) are not directly proportional to the state of completion of the actual program. One of the great system programmers Mickey worked with at Evans & Sutherland designed and wrote every line of code of a very complicated device driver over a period of many months before compiling the program even once. At the other extreme, when Ron arrived at Fujitsu, the programming team had been telling management that the product was one week from being functionally complete every week for the previous three months. In both cases, there was no meaningful measure of progress that could predict successful completion. Even worse, a program can produce the desired results and be so poorly designed and/or executed that it cannot realistically be enhanced or maintained. These hidden, or intangible, aspects of the program may not be visible even to a seasoned programmer.

And frankly, many—perhaps most—programmers work on making changes to existing programs, the majority of which someone else wrote. Even if they themselves wrote a program, it was probably more than six months previously, so Eagleson's Law applies: "Any code of your own that you haven't looked at for six or more months might as well have been written by someone else." Which is to say, the code is gnarly and nearly impossible to figure out, and, again, there's no meaningful measure of progress that can predict successful completion.

Similarly, for too many managers (especially less technical managers, such as CEOs or CFOs) prototypes appear to be "done." The fact that software is so intangible makes it more difficult to judge its state of internal completion, regardless of the quality of the results the program produces. Through experience, tools, and looking "under the covers," managers must be able to gauge the actual progress of a program.

Ultimately it is best to avoid these problems by hiring great programmers —those special programmers who bring discipline and process to the art of producing computer programs. Are these great programmers artists, engineers, or craftsmen?

While there is much talk of the art of computer programming, few programmers would consider themselves artists in the purest sense of the word.

Similarly, while software engineering is a goal that we aspire to reach, few programmers today really are software engineers in the literal sense.

Though the IEEE[8] provides formalized certification programs for software engineers, in our experience not only are such programs ignored by most professional programmers, but these certification programs are largely unknown outside of academic circles and a very few companies. There is scant effort or desire among rank-and-file programmers to pursue the discipline of software engineering.[9]

What about "craftsmen"? A core group of programmers think that a better metaphor for programmers is that of a craftsman.[10] A craftsman doesn't start out as a master craftsman but rather must spend years as an apprentice and years as a journeyman and have proven skills and a portfolio to earn the title of master craftsman. Knowledge, experience, and a proven track record provide a means of tangible certification that cannot be easily assessed in a formal certification program. We think that this metaphor, more than others, suits the type of programmer we like to call a "great programmer."

What is it that makes a great programmer? It is much more than just raw programming talent. In fact, raw programming talent often detracts from the skills of the great programmer. Rather, a great programmer is a master of the medium and is methodical and disciplined. That is, a great programmer has an intuitive sense for structuring code and programs, is disciplined enough to design before coding, and writes code in a minimal amount of time that is clear, concise, functional, of high quality, and produces the desired result. In other words, a great programmer is a master craftsman of the medium.

Programmers who are motivated primarily by schedules, management pressure, or money are usually not great programmers. Most great programmers are actually motivated by a higher calling: making a difference in the world and making programs or products that people actually use. Great programmers want and need to work on projects that make a difference in the world. They want to feel their work is meaningful, even if only in some small way. Great programmers gravitate to companies and projects

---

8. The Institute of Electrical and Electronic Engineers (IEEE) professional society offers the Certified Software Development Professional (CSDP) certification, which is mostly based on practices outlined in the SWEBOK (Software Engineering Body of Knowledge, www.swebok.org). Whether such certifications should be sought is a topic that generates considerable debate, but it's worth noting that certification is the norm in "real" engineering fields.

9. For a pragmatic look at certification, see Jack Ganssle, "More on Certification," September 7, 2005, www.embedded.com/columns/embeddedpulse/170701175.

10. Pete McBreen, *Software Craftsmanship* (Addison-Wesley, 2001).

that fulfill their higher calling. Great programmers care intensely about what they are doing and work beyond normal limits to deliver desired results.

A great programmer can often be an order of magnitude (i.e., ten times or greater) more effective than an average competent programmer.

But there are too few great programmers in the world for every project team to have even just one. Furthermore, most teams cannot tolerate more than one or two great programmers in their midst. We find that we rely primarily on ordinary programmers, not truly great programmers, to create most programs and projects. The ordinary programmer, while competent and distinctly professional and very capable, may look at programming as a job.

The challenge, then, is how to find and hire a capable team of programmers, how to motivate and coach a few of them to be great programmers, how to manage the rest to deliver successful results, and how to deliver continuous improvement even if most or all of your team are merely competent.

Why Is Becoming a Successful Programming Manager Hard?

Most great programmers do not campaign to be managers of other programmers. Most ultimately recognize the need to have software managers but feel most comfortable allowing others to do the actual management. They are usually not truly happy managing people or projects.

Managing programmers is hard! The often-quoted line "Managing programmers is a lot like herding cats" captures the essence of why it is so hard to become an effective and successful programming manager. Cats are free-spirited, individualistic, wily, playful, curious, independent creatures. All of these adjectives can be applied to programmers as well.

In our experience highly capable software managers are rare. And it is the rare software manager who can actually succeed at and find joy in herding the free spirits who are the majority of programmers.

Because programmers are free spirits, typical motivational techniques are not usually successful. It is critical to be able to appeal to a programmer's sense of self and desire to change the world, in addition to providing the right amount of technical oversight and putting development practices and process in place. It requires a special type of manager, one who both understands how programmers work and understands the work, to be able both to effectively motivate them to perform exceptionally and to deliver results on time.

Unlike many jobs where compensation is a primary motivator, the work itself and the work environment tend to be much more important. Programming is a creative process that requires special handling to be done effectively. Good managers have to pay attention to these things while establishing a programming-positive culture, too.

As described throughout this book, becoming an effective and successful programming manager is possible, but we think it usually takes having been a good or great programmer to succeed as a programming manager.

Of course, that is usually part of the problem. Most programming managers were promoted to be managers because they were good or great programmers and showed some people skills—they demonstrated a capacity, and perhaps even an inclination, to direct the activity of other programmers.

Few programming managers have any formal management training, and what management experience they have is usually gained on the job and "under fire." Some of these rookie managers succeed. Some fail immediately. Many fail over time.

The ones who succeed are likely to have a mentor in their organization or network who can help guide them and protect them as they earn their stripes and make their mistakes along the way. Having been programmers and managers of programmers for almost 40 years, we have had the opportunity to hire and manage thousands of talented programmers and mentor many of them. We hope, with this book, to provide the kind of guidance a mentor would provide—to provide a surrogate mentor for those who must struggle alone to manage programmers.

This book does not and cannot "fix" programmers. They will continue to code before they design, and they will continue to produce tangible results only when necessary. Our goal is to provide some insights, suggestions, tools and techniques, and rules of thumb that may help you "herd the cats" you have on your software projects, and to successfully manage the seemingly unmanageable programmers on your team.

2

Understanding Programmers

PROGRAMMERS ARE VERY DIFFERENT from one another across many dimensions, something that you must be close to programming to fully appreciate. In most companies, the executive management views all programmers as being alike, which is a terrible mistake. Bill Gates at Microsoft and John Warnock at Adobe Systems avoided falling into this trap because both were programmers at heart.

Why does it matter? Maybe it shouldn't, but it does. After years of managing programmers we still marvel at the substantial differences among them, and how we must approach problems and motivation differently. To us, one thing is clear: In order to successfully manage programmers you must first understand who each programmer really is.

One thing to note, which is very important, is that in general we have found no great differences in programmers based on age, gender, ethnic group, or culture. Our experience with the hundreds of programmers we have hired or managed is that what differentiates programmers is what is inside each person, not outside attributes. Of course, training and experience have a bearing. But individual talents and innate characteristics are the real differentiators.

There are different ways to understand programmers. We approach this in several ways, by looking at programmers through different lenses. These are

- Programming disciplines
- Types of programmers
- Domain expertise

- Programmer job requirements and abilities
- Proximity and relationship
- Generational styles
- Personality styles

Programming Disciplines

The first way to think about programmers is to understand the various programming disciplines into which they can be grouped. We tend to think of these groupings as

- Client programmers
- Server programmers
- Database programmers
- Web developers and other scripters

There are, of course, many programming specialties that may not fit neatly into these programming groups. But in general, these four categories cover the vast majority of programmers in the world. Each of these types of programmers uses and focuses on different approaches to problems, different tools, and different deliverables. Some very talented programmers can do all of these tasks; however, it is more common that programmers *think* they can do all of these programming tasks but really do only one of them well.

Generally, we recommend that you staff different programmers for each of these different types of activities and don't expect any of your programmers to span more than one of them, or you will likely end up regretting that decision. Therefore, it is paramount that before you hire a programmer or staff a project, you clearly identify the types of programmers you need.

Client Programmers

A majority of all the programmers who have ever done programming are client programmers. The term *client* in this context refers to the location where the program resides and is often taken to be the end user's computer. The advent of the personal computer led to the development of innumerable "client programs"—word processors, spreadsheets, productivity applications, games, and utilities ranging from Microsoft's Word and Excel to Brøderbund's game Myst and Lemke's GraphicConverter utility. However, before there were dedicated personal computers, most of the programs that were written ran on a central system. The developers of programs that delivered "client results" to a dumb or intelligent terminal or via printed reports were client programmers as well.

With the proliferation of low-cost microprocessors, client programmers have expanded into developing and delivering embedded applications that run on game consoles, mobile phones, iPads, and other consumer and end user devices.

The reason for grouping all of these programmers together as client programmers is that they tend to have assignments where they have near-complete control over their resources. If a client programmer has a task to do, it is generally of finite scope with a defined set of deliverables for which the client programmer/team has clear responsibility and few dependencies other than on server-delivered data.

Server Programmers

The term *server* in this context refers not only to the location where the program resides but also to the fact that the program often is written to serve up information and data to remote clients. Server programs reside on machines that are generally remote from the end user, and most of these programs must be written to handle multiple activities from a number of clients at the same time. This creates a level of complexity that is often not part of the programs that client programmers must deliver. Server programs often must be written and deployed such that additional machines and resources can be added without changing the fundamental architecture of the program, which adds even more complexity to developing server programs.

With the advent of the Web, the term *client/server* has become synonymous with the manner in which a Web browser interacts with a Web server ("somewhere on the net"). The client-based Web browser is complex, but creating server programs that can provide scalable access for hundreds or thousands of simultaneous end users who are accessing the same Web server has proven to be a very complex programming task, indeed. Building these systems typically involves interfacing, data transfer, and synchronization among many different programs and server systems. These are the types of tasks undertaken by server programmers.

Database Programmers

Database programmers are a different breed of cat from client or server programmers. Database programmers typically "speak" a completely different programming language, use completely different tools, and write programs that deliver distinctly different results from client or server programmers. Database programmers typically deal exclusively with the organization, storage, and extraction of data for or by an end user or by an application.

The differences between database systems have diminished over the years, and many of the "basic" technical skills of a database programmer are more transferable from database system to database system. While "big data" systems like Hadoop are emerging for accessing terabytes of content, the most popular database systems are relational ones, which include Oracle, Microsoft SQL Server, IBM DB2, MySQL, Postgres, and Berkeley DB. Most of the key concepts are the same for all of these systems, which all use SQL statements (and API equivalents) to access data. So one would think that an expert on one of these systems would most likely be an expert on another. However, our observation is that direct experience with your particular database system is required if you expect any but fairly rudimentary database tasks to be performed.

Database programmers are like auto mechanics. You might trust any mechanic to change a tire or a wiper blade, but for any serious work that needs to be done, you would never consider taking a Porsche to a mechanic who knows nothing about Porsches.

Similarly for database programmers: We might trust any database programmer to write a report to access data from, say, an Oracle database, but we wouldn't think of having one do any serious database development without considerable direct experience on the database system on which the development is to be deployed (e.g., Oracle, SQL Server).

Web Developers and Other Scripters

Many Web developers use a completely different set of development tools from any of the other types of programmers, who usually use hardcore programming languages like C, C++, C#, Java, and Ruby for most of their development tasks. Web developers, on the other hand, mostly use formatting markup (e.g., HTML, XML, CSS, ASP/JSP) and scripting tools (e.g., Perl, PHP, JavaScript) to accomplish their tasks. Some of their development is "cut, paste, and modify" (copying some code that works, sometimes modifying it to perform a different task). They may also use even higher-level tools that make scripting and deployment easier, such as Flash,

Dreamweaver, or Cold Fusion. This means that programmers doing only Web development would benefit from formal computer science training but need it less than other programmers.

On the other hand, the movement to push more of the processing out of the server and into the browser, using JavaScript and frameworks based on AJAX, has changed Web development. Web developers had long faced problematic browser compatibility issues. Pushing more intelligence into the client has exacerbated such issues, forced more traditional programming discipline onto Web developers, and created the need for a new breed who are as skilled as client programmers. Web developers are fast having to learn client programming and the issues it entails.

The descriptions of the previous four types of programmers are generalizations, and some highly skilled programmers can actually do all four types of work. However, most programmers gravitate to one of these areas and perform best when working on "their" type of code. Expecting one kind of programmer to work on a different kind of project is often a recipe for disaster in a project. A programmer may be capable of doing the other type of work, but most programmers aren't interested in doing so. And a programmer who is not interested in what he is doing is a problem waiting to happen.

Types of Programmers

There is another way of looking at programmers that you should also understand in order to select the right staff. In looking at the types of programmers in the previous section, we focused on the type of work they do (i.e., client, server, database, Web). It is also important to look at the technical knowledge, depth of experience, and expertise that programmers bring. One way to categorize programmers in this way is as

- System engineers/architects
- System programmers
- Application programmers
- Not really programmers

System Engineers/Architects

System engineers/architects are the most highly skilled and experienced programmers on any development staff. The ability to understand the complex relationships among all the relevant system components (operating systems, communication systems, databases, online/offline access, security, hardware, etc.) requires extensive expertise in all the various technologies and systems. Typically, there are only one or two "true" system engineers/architects in any reasonably sized group. Having great system engineers/architects will make everyone else on the team look good. Their systems will be designed to work reliably and will usually seem elegantly simple.

Gracenote was founded by one of these highly skilled and experienced system engineers/architects. His purity of design and implementation has created an incredible service that is reliable, scalable, and flexible. Larry Page and Sergey Brin, cofounders of Google, appear to be similar types who have fostered the elegance of design and implementation that has been the driver of Google's technical and business success.

System Programmers

Most system engineers/architects started out as system programmers. System programmers understand how all the components in a system work, including the operating system(s) and communication system(s) on the client and/or server. A Bob Barton quote in Alan Kay's Ph.D. thesis[1] sums up how system programmers are seen by their programming counterparts:

....

System Programmers are the high priests of a low cult.

—BOB BARTON[2]

System programmers write the device drivers that interface with hardware, create the operating systems that provide the runtime environment

---

1. Alan Kay is an influential computer scientist most widely known for Smalltalk and his contributions to Object-Oriented Programming. See www.vpri.org/html/people/founders.htm.

2. Bob Barton was chief architect of the Burroughs 5000 and a professor at the University of Utah where Alan Kay earned his Ph.D. thesis. See www.computer.org/portal/web/awards/barton.

in which the device drivers and applications execute, create compilers and debugging tools for other programmers, and generally provide tools and services that the other programmers use to deliver programs.

In the past, being called a system programmer was almost an insult to anyone with reasonable social skills. The T-shirts and demeanor of many of the system programmers we have known are iconic of the geeky look that has become fashionable. The statement "I was geeky when geeky wasn't cool" comes to mind whenever we think of many of the system programmers we have known (and by the way, we were both system programmers ourselves).

Application Programmers

Application programmers make up the vast majority of professional programmers, students, and hobbyists who call themselves programmers. Application programmers typically develop programs that are used directly by end users or whose results are used directly by end users. Examples of applications developed by application programmers include word processors, spreadsheets, calendars, Web browsers, media players like iTunes and Windows Media Player, and games. Applications can also be developed by database developers to perform specific functions on data extracted or stored in a database. Examples of database applications include financial packages, airline reservation systems, and data-mining tools like Oracle Financials.

Certain application programmers have the ability to rise above the practicalities of the code and are able to actually empathize with the users of the application and appreciate the nuances of visual and interactive design. Such application programmers are best equipped to become user interface (UI) developers. If you pair one of these gifted application programmers with a UI designer, who will typically have a background in graphic design as well as human factors and possibly cognitive psychology, the results will far exceed the results that can be produced by either the programmer or the UI designer alone.

There are projects so focused on UI, such as the Mac Finder (the MacOS desktop UI), that they require the entire team to be made up of these gifted application programmers. Thus when Ron managed the Mac Finder team at Apple, he specifically sought out and carefully interviewed candidates to identify a high level of user empathy in addition to stellar programming skills. "Coding skill alone could not have made a programmer successful on that team," he notes.

Not Really Programmers

There are members of the technical staff on development teams who are referred to as "programmers" who are not really programmers. Some specify program or business logic using graphical user interface (GUI) tools that then generate user-accessible applications. Others create scripts or modify configuration files that result in customized content display. The chief distinction in the role these "programmers" serve is that they are using preprogrammed tools and applications and not directly crafting code.

These "programmers" are important and valuable; however, generally their depth of technical skills is not a match for that of the other types of programmers we discussed. The world is becoming increasingly populated with programmers such as these, as the tools evolve and become more powerful and effective. However, we will not directly discuss them in this book.

Many of the techniques we describe for programmers can be used with these other "programmers," but our experience has shown that many are content with just doing their job. Most are not as eager to learn and are less motivated than "real" programmers.

Domain Expertise

Programmers also vary by background and expertise in your organization's domain, or line of business.

We find that the extent to which experience is called out in job classifications, descriptions, and requirements varies according to the economy. In good economies, organizations seek out technical people (as well as managers) with broad domain expertise, hoping that they will contribute out-of-the-box thinking and cross-pollinate ideas and approaches and best practices that have come into use in other domains. As an example, when Ron was hired into financial services IT, it was from the product world, where his teams had been crafting highly interactive computing experiences (the Mac OS) and entertainment products (games and multimedia tools). Because the Web was new in 1996, Schwab needed an outside technologist to lead its team building highly interactive Web tools for investors.

In bad economies, on the other hand, organizations are hunkered down, cutting costs, driving efficiency, limiting development to core domain functionality—and they tend to look for years and years of domain-specific expertise to reduce the risk of the few new hires they're able to make.

Regardless of the state of the economy, every team can use a mix of great programming talent, domain expertise, analysis, and technical communication.

And domain expertise is an important consideration in hiring the right team of programmers.

Programmer Job Requirements and Abilities

Successfully hiring and managing a programmer starts with understanding that each programmer has unique abilities. Like snowflakes, no two are alike. We have often said that there can be an order-of-magnitude difference among programmers in the ability to "crank out code." What can make such a difference? Several factors do, including education, experience, talent, and intuition, as well as many other intangible factors.

Most programmers understand the distinctions among their peers intuitively; they don't need explicit rank or title designations to differentiate. But having a formalized set of programmer types and levels (see Table 2.1), each with a minimum set of job requirements and abilities, will make your management job much easier, help project managers identify who is best suited for various tasks and projects, and give senior management more insight into your organization and how it's structured.

Associated with each of these programming levels[3] is a set of criteria that each programmer must meet to be hired or promoted into that level. Of course, the years of experience are not mandatory but are used as rough guidelines to indicate the experience expected for the programming level. Each programmer's skills and experience are unique, and these guidelines should not dictate that very talented and experienced programmers be held

Table 2.1   Client Programming Level Guidelines

Programming Levels	Client Programmers
Entry level	Programmer 3
1–5 years' experience	Programmer 2
Experienced (5–10 years)	Programmer 1
Experienced (10–20 years)	Senior Programmer 2
Very experienced (12+ years)	Senior Programmer 1/Architect

---

3. These programming levels are consistent with most compensation-related services, such as Radford Surveys and Salary.com. These services provide comparative salary and total compensation information that is invaluable in managing your software team. By aligning your programming levels with the compensation survey service used by your company, you can ensure that you have the best information at your disposal for managing your team.

back just because they do not have the requisite number of years' experience. Ultimately, you must measure programmers based not on what they bring, but on what they produce.

Both Ron and Mickey have had experiences where the best programmer is not the most experienced or highly paid programmer. We encourage you to see such circumstances not as a problem, but as an opportunity, that is, an opportunity to reward your exceptional programmers with considerably higher salaries or perks. Having programmer levels in place will be additional ammunition in your battle to reward them appropriately. We have seldom encountered resistance from executive management when we have campaigned to reward clearly outstanding programmers, though your actions may affect what you can do for underperforming programmers.

Table 2.2 shows how programming levels can be implemented for the types of programmers discussed previously.

It is important to craft a set of criteria that build as a programmer progresses through the programming levels. Table 2.3 shows how this works for client programmers. The Tools section provides a complete build-out of the system that you can adapt to your organization.

Of course, what you really want to go along with this programming level summary is a detailed job description for each of the positions. Programmers have a reputation for being free spirits and for being disdainful of formal documents. However, it is our experience that programmers also desperately want to have a job description and a clear understanding of what it will take for them to rise in the organization. There are exceptions to this, but the vast majority of programmers will work better with this system in place and a clear understanding of where you and other management in the overall organization perceive them to fit.

Table 2.2 Programming Level Guidelines		
Client Programmers	**System Programmers**	**Database Programmers**
Programmer 3	System Programmer 3	Database Developer 3
Programmer 2	System Programmer 2	Database Developer 2
Programmer 1	System Programmer 1	Database Developer 1
Senior Programmer 2	Senior System Programmer 2	Senior Database Developer 2
Senior Programmer 1/ Architect	Senior System Programmer 1/ Architect	Senior Database Developer 1/ Architect

Table 2.3   Client Programmers: Level Criteria

Programmer 3 (Entry Level)

Knowledge of Windows, Mac, or Linux

Basic knowledge of good coding practices

Aware of/interested in Internet technologies

Aware of/interested in database technologies

Knowledge of C/C++

Ability to work in a team and take direction

Can work with supervisor to plan tasks

Programmer 2 (Some Experience)

Produced one or more commercial apps

Proficiency on Windows, Mac, or Linux

Experience with good coding practices

Conversant with Internet technologies

Conversant with database technologies

Solid understanding of C/C++

Self-motivated and can take direction

Can independently plan tasks

Programmer 1 (Experienced)

Produced two or more commercial apps

Proficiency on two platforms

Familiar with Internet technologies

Familiar with database technologies

Well versed in C/C++

Good communication skills

Self-motivated, minimal direction

Good project-planning and schedule-estimating skills

Recognizes problems and helps group adapt

Senior Programmer 2

Produced two or more commercial apps

Proficiency on two platforms

Understands cross-platform issues

Knowledgeable about Internet technologies

Knowledgeable about database technologies

In-depth knowledge of C/C++

Strong communication skills

Self-motivated, minimal direction

Excellent analysis, project-planning, and schedule-estimating skills

Watches for changing conditions and plans adaptations

Senior Programmer 1

Produced two or more complex commercial apps or technologies

Thorough knowledge of two platforms

Understands cross-platform issues

Excellent knowledge of Internet technologies

Knowledgeable about database technologies

Expert knowledge of C/C++

Expert in software design practices

Strong communication skills, industry relationships

Self-motivated, works independently

Excellent analysis, project-planning, and schedule-estimating skills

Generates, enhances, and promotes new ideas

Watches for changing conditions and plans adaptations

Creating detailed job descriptions is a very difficult task. For the past 15 years Mickey has been developing a structured set of job descriptions that reflect the programming level summary discussed above. The basic format of these job descriptions is illustrated by the Programmer 3 example shown in Figure 2.1.

As this example shows, there are three sections to the job description:

- What the job is (the facts: title, department, reports to, status, and location)
- A narrative position summary that includes job responsibilities and expectations
- Minimum job requirements

It is easy to adapt this format to almost any job description, but we strongly encourage you to write not just one job description but sets of job descriptions that describe levels of job capabilities. We find it does not take much longer to create a set of job descriptions than it does to create just one. By creating a set of job descriptions for a position you will easily address questions regarding job growth and promotion. The few extra minutes you spend up front will save many hours later on. Do this and you will become a hero to your HR department, and you will also have an excellent tool to help manage your programming staff.

Included with the Tools for this chapter are sets of example job descriptions that you can modify and adapt to meet your specific organization, department, and job requirements.

Proximity and Relationship

Managing software development has gotten considerably more complex over the past years. If you are lucky, your world remains simple, but those days are rapidly disappearing. If you are not impacted now, you will be. That, or your business will not be competitive.

In days gone by, there was only one question that was asked: "Where do I find a programmer to work on my project?" Then the choice between hiring an on-site, full-time employee and a contractor emerged. These days, where and how you get work done involves a whole host of choices that must be carefully considered.

TITLE:	Programmer 3
DEPARTMENT:	Client Programming
REPORTS TO:	Director, Client Programming
STATUS:	Full-time, exempt
LOCATION:	San Francisco, CA

POSITION SUMMARY: Entry-level position. Responsible for code and/or asset management, conversion, verification, and maintenance. Responsible for writing well-defined portions of source code adhering to established standards of quality for documentation and coding. Works well in a group, and follows direction from manager and senior team members. Expected to work under direct supervision, communicating issues and problems that arise.

JOB REQUIREMENTS

- Four-year college degree in computer science or equivalent experience.
- Knowledge of Windows, Mac, or Linux/UNIX with more than one platform preferable.
- Knowledge of C/C++ and debugging techniques.
- Basic knowledge of good coding practices and fundamental computer science principles.
- Aware of and interested in Internet technologies, communication protocols, and techniques.
- Aware of and interested in database methodologies and database systems.
- Ability to work in a team and take direction well.
- Self-motivated and responds to supervision. Asks relevant questions.
- Enthusiastic about company and programming company products.
- Can work with supervisor to plan tasks and estimate their completion.
- Can adapt to changing conditions.

Figure 2.1   Sample job description

Often, these are not choices you get to make. They may be dictated by your management or by project circumstances. Regardless, to succeed you must effectively manage geographical and relational diversity.

The five types of programmer proximity and relationships you will be called upon to manage are

- In-house employees
- Geographically distant employees
- Contractors
- Contracted managed teams
- Outsourcing companies

You can think about these types of relationships as the "ties that bind," and these are ranked accordingly. The closer the tie (in-house employees being the closest), the more control and visibility you will have into the work of the programmer. The looser the tie (the outsourcing company being the loosest), the more you will be called upon to manage vicariously, often through specifications and deliverables rather than by managing people directly.

In-House Employees

The majority of the tools discussed previously in this chapter are designed for use with in-house employees. Having an in-house employee is an explicit commitment by you and your company to provide an agreed-upon set of benefits and a dedicated working environment, in addition to compensation, in exchange for satisfactory work by the employee. It's a contract of sorts.

But there are a lot of implicit assumptions built into that contract, at least in our experience. In-house employees expect a career, not just a job. So, you must also worry about providing

- Professional and career growth, and opportunities that will enable that growth
- Regular feedback
- Communication about company news and events
- An almost unlimited number of other expectations that you may have to discover

However, you and the in-house employee have the opportunity to forge a close relationship, which can minimize the communication required to manage effectively.

Geographically Distant Employees

Fundamentally, you must manage a geographically distant employee in the same manner that you manage in-house employees. You still have expectations and they must still perform. However, managing an employee whom you do not see often, or physically meet with regularly, places an increased burden on you to communicate to, and with, the employee.

The founder of Evans & Sutherland (E&S), once told Mickey a way to think about successful interpersonal communication:

....

Communication is a factor of the inverse square of the distance domestically, and the inverse cube of the distance internationally.

—*DAVID C. EVANS*

In our experience, this rule of thumb is very true. We have seen too many communication breakdowns just because someone is not sitting nearby. The farther apart people are (down the hall, in the next building, in the next time zone, halfway around the world), the more difficult the problem. And when the distance is international, the communication is often further impeded because of extreme time zone differences, language and accent challenges, and cultural barriers.

So, before you decide to hire or take on a geographically distant employee —or to keep on an employee who is moving to another state or country— understand the implicit commitment to ensure adequate communication with that distant employee. It will be harder than you expect, regardless of how hard you expect it to be.

Another problem with distant employees is that you are, almost by default, limited in the types of projects they can take on. Your company or organization may have an unlimited supply of projects that a programmer can undertake in isolation, but most do not. It takes a special programmer to be able to rise above the constraints imposed by time and distance to produce results effectively in a close-knit fashion with a team of distant peers. Make sure you have such an employee, or a suitable crop of projects that can be done largely independently, before hiring or taking on a distant employee.

Contractors

The decision to hire a contractor rather than a full-time employee is not one to be made lightly. Often, the situation dictates this. If a task is finite or no employee is available to do the task, the simple decision is to hire a contractor.

Contractors are, by definition, "hired guns" who are called upon to do the task(s) you ask them to do in return for compensation. Contractors should have no implicit expectations. Any expectations *must* be spelled out in a contract you execute with the contractor before services begin.

This relationship, company to contractor, is usually the simplest of all the relationships we will discuss. It is simple because it can be terminated at any time, without reason or warning.[4] However, that doesn't mean it can't get complex. If it does, it is undoubtedly your fault. You get to make the rules, and you get to call the shots.

So how does this simple relationship become complex? Often it is because you are not actually trying to find a contractor to perform a specific task, which is the classic definition of a contracting assignment. Too often, you are looking to hire a full-time employee and either cannot find someone suitable to hire or are not sure you have found the right person to hire. So you take on a contractor but begin treating the contractor like an employee. This leads to implicit expectations that are akin to those of a full-time employee, expectations that have sometimes been upheld by courts as a result of lawsuits. As a result, in companies in which we have managed, HR and legal departments have been quite clear and very directive that programming managers not provide employee perks—whether shirts or team offsite attendance—to contractors.

So beware of what expectations you set for contractors and how you treat them. Treat them as the hired guns they are paid to be, and don't feel bad if you treat them differently from employees. They are not employees.

Contracted Managed Teams and Outsourcing Companies

We believe that first-line programming managers should not be saddled with managing outsourcing relationships, so the topics of outsourcing and

---

4. This assumes you have put an appropriate contract in place with the contractor that includes the right to "terminate at will," without reason or notice. Any good standard contractor's agreement should include such language. Included in the Tools for this chapter is a sample independent contractor agreement that has such language in it.

of managing outsourced teams and organizations are not in the scope of this book. Outsourcing takes special attention and skills. If you find yourself faced with outsourcing some part of a project, take it on *only* if you can also get help and support from someone who is experienced in managing such staff or teams. Otherwise you could well fail in your primary role as a programming manager.

Managing outsourced resources can be a full-time job all by itself, but in Chapter 5 we will discuss the challenges of getting value from offshore contractors.

Generational Styles

There have always been generational differences among engineers and programmers, but these generational differences are now having a marked impact on the workplace. There are now three distinct generations that must work well together if they are going to succeed as a team. But these generations also have different values and views, and different things motivate them.

It is helpful to identify not only your own work style, but also the styles of those you hire and manage. One way to do so is to take a generational view. The problem is that there is no broad agreement about what delineates the generations. Traditionally, the generations have been characterized by their birth dates:

- Baby Boomers (born 1946–64)
- Generation X (born 1965–79)
- Millennials (born 1980–2000), sometimes called Generation Y, Echo Boomers, Next-Gens, or Net-Gens

But this probably doesn't do the generational differences justice; it's not just when you're born but also how you think that determines your "true" age. We've all known people who do not act their age, either by being "mature beyond their years" or "immature for their age," so it is dangerous to react to someone simply on the basis of age in chronological years.

But there are some characteristics and values that members of generations share, regardless of their actual age. Table 2.4 shows some ways to classify members of these generations.

Table 2.4   Generational Differences

Generation*	Year Born	Music	Mass Media	Technologies†	Characteristics†	Core Values§
Older Boomers	1945–55	Vinyl LPs	AM radio, broadcast TV, newspapers	Analog (e.g., electric guitars), telephone, U.S. Mail	Willing to use technology, but often only to communicate with family and friends.	Rebel against conformity and strive for a perfectionist lifestyle based on personal values and spiritual growth.
Younger Boomers	1956–65	Cassette tapes	FM radio, cable TV, newspapers	PCs, FAX, e-mail	Comfortable with Internet, social media, and mobile; they embrace technology but seldom fanatically.	Welcome team-based work and have had stable careers marked by loyalty to companies.
Gen X	1966–85	CDs	Cable TV, Web sites	Internet, e-mail, text messages	Love technology that helps them be independent, and digital stuff that improves their lives.	Economic and psychological "survivor" mentality; they tend to be skeptical of authority and cautious in their commitments. Ambitious and independent, they're now striving to balance the competing demands of work, family, and personal life.
Millennials	1986–2005	iPod/Pandora	Web sites, Facebook, Twitter	Mobile, text messages, Facebook, Twitter	Mobile is their defining characteristic: texting, making party plans on the fly while out, carrying their identity around in their phones.	Coming of age during a shift toward virtue and values, they're attracted to organizations whose missions speak to a purpose greater than a bottom line. They're technologically savvy with a positive, can-do attitude that says, "I'm here to make a difference."

* There are many definitions of generations, but little agreement on what they are. These generational definitions combine and integrate those that seem most useful and consistent for the topic being discussed in this chapter.

† Charles S. Golvin et al., The State of Consumers and Technology: Benchmark 2009, US (Forrester Research, 2009).

§ Dan King, "Defining a Generation: Tips for Uniting Our Multi-Generational Workforce," www.careerfirm.com/generations.htm.

The important takeaway from this table is that these different generations have distinctly different influences that form the individual while growing up, and more importantly different core values that make them react differently in the workplace.

- Baby Boomers tend to be optimistic and loyal, and they long to stabilize their careers. Many Boomers are workaholics, willing to do more than is required to help their company and advance their careers.
- Members of Generation X tend to be cynical and have a self-reliance that has led them to embrace "free agency" over company loyalty. They view time as a commodity they are unwilling to share or give away.
- Millennials tend to be individualistic, yet with a group orientation. Ambitious and confident, they have a collective sense of optimism, tenacity, and heroic spirit, traits reinforced by the national unity following the 9/11 tragedy. Like the Gen Xers, the Millennials view time as a commodity they are unwilling to share or give away—they see work as something to do between the weekends.

One can see how this dissonance of core values can create havoc in an office where work must be shared equally in a team environment. Being able to recognize and personalize your approach to these vastly different generations will be important in being a successful manager.

Personality Styles

In addition to the different types of programmers, there are also personality styles, traits, and habits that seem prevalent among programmers, each with its own set of challenges.

The literature is rife with theories about personalities, how to categorize them, and how to deal with them. Of those theories, it would be time well spent for you to understand the work of Myers and Briggs, who from 1942 to 1962 laid the foundation for personality tests and developed a framework for categorizing personalities. The purpose of the Myers-Briggs Type Indicator (MBTI) personality inventory is to make the theory of psychological types described by C. G. Jung understandable and useful in people's lives.[5]

---

5. The Myers & Briggs Foundation, MBTI Basics, www.myersbriggs.org/my-mbti-personality-type/mbti-basics/.

Their work was popularized in the 1984 book *Please Understand Me*[6] that packaged the Myers-Briggs methodology in a very accessible form.

The types originally described by Jung are extroversion (E)/introversion (I), sensation (S)/intuition (N), thinking (T)/feeling (F), and perceiving (P)/judging (J). It is worth noting that studies[7] have shown that a disproportionate number of programmers tend to be INTJ (introversion/intuition/thinking/judging), with Mickey and Ron both tending to this personality type.

There is much you can learn from this book that is worth exploring, especially in your own personal relationships. However, dealing with diverse technical personalities like those we have encountered in such formulaic fashion is fraught with danger, and we haven't found it particularly useful in managing our teams. We recommend that you avoid the formalized personality classifications and focus on managing the personality types as you see them.

We have provided a set of personality types that our experience tells us you will likely encounter when managing programmers. Though this list is not exhaustive, it is illustrative of the different kinds of personality types you may have to manage with some suggestions on recognizing them.

Left-Brain versus Right-Brain People

The right-brain versus left-brain theory grew out of the work of Roger W. Sperry,[8] whose studies demonstrated that the left and right hemispheres are specialized in different tasks. The left side of the brain is normally specialized in taking care of analytical and verbal tasks. The left side speaks much better than the right side, while the right takes care of space perception tasks and music, for example.

---

6. David Keirsey and Marilyn Bates, *Please Understand Me: Character & Temperament Types* (B & D Books, 1984).

7. C. Bishop-Clark and D. Wheeler, "The Myers-Briggs Personality Type and Its Relationship to Computer Programming," *Journal of Research on Computing in Education 26*, no. 3 (Spring 1994): 358–70.

8. The Nobel Prize in Physiology or Medicine 1981 was divided, one half awarded to Roger W. Sperry "for his discoveries concerning the functional specialization of the cerebral hemispheres," the other half jointly to David H. Hubel and Torsten N. Wiesel "for their discoveries concerning information processing in the visual system." See www.nobelprize.org/nobel_prizes/medicine/laureates/1981/.

If you are a programmer or technical person, you've probably been labeled as being "left-brained," which is said to be more verbal, logical, analytical, and objective and is more appropriately called "left-brain dominant," since we have only one brain and both sides are working at all times. So you can be "left-brained" and still have strong "right-brained" tendencies that are more nonverbal, intuitive, thoughtful, and subjective—tendencies more often associated with creative types such as musicians, writers, and artists.

While strong left-brained analytical skills are necessary for a good programmer, activities associated with the right brain are often equally important since programming is a very creative act (more akin to writing a novel as we discussed in the first chapter). In fact we, along with others, have found that some of the best programmers are also musicians. Mickey was a dedicated musician himself at the point he discovered programming during his first year in college. "When I first began programming, I was instantly comfortable with the medium. I was already a musician. Music theory is all based upon mathematics, the hours of practice require dedication and discipline, and I found the creative part of playing and/or composing music and songs very similar to the creative part of designing and implementing a program. Surprisingly, even debugging a program is similar in some ways to learning to play a song well—you need to play the portion of the song over and over until you get it right, not unlike running and rerunning a program again and again until it works right. I even found myself losing all track of time when programming, much as I did when practicing my guitar. Thereafter, programming became my primary creative outlet, though I still continue to play and compose music and songs."

This story is not unique among many of the programmers we know. In fact, it has become a common line of interview questioning when meeting a prospective candidate for the first time. If candidates are musicians, discussing what music they like and play, music theory, and what place music has in their lives not only provides valuable insight but also can help set them at ease at the beginning of the interview. While being a musician isn't a requirement for being a great programmer, we have never seen it to be an impediment!

Night versus Morning People

Unlike the majority of employees in most organizations who are morning people, a preponderance of programmers are night people. They tend to show up well into normal working hours and work much later, often into the night when in the middle of a critical or interesting project. Generally, if you are focused on results, this is not a problem if these late risers are delivering what you expected or more. However, the issue that usually arises is communication; that is, they need to be available for meetings and exchange of information.

In *The Tao of Programming*,[9] Geoffrey James recounts:

> *A manager went to his programmers and told them: "As regards to your working hours: you are going to have to come in at nine in the morning and leave at five in the afternoon." At this, all of them became angry and several resigned on the spot.*

> *So the manager said: "All right, in that case you may set your own working hours, as long as you finish your projects on schedule." The programmers, now satisfied, began to come in at noon and work until the wee hours of the morning.*

To avoid such problems, we strongly recommend that you do *not* make your night people show up at 9:00 A.M. What we do recommend is that you establish a set of "core hours" that you expect everyone to observe to ensure a minimum, reasonable level of communication across your entire team.[10] Having agreed-upon core hours will save everyone a lot of time and anguish that can easily be avoided. Note that you usually have to revisit the core hours periodically, since these programmers will find their schedules drifting and their adherence to the core hours slipping.

The other issue you need to deal with is the rest of the company's perception of your team. "Your guys don't show up until noon" is a criticism both of us have heard in every organization where we have been. To counter such talk, you need to be proactive in highlighting how many hours your team puts in and how late they are cranking out and checking in code. Make sure you single out some of the most notorious night people for recognition and call out the focus they gained through their work habits. Be proactive in doing this; don't wait for the comments to start.

---

9. Geoffrey James, *The Tao of Programming* (Info Books, 1986).

10. This same recommendation is made for members of your staff who work in different time zones or offshore.

Cowboys versus Farmers

Most programmers have a built-in bias toward being cowboys rather than farmers. That is, when a problem arises, their first inclination is to "jump on their horse and ride off" to solve the problem single-handedly. They too often skip planning, and that results in one-off solutions that could have better leveraged standards, practices, and their team.

You want your software development to be more like farming. Farmers are methodical in knowing the lay of the land, studying its current chemical makeup, planting, watering, weeding, and harvesting their crops. Software that is reliable, extensible, and maintainable is developed just as methodically.

Hence it is important to identify the cowboys and make sure they are kept in check and not charging off to develop solutions that will ultimately lead to other problems.

Since many programmers have cowboy tendencies, it is all the more imperative to establish a software development culture where cowboy behavior is not tolerated and where there is a methodical software development lifecycle that is followed for all major projects.

There are occasions, however, when you really do want a cowboy and not a farmer, typically in small, one-programmer proof-of-concept or prototype projects. We have found that having a "gunslinger" around who can tackle such projects is great for that person and for you. Matching your needs with a programmer's basic personality will make both of you happier and more successful.

Many cowboys are great programmers, but you must manage them carefully to get what you need from them. They tend to be prima donnas and divisive to an organization, so keep a careful eye on them and act quickly if issues arise.

Programmers who will only ever be cowboys usually will not last long in the organization. Either you will get tired of them charging off on their own and get rid of them, or they will get tired of being kept in check all the time and leave.

Heroes

A hero is someone who takes on work that requires superhuman effort to complete—and who delivers. Heroes are similar to cowboys in taking on superhuman efforts but can work successfully in teams and within the development process. Heroes need to be nurtured and usually rise as super-stars within your organization.

The challenge for you in managing heroes is that you can easily burn them out by expecting superhuman efforts all the time. Occasionally, yes, but all the time, no. Look after their welfare carefully and use them selectively to move forward important initiatives or critical projects.

Both Mickey and Ron from time to time during their programming years took on difficult projects and delivered results beyond expectations (often after pulling all-nighters or delivering marathon efforts). These resulted in good things for the companies we worked for, making key product deliveries for Kenway and E&S, completing a landmark Apple Computer product demo that was key to selling Apple's then-newest computer line, garnering patents for our companies, and pushing our limits and the known limits of our technologies and tools for the benefit of our clients and companies. The experience became extraordinarily useful to us when we became managers in defining the line between selective superhuman effort and burnout.

Introverts

Some members of your staff are so quiet and reserved as to be almost invisible. They can and do perform well but contribute little to the team dynamics or in meetings. One-on-one you can draw them out, but they step back and almost disappear when part of a group.

By drawing them out in meetings, and giving them positive reinforcement when sharing comments or insights, you can begin to build their confidence that they have something to contribute to the team. Look for opportunities to bring them into conversations and acknowledge their contributions. Seek them out one-on-one. Establish a special relationship on some small level, such as sharing an experience or a book. That is, find ways to connect more deeply.

Mickey recalls an introverted technical writer at Brøderbund with whom he connected over role-playing games. Mickey's encouragement led the tech writer to pursue game design; he eventually became a lead game designer at Brøderbund and later a published author and game designer of some renown at other companies.

This and other similar connections have been personally rewarding to both of us over the years, as we have seen unassuming individuals we have encouraged grow and demonstrate their talent.

Cynics

Avoid at all cost hiring individuals who are deeply cynical. They can poison a development team and create havoc in your organization by sowing dissension and dissatisfaction where those feelings might otherwise never grow.

The problem with cynicism is that it is rooted in reality but blown out of proportion in its impact and depth within an organization. For example, "Management doesn't care about programmers" may be true. However, cynics will find every opportunity to illustrate how this is true, even when it is not. They will point out every unintended slight, such as a change of drinks in the office refrigerator, as a "plot by management to punish the programming staff." Such comments are blatantly not true and demoralizing, at best. You will find yourself unable to even go on vacation without coming back to find your team in turmoil, off track, and perhaps even in revolt.

Jerks

Some people are just simply jerks. They are abrasive, caustic, toxic people. Of course they may also have some redeeming qualities. They may be brilliant, technically talented, great programmers. But brilliance doesn't justify the price you have to pay for having them in your organization. Having them in proximity is the problem.

Adopt a "no jerks" rule. Judging from our experience, you'll be sorry if you don't. Expand the rule to apply to cynics and bozos as well. Your staff will appreciate it and your job will be a lot easier.

There will be more discussion of dealing with cynics, bozos, and jerks in Chapters 5 and 7.

Summary

The purpose of this chapter was to help you see that understanding programmers is not a simple task, even if you've been one. The different lenses we provide can only help you find the ways that work best for you in dealing with the programmers whom you must hire and manage. Managing people is hard, and some of the most talented programmers are also the most challenging people to manage. It's a double-edged sword.

We listed the various personality types so that you can be aware of them, but we strongly discourage you from simply putting people into these boxes. Deal with each person as the unique individual each is, and you will be more successful as a programming manager.

Tools

We have prepared a number of tools to assist you in managing your team. The spreadsheets and Word documents provide full examples that you can easily adapt for your organization. See the Tools section, after the chapters, for the link to the Tools Web site, from which you can download the following tools:

- Sample programmer levels
- Sample job descriptions for all programmer levels
- Sample independent contractor agreement
- Roles and ranking system

3
Finding and Hiring Great Programmers

THERE ARE MANY PROGRAMMERS. However, there are not that many *great* programmers.

> *"Exceptional engineers are more likely than non-exceptional engineers to maintain a 'big picture,' have a bias for action, be driven by a sense of mission, exhibit and articulate strong convictions, play a pro-active role with management, and help other engineers," said an insightful 1993 study of software engineers.*[1]

Frederick Brooks in his classic work *The Mythical Man-Month*[2] cited a study[3] from 25 years earlier that showed, among programmers with two years' experience and similar training, that the best professional programmers are ten times as productive as the poorest of them. The researchers had started out to determine if changing from punch cards to interactive programming would make a productivity difference, only to find their results overwhelmed by the productivity differences among individuals. They found 20:1 differences in initial coding time, 5:1 differences in code size (!), and 25:1 differences in debugging time!

---

1. Richard Turley and James Bieman, *Competencies of Exceptional and Non-Exceptional Software Engineers* (Colorado State University, 1993).

2. Brooks, *The Mythical Man-Month*.

3. H. Sackman, W. J. Erikson, and E. E. Grant, "Exploratory Experimental Studies Comparing Online and Offline Programming Performance," *CACM*, January 1968.

Barry Boehm, 20 years later, reported a 25:1 difference between the most and least productive software developers, and a 10:1 difference in the number of bugs they generated.[4] In 2000, Boehm and coauthors updated their study to examine teams and concluded that teams of experienced top-tier programmers could be expected to be 5.3 times more productive than teams of inexperienced bottom-tier programmers.[5]

....

Good programmers are up to 30 times better than mediocre programmers, according to "individual differences" research. Given that their pay is never commensurate, they are the biggest bargains in the software field.

—ROBERT L. GLASS, *Software Practitioner, Pioneer, and Author*[6]

While there are some IT organizations that pride themselves on hiring "ordinary" programmers, there are few product companies and professional services organizations where you can be successful managing a software team without the ability to staff some part of your team with "great" ones. It's no wonder, given the kinds of people programmers can be, that finding and identifying exceptional engineers can be a challenge.

....

The single most important job of a programming manager is to hire the right people.

Hiring is far and away the most difficult-to-undo decision that managers make. Being successful at staffing will ease the rest of your job. The worst of unsuccessful hires can cast a plague upon your team for months, undermine your leadership, incite dissension and strife, delay or derail your deliverables, and in these ways and in every other way demotivate and demoralize your entire organization. Not to mention how hard it is to get rid of underperformers and other bad hires.

---

4. Barry Boehm, "Understanding and Controlling Software Costs," *IEEE Transactions on Software Engineering*, October 1988.

5. Barry Boehm et al., *Software Cost Estimation with Cocomo II* (Addison-Wesley, 2000).

6. Glass, "Frequently Forgotten Fundamental Facts about Software Engineering."

If you're hiring not only programmers but also managers of programmers, remember the rule Ron heard at Apple and Mickey heard directly from Steve Jobs:

....

A's hire A's. B's hire C's.

—*STEVE JOBS*

Steve's point was to emphasize how essential it is to hire top-notch managers, for the combinatorial effect they have as they make hires.

We've both been fooled. Ron had already been hiring for a decade when he interviewed a manager he was convinced would be a stellar contributor to his organization: "I was certain, given how well he talked the talk, that this was a guy who would really deliver. I called two of his references, and both shared stories and anecdotes that convinced me he'd walked the talk many a time before.[7] My interview team was unanimous in making a 'hire' recommendation. It was a time when I'd inherited a bad apple or two, but I'd never hired one. Until then. I realized it fast and I acted quickly to communicate the change I wanted to see in his behavior. Luckily, when I called him into my office, not even two months on the job, for a change-or-leave meeting, it was he who opened the conversation: He didn't feel like he fit; he was giving notice; he needed to leave. I was lucky."

While it can happen, we've figured out a few principles that have resulted in the vast majority of our hires being good ones.

Determining What Kind of Programmer to Hire

It all starts with knowing whom you want to hire. You're hiring not just a programmer, but also someone to fill a role and a need in your organization.

We outlined in Chapter 2 how to build a job description for the kinds and levels of programmers you need in your organization. But those are generic descriptions.

For individual hires, only by consciously thinking through the skill sets, values, ethics, and orientation you need are you likely to hire the right programmers for the slots you need to fill out your team.

---

7. "You can't just talk the talk and walk the walk; you've got to walk the talk." This frequent theme of Cecil Williams, renowned pastor of San Francisco's Glide Memorial Church, I realized later, turns out to be the very definition of integrity.

Think through whether your focus will be on experience, or on energy and passion.

Do you need

- A programmer who can mentor the team in best practices?
- A coder with a mind wired to ferret out the gnarliest design flaw?
- A designer who can sense the big picture and envision how your requirements can be broken up into modules and components?
- An engineer who is comfortable being proactive and collaborative with management?

Or do you need

- To churn out thousands of lines of code in short order?
- To prototype features important to your customers that your veteran programmers blow off as "fluff"?
- The flexibility and speed to iterate routines over and over as their essence becomes clear?

These are not mutually exclusive sets of characteristics. But the former type of programmer is more likely highly experienced. And the latter type is more likely a fresh, passionate one. Be conscious of which you need.

....

When it comes to getting things done, we need fewer architects and more bricklayers.

> —COLLEEN C. BARRETT, *President and*
> *Corporate Secretary of Southwest Airlines*

You also need to know whether you are better off with a full-time employee or a contractor.

Do you need

- A programmer for the long term?
- A fully integrated member of the development team?
- A developer with an evolving set of skills and tools whom you expect (and are willing) to train and grow over time, as needs or technologies change?

Or do you need

- A highly developed set of specialized skills and tools now?
- To fill a short-term need?

The former is likely an employee; the latter, a contractor.

Finally, will you consider distant candidates, either to move them to your location or to have them work remotely? Are you unable to find the candidates you want in the local pool, or is the skill set you need so rare that there is no pool of candidates, short of thinking regionally or nationally? Can you afford to pay moving costs? Or are you up to managing a geographically distributed team?

....

Distributed development can be made to work, but a distributed team will never perform as well as a collocated team.

—*MIKE COHN, Agile and Scrum Thought Leader*[8]

If so, you're likely to find yourself conducting some or all of your interviews by phone or videoconference. Conversely, you can leverage national trade shows and conferences to meet and recruit programmers who are uniquely qualified.

While at Apple, Ron frequently sought out hires at the Applefest and MacWorld and OOPSLA conferences. After giving a talk one year, he was approached by a programmer with laryngitis who was madly scribbling messages on pages of a 3-by-5 pad to communicate his interest in Apple. It was an odd approach, but he soon became a stellar Apple hire.

Writing the Job Description

Your hiring effort begins with writing a job description suitable for posting. Keep in mind that the objective of this description is to attract the largest number of qualified candidates—it's a marketing brochure for the position. It should be specific about what you're looking for to discourage the unqualified, broad where you're open to a wider set of talents, and persuasive about the company as a great place to work and the position as an ideal

---

8. Mike Cohn, *Succeeding with Agile* (Addison-Wesley, 2010), p. 387.

opportunity for your kind of programmer, highlighting the social significance, career visibility, and lasting value of the contribution the right candidate can make.

In a small company, writing job descriptions will likely fall to you. In
medium-size and larger companies, the staffing or HR organization will
prepare these, but you should plan to collaborate on or edit them if not outright provide all or most of the job description and requirements. Unless
you actually write the posting and are certain it will be run verbatim, it's
wise to ask to be included in a review cycle. We have seen job postings
(some of them appearing in expensive display advertising space in Sunday
newspapers) that are inadequate and sometimes downright embarrassing
due to rewrites of requirements and use of maddeningly ancient boiler-
plate by well-meaning but nontechnical recruiters.

If you're writing the posting yourself, you're probably thinking
you'll draw it from the internal job description; we showed you a sample
in Chapter 2. But that's really barely a start. It lacks both job-specific detail
and the sparkle to attract candidates.

....

*Your internal job description is only the starting place
for your external posting. Buff it up, add spice, make
it appealing.*

For example, while "Programmer 3" may be a fitting title within your
organization, you'll need one that is both more meaningful and more
descriptive of the background and technology experience you're looking
for candidates to have. The other key qualifier that most job seekers use to
determine if a job might be a fit is location. "San Francisco Bay Area" is
much too general; in a good economy, a programmer trying to minimize his
commute will skip right by your listing rather than try to figure out where
in the 100-plus-mile Bay Area the job actually is. Be specific.

That will lead to titles such as

- Entry-Level Java Server Programmer—SF Peninsula
- Experienced AJAX Programmer—Cambridge
- SQL Server 2005 Programmer with BI Experience—South Bay (SF)
- Java Architect—Denver
- Support Engineer, .Net/Sharepoint—Vancouver
- Principal Programmer, Engines Team, Search Technologies—Austin

(The latter title, since it doesn't specify C++ or Java or .Net, might be for a role where you're much more concerned about finding a candidate with strength in algorithms, data structures, and system software internals than with specific language or platform experience.)

If telecommuting three days a week is possible, the top of the listing is the place to put that, as the example in Figure 3.1 shows.

Now come the key elements of your job posting. The first is a brief summary of the company and its product(s) with your focus on why a programmer would want to join you there. This paragraph is about selling, so if you're not used to writing compelling copy, get one of your sales or marketing colleagues to help.

Next is a job description that is specific to the job for which you're hiring. Here again, the internal job descriptions in Chapter 2 are too general for recruiting purposes. What coding, design, and architecture do you need this programmer to create? What special technical skills and knowledge do you need? What best practices experience do you expect as a minimum qualification? Are you looking for someone to lead or mentor other programmers, or give them technical direction? Do you need a communicator who can collaborate with your business partner? A technical guru who can translate business requirements into technical ones, or even directly into architecture? A mathematical wizard who can turn business requirements into complex analytical algorithms? A UI designer who from business requirements can conjure up a brilliant UI that users just intuit?

Now you're ready to describe the skills you're looking for. This is the time to describe the language and platform experience you need, in detail, along with the level of skill and knowledge you expect. You should also be specific about the experience you need candidates to have with leadership, management, project management, communication, analysis, design, architecture, and coding. Are you hoping for a programmer who takes direction and just codes? Or a programmer who gives direction? How many years of experience? Education? (While Mickey and Ron disagree regarding the extent to which education is a predictor of programmer success, neither would make a degree an absolute requirement short of some statutory requirement, or some organizational quirk that would make lack of a degree a predictor of failure.)

Sometimes follow-through, attention to detail, and a sense of ownership can be more important than specific skills. Don't ignore these "soft skills" when crafting your job descriptions and during the interview.

PRINCIPAL PROGRAMMER, .NET

San Francisco/Oakland/ Berkeley •————————————— Specific location

(Note: significant telecommuting opportunity if desired) •——— Telecommuting?

Competitive salary, benefits, and options •———————— Not equity only

Forensic Logic, Inc. (www.forensiclogic.com), is an early-stage, growth-oriented company looking for a highly productive senior developer with the ability to lead a team and set its technical direction based on tons of experience designing, coding, and scaling .Net and SQL Server high-volume Web and analytics applications.

Forensic Logic develops Web-based applications that provide law enforcement agencies with tools that facilitate increased officer safety, early detection of crime trends, and interagency search capabilities. The successful candidate will have a unique opportunity to work with massive data sets, both structured and unstructured, and extensive association, geospatial, timeline, and pattern analysis and visualization, and application of matching and ranking algorithms for solving crimes. The position will provide a growth opportunity to the right individual who will be part of a great team of talented and motivated coworkers.

> The product, company, and opportunity: sales!

Forensic Logic's culture values respect, teamwork, and collaboration in achieving leading-edge functionality balanced with high usability.

> Company culture: more sales!

JOB DESCRIPTION

- Provide technical team leadership, direction, and mentoring to the small, existing remote programming team.
- Form the nucleus of a second Bay Area development team.

> Specifically, what the person you hire will do . . .

Figure 3.1   Sample job description (continued next page)

- Apply incisive design and exceptional coding skill to knocking features off the products' extensive and growing features list.
- Lead periodic rapid refactorings that keep the application code fresh, flexible, and reusable.
- Help define team development and engineering best practices.
- Lead the team's implementation of best practices.

Specifically, what the person you hire will do . . .

REQUIRED SKILLS

- Strong Web application architecture and design skills
- Fast, clean, efficient code implementation
- In-depth knowledge of Microsoft .Net and SQL Server
- 3+ years' experience designing, developing, and scaling high-volume Web applications on .Net and SQL Server platforms
- Leadership and mentorship of other developers, junior and senior alike
- Team orientation; ability to participate in lively engineering debate, making a strong case for well-considered opinions, while listening to, appreciating, and critiquing the opinions of peers
- Ability to analyze and improve the scalability and performance of high-volume, information-rich Web applications
- Strong verbal and written communication skills
- Strong customer empathy and customer experience sensitivity
- Must be highly self-motivated, ambitious, flexible, self-sufficient, and high-energy
- 8+ years' programming experience

Specifically, the skills you require

Figure 3.1   Sample job description (continued next page)

**EXPERIENCE WITH ANY OF THE
FOLLOWING A PLUS:**

- Algorithmic design and implementation; reasoning through algorithmic trade-offs
- Search/information retrieval
- Analytics, data warehousing, and business intelligence
- Information visualization
- Web services

The skills you consider a bonus

Some (but not extensive) travel will be required.

Travel?

Located adjacent to BART in the heart of the San Francisco Bay Area.

Location

www.ForensicLogic.com

Send résumés to:
Ron Lichty
VP, Products and Engineering
Forensic Logic, Inc.
RLichty@ForensicLogic.com

No phone calls

Principals only

Contact information

Figure 3.1   Sample job description

....

I emphasize communication, collaboration, energy, potential.

—MARK HIMELSTEIN, *Interim VP of Engineering,*
San Francisco Bay Area

Divide skills into "required"—what you absolutely won't hire without—and those that you would really consider a bonus in a candidate who has the required skill set.

Also consider whether travel will be required. Disclosing it here will increase your chances for a good fit long-term.

Finally, don't forget to give candidates a way to contact you—an e-mail address, usually, as well as your Web address.

Selling the Hire

Are you budgeted for another programmer? No? Then you're going to have to sell your management on why you need to hire. In most cases, that means making a business case.

Think through your need thoroughly first. Do you need the new person because the team is missing a specific expertise? Can you change technologies to mitigate the need or to make the resource easier to find? With the hybridization of applications—programs have not only become systems made up of multiple objects, components, and services, but of multiple languages—you don't have to convert your entire application. One of our colleagues recently stopped battling Ruby's scalability constraints by sectioning off the critical area and recoding it in Scala. Another got around a display-layer bottleneck of scarce XSLT coders by layering PHP Drupal on top.

When the expertise seems truly needed, you can make your case visually by taking a census of your team members and an inventory of their skills and presenting compelling visuals of your existing expertise against the expertise required by your customers, your products, or your marketplace.

On the other hand, perhaps there simply seems to be too much work. Be wary if that's a short-term need: Remember the Mythical Man-Month rule of thumb that adding resources to a late project will make it later. Your management may remember it if you don't, even if they're not reluctant to fund a hire.

Prepare to show that you have thought through every alternative to hiring. Instead of hiring, can you carve off a piece of functionality and have it programmed out of house/offshore to the lowest bidder? Can you convert your process to Agile and your product managers to Software by Numbers[9] to focus on limiting development to a smaller but earlier initial release of just the highest-return features using the team you already have? Can you improve productivity and throughput by improving your team's processes?

---

9. Mark Denne and Jane Cleland-Huang, *Software by Numbers: Low-Risk, High-Return Development* (Prentice Hall, 2003). This book introduced Minimum Marketable Features (MMFs) and an Incremental Funding Methodology (IFM) based on the notion that software is never complete, and it showed how to prioritize a project based on return so that it can become self-funding earlier.

Often enough, even with those analyses, you come up short and need to pitch resources. When Ron was faced at one firm with having a team of 30 programmers—a fifth of the firm's heads—and yet short what he needed to deliver customers' work, he helped make his case by drawing a new organization chart based on customers. The chart was, for the first time, visual evidence that once each of the most influential customers had been assigned the dedicated programmers its work deserved; the remaining customers were left without any. In another case, he gathered statistics of incoming requests for work and projects completed and graphed the rapidly growing backlog of work requests.

Regardless of the analysis, you may run up against the hard fact that your budget (or the department's budget or the company's budget) will not let you add headcount. To get the resource you need, you'll have to lay off someone or terminate a poor performer. If you're doing the right thing for your team and your project and your company, you'll likely sooner or later be faced with making tough decisions like this one to get the resource(s) you need.

Recruiting Full-Time Employees (FTEs)

Now that you can describe the type of employee you're looking for, you need to think through where you are going to find candidates, and how much you can spend to do so.

You may luck out. If you're in a large organization, there may be a programmer in another part of the company with an established reputation who wants to work for you. As with any other candidate, express enthusiasm while privately checking the facts, verifying the person's reputation, and satisfying yourself that their credentials and qualifications apply to and are a fit with your project and your needs.

Be aware that most large organizations have an established process for employees to check out opportunities elsewhere in the company. There may be requirements that they spend a year in the job into which they were hired before they're eligible to move. They may be required to give a heads-up to their current manager before talking to you. Or they may be allowed to talk with you informally about what you have available but be required to post a form to HR before they can apply. They may be required to resolve issues with their current organization before being allowed to look outside it. You as a hiring manager may have constraints. There may be rules to prevent or at least discourage the "cool" projects from "raiding" more mundane ones. Or you may be expected to consider internal candidates first. These are questions only HR can answer definitively, and you should always ask.

At Fujitsu, Ron found a "diamond in the rough" programmer in the quality assurance (QA) organization and worked with the business unit's executive director and his peer to ascertain the tester's interest in development and then to transition him gently. That and some mentoring made him a stellar hire.

Always Be Recruiting

To start your recruiting, post positions on your own Web site. Include not only the active positions you are recruiting to fill, but also positions for which you always seem to need new talent. "At Gracenote," says Mickey, "we were always looking for Oracle database developers and embedded client programmers. So we continued to collect résumés and review them even if we did not have positions open. If we saw a bona fide superstar, we would bring them in to interview and make the case for increasing headcount (which is always easier if you've found a bona fide superstar candidate)."

When Ron first went to Razorfish, his teams were working with almost every technology but Microsoft's. "I didn't even have a folder set up for Microsoft coders when an information architect from upstairs came by to give me a résumé of a guy she'd worked with before, a .Net senior coder. I took a look at the résumé and knew I couldn't use him—and I sure didn't anticipate that changing—but I also knew if I ever did need a C# programmer, I was looking at the résumé of one I'd want. It doesn't happen like this often, but a few weeks later one of our clients asked us to help them solve problems with one of their C# apps! I sure felt lucky."

Mickey has numerous examples of interviewing candidates but not having the right position for them at the time. One example comes from Brøderbund: "I interviewed a guy who was not right for the job we were recruiting to fill, but I liked him and stayed in touch with him occasionally. Almost three years later the right position opened up and he was hired almost immediately. He turned out to be a superstar and was well worth the patience and waiting for the right position to open up."

By thinking of recruiting not as a series of one-time challenges but as ongoing relationship building, you'll add value to your network in the short term and your recruiting in the long term. You should always be recruiting!

....

*You should always be thinking about building a network
of possible employees and referrers and staying in touch;
the person who turns you down this year may be next
year's awesome hire. And the candidate you would
think would never come and join your company may
have their own perspective, or may refer a friend.*

—TIM DIERKS, *Engineer, CTO, and VP of Engineering,
Apple, Google, and elsewhere*

If you're at a start-up, you may find that your own network, your list
of potential candidates, and referrals from your colleagues are all you have
to work with. You can make some great hires with nothing more; you'll just
have to work your limited paths harder.

Budgeting for Recruiting

One of the first things to know about hiring is how much you can spend to
find candidates. Marketing costs to attract and recruit full-time employees
can include

- Paying commissions to headhunters
- Engaging an internal recruiter or retaining an external one for this or a
  group of hires
- Paying employees bonuses for making successful referrals
- Paying for advertising in daily and Sunday newspapers, in trade and
  technical journals, and online
- Organizing a special recruiting event, perhaps around the time and
  location of a conference focused on a key technology in which you need
  expertise
- Paying to fly in remote candidates to interview (and potentially paying for moving expenses to relocate them, should you decide to go
  that route)

For any given hire, large companies will likely set strict limits on what
avenues you can pursue and how much you can spend (mitigated sometimes by providing recruiters in-house and by letting you recruit from those
already part of your organization—lateral hires). Smaller companies may be
more flexible with outside recruiting resources and dollars. Start-ups may
give you no budget whatsoever.

Resolve the headhunter question first. If you're in a rush to hire, or you're anxious to increase the certainty of making a hire, particularly in a fast economy, working with two or three effective headhunters can vastly improve your candidate pool.

There are lots of mediocre recruiters. The recruiter you want is one with whom you can do a quick mind-meld, one who will almost instantly understand your needs and mirror them back to you first verbally and then in the form of perfect candidates.

The cost of using headhunters—you don't pay "contingency recruiters" unless you hire a candidate whom you had not previously contacted regarding a specific position—is usually a percentage of the new hire's first-year salary. The percentage was once 15 percent, but these days it is seldom less than 20, and 25 percent is not uncommon.

Companies of any size will have their own standard contract stipulating the conditions under which candidates are presented and commissions are earned, including an absolute ceiling on the commission percentage. Just make sure you have a contract in place with a recruiter before you accept résumés or interview any of the recruiter's candidates—or risk heartbreak when your HR department tells you that you can't hire the perfect candidate whom you just had 12 people invest their time interviewing because the recruiter won't meet your company's terms.

Beware: There are some less-than-ethical recruiters. You're looking to engage only exceptional recruiters with absolute integrity.

Avoid boiler-room operations. These are people who would, but for the fortuitous offer of a job in recruiting, be calling you at home during dinnertime to sell you carpets or drapery cleaning or credit repair. When they interrupt you with phone calls at work, they're no less annoying. Some of them will lie and tell you that your colleague "Bob" (pick a name in your organization they just heard) pointed them to you. Some of them will lie and tell you they have a "perfect candidate" with the very set of skills you're looking for and a pedigree so perfect any manager would leap to hire the candidate. On the flip side, programmers get calls about "perfect jobs" that may or may not exist and soon realize the "recruiters" cold-calling them don't know anything.

The worst for you—worse even than being unable to shake a recruiter who hounds you with phone calls—is the recruiter who "introduces" a candidate to whom your organization is already talking, then accuses you of lying and threatens to sue you for a commission.

You can mostly avoid the bad apples and find stellar recruiters by relying on recommendations from other managers and being nothing more than polite to the cold callers.

Ron's feeling is that no interruption by an unsolicited recruiter on the telephone is acceptable. He is civil and asks them to e-mail him. He keeps expecting this to change, but so far it hasn't: The boiler-room operators never, ever e-mail. Their game is a telephone game. He won't hear from them for a month or more, when they phone again. He is always very cordial (until they try to keep him on the phone instead of listening to how he wants to communicate with them). He tells them he loves to communicate with recruiters—which generally truly throws them off their spiel—then after a pause says, "But until I get to know them, I only want to communicate via e-mail." They pester him with questions, to each of which he replies, "I'll look for your e-mail." And after a few of those, he says goodbye and hangs up the phone.

There are, of course, the rare real recruiters who cold-call, but they will be more than willing to contact you however you want. From them you'll see e-mails and candidates and interaction on your terms. And some of them will make it onto your personal list of preferred recruiters.

Recruiter Case Study

In late 2009, Elaine Wherry, one of the cofounders of Meebo, created a fictitious online persona, a JavaScript developer at her company. The fictitious programmer launched his own Web site, LinkedIn profile, and Facebook page. She was fishing for recruiters, hoping her persona would show her who were the best. Over the next 18 months, as her fictitious developer received 237 e-mails from 180 recruiters and 195 companies, she unexpectedly stumbled upon some great insights about recruiting.

Elaine was looking for prize JavaScript superstars; she needed to double the size of her team. She had already tried all the guerrilla recruiting tactics she could think of. She had placed Google AdWords (to pretty much no effect); embedded a "secretjobs" e-mail address into the gnarliest source code on her company's site to snare anyone daring enough to read it; put logo'd T-shirts on students' chairs during Stanford finals for the classes likeliest to deliver her talent; set up a jobs page chat widget (which she described as "useful"); devised JavaScript blog puzzlers and bingo; networked at JavaScript meetups; set up a résumé spider engine; spoke at events; participated in Stanford's computer science classes; advertised in student newspapers;

and placed Twitter keywords. And she created a map of the JavaScript community that proved useful to her recruiters. But when all that wasn't enough, she hit on creating the persona—a honeypot she hoped would attract recruiters who would be best able to find and deliver the coders she needed.

Initially, she gave her guy a great résumé and a good blog but got nothing for two months. Then she filled out a profile for him on LinkedIn—and was flooded. What she learned was that despite what every recruiter told her about how broadly they looked, in fact recruiters these days rely almost exclusively on LinkedIn. So she began turning over rocks for non-LinkedIn-listed programmers.

When she found that her competition for the coders she wanted was not just the big guys—Google and Amazon and Apple and their ilk—but predominantly the midsize and smaller companies, she began working harder to differentiate her company from the rest.

She found that every single recruiter her company had ever employed who was no longer contractually prevented from doing so tried to recruit away her "programmer"—and realized how important it is to keep your prized programmers happy: free food, great people to work with, and interesting stuff to work on.

When she realized how poorly prepared most recruiters were—how many were shotgunning impersonal, canned e-mails—she made sure her own recruiters were armed with her company's mission statement, had specifics about the role being recruited for, and referred to something in candidates' profiles and on their blogs that made them a good fit for the job requirements. Realizing how few stellar recruiters she came across, she determined to treat her few good ones like gems.[10]

Employee Referrals

While we think you should get your cards in order with respect to recruiters right away, in our opinion the number-one source of candidates (and in a start-up with limited funding, virtually your only source) is employee referrals. With referrals, you're leveraging the people you already have in your organization to recommend their friends and former colleagues. Every study we've seen supports our experience: Good people recommend other good

---

10. Elaine Wherry shared her lessons learned in her Code Camp 2011 session, "Winning the Engineering Talent War Online," and later in her blog at http://www.ewherry.com/2012/06/the-recruiter-honeypot/.

people. And you get a built-in reference, usually with contact information for other former colleagues who will vouch for the candidate as well.

....

If your current employees are happy, they will refer other great employees to you. So make your place a desirable place to work—including offices for programmers, good leadership, and perks.

—GREGORY CLOSE, *Manager, Project Manager, and Start-up Founder, San Francisco Bay Area*

It would be nice to think that everyone in your organization would recruit their friends onto your team every time you have an opening. But the fact is that people can be hesitant to solicit their friends; however, that can be overcome with money. You can expect to pay a headhunter a big commission to find a candidate who will be less predictable than the ones your own employees will recommend. If you were to offer a bonus of just half that for employee referrals ($10,000 for a $100,000 hire, say), employees would feel richly rewarded and highly motivated. Justified as they would be, we have never, ever seen referral bonuses that high. Nor have we seen a single study quantifying the difference between $2,000 and $500 bonuses, both of which are common. But we know referral bonuses work.

By the way, hiring managers are a special case when it comes to employee referrals. In every program we've seen, as the hiring manager you are not eligible for referral bonuses; you are expected to lure former employees from your network to your current team. It's not uncommon for managers to be asked, when interviewing, about their networks of programmers and their ability to hire from their own pool. Like many job expectations, doing so is not bonusable.

It is important to keep in touch with peers and former employees. In fact, a large number of employers, possibly a majority, would not hire you if they knew you hadn't stayed networked with the best of the developers with whom you've worked throughout your career. That said, don't solicit developers from the last company you worked for. Even if you didn't sign a nonsolicitation agreement, it's bad form. But stay in touch, connect with your former colleagues on LinkedIn, be friendly, let everyone know where you are, and let them contact you. That is OK. So is nonspecific recruiting like posting an update on your LinkedIn profile and other social networks to broadcast your need.

One note of caution: While the rule is that good people recommend good people, always, always, always listen to your "gut." Ron recalls, "I progressed through one employee's referrals from one of my best hires to one of my worst. My employee had been stellar at his job, so when he told me that his referral candidate was even better, I was skeptical; but after interviews I thought she would at least be good. She was better. She knocked my socks off. So when I next needed a hire and the guy had another 'even better than me' candidate, I ignored the odd feeling in my gut and chose his candidate over another that my team and my gut really liked. My entire group suffered when he turned out not to be stellar—and in fact was not even competent; it was a month of pain until he made it easy for me and left the company." The rule of thumb: Trust your gut about the candidate, not about the referrer.

One more note of caution: You must avoid cronyism and the appearance of cronyism. Your job is to make great hires of people who are a superb fit, not to hire a team of your friends. Your hires should be the best candidates. Yes, that's a subjective decision, and you're the one making the decision, and you have experience with your candidates that no one else in the organization has, and all that is worth something. But if you have a history with a candidate, you should be explicit about communicating why that candidate is your choice; you should share the experience you had with the individual that makes you confident he is the right hire, especially in the face of a competing candidate who interviewed well. As always, communication is your "job one" as a manager, and maintaining interpersonal trust is essential.

Effective Recruiting

Our experience with advertising tech jobs in print media has been to do it rarely, only when the company has a large number of positions to fill, ideally when the number is large enough that it leads you to hold a recruiting event (perhaps in connection with a tech conference nearby) so that the advertising can focus on getting candidates to the recruiting event.

One way to be cost-effective with your recruiting budget, if you have time, is to tier your efforts. Give employees a two-week lead to bring in candidates (and you might make the bonus higher for candidates they bring in during that initial period, possibly saving you the additional work of the next steps). During that time, see if you can scare up candidates yourself from your own network of former employees and colleagues.

After two weeks, turn the recruiting over to your internal staffing department recruiters; if they're any good, the number of résumés you will now have to read will multiply fourfold if not tenfold.

If you still aren't finding your hire, advertise on low-cost local classified networks like Craig's List and free software-jobs-specific job boards like the Bay Area's SWAPjobs Yahoo! Group (SWAPjobs stands for SoftWare Architecture Professionals' jobs list). Your résumé reading list should increase again. Then consider LinkedIn and the large commercial boards like Dice.

Finally, go to a few contingency headhunters. If they're good, your résumé pile will grow by only a small number, but the candidates will be perfect and you'll owe the recruiter a lot of money. (If your organization has a lot of money and little time, skip directly from employee referrals, head-start or not, to headhunters.) If you find yourself working with a headhunter who doesn't "get" what you're looking for—who sends you one inappropriate résumé after another—drop that recruiter. Your time is too valuable.

Recruiting Tips

There are a few other items to pay heed to when recruiting full-time employees.

First, given that your most important jobs are to recruit and retain the right people, the staffing and HR departments are the most important groups in your company to bond with. Staffing will play more of a role in your success than any other group. Make internal recruiters your friends. Their care and feeding should be a top priority for you.

The typical staffing department is wildly understaffed. And with your technical positions to fill, you're at an additional disadvantage, since 95 percent of recruiters barely have a technical bone in their bodies, truly struggle to make sense of your list of required skill sets, and don't really understand the people you're looking for (even if they're good at finding them!). Internal recruiters are typically either touchy-feely HR people who happen to demonstrate a bent for external networking, or marketing people who wish their colleagues would stop typecasting them as HR people. Either way, they have little in common with you.

Make it your mission to make these people your friends. Drop by. Be a friendly face; bring them a smile, flowers, a stuffed animal, or perhaps food (but not to recruiters who are dieting); learn to explain what you're looking for in their lingo; ask about their kids and their hobbies and their interests; help them to figure out where to look for the candidates you're seeking;

review résumés with them to show them the words and phrases that jump out at you (both positive and negative). If they ask you for anything, get it to them by return mail. If they give you résumés to review, return them within hours, commented and prioritized by desirability against your criteria. Don't ever make them track you down. Make their job easier in every way. Be their best friend. Figure out how to genuinely like them, and they'll like you back.

Don't ever assume, when you don't hear from them, that they're working on your hire. Ask them how it's going. Ask if there's anything you can do to help, or if there's any additional information you can supply that would help. Follow these suggestions, and you'll be one of their favorite managers.

Staffing may be located elsewhere. Find excuses to wander by. Schwab's staffing department was on the same floor as its cafeteria, making it easy for Ron to drop by before or after lunch, or when visiting the vending machines at snack time. At Razorfish, Ron formed deeper bonds with the team upstairs when his recruiter was relocated to an office there. It worked. His job requisitions got the attention they needed.

Mickey has used contract recruiters quite successfully at Brøderbund and Gracenote: "When I have a bubble of critical positions to fill, I have worked with HR to bring in a contract recruiter who can focus on those positions. Such recruiters work for a lower fixed fee or on an hourly basis, which can greatly reduce the recruiting costs and result in more progress by focusing strictly on the critical positions. Like programmers, you can sometimes find contract recruiters who are passionate about their areas of interest. You can work closely with these contract recruiters to make sure they thoroughly understand the ideal candidate profiles and the critical skill sets, and they work very closely with hiring managers to optimize their time by presenting only highly qualified candidates. At Brøderbund we had one contract recruiter who became a specialist in locating great multimedia talent. He immersed himself in the technologies and prowled the technical forums and special-interest groups looking for talented individuals. He became almost obsessive about looking for and being successful at finding talent. I saw him recently at a SIGGRAPH trade show where he was working for Intel recruiting 3-D graphics specialists and still obsessed by his mission. He was a special recruiter."

Finding such passionate recruiters is hard, but when you do, your life will be easier and your recruiting almost a pleasure.

There's another class of headhunters besides those who work on commission, but they mostly don't apply to you. Retained recruiters are ones you retain and pay regardless of whether they find the candidate you hire.

Retained recruiters mostly work on senior management positions, where they specialize in having senior-level networks they can access to find candidates. Sometimes they specialize in or undertake searches in secrecy, to avoid putting the word on the street that someone senior is being replaced. For programmers, though, you'll almost always pay recruiters a commission only if they find the right candidate for you—a contingency search.

Recruiting Contractors

Recruiting contractors is different from recruiting employees.

A large organization may well have a list of six, eight, or ten "preferred vendors" of contractors through which you will be required to hire contractors. One or more of them will be designated as "pass-through" vendors; should you find an independent contractor you want to bring in, you'll be required to bring them in through one of the pass-through vendors, which will provide payroll services and bill you enough more to pay taxes and take a cut themselves.

If you're lucky enough to have this system in place and enforced in your company, your phone won't ring except with legitimate business. You'll never be plagued by the swarm of job shops trying to be the one to find you contractors. On the other hand, there goes your largest source of free lunches and presents at Christmas. The real downside is that you'll have to leave behind the contractor recruiters who have served you so well in the past and whom you have long cultivated to bring you great people (and buy you lunches).

If you don't have a preferred vendor system in your company, ask your engineering manager peers and colleagues for referrals of good contractor houses and recruiters to work with.

Go out of your way to find a "boutique" contracting house that you can trust to find especially skilled contractors when you need them. Mickey says: "While at Gracenote I found a contract house that always seemed to find exactly the right 'specialty' contractor when I needed one. They had access to a network of contractors and had them categorized very well, because they found me a contractor in Seattle, a contractor in Toronto, and many locally with exactly the specific skills I was looking for at the time. These skills were not simply programming skills; they were as exotic as experience with Japanese *and* Korean Morphological Text Matching, or experience in implementing UPnP servers (when the technology was first emerging), and others. I was amazed at how quickly they could respond to my seemingly exotic requests for contractors."

Preferred or no, cultivate those relationships. You want these folks to see your needs as their top priority and to think of you when their best people become available.

Of course, the best place to look for contract talent is within your own network. LinkedIn provides instantaneous and always updated access to your network, though it is no real substitute for a carefully cultivated database of your contacts that you maintain throughout the years.

Mickey uses LinkedIn for his close set of personal contacts (hundreds, not thousands), but also the CardScan program religiously to maintain all his contacts, including those whom he would not dream of inviting into his personal LinkedIn network. CardScan is exactly what it says; it is a business card scanner and related personal contact management program. "This has been one of my best weapons in accelerating the recruiting process for employees and contractors."

Reviewing Résumés

If you're lucky, all that recruiting will result in a flood of résumés. But how do you identify the potential stars in a stack of résumés?

Reading résumés is an art. You need to look for your requirements expressed in someone else's words. You need to read between the lines. You need to connect the dots. You need to read the words and imagine the activities the candidate would have had to undertake to be able to write those words. You need to think through whether the range of experiences candidates have had will have readied them for your company and your position.

....

College degrees don't impress me, and lack of school doesn't scare me (see: Jobs, Steve, and Gates, Bill). At some point, when a person is far enough removed from school, the degree is all but meaningless. Experience is what matters most.

> —ERIC MULLER, *Software Architect and VP of Technology,*
> *San Francisco Bay Area*

Pretty soon, you have to make a value judgment regarding what requirements are truly required; how experienced a candidate really has to be with each of those technologies; how many applications you need to see and how big they need to be to prove a candidate truly has the skills you're looking for.

*I assume that a good candidate rewrites their résumé and
cover letter after reading my Web site. Checking them out
on LinkedIn tells me what their résumé really says.*

—*BRUCE ROSENBLUM, CEO of Inera, former VP of
Software Development at Turning Point*

If you're seeking arcane and unusual skills, the pickings may turn out to
be scarce. You'll have to decide whether to redouble or rethink your recruiting efforts in order to find the candidates you need or to scale back your
expectations and plan to train. Keep in mind that though you can train
FTEs, you should expect contractors to have each and every skill you need,
coming in the door.

*I want people who can write, because we spend a lot of
time writing to each other. We're writing e-mail or
documentation. We're writing plans. We're writing
specifications. I want to know that the people on my
team are capable of doing that, and that turns out to
be a really difficult skill. So I would actually rather
see people start as English majors than as math
majors to get into programming.*

—*DOUGLAS CROCKFORD, Inventor of JSON,
Software Architect, and Entrepreneur*[11]

As you read résumés, jot notes on your copy (not on the original, since
you want other interviewers to reach their own conclusions, not base their
judgments on yours). Highlight the skills and tools you're looking for, where
they appear. Draw arrows to gaps in employment history, so you can follow
up with a question. Circle spelling errors, bad grammar, and sloppy formatting; you may end up making a decision between two candidates based on
knowing that one can write well enough that you won't have to review every
word. Note where candidates have changed jobs frequently; if you're looking for someone to stay on your team long-term, you may need to formulate
a question that elicits why a candidate jumped around. And write questions on the résumé as you're reading it (e.g., "What was your role in this

---

11. Quoted in Peter Seibel, *Coders at Work: Reflections on the Craft of Programming* (Apress, 2009),
    p. 124.

accomplishment?" "What part of this project did you do?" "Why were you at this company for such a short time?" "What was the result of this effort for the company?" "What was the most difficult aspect of implementing this technology"? "What technologies and tools did you use on this project?" "What language did you write this in?" "What was the toughest challenge you overcame on this project?" "How did you learn this new skill?").

I often look for people that have done a lot of stuff on their own that wasn't asked of them. Not just their school project or just what their previous employer had them do. Somebody who was passionate about something and had some side project. How did they maintain it and how serious did they get with it? Or do they do a lot of quick hacks and abandon them?

—BRAD FITZPATRICK, *Founder of LiveJournal and Chief Architect at Six Apart*[12]

Résumé reading is a skill in which new managers will find it helpful to be mentored. Ask around to identify experienced and talented interviewers and hiring managers. Ask if you can help them read résumés for their next hire. Few managers will turn down that offer since even those skilled at it find reading résumés a thankless, but critical, chore.

You will find the résumé-reading checklist in the Tools section useful.

Narrowing the Field

In a slow economy or if you're hiring into a hot company, you may still have more candidates than you can interview.

IQ-like questions and quizzes are stupid.

—DAVE WILSON, *Software Architect, San Francisco Bay Area*

One way to narrow the field is to send candidates a programming challenge. Work with your team to identify a coding challenge that requires

---

12. Ibid., p. 77.

skills consistent with your team's needs, has a correct answer, and should be able to be coded in a reasonable amount of time. Ask candidates to send you their answer and their code.

When you get results, interview the candidates who submitted correct answers and whose code shows the kind of thinking, rigor, and documentation you expect.

A suggestion worth pursuing is to do the hands-on programming challenge live using WebEx, IM, or a Web site like http://i.seemikecode.com that allows you as the interviewer to watch the remote candidate type. It will give you a virtual hands-on feel for candidates before bringing them in for in-person interviews.

What ultimately narrows the field for us is simple: careful screening.

Preparing to Interview

Once you've got candidates who look like they might be a fit, it's time to interview.

The first interview is by phone, a screening interview. You need to find out

- If the candidate is still interested
- Whether the candidate is interviewing with other companies (and what the time frame is with those companies, whether the candidate already has other offers, is considering them seriously, and when a decision must be made)
- What kind of job the candidate is looking for
- What the candidate considers to be their areas of expertise
- What compensation is expected
- Why the candidate is looking for another job
- The candidate's availability to start working for you
- Whether the candidate is willing to commute to your location if working in your offices is a requirement

Ask candidates to describe in detail what they have worked on, both for you to gain confidence that they actually did what they said, but also to know that they can explain what they have done and what they know. Drill down into one or two of the accomplishments they cite to confirm that they have the skills you need.

....

*I avoid prima donnas. One candidate told me he only
needed to work two days per week because he could do
in 16 hours what everyone else would do in 40. No,
thank you.*

—BRUCE ROSENBLUM

For a highly specialized technical position, you may want to choose a highly technical team member to conduct a second screening to test expert knowledge the candidate claims to have and that you need.

Once you confirm that candidates are credible—that they appear to meet all your criteria—you'll assemble an interview team. Then bring in two or three leading candidates for one or more rounds of interviews with your team, your colleagues, and perhaps your boss.

The job description you prepared earlier, such as our sample one in Figure 3.1, should provide all the criteria you'll use to qualify a candidate and measure one against another. The challenge is to remember to test every candidate against all those criteria, and then keep track of how the candidates stack up against them and each other. Mickey long ago came up with the spreadsheet format in Figure 3.2 to help him do that. Enter your criteria into a similar spreadsheet to keep track of your candidates and their qualifications.

Plan a strategy for who will pursue which skills and qualities, and additionally who will help you sell the candidate on joining the company. (It works both ways.)

The interviewers you assemble may include

- You
- Your HR or staffing person
- Programmers who are the technical leadership on your team
- Programmers from related teams with whom your hire will need to interface
- Your UI designer
- The product manager
- The project manager
- Another development manager or two (particularly if you're green at hiring; another manager's observations and feedback can help you with what to look for and how to look for it)
- Others in the business from whom the programmer will get requirements or collaborate around product and support issues
- Your boss (or even your boss's boss)

Principal Programmer Interview Summary	Bill Smith	Cathy Llu	Arnold Lai	Lucy Miller	Andy Jones
Received résumé on					
Phone screen on					
First interview round on					
On time, early, or late?					
Second interview round on					
On time, early, or late?					
Bachelor's Degree (optional)					
Minimum 8 years programming experience					
Wrote first program ever in (year, language)					
Wrote first professional program in					
Experience with what languages					
Experience with what databases					
Minimum 3 years .Net programming experience					
Wrote first .Net program in					
Most recently wrote for .Net in					
Minimum 3 years SQL Server programming experience					
Wrote first SQL Server program in					
Most recently wrote for SQL Server v. (???) in (year)					
Web application architecture and design skills?					
Ability to analyze & improve scalability and performance					
Experience scaling high-volume, information-rich Web apps					
Fast, clean, efficient coder?					
Refactoring skills					
Has defined development and engineering best practices					
Experience leading and mentoring other developers					

Figure 3.2   Principal Programmer interview summary
(continued next page)

Principal Programmer Interview Summary	Bill Smith	Cathy Liu	Arnold Lai	Lucy Miller	Andy Jones
Communicates designs effectively					
Listens					
Critiques others' designs					
Writing skills					
Customer Experience empathy/ awareness/design sense					
Intangible qualities					
Energy					
Flexibility					
Self-direction					
Smart					
Articulate					
Passionate					
Fit in with team					
Overall desire to work at our company					
Experience w/algorithmic design, coding, trade-offs					
Search/information retrieval					
Analytics, data warehousing, and business intelligence					
Information visualization					
Web services					
Sent us a follow-up thank you?					

Figure 3.2   Principal Programmer interview summary

In one company Ron's CEO asked to interview every candidate to whom Ron thought he would want to make an offer (provided the CEO's travel plans or other conflicts did not hold up the hiring process); he wanted a head start with new hires for his goal to know everyone in the company, considered it a "touch test" to build confidence in his senior managers' hiring IQs, and offered the gift of his time to assist with the sometimes challenging task of luring highly qualified developers who were choosing among competing offers.

On the other hand, earlier in his career at a much larger company, Ron's midlevel boss gave him carte blanche to hire without the boss interviewing a single candidate. At a third company, not only his boss but also his boss's boss were on the interview schedule. You'll likely have managers of every stripe as well, but if they interview, they'll almost always want to be last to do so; most will want to see just the "keepers."

Mickey and Ron would both rather have more interviewers than fewer. When hiring FTEs, Ron typically selects two teams of four to five interviewers for a first and second round of 45- to 60-minute one-on-one interviews. Get to know how long your interviewers prefer for an interview. Some will be like Ron, who wants a full hour with candidates, whether his or another manager's candidates; others are happy with 30 minutes and uncomfortable with even five minutes longer than their requested time.

Programmers are critical interviewers. They will have to work with the new person and team with them. They also likely know the skills and experience that are needed or missing better than anyone. But programmers are also generally the least prepared to interview. You need to spend time with new interviewers to go through the technical and team qualities you want candidates to bring. Then you can work together on questions and exercises they can pose that will help reveal the candidate's facility.

Assign areas of focus for your interview team members: the various technical skills you need; analytical, problem-solving, communication, and interpersonal skills; and résumé red flags and omissions. Make sure you have interviewers who will ask technical questions that demand technical answers. Divide up the candidate's projects and companies among your interviewers, so that someone digs into the details of each one. And divide up the qualities you're looking for, both to ensure that among your team someone is pursuing understanding of that quality as well as to avoid a day of interviews where everyone asks the same questions. A wiki page or other collaborative online space is perfect for letting your team sign up for those areas about which they feel most competent or most passionate.

All that preparation will help ensure that your interviewers are prepared. Too many interviewers in too many companies read a résumé five minutes before the person comes in—or on their walk to the lobby to pick up the candidate—and end up contributing a fraction of the thoughtful, in-depth understanding that a well-grounded, well-thought-out interview should produce. The entire interviewing team must be clear on the need for this hire, with whom the new hire will work, and what the new employee will be tasked to contribute. Then each interviewer can create initial specific questions, using the résumé to guide further questions when probing into the candidate's experience and background. Interview training is something that is not often given to employees, but the cost of hiring the wrong people far outweighs that time and effort.

When you're hiring programmers, you have to get at their ability to code. It's essential to answer questions that elicit a picture of their understanding of programming. It's critical that you ask them to do some design and to write some code.

> *I have had a couple of profound wake-up-call cases lately that pointed out how important it is to ask a programmer candidate to write code. In both cases, we had candidates whom we considered to be A or A+ level matches to what we were looking for. They'd had all the right experience, listed just the right skills for the job, seemed to have the right people skills, and genuinely seemed like nice and well-rounded individuals. But then, almost as a formality, we asked them to write some code. The term* deer in the headlights *best describes the result. Both these guys fell flat on their faces. We couldn't believe it. They did so badly that it caused a stir throughout our whole department and led to multiple discussions about how this could have happened. Long story short: What we learned was that asking candidates to write code and to answer questions about code is absolutely critical.*
>
> —*STEVE JOHNSON, VP of R&D*

Encourage the candidate to bring a portfolio of projects—documentation they've written, designs they've created, samples of their work, and even demos on DVD-R/USB flash drive or online that demonstrate their prowess.

> *I invite the candidate to bring in a piece of code he's really proud of and walk us through it. I'm looking for quality of presentation . . . how effectively they can communicate, that's a skill that I'm hiring for.*
>
> —*DOUGLAS CROCKFORD*[13]

---

13. Quoted in Seibel, *Coders at Work*, p. 129.

*Ask a candidate to bring along some of their source code.
Inspect their code, and you'll know if they are any good.
Then ask the candidate to show you an app that they
built. Evaluate the user experience.*

—DAVE WILSON

Sometimes doing this can have unexpected effects. Ron's youngest hire was, at Apple, an intern just out of high school. Ron had heard, through a connection, about the young programmer's prowess but wasn't sure his team would embrace a high school kid. As it turned out, the young programmer brought in samples of random-dot wall-eyed auto-stereograms; he had read about the technique of hiding 3-D scenes in images that at first glance appear to be nothing but random dots, and he'd figured out how to reverse-engineer a program to create them. As Ron watched his team squint wall-eyed at the samples pinned to the team wall, willing the 3-D images to emerge, he knew he had a fit.

*Pair programming for half an hour during an interview
will save everyone's time.*

—DAVID VYDRA, *Continuous Delivery Advocate and
Software Craftsman, TestDriven.com*

As you set up a morning or afternoon or day of interviews, you need to plan for someone to be the first to greet the candidate, and someone to see them out. As the hiring manager, you're a strong candidate to fill at least one of those roles. Taking the closing role can be a great opportunity to debrief candidates on their perceptions of your company and your team, try to correct any misperceptions, and send the candidate off with a positive impression.

Ron also tries to have a trusted strong interviewer lead off—and report back at once if the candidate seems at all a bad fit. There's no use wasting the candidate's or the team's time further if you determine up front that the match isn't there.

If possible, take the candidate and at least part of your team to lunch. The interactions you'll see will be priceless for making a decision about whether the candidate has "team fit."

Mark Himelstein, an Interim VP of Engineering in the San Francisco Bay Area, prepares his interviewing teams by going over

- What the person is being hired for
- Issues/areas to be covered (making sure that someone is covering the basics)
- How to sell the company consistently

He notes, regarding selling the company, "I have used role-play to teach developers how to sell the company consistently. We agree on the point I want each to make, then I have them use that point to sell the company to a colleague in 120 seconds. I have the team offer critiques to their peers on how to improve the pitch."

Finally, do candidates a favor by presenting them with an interview schedule when they arrive that includes times and interviewers with their titles and (should the candidate want to follow up) e-mail addresses. Having your greeter not only present it but draw a verbal picture of the interviews ahead and who the interviewers are will put your candidate at ease and get logistics out of the way so that you can all focus on fit.

Take a look at the sample interview schedule in the Tools section.

Interviewing

Take notes! Walk into interviews prepared to take notes on what candidates say. It's amazing how a series of candidates will blur together without notes to tell them apart.

Make time before the interview to prepare your questions. Write them down. Carry them into the room with you.

Make eye contact (and make sure the candidate can make eye contact with you). Make note of what candidates communicate nonverbally; how they comport themselves; whether they're on time, early, or late; and afterward whether they send a thank-you. And make notes about what your team members, colleagues, and boss have to say about the candidates.

At the same time, don't be so busy writing down what candidates say that you don't notice who they are.

Ron makes it a practice never to interview a programmer in a room that doesn't have a whiteboard; he looks for candidates' willingness, even eagerness, to get up and explain to him how they approached a problem they faced in a previous company, to explain the architecture and design of one or another of their previous projects, or how they would face one of his team's problems now. It can help differentiate the talkers from the doers.

....

I like to talk about design patterns, like how would you design something. Candidates should be able to identify all the parts of objects. For example, if you were designing a game of blackjack, you have cards, hands, and players. They should be able to identify properties of these objects and their relationships. When would they use inheritance? When would they use "is-a" versus "has-a" relationships? There may be more than one correct answer, but the approach should be workable. I find I am usually willing to give answers and instruct so that it is not a "gotcha" interview, but more of a conversation. The goal is to determine how well we work together on a problem.

—PAUL OSSENBRUGGEN, *Senior Staff Developer*

You're going to want to know the answers to questions like these:

- "What aspects of your last job did you most like?"
- "What were your colleagues and your management like?"
- "Tell me about some of the things you and your supervisor disagreed about."
- "What led you to leave the companies you previously worked for?"
- "What attracts you to our company?"
- "Why are you looking for another job now?"
- "What do you want to get out of your job?"

Learn to ask questions that are open-ended—that candidates can't answer with a yes or no—questions like these:

- "Tell me about . . ."
- "How were you able to accomplish . . . ?"
- "What was your role in . . . ?"
- "If you had led the development effort on that project, what would you have done differently?"
- "What best practices are you most fond of?"
- "What are your strongest technical strengths?"
- "What are your strongest nontechnical strengths?"
- "If you think of the fabric of programming as triangular, with the points representing design, coding, and debugging, tell me about the part of the fabric on which you would most like to spend your time."

- "Where would you place yourself on a continuum where one end is developing gnarly algorithms and the other is developing customer-focused UI?"
- "Imagine a line. One end is leadership. On the other is teamwork that's so fully collaborative that leadership is totally shared and no one on the team would be able to identify a leader. Where on that line would you place yourself?"
- "How would your manager describe you?"
- "Tell me about your comfort level with asking for assistance from others."
- "Where do you fall on a continuum that ranges from highly structured, where your tasks are spelled out completely, to one that is entirely free-form and you have to make decisions, often without having all the information you'd like?"
- "How do you like to be managed?"

Ask for examples:

- "Think of a time when you knew you could not make a deadline. What did you do?"
- "What was the most interesting problem you faced in a former project? How did you solve it?"
- "Tell me about a time when you . . ."
- "Give me an example that illustrates your leadership style."
- "Think for a minute about the most stressful situations you've been in at work and tell me about the one you think was most stressful of all. What did you do to deal with it?"
- "Have there been times when you needed to formulate a new solution? Tell me about that time, and about what you devised."
- "Tell me about a best practice you played a role in getting your team to adopt."
- "Describe a time when you displayed extraordinary initiative."
- "Have you worked with a UI designer [product manager, business analyst . . .] to translate customer needs into technical requirements? Tell me about that collaboration."
- "Tell me about a time when your manager was annoyed with you or with your role on the team. How did you respond?"
- "Think about the teams you've been part of and tell me about a peak teamwork experience. What contributed to making that memorable?"

- "What have you done when you've had far too many tasks assigned to you than you can handle? When that's been the situation and you could see yet another task coming your way, what did you do?"
- "Tell me about a time when you successfully persuaded your manager or your team to adopt your position."
- "How have you handled making formal presentations in front of large and small groups? Tell me what that was like."
- "Have you had to present technical solutions to highly nontechnical audiences? How did that go?"
- "Describe a time when you advocated creating a better customer experience."
- "Describe a situation in which you had to tear down code and redesign and recode from the ground up."

I'm no longer a full-time developer and my skills have gotten a little rusty. When I'm interviewing someone, I focus on basic concepts. If I can stump them, they are done.

—ERIC MULLER

I have a "trick" for hiring that's proven to be pretty effective:

After a candidate has been through the interview process and has gotten to me (they've already proven their technical chops and the team likes them), I ask three questions:

1.   Do you run radio-controlled vehicles (cars, planes, boats)?
2.   Do you juggle?
3.   Do you play any musical instruments?

If they answer yes to one of the three, they are likely a good developer. To two, a better developer. To all three? A 20X developer. None? Likely not a good hire.

I know it sounds like a gimmick, but I've used it hundreds of times, and so far it's proven to be quite effective.

—SCOTT CONVERSE, VP of Engineering, Colorado

Get candidates to give you details. What role did they play in the projects they cite on their résumés? Get them to tell you how they accomplished the achievements they claim. Ask them about the most difficult problems they had to solve in accomplishing them, and ask them to walk you through their solutions.

I have always found that getting candidates to talk about a project they have done in detail brings me the best info: how well they communicate, what roles they actually had, do they have a big picture about what they did, do they really understand the technical details. . . .

—*MARK HIMELSTEIN*

Think of a problem situation that vexed a team you've managed (and would be appropriate for candidates to solve) and ask them to suggest how to solve it.

But don't ask leading questions. Do truly make your questions open-ended; give candidates room to answer as they think appropriate.

Ron writes questions with the intent not only to understand what candidates know and how they think, but to learn something from each and every candidate that he has the opportunity to interview, no matter for what job. "We're interviewing these candidates because we think they can bring something to our company. My attitude is to figure out what they know that I don't (yet), and to start learning from them. Sometimes it's technical; other times it's how other companies or managers have handled challenges or, from college hires, how the computer science curriculum is being taught these days."

If I can't learn something significant from a candidate in an hour's interview, it's almost certain I will decline to hire them.

There are also key logistical questions you'll want to ask:

- "What will commuting to our offices from where you live be like for you?"
- "How much travel do you like (and how does that fit with the amount of travel I foresee in the job)?"
- "What are your compensation expectations?"
- "What was your base salary in your last job?"

The latter questions are important for you (or your HR or staffing interviewer) to ask, ideally before you even bring the candidate in, since your
budget for the position or the need to maintain salary equity with the developers already on your team may not be a fit with what the candidate is
looking for. Make sure you know beforehand which interviewer will ask
them, so you don't come away still clueless. For those candidates reluctant
to respond, point out that your reference-checking process will get previous
salary information from prior companies anyway—this is their opportunity
to affect how you think about it.

One final note on preparing questions: Keep them legal. Your questions should never in any way suggest or encourage candidates to tell you
about their

- Marital status
- Parental status
- Age (particularly whether 40 or over, but don't go there with anyone)
- Ethnicity or nationality
- Disability or perceived disability
- Religion
- Sexual orientation

Making the Decision to Hire a Programmer

As each round of interviews completes, get timely feedback. Our experience is, unfortunately, that you will likely have to remind (even hound) your
interviewers to give you their feedback. You need to get it the same day, at
the latest the next day, while it's fresh and memorable, and also because, if
you like the candidate, you want to take action, whether to bring the candidate back for another round of interviews or to make an offer.

....

*Debriefing your interviewers, as a team, is critical: Not
only is it an opportunity for you to understand the
team's perspective, but for them, observing how others
can perceive different aspects of the candidate can help
each team member improve their interviewing skills.*

—PHAC LE TUAN, *VP of Engineering and CEO,*
San Francisco Bay Area

Ask your team to look for indicators and for red flags. An indicator might be a candidate who has programmed in a lot of languages. It's a rule of thumb: The more languages, the better the programmer. On the other hand, red flags might be that the candidate arrived late for the interview, took a call during the interview, never seemed to establish eye contact, was sharply critical of former managers and former companies, arrived knowing nothing about your company or your products, was unable to explain a previous design, didn't show interest in the work you do, didn't share anything from which you could learn, or didn't follow up with a note or e-mailed thank-you.

Will the candidate be able not only to contribute to the current need, but can you anticipate their skill set contributing for years to come? Make sure you're not hiring a narrow fit for a short-term task that, when complete, will leave you with a long-term problem requiring that you either train or terminate.

Weight the feedback from your interviewers. Some interviewers' feedback is worth a lot more, whether because they know the technical hiring requirements cold, or because they have proven themselves to have a great feel for hiring, or for one of a dozen other reasons. Think about the weighting *before* you hear the feedback.

....

If you're dithering, don't hire them.

—STEVE BURBECK, *Manager at Apple and IBM, a small wholesale company, two start-ups, and a research institute*

While dismissing candidates as not appropriate is easy, making a decision to hire is often difficult. Be clear with your interviewing team that the decision will be yours. (Actually, it will likely be yours in concert with your boss and HR.) It is *not* a consensus decision.

Sooner or later, you'll find yourself convinced that you have a stellar candidate, and every interviewer is on board but one—an interviewer who is adamant that hiring the candidate would be a mistake. Listen carefully to that person's feedback; it's possible the feedback is dead-on. It's also possible the interviewer is not looking at the same criteria you are. If you make it clear you're taking input (not looking for consensus), and you bring all your reflective listening skills to bear so that the person feels he is heard, you're likely on solid ground to hire the candidate based on all your other feedback that says "stellar." On the other hand, if the interviewer, or worse your entire interview team, gets it in their heads that it's a consensus decision, you'll never break a meeting deadlock without bad feelings, very possibly not only from the one person who demurs but from the team as a whole.

A quick meeting of all interviewers can be useful; a discussion can prompt memories and *ahas* that had been only subconscious. But meetings can also communicate to interviewers that they have more say than they do. And going on the record with one's input can make it more difficult for an interviewer to give you the power to make your own decision. These days Ron tends to get feedback one-on-one with each interviewer, ideally in person or by e-mail or phone.

You need to learn not only to listen to others who interviewed, but to trust your "gut" about what you heard and saw. At one company, Ron let his team talk him into hiring a candidate when all his internal signals were saying no. The candidate, who wanted onto the team for all the wrong reasons, turned out to be mediocre. While she in fact made some good project contributions, she never really fit in with the rest of the team and was at the top of the layoff list when times turned bad.

Ron made the first hiring decisions of his career at Apple, at a time when the company couldn't interview and hire fast enough. So it was memorable when CEO John Sculley, speaking to a full auditorium of Apple managers, urged everyone to hire carefully. His sage advice: "Hire people you want to sit next to, both tomorrow and a year from now."

Different organizations have different customs and practices around hiring. When Steve Jobs's NeXT Computer company hired technical staff, the decision to hire someone had to be unanimous; every person who interviewed the candidate had to agree that the candidate should be hired or they would pass ("thumbs up or thumbs down"). This led to some very intense interviews, and many of those who were hired survived grueling programming problems, one-on-five interviews, and a process that lasted many hours. The approach led to a team of extremely bright and talented members—but they were not that diverse. Make sure you clearly understand the culture you are working to staff.

To help you understand other hiring cultures, we suggest that you research some of the top technology companies to get some insight into how they work. Try Googling "interviewing at" and you'll get suggestions for several companies to review. There are some very interesting stories about interviewing experiences you can easily access online. Don't feel compelled to copy them, but learn from the good and the bad that are painted in these stories to help mold your own hiring culture.

....

Call references.

With a candidate chosen, it's time to check references. Ask the candidate to provide you with a list of references you can call. You're going to ask for at least two peers and two former managers, with phone numbers and e-mail addresses. If you're hiring a manager, also ask for two former employees. Pick and choose to call at least one from each category.

To the candidate's list you'll add your own "back-channel" references. The candidate presumably listed colleagues who will all deliver praise and recommendations. What you're looking for are random others to corroborate that feedback but also to fill in gaps. You may know someone or have a teammate who worked at a company at the same time the candidate did. The shortest route these days is to search LinkedIn to identify whom you know who worked there when the candidate did.

....

Never be satisfied talking only with the references your
candidate supplies. If they're a friend of the candidate, they
often won't mention the candidate's faults—and everyone
has them. Find an independent source—someone you know
who has worked with the candidate as a peer as well as
someone who managed or worked for them.

—*DAVE CURBOW, User Experience Architect, Cisco*

HR may volunteer to take care of reference checking, but you should always have at least two or three of the conversations yourself. After introducing yourself, begin by asking how and when the reference worked with the candidate.

Like interview questions, the best reference-check questions are open-ended. You want to know about the work that candidates did and about their skills, teamwork and collaboration, work habits, initiative, thoroughness, follow-through, reliability, need for supervision, ability to learn, strengths and weaknesses, and values and ethics. Ask for examples. Get the reference to be descriptive, to draw verbal pictures for you. Ask about any red flags that came up for you or your interviewers. Ask references where they would rank the candidate with the others on their team. Describe the job you're hiring for, and ask references whether they think the candidate is a fit. Ask former managers if they would hire the candidate again, former teammates if they would gladly work with the candidate again.

We suggest you use a reference checklist like the one we've provided in the Tools section.

Making the Right Offer to a Programmer

Making the right offer to a programmer starts with timeliness. Every day lost is an opportunity for your candidate to discover, interview with, and receive an offer from another shop. During the dot-com hiring frenzy, every hour lost was an hour risked.

Don't be hasty but be quick.

But how do you know what offer to make? Determining the right offer starts early in the interview process with the question "What are your compensation expectations?" You may want to follow up with "How much did you make in your last position?" or even more explicitly "What were your W-2 wages for last year?"

You might be thinking that your worst-case offer will be to maintain a programmer's last salary and your best offer will apply some single-digit-percentage increment. But last salary is less useful than it looks at first glance. It might have been exorbitant; salaries required to lure top programmers at the peak of the dot-com boom were downright unrealistic just a few months later, after the bust. Or it might be drastically below market; a programmer hired just before boom times probably didn't get raises to match the salaries of developers hired later. A programmer working for a struggling start-up may not have had a raise for years.

....

Salary compression is a fact of life. Don't let it make you miss a candidate.

—*MARK HIMELSTEIN*

Most programmers know if their last salary was out of line. In the first case, they may respond with expectations considerably lower than their last salary. In the second and third examples, their expectations may justifiably be a big increment from what their previous company got away with paying.

You may hear expectations that are out of your range. Be frank: "Our base salary ranges just don't go that high. We can offer <options, bonus

opportunity, special benefits>, but not that kind of base salary." If you end up cutting the phone screening short, you'll have saved your interviewing team a lot of time, trouble, and false hopes and given yourself back a little time you can use to scout for other candidates. Be aware, though, that while you'll run across an occasional candidate with an inflated sense of self-worth, more often you're getting a signal. It may be that you've overshot and are interviewing a candidate much more qualified than you need. On the other hand, you may be hearing a signal that salaries have moved. If the latter is the case, as you hear high expectations from subsequent candidates, you may kick yourself for dismissing the first.

Compensation is not just a salary number but a package. While some candidates won't lower their base salary expectations even for a great package that includes outstanding options, exceptional bonus potential, unusual and special benefits, or the like, some will. If you're excited about hiring them, then sell them on the company, the position, your team, and your package.

Every programmer's motivation is different.

If candidates are wary about telling you their compensation expectations, give them some time to think about it. Let it go during the interview, but follow up afterward if you're interested in pursuing them for your position. If you don't, you could end up negotiating with yourself by putting an offer on the table that is inappropriate—either too low or too high. In either case, you're now at a disadvantage in formulating the right offer for the candidate. Make sure you get wary candidates to clearly state their compensation expectations and consciously decide they are acceptable before moving forward in the hiring process.

Once you know what they expect and that it's a match for your range—and once all the feedback from interviewers and references has led you to want to hire—you need to think through a specific number and package. If the candidate's expectations are low, you may be tempted to make a lowball offer. We think you'll regret it.

We think your salary number has to be in line with the going rate in the market. The last thing you want is for a candidate—realizing, just after arriving, that many if not most companies are paying a lot more—to keep the pipeline of job opportunities open, leading to a departure for a better one after only a short time on your team. If possible, work with your HR department to verify your target number with an industry standard salary survey service such as Radford Surveys.[14] Radford, and other similar services, provides benchmark data comparing companies situated similarly to your own. This will help you determine if you are paying competitive market rates for the new hire and provide the ammunition you may need to help convince your management to hire someone for more than what is budgeted for the position.

We think your salary number also has to be in line with salaries you're already paying comparable programmers on your team and across your company. You can exhort your team all you want to keep their salary numbers to themselves, but sooner or later they'll all know what the others are making. Bad inequities will lead, at that point, to carping, bitterness, disgust, and an exodus of your best people.

....

I'd rather do big bonuses than out-of-range salaries.

—MARK HIMELSTEIN

However, sometimes you need to bring in a programmer who doesn't fit your current internal equity. You hate to do it, but you may choose to because you need the programmer desperately, or because your programming staff, in general, is paid below market rates. By bringing someone in above your internal equity rankings, you have ammunition to bring to HR and your management to try to increase the salaries of the top performers on the staff you already have. This is a painful tactic, but it's sometimes necessary to satisfy your short-term hiring needs.

The one exception where equity can be less of an issue is with geographically dispersed teams, since salary decisions may have been made based on geographical differences in both market and cost of living. You can get an idea of how to derive geographical equity—how to come up with a salary number for the same person in different locales—by using the research data at www.salary.com.

At some point you may find yourself hounded by management or HR to bring contractors on board as employees, a challenge made especially difficult by compensation numbers. Contractors' hourly net is almost always higher than the salary you could equitably pay them, and often more than

---

14. Radford is a market leader in compensation intelligence. www.radford.com/.

the salary and benefits put together. And if they have figured out a way to make their benefits work (e.g., getting benefits through their spouse's employer), such that they don't need those that come with an employee offer, converting them to employeehood becomes monetarily nearly impossible. On the other hand, contractors often face corporate policies, put in place to avoid tax and legal problems, that decree they can consult for only a year or two, then must be gone for six months to reestablish eligibility. If they like you and your team and your work, they may be willing to talk, at that point, about conversion.

Ron had one contractor who wanted $10,000 in salary above the rest of the company's engineers at his level. The company's pay system required breadth to qualify for the next engineering grade, but like many contractors his skill set was narrow and vertical. Ron created a win-win by formulating a package (which required his getting sign-off all the way to the general manager) including

- A salary at grade level
- A guaranteed $10,000 in training over the next 12 months that could be used only for coursework in related technologies that the company needed and would also broaden the contractor's narrow skill set to a much more versatile and valuable one
- A promise to provide him with mentoring support from one of the team's most senior architects
- A promise to evaluate him, in 12 months, for possible promotion to the higher grade and a possible $10,000 raise to go with it

Complicated as that was (and hard as it was to get HR to go along, which was where selling it to the general manager came in), it reduced Ron's personnel budget, extended the programmer's tenure, motivated the new employee both to deliver and to expand his skills, and gave Ron a productive, valuable resource on the team who was gratified at the investment being made in him and on his behalf—for less than he would have cost as a contractor.

You'll forget what you gave them in ten minutes so don't get too worried.

—MARK HIMELSTEIN

Once he has a salary number, Ron will sometimes test it: "I need someone to start Monday. It's difficult adjusting an offer later—I need to have an offer that I know you would accept before I go to get it approved. If I were able to get you an offer by Thursday of $xx,000 in base salary, along with n-thousand options and the opportunity to make a 20 percent increment over your base in bonuses, would you accept it and start Monday?"

Questions like that will help you to understand what a winning offer looks like, typically clue you in about competing interviews and offers, and often begin to build commitment on the part of the candidate—get them practiced in saying yes.

Before making and writing up the offer, you'll want to think about a start date. If the candidate is working, it will almost certainly be at least two weeks after giving notice. If you have flexibility, you may want to give candidates an opportunity to take a week or two between jobs. They'll come to you fresher, happier, and less needy.

Ready to make the offer? You'll actually make it in two ways, first verbally, followed by a written offer.

Staffing and HR organizations are often in the habit of making the verbal offer themselves, but we suggest you volunteer to present it. In our experience managers who ask for the task are seldom refused. From the standpoint of selling the candidate on taking the offer, unless your staffing person is an exceptional salesperson, we think the implied relationship of having the hiring manager present the offer makes the stronger sell. (There is also an argument to be made for having your boss make the offer, if he is willing; candidates are, in general, impressed that someone senior would know who they are and call to urge them to take your company's offer.)

Your goal, the moment you have the offer approved and have mentally rehearsed your pitch at least once, is to reach the candidate voice to voice. "I have exciting news. I'm calling to make you an offer to join <our company> as a Senior Software Engineer for Database Development. The salary is the one we discussed, $xx,000 annually. You'll have an n percent bonus potential. And you will be awarded n-thousand stock options, 25 percent of which will vest after the first year, with vesting monthly thereafter. In addition, you'll get <a few great/unexpected/unusual benefits>. Will you accept? Can we set your start date for <date>?"

If you hear hesitation, try to find out what the objection is and resolve it.

If you've done your homework well and have a good read on what really motivates the candidate and have made that part of the offer, he should accept without hesitation. However, some candidates always want to push the envelope by asking for more—even if you've met the compensation requirements they asked for when you had that discussion. When they hesitate or ask for more, don't get flustered. It is part of the hiring process. Take your time and determine what their objections to your offer really are and how deeply seated they are. Rarely, if ever, should you counter immediately with more than your standing offer. Mickey says: "Rarely is the hesitation really about money at this point. Often it is about the job title, or another desire that the candidate has surfaced since you verbally sounded out the offer with him. Title, office space, additional training, ability to attend technical conferences, and permission to work at home (at least occasionally) have all come up as I've presented offers over the years. The key is to stop and get the person to fully articulate these concerns; then you can see if you can address them."

Ron has promised unofficial days off (provided he is not reorg'd away from being the candidate's manager) when a candidate asked for vacation days that had already been set aside at the candidate's current employer. He has gone back through the approval process with a changed offer due to a just-arrived competing offer. He has clarified that telecommuting two or three days per week was absolutely acceptable (with the proviso of good communication, availability, and productivity). He has clarified to a known stellar candidate that starting at a later hour to accommodate a combined train/bike commute was perfectly acceptable. He has responded to questions about child care and flexibility for sick kids. He has reassured candidates that the job was not a dead end and has explained the opportunities for transfer and promotion that it could afford the candidate.

Many candidates will ask for a few days or even a week or more to consider your offer. It's seldom the answer you want to hear, but it is reasonable. Know beforehand how long you're willing to give them. Once you've arrived at a date, enter it into the written offer as the candidate's deadline to respond. And then stay in touch during that time.

Invite candidates with pending offers to team events, connect them to people on your team, and make them feel welcome and like they're already a team member. Have someone senior—CEO, CTO, VP of Engineering—make a special call to the candidate to sell him on the position and the company and really connect with the candidate, if possible. Often these calls are an opportunity to paint a more strategic picture of the position and how it fits into the organization and the company's goals. Help the candidate understand why the position you offered is the best they could ever encounter!

We recommend that you try all of these things before considering sweetening the offer in any way. If you can do creative things that do *not* add to inequities for your staff, do that. One-time hire-on bonuses are often the easiest. Such one-time actions can be effective at handling salary issues without causing internal inequity problems, but they may not address the fundamental issue (too low a starting salary). In such cases you may reach an impasse and the candidate may not, in the end, accept the offer. You have to know how far you can and will go to make the hire and stick by that, even at the risk of losing a potential new hire. Sometimes you've just got to let go.

Benefits questions will likely come up. Let your staffing or HR organization answer them. Those people are far more versed in the intricacies (and the questions candidates ask about them) than you will ever be. Make sure your benefits package includes links to all online benefits information that is available externally.

The written offer will be drafted by HR and will include salary and benefits information, a limit on how long the offer is good, and a proposed start date. Make sure you get a copy, preferably to quickly review and approve before it is FedExed to the candidate. With the offer should go a confidentiality agreement (which should include a nondisclosure agreement, along with the caveat that the company will own any inventions created at work), forms, and collateral that portrays the company as the terrific place to work that it is.

Follow Up Until the Programmer Accepts

Sending candidates a signed offer letter in a FedEx package for them to sign and return speaks volumes to how important the candidates are to you and getting the offer in their hands is to them. Often the letter will have been sent out in e-mail already, so this may seem like a needless expense. But you want to make sure they realize that you want their commitment to coming on board as soon as possible, and that your organization doesn't cut corners.

Also, since there is a FedEx tracking number, you can use that information to time your follow-up with the candidate to make sure the offer was received (you'll know it was delivered), and make sure that there are no other questions or issues. Use this as an opportunity to make sure the candidate is excited about joining you for the position they verbally accepted. Keep following up until your offer is finally accepted (or rejected).

The next chapter will elaborate on more follow-up activity even after an offer has been accepted.

Summary

Hiring is one of the most important jobs, if not the most important job, you'll do as a programming manager. It needs to be treated with both care and purpose. Just as in a project, you're unlikely to get it right without getting good requirements down first. In fact, for critical positions or in a hot hiring climate you'll need to treat it like a project, setting short deadlines for yourself for each step: identifying candidates, phone screening them, moving them along or rejecting them, interviewing them face-to-face, making a decision, and presenting your offer. Leverage your team and your network to bring in prequalified candidates. Choose your interviewing team with care. Mete out assignments—interviewing objectives—to each member of the team, and make sure they understand how important you think their participation is to hiring the right person.

And remember that while hiring is an event, recruiting is a part of your job you should always have turned "on."

Tools

We have prepared a number of tools to assist you in managing your team. The spreadsheets and Word documents provide full examples you can easily adapt for your organization. See the Tools section, after the chapters, for the link to the Tools Web site, from which you can download the following tools:

- Sample job description
- Résumé-reading checklist
- Candidate-screening spreadsheet
- Sample interview schedule
- Sample interview questions
- Sample interview summary
- Reference checklist
- Hiring checklist

4

Getting New Programmers Started Off Right

GETTING NEW HIRES STARTED OFF RIGHT is *very important*. It's a chance to demonstrate that your organization is well managed and well run and that your employees matter to you.

You have the opportunity, on your new programmers' first days, to set the tone, introduce the culture, establish expectations, and incorporate them into the team and organization. While this is true for employees of every kind, it's especially so for programmers, who will soon be immersed in thought-stuff and code. You have one chance to make a first impression. Exceed their expectations! It doesn't take that much planning to communicate that you're excited to have them on board and have planned appropriately.

If the employee you've hired will be working remotely, you have some decisions to make. Mickey likes to fly remote hires in to have them spend their first day in the home office. Aside from the expense, it makes for a great start.

If you decide to start the employee at a remote office, you'll communicate your expectations by phone, VoIP, teleconference, videoconference, or voice-IM. But assign the greeting, welcoming, and orienting tasks we're about to describe to employees in that office.

Getting contractors started is another matter. Contractors are guns for hire. You're not looking to inculcate culture, tone, orientation, or the long term but just to ensure their success delivering their statement of work. You'll explain the objectives and expectations, give them their tasks and tools and location, introduce them to the team and others they'll work with, explain to them how and when to invoice, and get them started working!

Get Them on Board Early

On-boarding employees should begin at their acceptance of your offer. Place a congratulations call. Welcome them to the team. Assign other team members to do the same.

Your new employee may have signed your paperwork and committed to join your firm, but new hires are as subject to buyer's remorse as home buyers. They will question themselves and go through angst about whether they've made the right choice. There may have been a second offer (or even a third or fourth) that your new hire is not entirely sure shouldn't have been their first choice. The other hiring manager may still be calling your new employee frequently, applying the hard sell and trying every ploy to lure them away. The larger threat, if they were employed when you hired them, is their current manager, who will likely be asking what incentives might yet convince them to stay.

It happens, even after signing and returning your offer letter. Ron learned this the hard way. When one of Ron's new hires at start-up mFactory got around to telling his boss he was leaving, it generated a flurry of arm twisting and promises. You have the opportunity, at a start-up, to paint a picture of opportunity and reward, but an established current employer can paint a corresponding picture of doom. Ron didn't know his hire had gone awry until the morning the programmer was to start—when he called to say that coming to a start-up seemed entirely too risky now that he'd had time to think about it.

We have tried to turn around resignations many times, ourselves, after a key member of our technical staff has given notice. For some employees such efforts are an exercise in futility, but several have been saved and not always by more money. It can come in the form of additional responsibility, a change in projects or manager, a commitment to training, or hiring a partner or an assistant for an overworked specialist, but it can be done. As the manager doing the hiring, you should assume your new hire's current boss will be doing the same!

....

Keeping candidates "warm" between acceptance and start is very important. Try to not have it be more than two weeks. Take them to dinners. Make calls. Invite them to meetings. Give them tasks.

—MARK HIMELSTEIN, *Interim VP of Engineering,*
San Francisco Bay Area

So a friendly call (or two or three) from you and your team can be reassuring and reconnecting. You can easily come up with excuses to call. Ask what you can do to make your new employees productive from day one. Present them with their desktop and software options. Ask if they have special needs: Deskalators to raise a tall hire's desk height? A footrest for a short hire? Other ergonomic needs? A phone headset for those hires who will be abysmally unproductive on the phone without one? Special software they have found makes them more organized and effective? Do you have options for offices that you can offer? Establish your hires' first-day arrival time, who will meet them, the schedule for the first morning, the introductions you would like to make.

The more eager of new hires will ask what they can do to prepare. Don't overwhelm them. Send just enough information to orient, set context, and intrigue. Ideally, send just enough to get them thinking about your projects and architecture.

Oh, and be sure to send HR's packet! Let them fill it out at home, where they keep their personal data and can be most efficient at the chore (and can complete things on their time, not yours), and bring it on their first day mostly completed except where they have questions.

Preparing for Their Arrival

In most companies you'll be responsible for identifying or at least suggesting a workspace location. Think about your team's configuration and where the new programmer fits within your team's personalities, its code responsibilities, and the locations of team leads, tech leads, and architects.

You may well be the one to specify the desktop computer configuration that's adequate for programming your team's deliverables, along with the appropriate development environments and tools, plus any productivity applications specific to your firm. What is the request process and what kind of lead time does it require so that your new hire's computer is in place, configured, and running upon their arrival?

Similarly, what steps are yours to take and what kind of lead time is required to guarantee that your new hire's e-mail address, network access, server accounts, and permissions are in place on the first day? Once the e-mail address is in place, get it added to the appropriate distribution lists for your team, your group, and your department, as well as to the appropriate meeting invitations in your calendaring system. Have the new person listed in the corporate directory.

Similarly, what steps are yours to take and what kind of lead time is required to ensure that your new hire's access badge will be ready, and that they have a mailbox for physical mail?

Even if your company doesn't have an official "buddy" program, you can create your own. Pick a first-day buddy to introduce the new employee to teammates, neighbors, other coworkers, and the management team. At Razorfish, Ron developed a contacts checklist of all the teammates from across the company (senior and junior alike, as well as HR, Facilities, Staffing, and IT) that a new programmer would need to meet, with checkboxes to remind the new hire's buddy to make and check off each introduction, along with phone numbers for each so the developer could easily follow up later.

In all but the smallest offices, assign someone to lead a tour that points out the bathrooms, emergency exits, fire extinguishers (one of Ron's programmers once had a PC literally self-combust and go up in flames), snacks, copy rooms, supply closet, and coffee/tea and break areas. If you don't have an office manager with that responsibility, the buddy is a good choice.

Think about whether to also assign a longer-term career mentor. Your more senior programmers or software architects can help look out for growth opportunities for your new hires and advise them how to advance their careers. Consider assigning an interviewer who connected with the candidate particularly well or a senior person whose weak spots could benefit from the new hire's expertise.

Don't just pick people; ask them and confirm their availability. For the first-day buddy program to work, buddies can't be slammed with work on your new hire's first day, or scheduled to see their dentist for a root canal that morning. Both buddies and mentors should display enthusiasm, or you may want to pick others. Give buddies and mentors a summary of how to deliver their roles: what tour stops for buddies to make, the initial (and subsequent) conversations for mentors to have.

First-Day Musts

Now spend a few minutes thinking through your new hire's first day. Create a checklist, such as the one shown in Figure 4.1, to help ensure that you do all the things that are necessary.

Do you have equipment, software licenses, logins, and passwords in place? Nothing is worse than a new hire being unable to accomplish even the most rudimentary tasks for lack of preparation by you or your organization. Even if you have others who are responsible for this, we recommend that you double- and triple-check to make sure preparation is complete.

Checklist:
New Hire:_____

☐ Sign "new hire" paperwork
☐ Assign Buddy:_____
☐ Assign Mentor:_____
☐ Show around new workspace
☐ Introduce to coworkers
☐ E-mail and social media accounts/passwords assigned?
☐ E-mail etiquette (To:, CC:, BCC:, distribution lists)
☐ Add to group mailing lists
☐ Explain use of group mailing lists, online chat, etc.
☐ Review calendar and meeting requests
☐ Invite to required meetings, one-on-ones, group gatherings
☐ Printers
☐ Licenses (if necessary) for SCM, IDEs, tools
☐ Intranet access
☐ Personnel Web site
www.intranet.company.com/personnel
☐ Public folders
/File/Public/xx_Department
☐ Internet access
Business purposes only?
Streaming music or videos allowed?
Downloading (music or applications) allowed?
☐ Establish initial goals:
1 - _____
2 - _____
3 - _____
4 - _____
5 - _____
☐ Describe required reports (i.e., status reports, etc.)
☐ Set one-week and one-month check-in meetings
☐ "The speech"
It's a marathon
Teamwork is one of our values
Customer satisfaction
Consulting demeanor
The rest of our values
Joining an outstanding team
Joining a team with a history of doing outstanding work (examples)
☐ Create "about me" message, send to supervisor to send to team
Solicit or take photo
☐ Get home e-mail, home address, mobile phone number for your records
☐ Inventory new employees' skills; add to knowledge bank
☐ Arrange invitation to "Company 101" orientation session

Figure 4.1   First-day preparation checklist

Ron's Razorfish office made new hires feel welcome with a colorful first-day agenda, reproduced in Figure 4.2 and available among this book's Tools. There was never ambiguity around start times; first days always started at 9:00 A.M., and that time was communicated to the new hire in the offer letter. HR prepared the agendas, which provided a reminder system for the development managers, themselves often buried in senior-level technical consulting projects, to spend the necessary time thinking through what would be needed for new arrivals.

WELCOME DAY SCHEDULE FOR RON LICHTY'S NEW EMPLOYEE, Bob	
9:00 a.m.	**Meet with Ron Lichty** Ron's office
9:30 a.m.	**Facilities Tour with Susan, our office manager** Meet in Lobby
10:00a.m.	**IT Training with Dennis** Your desk
10:30 a.m.	**HR Training with Gary** Conference Room: Days of Our Lives, 8th floor *Bring your new hire binder and a pen*
11:00 a.m.	**Meet with Career Manager, John Smith** John's office
12:00pm	**Lunch with Buddy - Jill Miller** Restaurant TBD - the firm is buying
1:30pm	**Meet with teammate on your first project, Arun Nguyen** Arun's cube
2:00 p.m.	**Meet with client-side teammate Johnny Arnold** Johnny's cube
2:30 p.m.	**Meet with best practices lead, Jim Starr** Jim's cube
3:00 p.m.	**Meet with business partner, Chris Barnstable** Chris's office
4:00 p.m.	**Time Tracking Tour with Jack, our finance guy** Jack's office

Figure 4.2   Sample first-day agenda

Never underestimate the importance of a proper welcome for a new employee. Mickey recalls a new Gracenote employee hired for his Tokyo office who had previously worked many years for Sony: "Deciding to leave a company such as Sony was a big decision for him, so he expected to be welcomed as an important member of the staff. Unfortunately, on the morning of his first day of work, the hiring manager and the general manager of the Tokyo office had to be out on a customer visit. He was greeted by the office manager, which was incredibly disappointing to him. This lack of appropriate welcome haunted him for many months and led to serious issues that I personally spent many hours helping to resolve."

The Razorfish agenda generally started with the department or hiring manager providing a half-hour welcome. The rest of the schedule was also mostly half-hours that included

- A buddy-led office tour focused on making a round of introductions
- An objectives kickoff with the new hire's direct manager
- A facilities tour from the office manager: restrooms, office supplies, copy areas, printer and fax machine locations, conference room maps, water coolers, coffee and how to make more, snack machines, break rooms, safety information, fire escapes, and other important locations
- A visit from IT to review final computer, printer, network, e-mail, and Web configurations, walk through voicemail and VPN instructions, and do Q&A
- A benefits overview delivered by HR; completion of the stacks of paperwork required to get new hires started these days, including the confidentiality agreement
- Meetings with team members—from other development leads to project and product managers—one of whom has been assigned responsibility for showing the new hire how to get to the servers, ideally on the new hire's own computer, as well as where in the file systems to find key team, department, and company assets; the corporate and department intranets; and bios and photos and directories of teammates and colleagues
- A long (hour-and-a-half) lunch with the buddy or career mentor (the other of the two should take the new hire to lunch later in the week); each has been clearly instructed that the firm is paying and reminded if necessary how to expense lunch
- A personal welcome by one or more senior managers of the organization

To pull all that off, you need to think through, identify, check with, and schedule an entire first-day cast of greeters and get them thinking about how they'll present the firm, the department, the team, and the project. Keep in mind your goals:

- Make the new hire feel special as well as that he's joined a very special team and a very special company.
- Help the new hire understand the importance of your project(s) and feel responsibility for their part in them: the tasks you've assigned.
- Communicate your culture and your expectations.
- Establish that you run a tight ship.
- Begin to incorporate the new hire into the team.
- Set the foundation to help the new hire be productive quickly.

Pay attention to the special equipment needs of programmers: high-end systems, large monitor screens, licenses, logins, network access, home access, and so on.

Paying special attention to programmers' equipment needs isn't reserved only for new hires. At Brøderbund Software, Mickey hired a dedicated "Programming Department IT Specialist" whose sole responsibility was to make sure that any hardware and software needs were addressed quickly, and any hardware and software problems were handled *immediately* without the need to go through the corporate IT staff (which often introduced hours or days of delay in addressing problems). The IT specialist doubled as the source control administrator, thereby ensuring that any source control issues were also handled expeditiously. "My direction to the IT specialist was simple. His job was to remove any roadblock that hampered the programming staff . . . if he needed to rent a bulldozer to do so, he had my permission."

Introductions

During the week—ideally on the first or second day—you'll want a senior manager to deliver a "Company 101" for your new hire. This is an opportunity to go over

- The corporate mission, vision, and values
- The metrics by which the department is measured
- The history of the company and its products, services, and business model

- An overview of the company's architecture and technology
- Important company milestones
- An organizational overview with relevant org charts, showing where the new hire fits in the employee universe (including in the context of employees just met)

Get the new hire to write a couple of short paragraphs of personal information and past history, or interview the hire so that you can write it. You will incorporate a photo of the new hire as you craft this personal welcome message that you'll send out to the department, region, or company. Urge recipients of your e-mail to introduce themselves, and include your new hire's phone number, location, and e-mail address so that they can do so.

Figure 4.3 shows an example of a welcome message like those that Mickey has used.

Ensuring Success

Get your new hires incorporated into the team quickly to help ensure their success. These three things will help:

- Get them started on achievable tasks quickly.
- Colocate them with team members who can also act as mentors.
- Make sure they have immediate access to relevant documentation.

....

On-boarding is simple:

1. *Some initial project starting day one that forces getting up to speed on source control, dev practices, etc.*
2. *Ideally some kind of dogfooding of the project. An engineer divorced from the use of the product is useless.*

—DIRK BESTER, VP of Engineering, San Francisco Bay Area

Have the project manager or project team lead prepped to meet with the new project member to discuss topics such as these:

- Project objectives and goals, plus project team objectives if they're a subset or different
- The key project stakeholders, their levels of involvement, and their priorities
- Software development approaches used by the project team
- Practices and working conventions adopted by the team

- Software development tools used by the team
- Current project status and other details to help the team member more quickly integrate into the team

Ensuring that new programmers are successful means integrating them into the team and the work as soon as possible. A good way to do this is to contrive situations that have new arrivals working closely with new teammates, contributing early, and working on a task that will give them a quick feeling of success.

MICKEY MANTLE
SENT: Thursday, June 9, 2009 12:50 P.M.
TO: All_Company
SUBJECT: Please help me welcome Mike xxx to Gracenote . . .

Mike has begun work as a software engineer, working for Gary and with Paul, Steve, and Peter on the "Music System" project. Mike brings a background in linguistics and programming and graduated from Stanford last year.

Mike is sitting in the programming area near the kitchen, so please stop by and introduce yourself when you get a chance and help me welcome him to the company.

—Mickey

Here's what he has to say about himself.

Hi, I'm Mike and I'm excited to work at Gracenote for a while. I'm excited to be working here because, like many of the people who work here, I have an extreme interest in music and providing new cool ways of managing my numerous digital audio files. I received my BS in Symbolic Systems from Stanford about a year ago and prior to this worked at Sun Microsystems.

I like linguistics, Giants baseball, red wine, shows in the city, and every now and then playing some golf. I'm on the south side of the programming department in a cubicle next to the kitchen, so feel free to come by and see my bare cubicle walls.

Figure 4.3   Sample welcome message

On-boarding is very important. Provide training. Identify mentors. I try to get [new hires] to accomplish something small quickly. When you don't do this, I have seen even experienced people get into a bad pattern early. When you do, it makes the new employee feel good and it starts building their clout with the rest of the team.

—MARK HIMELSTEIN

When Mickey colocated a new database developer next to his mentor, giving the new hire immediate access to the person best suited to answer his questions, the result was remarkable. The new developer became a significant contributor much sooner than expected. Because of this success, Mickey has since tried to locate every new hire appropriately. A remodel of the engineering space at Gracenote allowed the introduction of collaboration spaces, with couches, flat-panel TVs (for presentations), and floor-to-ceiling whiteboard walls, for informal meetings and work sessions to help address this need.

At Apple, Ron applied his team's candy jar to the integration challenge. As he began hiring, he moved the jar to reside in each new hire's cube for the first month. "The new hire was typically reading code, setting up his development environment and tools, poking around, trying out ideas. Candy-jar-prompted interruptions represented opportunities for the newbie to interact with his new teammates and to ask them questions. I made sure that happened by making a rule that the cost of each incursion into the new hire's cube for candy would be a 'free' question he could ask his more tenured teammate."

In consulting organizations one of the challenges of each new client is to understand its unique mix of tools and technology. At Razorfish, Ron developed a survey form he expected new developers to fill in on their first day that fed into a Skills and Experience Census he could consult to match up developers with needs. (See the example Census among the Tools.)

Something that we both have found to be of increasing importance for our teams is the use of a wiki as a repository of wisdom for departments, projects, and teams. For new hires it is a treasure trove of readily accessible information that can help them get up to speed and also provides an opportunity for them to contribute immediately by improving the content. Many companies, even small ones, are so thick with acronyms and code words and phrases that newcomers would universally value a wiki page set out to decode the lingo.

Initial Expectations

The new hire's manager should give the new hire a picture of his role on the team, his part in projects, and what he'll need to do for you to consider him successful. So you need to

- Build an action plan for the new hire's first involvement in projects
- Establish desired outcomes for the current review period

It's common to give a new programmer a first task to

- Set up a local copy of the environment and sandbox
- Install the tools
- Load up the code to be worked on
- Compile the code
- Check the result against the team's official build to confirm that the new hire's copy of the source is current and sourced from the right place and his tools and sandbox configuration match those the team is using

Ron remembers, "When I gave that assignment to the first programmer I hired onto the post-System-7 Finder team, our systems turned out to be so crufty that it took him a week to get everything in place and get the entire Finder built and validated. So the second task I gave him was to measurably shorten that for my next hire. I gave that same second task to every subsequent hire. Three years later, downloading the source and tools and creating and validating the build could be accomplished by a green new hire in less than 30 minutes."

You also want to give "the talk" on that first day: Go over your expectations—all of them. Explain the role of each member of the existing team and the role you'd like your new hire to take on. Give your new hire a vision to live up to. Reaffirm your commitment to your new hire's career growth, training, and advancement. Remind him of the importance of the confidentiality agreement he signed before starting.

....

Be really attentive in the initial probation period.

First day, first days, first week, first month . . .
Pair them up, read their code, and above all, treat them
with respect.

> —STEVE BURBECK, *Manager at Apple and*
> *IBM, a small wholesale company, two start-*
> *ups, and a nonprofit research institute*

Some of the expectations we've communicated to new hires on our teams include the following:

- The new hire is part of a team and a team effort.
- Team members need to maintain core hours, and teams need work schedules that overlap predictably to work together effectively.
- We expect our team members to work amicably with each other. Of each member, we expect cooperation, collaboration, contribution, communication, and initiative. We expect each to contribute to making the team a safe place to ask questions with a minimum of judgment and unhealthy competition.
- We expect our new programmer to make decisions. We expect our programmers to communicate decisions as they're being made.
- Programmers who telecommute must be as available as their teammates just down the hall (perhaps more so!). We expect them to let their teammates, colleagues, and manager know where and how to reach them and to repeatedly encourage them to do so.
- We expect interaction and engagement in our staff meetings.

And as Mickey has often told new hires to his teams:

- Projects should be run like marathons. You have to set a good pace that can win the race, and then expect to sprint for the finish line.

Depending on the company, the department, management, our core values, and so on, we have also made points like these:

- How the company's core values specifically apply to our teams and how they are meaningful to us personally.
- If we (or our boss) expect a status report, when (every Friday end-of-day?) it's due, how much (or how little) detail is required, and the format to use.

There are processes to walk your new hire through

- Your established software development lifecycle, and how projects are tracked and reported
- Time recording, if time is recorded
- Vacation approval and other time off
- The policy for reimbursement of expenses (we follow up by e-mail with the form or a URL to the online process)

- The performance review process: how often, how it works, what it means
- Your new hire's calendar and the meetings to expect—those set by you and those set by others
- Ordering business cards
- Applications for company credit cards and telephone credit cards
- Telephone conference calling

Communicate your commitments to your employees to

- Support and enable your new hire's professional growth while setting the expectation that each of your employees will take responsibility for their own growth
- Get them the tools they need to do their job

For me, the biggest challenge with new programmers is to size them up and figure out what it will take to make them effective contributors to the organization. The big challenge I always found was tight versus loose. For some programmers, you can give them a big-picture idea, they develop their own spec, you manage by objective; breathing over their shoulder will make them less effective. For others, you have to keep them on a shorter (or short) leash, monitoring a series of short-term deliverables. In particular, many programmers will argue they can be managed hands-off, but some of them are not telling the truth.

—*JOEL WEST, Professor, Innovation & Entrepreneurship, Keck Graduate Institute of Applied Life Sciences, The Claremont Colleges; former Programmer, Manager, and Entrepreneur in the software industry, California*

After you walk your new hire through the summary of your initial expectations, set up a follow-up appointment to make sure there are no issues.

In your follow-up appointment, if you detect any concerns that your new hire is not meeting your expectations, address those concerns directly and immediately. Chapters 5 and 7 will address managing performance issues and motivating your staff, but don't wait for issues to become a problem.

Summary

Hiring isn't complete when your candidate accepts your offer. Smart managers continue to nurture their candidates until the day they arrive—to avoid "buyer's remorse" and to anticipate an effort by their current manager to "save" them and safeguard their transition to your fold—and well into their tenure to successfully transition them onto your team.

The initial few days and weeks are critical to ensure that a new hire is productive, happy, and meeting your expectations. This ramp-up period is the time to make certain that issues are communicated and addressed and new hires become part of your team and adopt your culture.

Tools

We have prepared a number of tools to assist you in getting your new hires started. These spreadsheets and Word documents provide full examples that you can easily adapt for your organization. See the Tools section, after the chapters, for the link to the Tools Web site, from which you can download the following tools:

- Hiring follow-up checklist
- Need-to-meet checklist for new hires
- Sample contacts checklist: key teammates
- You're a new hire's first-day buddy: what to do
- You're a new hire's career mentor: what to do
- First-day checklist
- Sample first-day agenda
- Sample welcome message
- Developer skills census and inventory
- Skill sets and capabilities—an organizational dashboard

5

Becoming an Effective Programming Manager: Managing Down

Everything that has been presented in this book so far has only set the stage for the real heart of the information we hope to convey: how to manage programmers effectively on a day-to-day basis. Since most organizations are structured hierarchically, we have broken this information into four basic topics in relation to your position in the organization:

- Managing down
- Managing up
- Managing out
- Managing yourself

These topics deal with managing your staff, managing your boss(es), managing others inside or outside of your organization, and managing yourself. Chapter 6 covers the last three topics, which are critical to being an effective programming manager.

The most relevant topic here is the first one, and this chapter focuses solely on managing down. As a first-line programming manager, you should probably be spending the bulk of your time doing this. Managing down includes all those things you need to do to effectively manage the staff that reports directly, or indirectly, to you. One aspect of this, that of motivating your staff, is so important that Chapter 7 is devoted to it. The remainder of this chapter deals primarily with the mechanics of being an effective programming manager—what you need to do and how to do it.

Earning Technical Respect

Scott Adams has forever stained the reputation of every programming manager by making an icon of the Pointy-Haired Boss (or PHB, in programmer parlance). The PHB is a buffoon who is clueless at best and malicious or evil at his worst. We need not discuss what the PHB is but rather realize what he isn't—respected by Dilbert and his cohorts.

The PHB isn't respected because he does not understand, or care to understand, what Dilbert and his cohorts do, and he demonstrates that at every turn. Years of working in technical organizations have led us to believe that those who don't intimately understand programmers are going to make a mess if they try to manage, direct, or dictate actions for a programming team or project. It is the rare manager who has this understanding who has not been a programmer.

The single biggest key to successfully managing programmers is to have the technical respect of those you manage and your peers. Without technical respect, every attempt to manage will be thwarted actively or passively. This is why it is so hard for those who do not understand programmers (i.e., have not been programmers at some stage of their career) to manage programmers effectively. This is true of many technical disciplines but seems to be more of a truism in the world of programming.[1] Key aspects of earning technical respect are

- Understanding the art of computer programming
- Having a good track record
- Making some notable technical contribution
- Keeping up with technical trends and technologies
- Being an active member of technical or professional organizations
- Demonstrating strong personal values

To understand programmers, you must have a solid understanding of the tools, the processes, and the art of computer programming.[2] The deeper

---

1. We are not aware of any other vocation where there is a character such as Dilbert who throws such pointed barbs at his manager except, perhaps, the military.

2. Donald E. Knuth, *The Art of Computer Programming,* Volume 1, *Fundamental Algorithms, Third Edition* (Addison-Wesley, 1997); Volume 2, *Seminumerical Algorithms, Third Edition* (Addison-Wesley, 1997); Volume 3, *Sorting and Searching, Second Edition* (Addison-Wesley, 1998); Volume 4, *Combinatorial Algorithms, Part 1* (Addison-Wesley, 2011); Volume 5, *Syntactic Algorithms* (Addison-Wesley, forthcoming). If you don't have a copy of these books prominently displayed in your office, you should!

your understanding and the stronger your ability to engage in meaning-ful technical dialog with your staff, the more technical respect you will have from them. A Microsoft program architect once said of Bill Gates, "Gates relishes nothing as much as disassembling the bits and bytes of computer code with his programmers. He easily holds his own in the tech-nological trenches. . . . He gets respect because he can take those guys to the cleaners."[3]

The intangible elements of technical respect explain why it can be difficult to bring programming managers in from outside the company or organization and have them be effective. A key attribute of any candidate you consider to manage a programming team is having a set of "bona fides" (i.e., a proven track record in software) that the team they will be managing can respect.

There are many ways to build a solid set of bona fides, the simplest of which is to be an acknowledged outstanding programmer/technical leader and be promoted to be a programming manager in the same organiza-tion. This has its own challenges, but an outstanding programmer will be a known quantity and have the needed technical respect of his peers and those he will then be responsible for managing, and that will help foster a good team culture that is founded on respect. Having a deep understanding of the technical organization and its managers will also be an advantage, since that understanding can be communicated to the team.

Another way to increase your stature, and in turn gain technical respect, is by having developed or managed projects or products that are well known to the programmers you manage.

Mickey's own management career was built by first being recognized as a key contributor at Evans & Sutherland (E&S) after leading the Picture System graphics library project, being promoted as a manager of the team developing the company's next-generation graphics products, and then being recruited by Pixar where his E&S work was well known.[4] Thereafter, having E&S and Pixar on his résumé gained him some technical respect that has carried forward to this very day.

Ron's bona fides for a management role at Apple began with coauthoring the canonical assembly language reference for the emerging

---

3. Paul Maritz, Microsoft program architect, *Playboy* magazine profile of Bill Gates, 1991.

4. Pixar, and Lucasfilm from which Pixar was spun off, were both heavy users of E&S's 3-D graphics systems. Pixar's groundbreaking short film *Luxo Jr.* was animated by John Lassiter using an E&S Picture System.

65816 microprocessor. When Apple chose the 65816 as the core of what would be a hybrid between the Mac and the Apple II, the Apple IIGS, Ron was recruited to code the animated program by which the IIGS demoed itself to buyers in every Apple store in the world. That led to Ron being recruited for a programming role at Apple in system software, during which time he was repeatedly tapped to manage the groups developing first the Apple II and then the Macintosh UI. That led Berkeley Systems, which had invented the change-the-channel screen saver *After Dark*, to hire him as their Director of Engineering for entertainment products. This led to directing engineering at two other entertainment software companies (not to mention the opportunity for Ron and Mickey to meet).

Pixar and Apple were important bona fides for Mickey and Ron, but any career can be packaged or enhanced with a little effort. This is an important aspect of career management, which every programmer or programming manager should work hard to do. Look for opportunities to make contributions, stand out from the crowd, and create your own legend. It can be as simple as contributing to an open source project, or blogging about your experiences. Find the right thing that works for you.

Joining and participating in relevant technical societies and organizations can contribute to your bona fides. We strongly recommend joining ACM and/or IEEE, either of which will bring anyone a measure of technical credibility regardless of their degree of participation. Long-standing members of either organization command even more technical respect. Attending annual conferences sponsored by these organizations as well as local chapter meetings is a great way to keep in touch with technical advances and do some personal and professional networking.

Other ways to gain technical respect are to get advanced technical degrees; become professionally certified; author technical papers; create open source, commercial, or shareware software; apply for patents; write a book; build your own Web site; start your own company; have your own blog; be a "known" contributor to a technical community (e.g., Slashdot); invent an algorithm (e.g., Page Rank, Warnock's algorithm); postulate a law (e.g., Moore's Law); and so on.

During his tenure managing Apple's Macintosh team developing the Finder—Apple's desktop UI—Ron developed the Macintosh shareware reminders program Birthdays and Such. Exploring coding best practices for one particularly gnarly area of Mac UI programming, Ron realized that Apple's own documentation was wrong and authored two Apple Tech

Notes to make it easier for Apple's developers to get it right. Seeing how hard it was led him to a deep discussion with his tech lead, during which they opened the appropriate section of Finder code and discovered the Finder had gotten it wrong, too. It's the kind of activity that gives your team respect for your technical chops.

Regardless of what you do to build your professional stature, make sure it is known to those whom you must manage. That means making sure those things find their way to your résumé and get noted by the technical staff during the hiring process. Don't be shy about finding ways to make your personal achievements known. Simple suggestions include displaying degrees and certificates of achievement (this is why doctors do this in their offices), getting plaques for patents granted to hang on your wall, framing magazine covers where articles you wrote appear, and keeping a personal Web site that details your career and achievements.

One thing Mickey has done that has borne benefits over the years is to mount all of his business cards for presentation, as shown in Figure 5.1. He displayed this in his office and used it during interviews with prospective employees to make sure they understood his long-standing career and positions. His first business card (which he had to reconstruct via scanned artwork and a vague memory of the original layout) proudly shows the title System Programmer, and the other business cards trace his various positions to Senior Vice President of Development.

All of this was a thinly veiled attempt at gaining technical respect from his staff. But such attempts will only provide you with the opportunity to establish respect. You must gain that respect and cement it daily through interactions with your staff.

One important way to gain and maintain the technical respect of your staff and peers is by keeping up

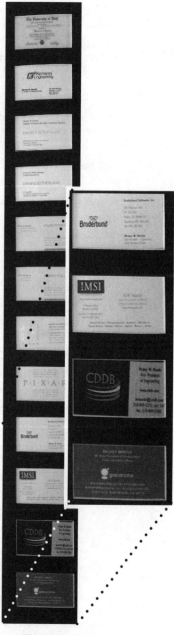

Figure 5.1 Mickey's business card display

with or getting ahead of them on technical trends and technology. Though clearly the oldest person in his company, Mickey worked hard to keep up with or get ahead of the "young Turks" who thought they knew it all. Though it is impossible to keep ahead of them on the details of every technology, he didn't find it that hard to stay ahead of them on major trends and technologies. Both Ron and Mickey read carefully selected electronic newsletters,[5] Web sites, and periodicals[6] voraciously; attend select technical conferences; and leverage their networks of other technologists to exchange insights and knowledge over breakfasts, lunches, dinners, e-mails, LinkedIn discussions, and ad hoc meetings.

By having a broad grasp of technical trends and technologies, taking selected deep dives into things that seem applicable or particularly interesting, and sharing selected highlights with their direct reports via e-mail and broader staff as part of monthly departmental or periodic company meetings, they nurture the respect of their staff and peers.

Mickey's long-standing memberships in ACM, IEEE, and IGDA (the International Game Developers Association) help him keep abreast of technical trends and information. Gaming trends tend to lead broad adoption of technologies by three to five years, so he continues to pay particular attention to the gaming industry and tries to attend its annual conference whenever possible.

Ron cofounded and cochaired SVForum's Software Architecture SIG (Special Interest Group) for five years, cochaired the East Bay Innovation Group's Software Development Best Practices SIG, has presented to SVForum's Engineering Leadership SIG, and currently cochairs SVForum's Emerging Technologies SIG. The SIGs drive him not only to stay abreast of but also to capture the best of architecture, technology, and management trends as they become known.

---

5. As one example, a great free electronic newsletter is the *Wave Report*, produced (occasionally) by John Latta. See www.wave-report.com. Each *Wave Report* is essentially a "trip report" for a trade show he attended, meaning he does all the legwork and you get to quickly digest the most interesting information.

6. Mickey and Ron both religiously read *Wired* (always a great source of entertainment and broad trends). Mickey also reads *EE Times* (the best compilation of hardware and software technologies and trends available, though the hardware trends tend to be early in their adoption cycle) and *eWeek*, which reviews software products and systems broadly. Ron was, until its demise in print form, a fan of *Dr. Dobb's Journal*. He continues to check in with it at www.drdobbs.com.

There are many subtle aspects to gaining your team's respect that include demonstrating integrity, fairness, trust in your staff, support, encouragement, and a balance of love and "tough love." These aspects are touched on in Chapters 7 and 8, which deal with motivation and establishing a good programming culture.

The real takeaway from this discussion is to strive to be a technical leader who can command the respect of your staff, not only by being good technically but by demonstrating strong personal values that your staff can and will respect.

But technical respect is not enough. It takes a lot more to successfully manage programmers and teams.

Hire Great Programmers

The next important thing is to inherit, hire, and/or build a good technical staff. As we are both fond of saying, "The single most important part of our job is to make sure we hire right." If you hire great staff members, the other parts of your job are easier. If you don't, you usually don't have time for other parts of your job since you're too busy dealing with the problems that always seem to be plaguing you. Chapter 3 covered this issue in great detail, so no further elaboration is needed. Just be sure you make this your single most important task.

Turbocharge the Team You Have

There are lots of teams made up entirely of average programmers—competent, decent, but unexceptional coders. We've all found ourselves inheriting teams like these. You may live in a region where few great programmers can be found. You may have hiring budgets that preclude the salaries that great programmers can demand. You may be managing teams charged with maintenance or evolving old or uninspiring systems that would drive any great programmer nuts. And over the first decade of the new millennium, plenty of us who hungered after adding a great programmer or two found ourselves in hiring freezes for years at a time; making hiring your single most important task in an era of stagnant hiring is a nonstarter.

Even if you're trying to hire the right great programmer, you always need to be thinking about the team you have—about how to drive continuous improvement and how to turbocharge your team. Either way, your work starts with understanding the different types of programmers and how to manage them differently. We'll talk about motivating them in Chapter 7.

Managing Different Types of Programmers

Few who are not acquainted with the different types of programmers described in Chapter 2 would believe that your approach to managing these various types of programmers would be different. But they probably should be. Of course, it really depends on the traits of the individuals you manage, but our experience has convinced us that you will be more successful if you manage different types of programmers slightly differently.

For example, *system programmers/architects* are typically the biggest "tomcats"—the most cantankerous and the most individualistic. This is also the group among whom individual results vary the most. The rare "great system programmer" is able to architect massively complex systems in such a way that they are elegant and conceptually simple. And such great systems will make all the other programmers' jobs less complicated as a result, leading to massive leverage from one individual.

As Mickey recalls, he had just such a great system programmer at Brøderbund: "This programmer created a system that allowed cross-platform development (supporting various versions of Windows *and* MacOS) for almost all of Brøderbund's multimedia products. It isolated the application programmers from dealing with all the gritty, low-level problems of making sound, graphics, and animations run on different operating systems and hardware platforms. It also removed the issue of hardware performance variability (300MHz versus 900MHz processors, for example, and 16X versus 64X CD-ROM drives). He named this system Mohawk (**Mo**st **h**einous **a**pplications **w**riting **k**it), not really because it was that nasty to program but mostly because if there was a problem, you had to deal with him. And he could be heinous to deal with!

"Having made the work of the application programmers doable, he also developed a system for creating page-oriented, animated storybooks that did not require programming per se, but rather used interpretive scripts. Analogous to Macromedia's Director in some ways but less general, it allowed animated storybooks to be created cost-effectively by a staff of animators, sound designers, and technicians. These animated storybooks became so successful that they spawned a joint venture between Brøderbund and

Random House to produce *Living Books* for notable children's authors such as Mercer Mayer, Marc Brown, Dr. Seuss, and others.

"I attribute much of Brøderbund's success in the early to mid-nineties to the largely single-handed efforts by this truly great system programmer. This is not meant to diminish the fantastic efforts of others at Brøderbund who also contributed (there were many talented designers, artists, animators, sound designers, product managers, programmers, etc.). But the contributions of this one programmer made all of their efforts easier and the products better.

"However, those who had to work directly with him would not say he made their efforts easier when dealing with him. He could be arrogant and defensive and make someone who had a problem with his systems truly miserable until it was proven the problem was actually his. Then he would fix the problem—often quickly and painlessly.

"Since he reported to me (directly at times), I felt the pain, too. But I recognized a true talent and rewarded him well for his efforts—never enough for the leverage he created at the company in my opinion, but well. But it was a balancing act, rewarding him yet coaching him to be *less heinous* to those he worked with. The effort I put in was well worth it."

Such a rare gift can only be likened to other greats, such as great pianists, architects, poets, and others. Because of this, we believe in giving broad latitude to such great system programmers, much more than we would to other programmers. However, this often takes tremendous trust without much insight or oversight along the way. We have spent many management hours justifying continued investment in projects being led by great system programmers without the "necessary" or "sufficient" requirements review, schedules, or milestones. The trust in these rare great individuals has seldom, in the long run, been misplaced. They have always delivered, though hardly ever on time or within budget. But the results have been more than worth the additional time or money required.

Application programmers typically are more easily managed than system programmers. By this we mean they are, in general, less cantankerous than system programmers, and their coding progress is usually more visible. That is because most applications have some sort of interface (UI or external interface) whereby a good manager can assess progress. Our experience shows us that application programmers usually have to be able to relate to the end user of the application to be successful. This makes them more sensitive to end user needs, which translates into fewer problems to manage.

Database programmers are more opaque than other programmers, though part of the opaqueness is derived from the special language they speak: schemas, tables, queries, and so forth. Managing database programmers effectively requires helping them to think like computer scientists—not just as custodians of rows and columns of tables accessed by SQL statements.

It is also our experience that the levels of abstraction from the raw hardware tend to insulate database programmers from the optimizations that database administrators (DBAs) must do to make relational databases run more efficiently. We believe database programmers should think about optimizations, too. All too often we hear the statement "With today's fast hardware, we don't need to think about optimizing," which can be true for small programs. But for large-scale databases or production systems that hope to scale effectively, optimizations and careful design to fully utilize the targeted production hardware systems need to be considered from the start.

Ron recalls a problem he encountered at Forensic Logic where the production database needed an order-of-magnitude performance improvement to run effectively. Rarely can an order-of-magnitude improvement be gained by simple DBA tuning. Ron asked his database guy if he had ever programmed in assembly language (he had), then walked him through how the performance problem could be better handled by accessing arrays of bytes in memory, not SQL statements, and the obviousness of how much faster it would run if coded that way. The DB guy had a real "aha" moment. "You're making me think outside the box," he exclaimed.

Another example of how database programmers often get constrained in their thinking came up at Gracenote, where the process of ingesting and matching metadata content from content partners—data such as record labels—is a continual challenge for the database team. As Mickey recalls, "We had many dozens of feeds that were continually being updated by our partners as they released new products, and these updates needed to be matched up with the vast Gracenote metadata database. This process required a lot of text matching, and this text matching was never a process of 'exact matching' since the same metadata can be expressed quite differently (e.g., The Beatles might appear as 'Beatles, The,' or misspelled as 'The Betles').

"A considerable portion of the time spent in the DBMS was strictly doing text matching. The database programmers continued to try to fine-tune the text-matching algorithms, but this did not achieve the orders-of-magnitude performance improvements that were desired. The solution in this case was literally an out-of-the-box solution: namely, move the text matching out of the DBMS environment entirely and onto a dedicated server. Custom algorithms tailored to this problem on dedicated text-matching systems provided the desired performance improvements, but the solution had to be imposed on the database programmers—they didn't come up with it on their own."

Like great system programmers, great database programmers are conscious of the systems on which their DBMS runs, paying special attention to the CPU and hardware hosting the DBMS, the massive file storage that hosts the DBMS files, the method of connection that the DBMS has to the file storage, and all the other details that make up the DBMS operational environment.

Mickey recalls an upgrade at Gracenote that caused serious problems for months because the details of the file storage system were not adequately determined before the upgrade began: "As with most upgrades, you undertake them to improve performance or capacity. So it was with this case when Gracenote needed to upgrade its network file storage system. Expectations were that this would lead to greater online capacity and better overall performance. As the system was tested and rolled out, it seemed to work fine and the expected new capacity was as promised. However, as all the DBMS applications were loaded and began running, the overall performance was much less than with the old file storage system that had been replaced. Consulting with the systems integrator, the vendor, and the hardware systems suppliers (Sun and Net App) led only to baffled head scratching. Test after test was run, but the cause of the performance degradation went unsolved for many weeks and months.

"At long last one of the system administrators determined that the raw block size of the new file storage system was 'non-optimal' for the virtual memory page sizes of the Sun machine, which caused a delay during data transfer from the file storage system to memory. This subtle parameter setting had a terrific impact on the overall performance of the system."

While this is an extreme case, it points out how lack of understanding of some of the minutest details of the DBMS environment can have a significant impact on the overall efficiency and performance of a DBMS system. All too few database programmers feel compelled to understand the broad spectrum of subsystems that make up a DBMS today.

Encourage your database programmers to dive deeper. Reward handsomely those blessed few who do span the spectrum of understanding of the DBMS world and excellent system programming.

UI and Web developers are like other programmers but typically use higher-level languages and tools for their development. This tends to make them less technical and more reliant on the performance of their tools—they are too often held hostage by their tools. These programmers must deal with iterative change much more often than the others we have discussed. This means you must ensure that you have the right staff who can take less-than-complete requirements and flesh them out, and then iterate to meet the rapidly evolving needs of end users and their requirements.

Ron recalls that "at Apple I would use newspaper layout as a metaphor to talk about UI design. When I was a newspaper reporter and editor, I had worked with a layout artist who would carefully paste up what was wanted but never hesitated to rip out everything and start over from scratch if either of us thought the page wasn't working." Similarly, good UI and Web developers must have the same "eye" to recognize when things are not working and the same responsiveness and willingness to back up or even start over when user testing or the product manager indicates another approach is called for.

Common to all of these types of programmers is the fact that a great programmer may out-produce his peers by as much as an order of magnitude or more. Countless stories abound in our own experience—the system programmer at Brøderbund described previously, for example—and throughout the industry that clearly demonstrate how effective the great programmer can be in getting things done.

But if you could have a team of only great programmers, you probably wouldn't want to manage it. Great programmers need to be surrounded by competent programmers who can be relied upon to do the day-to-day work of predictably making systems and products. Much like the blocking and tackling that make great football teams great, these competent programmers are the main staff of great programming teams.

Regardless of how a project is organized, managing programmers is not easy. It is often difficult to tell that progress is being made, since visible progress may not be possible. And even if it is possible, all you can see is the tip of the iceberg of the entire software project. So you must rely on proxies for visible progress: status reports, project schedules, primitive metrics, and verbal feedback. The most effective managers have staff who are not afraid to tell the truth about where a task stands and who will ask for help with resolving problems without the managers having prompted them. And the most effective managers are open, available, and accessible to meet with their staff and listen carefully to what they have to say.

Facilitation

An important part of any manager's job is to facilitate making the right things happen. This often means simply making sure the right communication is taking place among team members or teams. It also means identifying roadblocks and finding ways to remove them, usually by getting a programmer to start or finish a task.

Facilitation is more about getting something done than about how such a thing might be done. Some managers try to dictate decisions and activities. That may be appropriate on occasion. However, a manager is maximizing his time and skills when he facilitates getting the right decision, rather than dictating it. In doing this he builds the skills, experience, and confidence of his staff as well as ensuring buy-in from those who must implement the decisions.

If you find yourself giving specific directions often, you are not leveraging your skills well enough or empowering your staff. As a manager, you must communicate broad direction, and then check in sufficiently to ensure that the right decisions are being made and actualized. Make sure you check in on important decisions made by your staff early enough so that if you choose to step in and make any midcourse corrections, your staff will not have done needless work. A member of Ron's programming team at Social-text identified the essence of a great manager:

> *Any manager, when goals are not being met, identifies the impediments and whenever possible removes them. A good manager goes further by identifying and removing potential impediments before they lead to the goals not being met. A great manager makes this seem easy.*
>
> —TONY BOWDEN, Socialtext

Protection

One of the most important lessons a programming manager must learn is to protect his staff from the ebb and flow of problems, issues, and "opportunities" that wash over an organization on a daily basis. In larger companies and government organizations, bureaucracies ignore or buffer the daily flood of requests and issues by requiring paperwork ("Please submit Form 13804-A"). But in smaller companies and organizations you may be the only defense against the flood of sales-driven opportunities, customer-driven issues, and management-driven ideas that challenge your teams.

To be productive, a programming team must be buffered from the flood. You, as their manager, must take charge. A big part of your job will be understanding, evaluating, discussing, negotiating, deferring, documenting, and finally agreeing to or refusing to deal with these issues. If you allow your staff, or even your trusted lieutenants, to be swept up in this flood of items, you will greatly diminish their programming effectiveness.

....

This organization is drowning in data, but starved for information.

—DAVID DIBBLE, EVP, Schwab Technical Services

To adequately deal with some of the issues, you may need to involve some of your staff. Do this selectively and carefully. Our experience shows that seldom is a "fully baked" technical response necessary in the early stage of problems, issues, and opportunities. Often enough all that is needed is a basic technical assessment of feasibility. So usually such inquiries do not warrant involving your staff. Take a risk and give an answer, but make sure you have a caveat that lets you pursue further technical investigation if warranted.

Often enough, a few important items float to the top and the rest wash away. Pay more attention to those at the top. Over time learn to identify the ones that are truly important so that you can deal with those appropriately and not sweat the rest.

By providing this protection for your staff, you will avoid diverting their valuable time to transient issues. You will also make them happier because some of those issues could blossom into full-blown rumors about project changes or, worse, about acquisitions, reorgs, or layoffs—rumors that can be demoralizing and lead to productivity-sapping water-cooler speculation and chatter.

Do make sure that your staff is aware of the extent of your efforts to protect them from the murky stream of requests that wash across your desk. This can be done informally, in casual conversation with your staff, or even by sharing selective rumors in your staff meeting. In Mickey's monthly departmental meetings at Gracenote, attended by the technical staff that reported to him directly or indirectly, the last topic on the agenda was "hot rumors." Ron did the same at Apple and Schwab, organizations large enough to spawn no end of rumors.

As Mickey relates it, "At times I used the hot rumors slot to discuss recent customer inquiries, requests, opportunities, or discussions that might help motivate the staff depending on who the customer was or what the opportunity might be. By sharing these hot rumors, I tried to do two things: let them know there was more going on than they might know about, and implicitly let them know they were not being buffeted by the requests that came into the department. Both things were good for them to realize."

By protecting them, and letting them know you are protecting them, you will gain in stature on both counts. As Ron likes to say, "Provide an umbrella for your team. It's not so important that they think it's a sunny day as that they're kept dry. In fact, they'll appreciate you more when, knowing they are dry, they see rain all around them."

Your team also needs to be protected from inappropriate or bad communication from other departments or individuals in the organization. Such communication can be disruptive and demoralizing if it filters through your "deflector shields." Work hard to buffer your team from this kind of communication, as discussed later in Chapter 8.

Another aspect of protection that you must provide is to defend your staff from attacks by coworkers or departments outside of development. It is not unusual for marketing, sales, and finance executives and their staff—or even top executives—to take potshots at programming projects and staff. All too often, these potshots are taken without adequate information or facts to back them up. Some of these are good-natured, but some are malicious and may even include personal slams to some of your staff. Our advice is to be vigilant and notice when this is happening. Then, either at the time or offline and one-on-one soon after, call the person taking the potshot on his actions, pointing out that it is dysfunctional behavior that you will not tolerate.

There is a fine line between questioning actions and pointing out shortcomings, but a potshot is usually easily identified since there is a self-serving motivation for it. Don't hesitate to speak up and defend your staff from these potshots. You will gain respect from your peers, and (eventually) your staff will find out how strongly you stand up for and protect them, and you will gain stature in their eyes.

Judging and Improving Performance

One of the most important responsibilities you have as a manager is to judge the performance of your staff and improve their performance over time. Daily feedback, quarterly/annual performance reviews, and monthly or quarterly objectives are all tools to help you do a great job assessing and improving performance.

....

> *Be a yardstick of quality. Some people aren't used to an*
> *environment where excellence is expected.*
>
> —STEVE JOBS

Setting Objectives

A simple way to improve nearly anyone's performance is to mutually agree upon a list of goals to be attained or tasks to be completed and by when. Then periodically review progress toward completing those objectives. While most objectives are set with a quarterly or annual time frame for measurement—annual objectives tend to be more general and quarterly objectives more specific—even quarterly may be too long a time period for many programmers. Weekly, biweekly, or monthly objectives may be more practical, especially for certain programmers.

Objectives may be general in nature (e.g., "Improve coding skills") but are more effective when crafted to be clearly measurable (e.g., "Complete module xx with code-reviewable proven quality by the end of April"). The more measurable the objectives, the easier time you will both have assessing the progress toward their attainment.

....

> *Make sure the team understands that you evaluate them*
> *not only for what they do, but also on how they do it . . .*
> *and that the how in this case relates to transparency,*
> *clean code, documentation and respect for others.*
>
> —MARILSON CAMPOS, VP of Engineering,
> San Francisco Bay Area

Devising a simple-to-use form for crafting and evaluating a person's objectives is key to making sure that implementing, monitoring, and measuring progress does not become a huge task for you. Mickey used a spreadsheet for quarterly objectives for many years at Gracenote. His form allows a numerical score (percent complete) for each of the items being tracked; the overall score is a rollup from the individual objectives. A generic version of an objectives form is shown in Figure 5.2 and is included among the tools for this chapter.

Employee Name:	Name
Title:	Title (e.g., Sr. System Programmer)
Manager:	Supervisor's Name
Quarter / Year:	Q1 2011

Salary:	80,000
Annual Bonus $:	$8,000
Total Cash Comp $:	$88,000
Bonus %:	10%

Approval: Approving Manager's Name

Quarterly Individual Objectives

Individual Performance Objectives: {MAX OF 5}

	% of All Objectives	% Achieved	Results Description
	100%	0%	Individual Objective Results
Objective 1: Objective 1 Description — Describe details of Objective 1 here.	25%	0%	
Objective 2: Objective 2 Description — Describe details of Objective 2 here.	25%	0%	
Objective 3: Objective 3 Description — Describe details of Objective 3 here.	20%	0%	
Objective 4: Objective 4 Description — Describe details of Objective 4 here.	15%	0%	
Objective 5: Objective 5 Description — Describe details of Objective 5 here.	15%	0%	

Figure 5.2   Quarterly objectives form

It is particularly advisable to set objectives for new hires. Most companies have a probationary period (typically 90 to 180 days after a person is hired) when a new employee's performance is scrutinized closely; those who are not performing adequately can be summarily dismissed with little concern for performance improvement or company termination policies that will later force a more rigorous process for dismissal. By sitting down up front with new employees and establishing a clear set of objectives to be completed during the probationary period, you can establish measurable objectives that will help you assess their progress in the early weeks and months of their employment. Since hiring the right people should be your most important responsibility, getting rid of the wrong people quickly should be of equal importance. Use the probationary period to eject those bad hires you will undoubtedly make over time.

Be careful about tying financial rewards to the objectives you set for your staff. Recent motivational theory shows that, contrary to popular belief, rewards in creative environments like programming teams are counterproductive.

Research with both children and adults starting in the 1970s showed that contingent rewards (if you do this, you get this) turn play into work and drain motivation. Larger rewards lead to poorer performance. Furthermore, rewards narrow focus; they're useful for mechanical work (putting nuts on bolts, for example) but not for heuristic, complex, and conceptual work like programming, where narrowing focus lengthens the time required to find solutions.

Those of us challenged by complex tasks are driven by autonomy, mastery, purpose, urgency, praise, sense of accomplishment, and positive feedback (about effort and strategy but not about outcome). "Intrinsically motivated people usually achieve more than their reward-seeking counterparts," says Daniel Pink in his eye-opening best seller *Drive: The Surprising Truth about What Motivates Us.*[7] "When people use rewards to motivate, that's when they're most demotivating."

Our own experience shows that money is seldom a true motivator for programmers. A one-time cash reward can inspire focused effort to complete a critical project. But make rewards an expectation and the bottom falls out of all the other motivators that we think drive great efforts the rest of the time. Pink has convinced us to severely limit contingent rewards, to give unexpected rewards more frequently, and to focus on helping our teams find their own intrinsic motivators.

---

7. Daniel Pink, *Drive: The Surprising Truth about What Motivates Us* (Riverhead Books, 2009).

It's worth noting this about objectives: A by-product of having clearly defined objectives for your staff is the ability to clearly communicate a well-articulated method for measuring the performance of your team to your boss and others in the organization.

Performance Reviews

Everyone desires feedback on their performance. This is best done daily by walking around or weekly in scheduled one-on-one meetings to let members of your staff know how you feel about the work they have recently done.

However, such informal communication is not a substitute for a periodic (at least annual) detailed, written performance review. The jury is out on performance reviews. Robert Sutton, author of *Good Boss, Bad Boss*,[8] claims that "if performance reviews were a drug, they would not receive FDA approval: about half the time they make things better; about half the time they make things worse." Nonetheless, most large organizations require them. Both of us have found our developers craving the feedback a written review can provide—and such reviews to be an excellent vehicle for encouraging good outcomes and discouraging inappropriate behavior and bad results. Additionally, a formal review provides a written record should performance become an issue and a performance improvement plan needs to be undertaken.

Giving regular feedback and formal performance reviews ranks right up there among your most important tasks as a manager of a programming team or department, right after hiring the right people. However, it also seems to be one of the most difficult tasks to do well and on time.

....

Have your annual reviews done on time. Nothing undermines your credibility as a manager more completely than pounding on your team all year to get their work done on time and then telling them you don't have their reviews done because you were busy. Whatever you were busy with likely wasn't managing your people, so you've just proven to them that they don't matter. Good luck motivating them next year.

> —TIM SWIHART, *Engineering Director,*
>   *Apple Computer*

---

8. Robert I. Sutton, *Good Boss, Bad Boss: How to Be the Best . . . and Learn from the Worst* (Business Plus/Hachette Book Group, 2010).

One of the things that will help you to do this well is to have a system that you like, and that your direct reports understand and appreciate.

Anniversary Date Performance Reviews

The timing of a performance review is usually dictated by the company or organization. Often the timing is on the anniversary date of the person's hire or the anniversary of their last salary action. Since some salary actions (such as promotions) can occur out of cycle, an anniversary date might change to that new date from the person's original or previous anniversary date.

Focal Point Performance Reviews

The problem with having performance reviews tied to anniversary dates is that the anniversary dates of your staff are sprinkled throughout the year, and you must

- Make time to complete the performance reviews when they become due
- Find ways to complete each performance review fairly, taking into account comparisons with other direct reports for whom you are not currently completing a performance review

Because these two issues are not easy ones to deal with, many organizations implement "focal point performance reviews" that occur for all individuals at the same time each year.

Focal point reviews generally make it easier for managers to do a good job of completing and delivering performance reviews. The organization expects you to spend "significant time" preparing all your reviews, and so you budget time for them appropriately, something that seldom seems to happen with anniversary date reviews. Also, since you are evaluating all of your direct reports concurrently, it is easier to make a fair evaluation of each individual's performance. We are big advocates of focal point performance reviews and try to drive any organization we are in to adopt them if they have not done so already.[9]

---

9. In start-up companies where cash is tight and financing tenuous, there is a good reason to avoid focal point reviews. Since all the salary adjustments will be effective at the same time and for the same payroll period, they will place a sudden incremental burden on the finances of the company. One response from management may be to freeze salaries rather than proceed with all those salary increases. The occasional burden of anniversary date reviews will not likely trigger this response. Focal point reviews belong in more mature organizations.

Performance Review Process

Regardless of the timing of the review, the process is typically the same:

- Solicit feedback from the person who will be reviewed regarding their performance over the interval since their last formal performance review.
- Prepare a 360-degree review by soliciting feedback from their peers and teammates regarding the person's performance since their last formal performance review or hire date.
- Write the review, incorporating peer and self-feedback in addition to your own comments and direct feedback.
- Give your supervisor a chance to look over and approve the review, incorporating any suggestions you feel are appropriate.
- Send the completed formal performance review to the person to be reviewed so they can read it over in preparation for meeting with you to discuss it. Alternatively, hold the review to present during your meeting with the person. This will ensure that questions regarding the review are discussed immediately and there is no room for misinterpretation. However, some managers and employees would prefer to have an opportunity to absorb the content before you meet.
- Meet with the person to be reviewed to present the performance review and discuss its content and the points you need to reinforce or areas the person wishes to discuss.
- Have the person sign the review. Allow the person to attach any comments they feel are appropriate, if necessary.
- Submit it along with any recommended salary action to your HR department for processing.

Having a good framework for crafting a formal performance review can make the task of completing a solid review much easier. Often this framework is provided by your HR organization as forms to fill out, questionnaires to give focus to key performance metrics, and templates for the actual performance review.

Depending on the maturity of the organization, the effectiveness of your HR staff, and how in tune they are with the art of programming, the framework provided may or may not be very helpful.

Brøderbund had an exemplary HR staff, but even so the programming management found HR's review framework sorely lacking. "The performance metrics did not actually line up well with how we wanted to evaluate the performance of the programming staff." So Mickey, along with the directors of each of the programming departments, created a new framework that in form resembled HR's framework but refined the performance metrics to better address the needs and objectives of programmers.

He adapted the performance review framework further and used it as the basis for a customized performance review framework for the programming staff at Gracenote. You can find a generic version of this programmer-specific review framework in the tools for this chapter.

The most important rule, unless you're managing someone out—and sometimes even if you are: Deliver more positive than negative feedback. *Good Boss, Bad Boss* author Robert Sutton claims you have to give five positive messages to counteract each negative one.

Deliver more positive than negative feedback.

  —*ROBERT SUTTON*

My job is to not be easy on people. My job is to make them better.

  —*STEVE JOBS*

Completing a solid performance review on time is an important accomplishment. Pat yourself on the back each time you complete one; this accomplishment is often underappreciated by your manager and all others except the people being reviewed. They will appreciate it and it will contribute to their view of you as an excellent manager.

Contractors: No Performance Reviews Necessary

For work-for-hire contractors (that is, individuals who are contracted to perform a specific job or project for direct compensation), no performance review is necessary. Because you can send them home at any time, each payment they receive for their work represents a mini performance review. So keep a close rein on all your work-for-hire contractors. If they are performing well and delivering on their milestones and deliverables, keep them on and reinforce their performance verbally or even in writing. But at the first sign of problems with their work, dismiss them or give them a very short time (one to two weeks max) to improve their work. They work "at your pleasure" and must continue to deliver successfully to enjoy that privilege.

Often you pay a premium for their expertise or contracting flexibility, so don't feel bad about dismissing contractors at a moment's notice. As mercenaries, they understand this characteristic of their work.

For independent contractors with whom there is a deeper relationship, you will gravitate toward treating them like employees. However, be aware that there are state and federal laws that prohibit you from doing long-term staffing with contractors who are treated as employees. Most companies have rules that prohibit hiring independent contractors for more than six months without converting them to full-time employees. There are existing legal precedents where contractors who were treated as if they were employees for an extended period of time have been awarded back pay for benefits and other compensation. Be sure you understand the "20 Rules of contracting"[10] that define the difference between employees and contractors.

Contracting through a services agency usually avoids the concerns about treating contractors as employees. Contractors hired in this way are employed by the services agency, to which you pay the consulting fee, which is in turn disbursed to the contractor as salary. There are many services agencies around that are all too happy to supply contractors for long-term services. These agencies may charge significantly more to broker the contractors' services (typically 20 percent or more) than you would pay if you were hiring them directly as independent contractors. This is a viable option for many organizations, to ensure that issues do not arise from hiring independent contractors.

Be conscious of when you are using contractors instead of expanding your headcount. A later section will discuss organizational thinking and staffing that can influence these decisions.

A special case to pay attention to is offshore contracting. Many companies now retain extensive technical resources in India, China, Eastern Europe, and elsewhere that are contracted through a company that specializes in providing technical resources in a "captive" fashion. By captive, we mean the offshore technical staff is dedicated and working directly for you and under your direction "as if they are employed by your company." Many

---

10. The IRS uses 20 standard questions as guidelines to determine whether a person is a full-time contractor or an employee. If your contractor does not meet a majority of these provisos, you may be in danger of assuming the legal liability for an employee. And that may become a problem lying in wait for you. Guidelines for determining whether a person is an independent contractor or an employee are contained in IRS Publication 15-A, *Employer's Supplemental Tax Guide.*

of these offshore arrangements include a clause whereby the offshore technical staff can become your employees at some mutually agreed-upon time and for an agreed-upon fee.

In captive offshore contracting, the contractor relationship is minimized in an attempt to integrate the offshore staff into your organization. The challenges of time, distance, and culture are big enough alone without adding artificial barriers by treating them as work-for-hire contractors. Performance reviews for these offshore technical staff will likely fall to their local management. But do not lose the opportunity to provide the bulk of the input to these performance reviews. You are paying the salaries and should have a large say in who is judged as performing well and who is not. Make sure you are aware of when the performance reviews are given (anniversary or focal point), and make sure you provide timely feedback on performance to their managers and to them directly.

Know When to Cut Your Losses

We believe that you should err on the side of dismissing anyone who is not performing well or who demonstrates a disruptive influence on the organization. We always follow due process for dismissal, giving the programmer a chance to turn a situation around. But when it becomes clear that a programmer is not going to make a turnaround and become an acceptable performer, you should move as quickly as possible to dismiss them.

Poor performers cause a drag on an organization in many ways. They use up an expense line in your budget without pulling their weight on the delivery side. Others who observe their poor performance become unmotivated themselves or, perhaps worse, lose respect for you as a manager. Poor performers impact project schedules by missing milestones, thereby penalizing everyone on the project. Poor performance discussions eat up agenda time in managers' meetings. Regardless, the situation must be addressed quickly.

....

Executives owe it to the organization and to their fellow workers not to tolerate nonperforming individuals in important jobs.

—PETER DRUCKER

Though difficult to broach, termination is usually a good thing for both you and the employee. Most poorly performing employees know they are performing poorly. Few have delusions that they are performing at an outstanding, or even adequate, level. They carry this burden with them to work each day and go to sleep with it each night. It is a heavy burden for most people to bear. So, when you at last confront them and begin the termination process (it usually starts with some sort of performance improvement notice), the employee is usually relieved. Many at that point choose to leave immediately, but others choose to try the performance improvement route. Make sure that if the performance improvement path is taken, you meet with the employee regularly—even frequently—to review and discuss results.

When termination remains the only option, engage your HR department to help prepare the final paperwork and paycheck. Then meet with the employee, usually on a Monday, not a Friday. This will give you a whole work week to meet with your remaining employees and make sure they have sufficient information to know the termination was handled humanely and that no more are currently pending (even if they may be).

Exit Checklist

It is helpful to have a checklist of items to review when you meet with an employee you are going to terminate. These situations can get emotional and are at least universally uncomfortable for all. So having something to go over gives both of you a purpose, and completing the checklist provides a clear end to the meeting.

While the exact checklist will vary from organization to organization, the exit checklist provided as a tool for this chapter is a good starting place if your organization does not provide one. Review it and add any specialized items that may be appropriate.

Organizational Thinking

It may seem unusual to step back and consider what we refer to as organizational thinking. However, it is useful to consider the pros and cons of the various ways you might (re)organize your staff. Often, such decisions are not delegated to a programming manager, and you will be forced to live with whatever organization you have inherited or were given. But even then you can help influence the organizational thinking of your management. And to the extent that you are empowered to do so, you can directly structure how your team interacts—and ultimately its effectiveness.

Sometimes organizational changes happen small and grow over time. Large organizational changes usually require buy-in from, or will be done by, your senior management. We highly recommend that you get buy-in before planning radical changes, and then socialize the specifics of your plan (that is, talk about it beforehand in a low-key fashion) with your management and peers. Otherwise, any changes you make may come back to haunt you.

Staffing

Traditionally, programming organizations have been staffed with full-time employees working at or near the same location, colocated with their peers. However, this traditional organization has changed over the past few decades to mix in work-for-hire contractors. In the past decade change has accelerated with large-scale use of offshore staffing. The advanced communication capabilities of the Internet and World Wide Web have now been embraced by innovative companies large and small that have combined the best of dedicated staff with the advantages of remote contractors or employees to form "virtual offices." We'll discuss many of your staffing options in the next sections, before we get into how to craft an organization from them.

Full-Time versus Contractors

The most important asset of nearly every company is its intellectual capital—that is, the full-time employees who carry in their heads the information and know-how that have built the company. Full-time employees usually have benefits and perks that part-time employees and contractors do not, such as paid vacation and sick time, medical and dental and vision insurance, savings and retirement plans, stock options, and (arguably) job security. Most programmers long to find a great full-time position with benefits and perks where they get to do work they find interesting and/or exciting. Many programmers now additionally include geographic and/or working-hours flexibility on the list of perks they seek.

The difficulty of finding long-term, full-time jobs that offer all those perks leads many experienced programmers to instead become contract "guns for hire" and accept the downsides, the biggest being the need to repeatedly secure ongoing work, pay additional taxes, provide their own benefits, and forgo stock options, paid holidays, and vacations.

It seems like there is always a need to complement your full-time staff with other technical talent. If you have the budget, the single best source for staff augmentation is trusted independent contractors. Because company budgets typically treat employee and contractor expense lines quite differently, it is sometimes much easier to bring on contractors even when hiring is frozen.

Mickey has used contractors to great advantage in every company he has ever worked in. "I use contractors to fill in when we are short-handed in specific skills or talent, or to add critical expertise to critical projects. I would not be able to respond to new company needs or projects if I could not draw upon contractors to help me respond quickly and effectively." Mickey's electronic Rolodex is filled with past employees, associates, acquaintances, and agencies that can help him fill critical positions on short notice. To this end, Mickey goes out of his way to network and keep in touch with those he has worked with.

LinkedIn is a great service that helps Mickey and Ron keep in touch with their numerous past acquaintances, but it is no substitute for a well-maintained electronic Rolodex with names, numbers, e-mail addresses, and notes on the capabilities of those they have worked with.

Mickey uses CardScan's electronic Rolodex program to keep track of all of his contacts—personal, business, and professional—plus talent whom he hopes to meet at some point. It has great word indexing and also allows him to scan the business cards he collects; it also performs automatic character recognition and indexing of the data. This has become one of Mickey's secret weapons in managing effectively (see www.cardscan.com). Ron has used a similar Mac electronic Rolodex program, now known as iData, for over 20 years. Outlook now performs many of these same functions, with plug-ins for additional features such as business card scanning. Other people are fans of Microsoft's OneNote and the Web-based Evernote.

We strongly recommend that you work diligently to maintain a stable of consultants and independent contractors whom you can call upon to staff critical openings or projects. This stable should include past work associates, past company employees, friends, those you may not know but think might be capable, and even rejected prospective employees whom you did not hire but seem capable.

Many of Mickey's Gracenote associates were in his Rolodex as potential consultants before they were hired as contractors for a project. They became full-time employees as they proved their capabilities and demonstrated their ongoing contributions to the company.

However, even a well-filled electronic Rolodex is not capable of providing programmers to fill all the openings you might have for contractors. To help bridge that gap, we have turned to capable contract staffing agencies to provide critical talent when needed. There are too many of these agencies out there, so we recommend that you shop around and find one, two, or a few that you can get to know and trust to help you fill critical openings. Such agencies allow you to have preexisting contracts in place and arrangements made so that adding contractors is relatively painless and convenient. They can also vet any candidates, making sure that only those who really are qualified are presented for your evaluation. The more you work with an agency, the more you can work effectively with the agency principal, who will learn your style and needs and respond effectively once you establish a pattern with them.

Before you call in an agency for help, make sure you have thought carefully about what kind of talent you need and have drafted a "job spec" tailored to your needs. This job spec is similar to but different from the job descriptions we discussed in Chapter 3. You'll remove the long-term job responsibilities and focus on current technical skills and experience. Don't waste your time or your recruiter's on half-baked ideas about what you need. If you can't take the time to create a well-crafted job spec, don't bother to pick up the phone.

When you hire a full-time employee, you usually invest considerable time and energy in giving them generalized and specialized training about the company as well as its technology. There should be little or no ramp-up for a contractor.

At any point in time, you should expect some percentage of your staff to be contractors working on short-term critical projects. If you do not find this to be the case, you may be lucky that you don't need that kind of help. However, it might also indicate that you are not being proactive or effective at responding to critical needs without impacting your own staff.

In-House versus Offshore Contractors

An in-house technical staff dedicated to your development work and projects is the easiest kind of organization to deal with. You have either inherited or handpicked them for the work you need to get done. Whether they are full-time employees or contractors, they likely speak the same language and work on (mostly) the same time schedule. Though some may work off-site at another location or at home, scheduling face-to-face or virtual meetings is usually possible for most of the team members during some core office hours you set for your staff.

Though individual agendas always vary, your in-house technical staff usually have a shared vision and agendas. All are on the same team, and you have the hope of getting "all the oars in the water at the same time and pulling together" for common goals.

Adding offshore contractors to the mix changes this dynamic. It is possible to change it for the better, most obviously by extending the working day across time zones, but our experience shows that it takes an incredible amount of time and energy to make offshore contractors work as well as in-house staff. In fact, if you can make them work 70 percent as effectively as in-house staff, you are either lucky or working tremendously hard to make it happen.

The challenge of vetting and selecting offshore contractors is beyond the scope of this book; first-line programming managers should not be saddled with managing outsourcing relationships. However, understanding the differences between in-house and offshore technical staff is worth touching on in our discussion of organizational thinking.

Offshore contractors are typically part of a larger company agenda than just one programming department. So usually you are given a directive to make use of offshore contractors in order to save costs, scale development capabilities, increase throughput, or improve your company's ability to design for and reach customers in other parts of the world.

The issues with offshore contractors, on the other hand, usually start with time, distance, and culture. Offshore contractors have thus far been preponderantly in India, China, Russia, Eastern Europe, and Southeast Asia,[11] all of which typically manifest all three issues.

TIME.   In these regions, the time difference from North America is usually 6 to 13 hours, depending on where you are and where the offshore contractors are located. This means that either you or they are inconvenienced whenever you actually need to talk to them. If all communication can be done via e-mail, it is less problematic (conceptually) but still a problem because a full day can pass before e-mail messages are exchanged. This drives you and your staff to work into the night or early in your day to ensure that your schedules overlap sufficiently for effective communication.

---

11. Hiring offshore contractors located in Canada and Central and South America may mitigate some of these issues (e.g., time or culture), but all of these issues will likely still be present to some degree.

DISTANCE.   You need to find mechanisms that effectively bridge the distance and commit liberal calendar time to them: face-to-face meetings occasionally, video or voice conferences frequently, and e-mail/IM (instant messaging) often. Mickey has used videoconferencing to try to bridge the distance and, while impressed with the current state of equipment,[12] is still convinced that there is no substitute for face-to-face meetings: "Over the years I have always been deeply impressed with the difference it makes once you have had a face-to-face meeting with someone. There is some kind of bond that occurs from at least once having eye-to-eye contact, and even better if some social bonding can be involved as well, such as dinner together, drinks and music, karaoke, and so on. Forever after, communication is dramatically improved."

If you are going to be doing any serious offshore development, we highly recommend you plan on having technical staff exchanges for considerable periods of time—weeks, not days—to build the communication and accelerate information transfer and exchange.

....

Air travel from site to site is a costly yet necessary part of global teams.

—ERRAN CARMEL, *Professor of Information Technology, American University*[13]

....

An increased travel budget should be part of any distributed project.

—MIKE COHN[14]

CULTURE.   Culture is another difficult issue without easy answers. The heart of this issue is that language- and country- (and sometimes region-) specific behaviors can cause barriers that are very difficult to overcome. This is one of the reasons why India has been a leading offshore area, since English is a second language for most of the educated population. That makes it a better choice than China, Russia, Eastern Europe, or Southeast Asia where

---

12. Skype is tremendously effective now, and *free*! Also, the new generation of Polycom Internet-based videoconferencing equipment is very affordable and effective, with superior video and audio capabilities.

13. Erran Carmel, *Global Software Teams* (Prentice Hall, 1998), p.157.

14. Cohn, *Succeeding with Agile*, p. 368.

English proficiency is more rare. Nonetheless, the language barrier remains a problem in India that is difficult to overcome because of accents and lack of language proficiency. In China, Russia, Eastern Europe, and Southeast Asia, even with excellent translators the verbal/nonverbal and cultural communication difficulties are very, very challenging. There is a tendency in many cultures for technical people to appear to understand information, only to reveal later that they clearly did not. In India, this is exacerbated by the opposite-from-Western-style headshake: side-to-side for agreement and up-to-down for disagreement. Communicating verbally and nonverbally with offshore staff can be several times more difficult than with your in-house staff.

All of these challenges—time, distance, and culture—combine to make offshore contractors more difficult to manage than in-house technical staff.

AGENDAS.   Additionally, inherent in offshoring is an issue specific to outsourcing to any partner: Their technical staff has a different agenda from yours. Most are more interested in their career advancement than in delivering results for your project. Too often in offshoring, contractors advance on the basis of time spent and companies worked for, *not* quality of work or results delivered.[15] And with title inflation rampant, architect roles are too often awarded to comparatively junior technical staff, as are numerous other similarly inflated positions.

The issues of time, distance, culture, and agendas, compounded by the burden placed upon you and your staff to ensure that communication happens effectively, mean that you will have to invest significant time and energy before any return can be harvested from offshore contractors. Make sure you are clear about what tools and processes you expect them to use, and be prepared to spend twice the time or more on requirements and specifications for the work you want done. For less critical functions or projects, expect a long ramp-up and significant investment before you reap rewards. For critical projects, expecting reasonable results in a short time carries high risk.

Mickey's experience working with offshore teams in India, Russia, Eastern Europe, and Canada has proven to him that offshore contractors are a major undertaking. There should be a serious strategic advantage identified (not just cost benefits) before even considering the investment of time and energy required to make offshoring work.

---

15. It has also been our experience that references for offshore workers are nearly impossible to check reliably.

....

*If you find yourself working with an offshore team, find
someone—whether a trusted coworker from that country
or an online resource—to help you understand how the
team's national culture affects programming practices.
Take notes about the culture's approach to asking and
answering questions, work ethic, motivation, and
ways they can work better with your team and you
can accelerate your ramp-up with them.*

Organizing

Your staff, full-time employees and contractors, will make up your organization. Your mix of staff and contractors, local and remote, their overall number, and the projects you need to complete all will help dictate how you organize your staff and programming teams. Various ways of organizing your programming teams are discussed below.

Office-Based versus Virtual Teams

A growing trend in software development is the use of "virtual teams" rather than centralized offices where teams work together in geographic proximity.

The Internet with its wealth of communication and collaboration tools has contributed to the rise in popularity of virtual teams. High-speed connectivity and WANs, e-mail, IM, VoIP, wikis, blogs, microblogs, distributed source control, project control centers, distributed bug-tracking systems, shared "whiteboards," and other tools have all helped spawn the rise of virtual teams.

Virtual teams can make recruiting easier. The allure of working in your own home, or from almost anywhere, as part of a team with a shared vision and focus is strong. For you, this means a vast pool of talent, some portion of whom will be less expensive hires because they live in areas with lower costs of living and lower salaries. And because the concept of virtual teams is still leading-edge and not yet widely adopted in today's business world, you may attract cutting-edge talent to your virtual team that you may never have been able to attract otherwise.

However, managing virtual teams brings a whole set of issues, many of them similar to the challenges of managing offshore contractors. While time and culture differences can also complicate managing virtual teams, for this discussion let's focus on the major issue, distance.

We are continually amazed at the amount of ambient information that is communicated, shared, and exchanged in a colocated environment. When teams are distributed even short distances from each other, ambient communication drops off. If they are spread over different floors of a building or different buildings on a campus, communication suffers even more. As the distance between two people increases, the information communicated between them decreases dramatically—even more dramatically when they're in different countries.

With virtual teams, you must provide alternative channels to replace the loss of informal ambient information flow. You can compensate to a certain degree not only by insisting on more formalized communication, but also by establishing and encouraging the use of wikis, blogs, and forums for discussing technical (and other) topics.

However, even with the use of these alternate channels of information, making sure that communication occurs still requires extraordinary efforts to make virtual teams successful.

At Socialtext, virtual technical teams were the norm; Ron was frequently the only technologist on-site at headquarters to communicate and coordinate with corporate management on a frequent basis. To overcome some of the communication issues, Socialtext institutionalized quarterly travel budgets for each member of the programming team to visit peers and instituted semiannual weeklong developer huddles for team members to interact in person and overcome some of the barriers that isolated development habits can instill.

There's no substitute for face-to-face communication, particularly at pivotal points in the project.

—ADE MILLER, Development Manager, Microsoft patterns & practices group[16]

While its travel policy wasn't quite so liberal, Check Point considered it unacceptable to blame distance as the culprit for not getting projects planned and products completed. Headquartered in Israel and spread across Europe and North America, Check Point intentionally forged virtual teams whenever needed.

---

16. Ade Miller, "Distributed Agile Development at Microsoft patterns & practices," October 2008, p. 10.

At Forensic Logic, where all of development was colocated in Vancouver but all of management in California, Ron found he needed to fly to Canada for two days of intensive meetings to get product plans in sync and everyone on the same page. There is probably no point more critical to temporarily colocating everyone than kicking off and planning a new project.

On the other hand, when a deep design issue emerged, he found, remarkably, that a two-hour one-on-one Skype call, even without a whiteboard, could drill down to elicit the design assumptions responsible for dragging down performance and to work through alternative approaches. Good intentions on everyone's part count for a lot when communication bandwidth is limited.

Employees don't have to be that geographically distant to experience virtual team issues. Even letting employees work at home a day or more per week can be challenging in ways you may not expect.

Most code is written by teams these days. Ron has repeatedly seen teams stalled because they were reluctant to call their teammates who were working at home. It has led him to take special measures: He approves working at home only with the caveat that home workers must *every day* send messages to their teammates that they should have no more hesitation to phone them at home than they would have to phone or come by in the office. The home worker must actually be reachable or the privilege can be canceled. Even with explicit encouragement, team interactions are dramatically reduced—but for the most part the urgent and critical ones do happen.

The flip side is that even with explicit encouragement to be contacted when needed, the home worker gets dramatically fewer interruptions and should be more productive. That said, there are individuals for whom the distractions at home are far more seductive than those at work—and at least a few individuals who clearly take advantage of the looser supervision.

....

The more distance between teammates, the more you have
to formalize communication and make it explicit.

> —TED YOUNG, *Development Manager/Agile Coach,*
> *GuideWirE*

Virtual teams can succeed, but they carry their own increased burden of communication overhead necessary to make them effective. E-mail and IM have improved the challenges of working remotely but have not eliminated them. Sometimes it appears that messaging has actually worsened the problem because people equate e-mail and IM with communication, which they are often not. Ron finds that switching from messaging to voice when the interchange gets complex can help dramatically. Videoconferencing is beginning to have a real impact on improving communication, but it is not currently widespread enough or used frequently enough by us to say it has solved much if any of the communication problem.

We suggest that you schedule regular face-to-face interaction with all distant employees, whether by having them visit you (and others on their team who work in your location) or by you and others on their team visiting them. Mickey requires at least quarterly visits by all distant employees, plus participation via regular videoconferences. E-mail and IM communication is a given.

It may be possible to achieve productivity gains from focused developers working in solitude; however, the added communication overhead is a heavy burden to overcome.

In the end, it will come down to the individuals and the tasks they are assigned to dictate whether virtual teams work for you. As a manager, you need to stay on top of your staff's productivity regardless of where or how they're working, ensure they're staying productive, and act quickly when results fall off.

Programmer Teams—Small versus Large Teams

Most programming projects require a team of programmers, usually working together in a coordinated fashion, to complete the desired tasks. In our experience, the ideal development team is two or three programmers. With a small team of two or three programmers, amazing projects can be completed, especially if one or more are solid, experienced programmers. But even small teams of relatively inexperienced programmers can move mountains. Our experience shows that teams of two programmers can be exceptionally effective.

Agile programming speaks to the effectiveness of "pair programming:" two programmers, one monitor/one keyboard. One of Ron's programmers at Socialtext, already a fan of pairing, expressed real pleasure when he moved from pairing physically to pairing virtually. Suddenly he wasn't scrunching around to see the same monitor and keyboard—yet with Skype and a shared editing environment he was experiencing the collaborative productivity gains of pairing. He sometimes paired with a peer who liked to use a Dvorak keyboard layout, and with virtual pairing the team was productive both singly and collaboratively. As this programmer related it, "In this distributed mode each of us just keeps working in the environment we're most productive in!"

Why are small teams so effective?

Experience shows that a small team can be colocated, often in one office together. Agile teams are typically larger but use colocation as a principle for this very reason.

In today's virtual offices, small teams can experience much of colocation and have similar effectiveness by being parked in teleconference all day on VoIP via headsets.

Effective small teams share communication equally among all members of the team. They commit to being immediately available to answer questions, resolve design dilemmas as they arise, and provide collegial debugging advice and assistance. Steps and cycles aren't wasted trying to find someone to help.

As teams grow, communication becomes more difficult. Interactions become fragmented. And that leads to an increased level of false assumptions and missteps that would otherwise be avoided in a small team.

Unfortunately, many programming projects are just too big to be tackled by a small team. We've both led projects that required dozens or even legions of programmers to work together without the benefit of colocation or even walking-distance proximity. Projects of this size require considerably more rigorous project planning, formalized communication, extensive documentation, and integrated systems testing.

> *Large teams (29 people) create around six times as many defects as small teams (three people) and obviously burn through a lot more money. Yet, the large team appears to produce about the same amount of output in only an average of 12 days' less time. This is a truly astonishing finding, though it fits with my personal experience on projects over 35 years.*
>
> —PHILLIP ARMOUR, *Longtime Industry Veteran*[17]

---

17. Phillip Armour, "Privacy and Security in Highly Dynamic Systems," *Communications of the ACM* 49, no. 9 (September 2006): 16.

If you are embarking on a large software project, you should do so with a copy of Fred Brooks's *Mythical Man-Month*,[18] the seminal book on managing large software projects, by your side. It contains wisdom that is as relevant today as when Brooks first wrote it in 1975 about his experiences creating OS/360, the first large-scale operating system for IBM.

That said, even big programming projects can benefit from having small programming teams colocated and working together on "their piece" of the overall project. Put small teams together whenever possible and have them focus on clearly defined deliverables, and your overall project will definitely benefit.

....

Small teams are more productive than large teams . . . a five- to seven-person team will complete an equivalently sized project in the shortest amount of time.

—*MIKE COHN*[19]

Managing Larger Organizations

Large organizations present serious challenges, but for the manager of such an organization they typically revolve around managing managers, not just programmers.

You may be promoted into a position where you are now managing others, including other managers. But it is more likely the case that you will grow an organization to a size that exceeds your ability to manage it directly. At that time you will need to either promote one of your staff to management to help you manage your team or hire someone from outside.

Managing large organizations is a more traditional management problem. Many books have been written to address the topic, so we won't delve into it here except to provide a few hints about hiring managers and delegating to them.

Hiring a manager is similar to hiring an individual contributor, but the stakes are much higher because more of the organization will interact with your hire. If you consider outside candidates, the interview process must be quite inclusive: You will want all the key stakeholders to be part of the hiring process. In addition to your own key team members, you'll include

18. Brooks, *The Mythical Man-Month*.
19. Cohn, *Succeeding with Agile*, p. 181.

your supervisor plus stakeholders in those other parts of the organization who will interact with this new manager: product managers, program/project managers, and QA managers, for example. Solicit feedback on the interviews that you arrange, and tally the results in a spreadsheet or other tool for tracking interview feedback.

One of the most important things to assess when hiring a manager from outside your company is how well he has been able to manage his team's personalities and quirks and successfully deliver projects. This cannot effectively be assessed during the interview, though you can get a sense from your interview questions how he views himself as a manager. You must talk to the references that are provided and make sure they can attest to the performance in the two areas mentioned above.

Also, if at all possible, find others who have worked with or for the person in the past, and find out how they would judge his performance in the two areas. Such "back-channel" reference checks can often be the most telling. Since so much is at stake when hiring a new manager, it pays big dividends to dig deep to find back-channel references whenever possible. LinkedIn has dramatically simplified finding back-channel connections to quiz, but if you still can't find any you can rely on, work the references provided to you. Sometimes a follow-up reference check will tell you more than an initial one. They know you are serious and that you are looking to them to help you. Mickey has been known to "chat up" a reference, finding common acquaintances or background to help bring the whole truth to the surface during a reference check.

If you promote from within, you have a good idea if it will work out before you promote the person, but most of the same principles apply. The reference checking is not relevant, but the rigor of the process is important. It is too easy to be blind to the limitations or faults of a favored team member in your desire to promote them. You should make sure you follow a formalized interview process to get a more balanced perspective on the candidate—and if nothing else to make sure you CYA should things turn out less than ideally.

One final observation about recruiting managers: Generally, good programmers who make great managers are rare. Those good programmers who do have the talent and inclination to manage effectively should be encouraged, nurtured, and rewarded. They can have a markedly positive effect on your organization as it grows. In almost 40 years of managing software development in numerous organizations, we have never been in a situation where we had too many great technical managers.

Hiring one or more managers provides the opportunity to delegate some of your management tasks. We both know first-level development managers who delegate to coders, but short of the situation where you're grooming one of your programmers for management, we think it's a waste of talent. On the other hand, hire a manager into your staff and you've added a partner—another resource whose tasks resemble yours and to whom you can give part of what's on your plate.

Hiring one or more managers presents new challenges for virtually the same reason. To delegate work, you have to be willing to let go—you have to accept that tasks will be done in ways different from how you would have tackled them. For one thing, do not expect everyone to manage the same way you do. Everyone has their own style and approach to work and management. What is important is to focus on the results, and not on the method. There are certain things that you must insist on, but those are generally basic leadership qualities and not specific management methods.

Make sure you formalize management responsibilities and span of control. Let your new manager make mistakes, but make sure they are small mistakes, not costly big ones. Coach and guide, as you would with an individual contributor. Emphasize helping your manager(s) with issues they raise and with guiding them through the maze of organizational minefields that you have learned to navigate successfully yourself.

By delegating appropriately as we've described, you will free yourself to step back and think more strategically about your organization, teams, goals, problems, and projects. Only by actually delegating and leveraging the opportunity do you rise to a more senior level of management and contribution.

FUNCTIONAL PROGRAMMING DEPARTMENTS. Depending on the size of your organization, your programming team may grow to be specialized in more than one functional area—that is, system programming, application programming, database programming, and so on. Grouping "like-minded" programmers together allows them to help each other and, to a certain degree, be more self-managed. The more experienced programmers can provide technical direction.

Technical direction does not include typical managerial functions like hiring, firing, salary/compensation, and dealing with performance problems. But technical direction does include making sure that programs are developed in the proper manner, with attention to design, implementation practices, debugging, and testing. Experience, of course, is especially helpful in solving difficult design and debugging challenges. And that is the considerable value gained from functional programming departments.

Functional programming departments pool the talent needed to solve sticky problems and are much easier to manage and run than most other organizational structures. At Gracenote, Mickey had three functional programming departments:

- UNIX System Programming
- Client Programming
- Database Programming

"Over time I grew the programming teams into three distinct programming departments. The managers of those departments were the most experienced and best programmers, who had also grown into excellent managers. All continued to be hands-on programmers as well, though they spent only a small fraction of their time actually programming."

Functional programming departments evolve naturally, which speaks to their effectiveness and universality. "Like seeks like" is an old rule of thumb, but it is certainly true in every organization we have been in. Even in an organization that moves to cross-functional teams, the "like seeks like" rule of thumb emerges. Mickey says, "At Brøderbund we broke our applications programming organization into cross-functional teams working on specific market segments (i.e., games, productivity apps, educational apps, etc.). But even within these small cross-functional teams, the application programmers tended to sit together and eventually became a very functionally oriented team as well. I was surprised at how quickly their functional organization tendencies reappeared."

CROSS-FUNCTIONAL TEAMS. Often a project requires participation from not only a single programming department but all of them plus other functional departments as well. Creating the first online investor tools in Java for Schwab.com didn't just mean collaboration between Java client and server groups, but also engaging middleware, mainframe, change management, release management, information security, corporate architecture and oversight, networking, testing services, data center production services, data center operations, UNIX design and engineering, data modeling, database services, corporate data solutions, and performance engineering. As Ron recalls, "It took a stellar technical project manager just to keep the tech side on track."

Even developing shrink-wrapped products at Brøderbund often required pulling in team members from more than seven different functional departments: "Making multimedia products required team members from the system programming, application programming, animation, art, sound design, QA, and product management departments, plus product marketing, marketing, sales, technical support, manufacturing, and other departments as well. Creating such a cross-functional team and making sure communication was happening appropriately and roadblocks were being removed expeditiously was a full-time job for one or more assistant product managers for each project."

Cross-functional teams like these are usually referred to as "matrix managed," meaning that the team members have a home in a functional area (e.g., the Application Programming Department) but are assigned "temporarily" to be part of a matrixed team for the span of a given project. This maximizes flexibility in staffing projects, since team members may be members of more than one team (though ideally working "mostly" on one project).

Managing "heavily matrixed" teams can be a challenge, however, because no one actually works for the person managing the project—usually known as the project or program manager—who has only indirect influence over the person's performance review or compensation adjustments. When team members are good, that is usually not much of an issue. But when team members perform poorly, they can be a major headache for the project/program manager. The problem is often referred to as *responsibility but no authority*.

At Brøderbund, the cross-functional projects became so problematic that the company reorganized to solve the problem. Mickey observes, "As the functional departments grew, staffing the heavily matrixed projects became more and more of a nightmare. To address this, the company reorganized itself into 'Studios,' each with dedicated resources for each of the major functional areas reporting up to a Studio manager. Given direct responsibility for performance and compensation, Studio managers could allocate resources freely.

"The Studios were able to exert more direct control on the projects and team members, but not without a cost. The major problem that emerged from Brøderbund's Studio reorganization was that members of the various functional disciplines began to lose touch with their functional counterparts. Experience wasn't shared as easily. Over time, duplication of effort began to appear."

The move from functional programming teams to cross-functional, product-focused teams is common as organizations grow or retract. This serves the business for a while, but eventually the "like seeks like" tendencies reemerge and mini functional departments appear. Eventually, larger functional programming teams are reestablished. This is a pendulum that swings back and forth, rarely reaching equilibrium.

Troubleshooting a Dysfunctional Organization

Be alert for "canaries in the coal mine" that can help you identify the early signs of a dysfunctional organization. One such canary is open and often rampant cynicism. Cynicism breeds negative morale and should be dealt with as soon as humanly possible.

In tandem, you must also identify the root cause of the dysfunction. Listing the issues that are the main focus of the cynicism will typically lead you to the issue(s) at the heart of the dysfunction. Then you must step back and take stock of the issues and determine which to attack and how to attack them.

....

You can't have great software without a great team, and most software teams behave like dysfunctional families.

—*JIM MCCARTHY, Coauthor, Dynamics of Software Development*[20]

Many difficult dysfunctional organization issues are outside your ability to address. All too frequent examples are

- Management-mandated unrealistic programming/product schedules
- Sales of products that have not been finished (or started, or even planned) combined with customer expectations that cannot be met
- Quality assurance testing that's nonexistent—not budgeted and not appreciated

To address such issues, your only hope is to enlist appropriate management support. Your role is all too often limited: Educate, evangelize, agitate, demand, and otherwise make a nuisance of yourself until the fundamental issues are addressed.

---

20. Quoted by Paul Roberts, "Drop and Code Me Twenty!," *Fast Company*, December 31, 1996.

For more local issues that you may identify, keep track of them and do not succumb to just accepting them as the way things are going to be. Examples of such local issues are

- Lack of adequate design during development projects
- Rampant poor programming practices
- Programmers refusing to participate in (or showing passive resistance to) an agreed-upon software development process

All of these kinds of issues are within your control, and you do not need approval or help from anyone to address them. Simply make sure that your staff understands the need to address the issue and follow up with them when they do not.

Address the issue of those programmers who actively or passively resist your efforts to deal with dysfunctional organizational issues. Normally, that means you must terminate them.

Deliver Results and Celebrate Success

Remember the reason why you are doing all this: to deliver great results. When that occurs, make sure you also find time to thank the team appropriately by sending a congratulatory e-mail to your team, and to the entire organization if at all possible. Make sure you CC the important people in the organization you want to be sure are aware of the team's success.

> *People often resist change for reasons that make good*
> *sense to them, even if those reasons don't correspond to*
> *organizational goals. So it is crucial to recognize, reward,*
> *and celebrate accomplishments.*
>
> —ROSABETH MOSS Kanter, *Business Professor, Harvard*
> *Business School, and Author, Speaker, and Consultant*

Also celebrate their success! Such a celebration does not need to be lavish but must be out of the ordinary. Go out of your way to be part of the celebration and even host it if that makes sense. Good ways to celebrate success include setting up a special Friday afternoon "happy hour" to thank the team for their efforts, buying a round of drinks at the local watering hole for the entire team, hosting a team lunch, or providing a special thank-you gift.

Summary

Managing down is hard, but it can also be very rewarding, both personally and professionally, if you do it successfully. There are never enough great programming managers, and your career is assured if you can do this and do it well.

Keys to ensuring this are to make sure you gain and retain the technical respect of your staff, hire great programmers and manage them as the unique individuals they are, facilitate and protect them, provide good feedback often and also as part of a formal performance review (at least annually), and make sure they are organized into teams appropriate for the tasks at hand and for the composition of your staff. The sections in this chapter will help you do this, building on the experience we have gained in our careers.

Look forward to a lot of hard work, and good luck.

Tools

We have prepared a number of tools to assist you in managing your staff. The spreadsheets and Word documents provide full examples that you can easily adapt for your organization. See the Tools section, after the chapters, for the link to the Tools Web site, from which you can download the following tools:

- Performance review templates
- Quarterly objectives workbook
- Employee termination and exit checklist
- Sample status report
- Training log

Rules of Thumb
and
Nuggets of Wisdom

WE ALL MANAGE BY USING RULES OF THUMB. Sometimes we create them ourselves—we have some hard experience that teaches a big lesson, from our having squeezed through it, or perhaps because we failed to. Sometimes the lesson comes to us already fully formed, and so succinct we can communicate it in a phrase or a sentence. Other times we struggle to boil complexity down to its pith.

Benjamin Franklin collected and published one of the first well-known sets of maxims, proverbs, and rules of thumb in *Poor Richard's Almanack.*[1] Around the same time, in 1732, Thomas Fuller published his own book of proverbs that included the ubiquitous "A stitch in time saves nine," a rule of thumb for much of life.

Rules of thumb we learned growing up and others are often as applicable to managing software development as to the rest of life. More than one software development manager has used "Measure twice, cut once," even though code is probably the most resilient of materials. Here are a few that predate our profession, many by hundreds of years, yet apply to us:

Measure twice, cut once.

> —*TRADITIONAL*

This is perhaps the simplest and clearest example of a rule of thumb. Nearly everyone has failed to follow this rule, and most of us have regretted doing so at least once, perhaps none so much as the space scientists whose metric-system-based Mars Climate Orbiter spacecraft disintegrated when the ground-based system sent its Mars orbit trajectory in English units.

Life is simpler when you plow around the stump.

> —*TRADITIONAL*

Sometimes bad practices are so deeply rooted that you need to route learning and the introduction of better practices around them.

---

1. http://en.wikipedia.org/wiki/Poor_Richards_Almanack.

*Do not corner something that you know is meaner
than you.*

      —TRADITIONAL

The corollary would have to be "Do not corner anything if you're
not willing to find out just how mean it can be." As applied to corporate politics, the rule is simple: "Don't corner your people, don't
corner your peers, and whatever you do, don't corner someone
who outranks you!"

*Don't interfere with somethin' that ain't botherin'
you none.*

      —TRADITIONAL

There's way too much to fix to fool with the stuff that works.

When you wallow with pigs, expect to get dirty.

      —TRADITIONAL

A corollary to "Do not corner anything."

Save early, save often.

      —LEARNED COMMON WISDOM

Recommended always, and especially when running beta software, or version 1 of anything.

While we learned some rules of thumb growing up, we learn others
from the counsel of managers and peers, whether to give us solace from
having had similar experiences, to counsel us in how to identify and avoid
future problems, or to mentor us with their hard-won wisdom.

We characterize two different forms of these seeds of advice:

- Rules of thumb—proven, pithy wisdom for making things work
- Nuggets of wisdom—concise insights to guide your actions and thinking

Separately and then together, we have long collected and used rules and nuggets to help us understand and manage programmers. Some come from our reading, some from our mentors and colleagues, some from the famous, some from our own experience. Many are well known and widely circulated. More than one software development manager has used "Underpromise, overdeliver," even though when first said it was probably not about software. Others are less well known. We find all of them relevant.

We hope you too will find them useful for understanding and managing programmers and teams.

The Challenges of Managing

Managers must manage.

> —ANDY GROVE, Former Intel Chairman and CEO[1]

I've used Andy Grove's phrase innumerable times to coach my managers and directors of programming teams. When confronted with a problem, they can't just "raise a red flag." I'm always available when needed, but good software managers find ways to solve problems without my involvement or executive management direction.

Management is about human beings. Its task is to make people capable of joint performance, to make their strengths effective and their weaknesses irrelevant.

> —PETER DRUCKER[2]

Drucker, born in 1909, is the man who has been called the "father of modern management." He coined the term *knowledge worker* and predicted the rise of today's information society and its need for lifelong learning.

---

1. Paraphrased from Andrew S. Grove, *High-Output Management* (Vintage Books, 1995).
2. Peter Drucker, "Management as Social Function and Liberal Art," in *The Essential Drucker* (Harper Business, 2001), p. 10.

A manager of years ago gave sage career advice:
When you land at a new company, pick a gnarly
problem—one that people have been avoiding—
and solve it. It gets you up the learning curve,
and it gains you credibility and respect, both
of which you'll need to be an effective developer
and influencer.

> —DAVE SMITH, *Agile Software Development Coach*[3]

People hate change but love progress.

> —TERRY PEARCE, *Author,* Leading Out Loud

It is not enough to respond to change; we must lead
change or be left behind.

> —POLLYANNA PIXTON, *Founder, Agile Leadership*
> *Network (ALN)*[4]

You miss 100 percent of the shots you never take.

> —WAYNE GRETZKY, *Hockey Phenom*

I have missed more than 9,000 shots in my career.
I have lost almost 300 games. On 26 occasions I
have been entrusted to take the game-winning shot
and I missed. I have failed over and over again in
my life. And that's precisely why I succeed.

> —MICHAEL JORDAN, *Basketball Phenom*[5]

Nothing stops a witch hunt faster than owning up
to being the culprit.

> —TIM SWIHART, *Engineering Director, Apple Computer*

You know when it's you (or your team) that the angry mob is
searching for. Stand up, succinctly explain what went wrong, why

---

3. http://c2.com/cgi/wiki?WorstThingsFirst.

4. Spoken at BayALN, the Bay Area chapter, January 2007.

5. Quoted in *Guideposts*, August 2002.

it went wrong, and what's being done to correct the situation. Too often in business, witch hunts start because those in charge can't get straight answers when things aren't going well. Providing timely insight into what went wrong and what's being changed to minimize the chance of it happening again provides them with the knowledge needed to accurately assess the impact of that problem.

Don't let the day-to-day eat you up.

> —DAVID DIBBLE, *Schwab and Yahoo EVP and*
> *First Data CIO*

David made this statement to make the point to his management team that managers have "real" work to do; that the seemingly urgent—e-mail, meetings, the routine—could easily fill a day. Only by being intentional about how we use our days can managers overcome letting that happen.

Every hour of planning saves about a day of wasted time and effort.

> —STEVE MCCONNELL, *CEO and Chief Software*
> *Engineer, Construx Software, and Author,* Code
> Complete *and* Rapid Development [6]

Prioritize. Sometimes, it is urgent to wait.

> —PHAC LE TUAN, *VP of Engineering and CEO,*
> *San Francisco Bay Area*

Chairman and CEO, Kinemo International, Phac explains: "When an unexpected issue comes up, engineers (mostly) tend to want to fix it right away to show their mettle, forgetting their actual priorities. It is actually more difficult to sit back and wait first to understand the actual priority of the new issue."

---

6. Steve McConnell, *Software Project Survival Guide* (Microsoft Press, 1998), p. 36.

The journey begins with a single step. The whole journey can be accomplished even with a series of baby steps.

—ANONYMOUS

I'm a strong advocate of baby steps. You'll get criticized for not solving the whole big problem at once. But in my experience, you're in a lot more danger of biting off more than you can chew. Baby steps are like Agile sprints: just enough to get everyone on board and rapid iterative change giving you a new context to see both the next priority and the next low-hanging fruit (and, ideally, where they intersect).

Don't boil the ocean.

—FREQUENTLY USED AT SCHWAB

The corollary to taking baby steps is this warning not to try to solve everything at once because of the impossibility of doing so.

No surprises!

—KARIN HARDISON, *Director, Software Development*

Every manager we've ever had whom we respected, must have had this as a rule of thumb, it seems so universal. Tell your employees the value of giving you the earliest warning possible. And do the same for your manager.

All you have to do is draw a picture.

—JOHN WARNOCK, *Cofounder, Adobe Systems*

While working with John on a project at Evans & Sutherland, every time I encountered a problem I would wander into his office and he would repeat this rule of thumb, and then we would sketch out the problem on a whiteboard and attempt to find a solution. It always started with a picture, regardless of the problem. As John's rule of thumb says and as I've found ever since, if you can't draw a picture of a problem, you probably don't understand the problem.

Ask any group of reasonably intelligent adults for advice on how to shave off a few pounds and they come up with some great dieting advice like "Eat less, exercise more." It's common sense, right? Common sense, but NOT common practice. I am reminded of a conversation I had with one senior exec some time ago. We were discussing the motivations for companies who routinely work on almost twice as many projects as they have the resources to efficiently staff (which is most companies). Key projects are routinely understaffed, and many individuals multi-task among various projects, resulting in task-switching inefficiencies known to decrease productivity by as much as 60%. Lack of planning and lack of focus routinely lead to predictable delays in product launches as well as severe quality problems with those products that do manage to launch. Why wouldn't business leaders just cut or put on hold the least important and least urgent projects, focusing on the critical few? Why would they persist in spreading precious resources ineffectively over too many projects, thus getting less done overall than if they focused their efforts?[7]

—KIMBERLY WIEFLING

Rule of 3: In a discussion: Limit two-way interchanges to three back-and-forths. Use the "Rule of 3" to get out of ratholes.

—ELECTRONIC BROKERAGE TECHNOLOGY, Schwab

It's a well-known problem in management teams that any two technologists can take a discussion down a rathole in seconds. The means of recognizing—and stopping—it, at Schwab, was to watch for an interchange that became just two people and to end it after each had spoken three times by requiring another voice to be the next to speak.

---

7. Kimberly Wiefling, "Why Common Sense is NOT Common Practice," http://wiefling.com/newsletter-why-common-sense-is-no-common-practice/.

Common sense is not common practice.

> — KIMBERLY WIEFLING, *Leadership and Program*
> *Management Consultant*

Example is not the most important way of
influencing other people. It's the only way.

> —ALBERT SCHWEITZER

Leading by example occurs whether you like it
or not.

> —JATEEN PAREKH, *Founder and CTO of Jelli*
> *Crowdsourced Radio*[8]

If you're a people manager, your people are far more
important than anything else you're working on.

> —TIM SWIHART

Tim notes, "If a team member drops by at an awkward time and wants to chat, set aside what you're doing and pay attention. They may be building up the courage to tell you something big. I've noticed this to be especially true when the sudden chatter isn't somebody who normally drops by for idle conversation. It might be as simple as being unable to get a piece of information needed to complete a task or might be as big as an impending divorce, the death of a loved one, or something equally devastating on a personal level to them . . . things that can throw a real monkey wrench into your carefully laid schedule. If they know you'll make them your top priority when they drop by, they're more likely to drop by sooner when things are about to go very wrong."

The major incentive to productivity and efficiency
are social and moral rather than financial.

> —PETER DRUCKER[9]

---

8. Spoken at the Engineering Leadership SIG of SVForum in January 2011 on the topic of "Lessons Learned on the Journey from Engineer to Company Founder."

9. Peter Drucker, *The New Society* (Harper & Row, 1950).

Conscious confidence moves mountains.
Unconscious ignorance sinks ships.

—*PHAC LE TUAN*

Phac adds: "With the right knowledge and awareness of what's still unknown (and therefore needs to be investigated), one can build the confidence to accomplish what seems impossible at first. However, fatal errors by the best teams often stem from unquestioned beliefs that are in fact wrong. Ignorance of the potential flaws in such beliefs is usually unconscious. It's a message about modesty (cf. the 'Invincible Armada' story)."

Adequacy is sufficient.

—*ADAM OSBORNE, Author, Publisher, Computer Designer, and Founder, Osborne Computers*[10]

This fits with another quote we have subscribed to, Voltaire's "The perfect is the enemy of the good." Programmers tend either to "finish" too soon and "throw it over the wall"—or to polish and polish and polish—and never finish. Scrum is all about delivering over and over and letting the product owner decide when to begin deriving value from it.

I praise loudly; I blame softly.

—*CATHERINE THE GREAT OF RUSSIA*

A manager who gets agreement by dominating conversations ends up not with a team but a coalition of the coerced.

—*JIM NISBET, CTO, HighWire and Loggly*

---

10. http://kurthaeusler.wordpress.com/2009/05/09/quotes/.

*Most teams aren't teams at all but merely collections
of individual relationships with the boss. Each
individual vying with the others for power,
prestige and position.*

> —DOUGLAS MCGREGOR, Professor,
> MIT Sloan School of Management[11]

McGregor was the formulator of the Theory X/Theory Y models
of management and motivation.

Behavior revolves around what you measure.

> —JIM HIGHSMITH, Agile Guru[12]

He pointed out that "all measurements are dysfunctional and
drive the opposite of what you intend"; therefore it's a best
practice to have a spectrum of things you measure.

Firefighters who get rewarded carry matches.

> —KIMBERLY WIEFLING

Wiefling says, "Never reward firefighters. Don't encourage them!
Reward is a double-edged sword: what gets rewarded is what
gets done . . . Firefighting, diving catches, and heroics are
symptoms of a problem, not signs of a cure. Don't spread this
disease by rewarding the carriers. Find the person who is planning ahead, preventing disaster, executing with excellence, and
recovering from setbacks without setting their hair on fire,
and without glitz or fanfare. Whip out a Starbucks gift certifi-
cate for this everyday hero and send them home at 3 P.M. to
enjoy some time with their kids."[13]

You cannot overcommunicate.

> —RON LICHTY

---

11. Quoted in Cohn, *Succeeding with Agile*, p. 175.

12. Shared February 16, 2010, to BayALN, the Bay Area chapter of the Agile Leadership
    Network.

13. www.projectconnections.com/articles/060507-wiefling.html.

The work that I don't do (that is, the work that is assigned to others) is not that tough.

—DAVID WYLIE, Engagement Manager, SolutionsIQ[14]

He pointed out that while people perceive their own work as challenging and hard, they can't figure out why other teams can't get their work finished, since it seems so much simpler.

It's a delicate dance to be an engineering manager: to communicate enough while filtering out distractions.

—EMILIO ROJAS, Software Developer, Manager,
and Engineering Performance Coach

There is nothing more difficult to carry out, nor more doubtful of success, nor more dangerous to handle, than to initiate a new order of things. For the reformer has enemies in all those who profit by the old order, and only lukewarm defenders in all those who would profit by the new . . .

—NICCOLO MACCHIAVELLI[15]

The more prominent salary, perks, and benefits are in someone's work life, the more they can inhibit creativity and unravel performance. . . . Effective organizations compensate people in amounts and in ways that allow individuals to mostly forget about compensation and instead focus on the work itself. Here are three key techniques: Ensure internal and external fairness . . . Pay [a little] more than average . . . If you use performance metrics, make them wide-ranging, relevant, and hard to game.

—DANIEL H. PINK, Author[16]

---

14. Shared during the March 2010 Agile in Action Road Show.
15. Niccolo Macchiavelli, *The Prince* (1532).
16. Pink, *Drive: The Surprising Truth about What Motivates Us.*

My job is to pay people as much as I can, not as little as possible.

—M. W. MANTLE

Compensation is a complex function made up not only of salary but of other important items like what you get to work on, who you get to work with, what new technology you get to use, whether you can help change the world, etc.

—M. W. MANTLE

When hiring people, I often ask what the person's expectations are for compensation. This usually results in an answer that is a salary number or sometimes salary plus stock options. I often launch into a discussion about how each person is individual, and how compensation is really a complex formula where

Compensation = i*salary + j*stock options + k*benefits + l*who they get to work with + m*where they get to work + n*what they get to work on + . . .

Each of the variables has a scalar associated with it, and the value of the scalar modifies the formula appropriately. Each individual has to decide what is important to them and how much it matters, so that the scalars range from 0 to 1. This then leads to a healthy discussion of what is really important to them, which often isn't really salary, thereby making the actual salary offered less of a competitive factor.

Manage salaries as if you had to post them outside your office door.

—M. W. MANTLE

Since my earliest days of being a manager, I have always tried to manage as if I had to post the salaries of all the people who report to me outside my office door. This means that I try to make sure that those who are generally accepted as the best performers are the most highly compensated. Of course, I would never want to post the salaries outside my office door. This is because there are always inequities, which leads to the next rule of thumb.

There are always salary inequities.

—M. W. MANTLE

Knowing that there will always be inequities, I manage programmers so that over time the inequities will be eliminated. That is, the rate of salary increases should be greater for those who are the best performers, and the rate of increase for the higher-paid of the lower-performing staff is less, zero, or negative. This was the hardest lesson I needed to learn when first managing programmers. Understanding that there will always be inequities and that my job is to correct those inequities over time made my job easier for me to handle.

Salary compression is a fact of life. Don't let it make you miss a candidate.

I'd rather do big bonuses than out-of-range salaries.

You'll forget what you gave them in ten minutes so don't get too worried.

—MARK HIMELSTEIN, Interim VP of Engineering, San Francisco Bay Area

Few recruiters are stellar; treat yours like gems.

—ELAINE WHERRY, Cofounder, Meebo[17]

If your current employees are happy, they will refer other great employees to you. So make your place a desirable place to work—including offices for programmers, good leadership, and perks.

—GREGORY CLOSE, Manager, Project Manager, and Start-up Founder, San Francisco Bay Area

---

17. From a talk at Code Camp 2011: "Winning the Engineering Talent War Online," October 9, 2011, later shared in her blog at http://www.ewherry.com/2012/06/the-recruiter-honeypot/.

Treat hiring like a project: Define times between events:

- *24 hours to phone screen or reject*
- *48 hours until face-to-face interview*
- *24 hours until decision*

    —MARK HIMELSTEIN

Sign up to interview high school students applying to your alma mater. I've hired some fantastic summer interns from those interviews.

    —BRUCE ROSENBLUM, CEO of Inera, Former VP of
    Software Development at Turning Point

Hire interns early and often. They're relatively cheap and they're energetic.

    —MARK HIMELSTEIN

Mark notes, "I have often hired new college grads with incomplete skills as interns and trained them in exchange for doing QA for a year."

R&D teams do need an influx of new talent to maintain creativity and freshness—but only at the rate of one person every three or four years.

    —RICHARD HACKMAN, Harvard professor and
    authority on teamwork, and Diane Coutu[18]

Making two OK hires is way behind making one great hire.

    —TIM DIERKS, Engineer, CTO, and VP of Engineering,
    Apple, Google, and elsewhere

---

18. From *Harvard Business Review*, May 2009, pp. 98–105, as quoted in Cohn, *Succeeding with Agile*, pp. 209–10.

A's hire A's. B's hire C's.

—STEVE JOBS

Shortly after Pixar was spun out of Lucasfilm in 1986 and while
Steve was actively involved in the company as CEO, he discussed
this management philosophy at a Pixar management meeting,
reinforcing how it is imperative to hire the right people (the"A's")
because allowing"B's"into the organization erodes the organization much more than just that one wrong hire.

*The challenge in hiring is that everyone has a place
they come from. You have to figure that out. The
baggage candidates carry can be hard for a manager
to negotiate.*

—MARK FRIEDMAN, CEO, *GreenAxle Solutions*

Mark, who founded the Best Practices SIG of the East Bay
Innovation Group, adds,"They could come in with a chip on
their shoulder if they just came from a project that was canceled.
They could be coming from a team that worked well but in a very
different way from your way of working. They may have a high
level of skepticism. They may have been on projects that repeatedly went south. You're constantly trying to figure out how to
work all those things."

*I often look for people that have done a lot of
stuff on their own that wasn't asked of them.
Not just their school project or just what their
previous employer had them do. Somebody who
was passionate about something and had some side
project. How did they maintain it and how serious
did they get with it? Or do they do a lot of quick
hacks and abandon them?*

—BRAD FITZPATRICK, *Founder of* LiveJournal *and*
Chief Architect at Six Apart[19]

---

19. Quoted in Seibel, *Coders at Work*, p. 77.

Let me offer a humble proposal: Don't interview anyone who hasn't accomplished anything. Ever. Certificates and degrees are not accomplishments; I mean real-world projects with real-world users. There is no excuse for software developers who don't have a site, app, or service they can point to and say, "I did this, all by myself!" in a world where Google App Engine and Amazon Web Services have free service tiers, and it costs all of $25 to register as an Android developer and publish an app on the Android Market.

—JON EVANS, *Author, Journalist, Adventure Traveler, Software Engineer, and* TechCrunch *Columnist*[20]

Hire people who built stuff on their own time, just for fun.

—DAVE WILSON, *Software Architect, San Francisco Bay Area*

College degrees don't impress me, and lack of school doesn't scare me (see: Jobs, Steve, and Gates, Bill). At some point, when a person is far enough removed from school, the degree is all but meaningless. Experience is what matters most.

—ERIC MULLER, *Software Architect and VP of Technology, San Francisco Bay Area*

I avoid prima donnas. One candidate told me he only needed to work two days per week because he could do in 16 hours what everyone else would do in 40. No, thank you.

—BRUCE ROSENBLUM

---

20. http://techcrunch.com/2011/05/07/why-the-new-guy-cant-code/.

It is far better to hire developers who are courteous, can blend in with the team, and seek stability than a superstar developer who during the interview appears ambitious and defensive.

—JERRY CHENG, *Engineering Manager, Yahoo! Mobile*

Jerry notes, "First, developers who have their own habits that they have developed over the years can have a hard time adjusting to a new system. This is why it is so important to hire courteous developers who are not going to be defensive and will be willing to adapt. Second, developers change jobs too much these days. Teaching a developer a new system takes time—it really is not worthwhile to see them leave right after. The constant churn of developers can break down any system. So, I look for developers who seek stability."

I emphasize communication, collaboration, energy, potential.

—MARK HIMELSTEIN

*The one interview question—to ask **every** candidate—that is important even though it has nothing directly to do with technology:*

What do you do for fun outside of work?

—PAUL MELMON

VP of Engineering Paul Melmon makes it a point to ask this question of every candidate his team interviews, noting that it gives him the opportunity to look for patterns of *passion*. When he finds programmers who have passion around some activity in their lives, he finds he can frequently translate their passion to the passion for product and engineering excellence he wants his team brimming with.

When I'm interviewing candidates, I like to talk about design patterns. Like how would you design something like a game of cards. They should be able to identify all the parts of objects. For example, in blackjack you have cards, hands, and players. They should be able to identify properties on these objects and their relationships. When would they use inheritance and when would they use "is-a" versus "has-a" relationships. There may be more than one correct answer but the approach should be workable. I find I am usually willing to give answers and instruct so that it is not a gotcha interview, but more of a conversation and we are working together on a problem. Finding out how well we would work together is the goal.

—PAUL OSSENBRUGGEN, *Lead Developer*

It's so important when interviewing developers to see how they think. I schedule interviews in rooms with whiteboards. My goal is to get a programmer talking about how they approached a problem, then get them to get up and show me. I want to know that we can work together, that they can explain it such that they draw me in and engage me.

Ask candidates to tell you what your company should do better than it does now.

—DAVE WILSON

I want people who can write, because we spend a lot of time writing to each other. We're writing e-mail or documentation. We're writing plans. We're writing specifications, I want to know that the people on my team are capable of doing that, and that turns out to be a really difficult skill. So I would actually rather see people start as English majors than as math majors to get into programming.

—DOUGLAS CROCKFORD, *Software Architect, Entrepreneur, and Inventor of JSON*[21]

---

21. Quoted in Seibel, *Coders at Work*, p. 124.

Pair programming for half an hour during an interview will save everyone's time.

—DAVID VYDRA

David has been an advocate of Agile practices, patterns, and test-driven development at various points in his career.

I invite the candidate to bring in a piece of code he's really proud of and walk us through it. I'm looking for quality of presentation . . . how effectively they can communicate, that's a skill that I'm hiring for.

—DOUGLAS CROCKFORD[22]

Ask a candidate to bring along some of their source code. Inspect their code, and you'll know if they are any good. Then ask the candidate to show you an app that they built. Evaluate the user experience.

—DAVE WILSON

IQ-like questions and quizzes are stupid.

—DAVE WILSON

Interview teams should be small, limited to four people: three people you trust and you, the manager. If you can't make a decision with four, you shouldn't hire. You waste your employees' time, the odds of a bad interview grow with the number of interviewers, and you can lose a candidate in a hot market.

—MARK HIMELSTEIN

For new college grads, two interviewers: one developer, one manager.

—MARK HIMELSTEIN

---

22. Ibid., p. 129.

For senior folks or managers, if they want to talk to more people before taking a job, that's fine. Make it clear to your team it is no longer an interview but a sell job.

—MARK HIMELSTEIN

Debriefing your interviewers, as a team, is critical: Not only is it an opportunity for you to understand the team's perspective, but for them, observing how others can perceive different aspects of the candidate can help each team member improve their interviewing skills.

—PHAC LE TUAN

Everyone should have their opinion heard. Then one person should decide.

—JOHN-ALISTAIR GEORGE, VP of R&D,
San Francisco Bay Area

Call references. It sounds simple, but this best practice is routinely ignored.

—GREGORY CLOSE

Never be satisfied talking only with the references your candidate supplies. If they're a friend of the candidate, they often won't mention the candidate's faults—and everyone has them. Find an independent source—someone you know who has worked with the candidate as a peer as well as someone who managed or worked for them.

—DAVE CURBOW, User Experience Architect, Cisco

Dave notes that while it's really too long to be a rule of thumb, "it's a lesson I learned the hard way."

I assume that a good candidate rewrites their résumé and cover letter after reading my Web site. Checking them out on LinkedIn tells me what their résumé really says.

—BRUCE ROSENBLUM

The best executive is the one who has enough sense to pick good people to do what he wants done, and self-restraint enough to keep from meddling with them while they do it.

—THEODORE ROOSEVELT

If you think it's expensive to hire a professional to do the job, wait until you hire an amateur.

—RED ADAIR

Regarding his fee for extinguishing oil well fires after the Gulf War.

If you're dithering, don't hire them.

—STEVE BURBECK, Manager at Apple and IBM

Steve also managed and hired developers in a small wholesale company (10 people); two start-ups, one of which grew to about 70 people before imploding; and a nonprofit research institute of 30 to 40 people; as well as leading tools product development at Apple and research at IBM North Carolina.

Keeping candidates "warm" between acceptance and start is very important. Try to not have it be more than two weeks. Take them to dinners. Make calls. Invite them to meetings. Give them tasks.

—MARK HIMELSTEIN

Wherever possible, make a three-month "evaluation" period part of your employment contract to hire. This way, you will not be stuck with someone who is a poor fit.

—GREGORY CLOSE

Be really attentive in the initial probation period. First day, first days, first week, first month. . . : Pair them up, read their code, and above all, treat them with respect.

—STEVE BURBECK

On-boarding is simple:

1. *Some initial project starting day one which forces getting up to speed on source control, dev practices, etc.*

2. *Ideally some kind of dogfooding of the project. An engineer divorced from the use of the product is useless.*

—DIRK BESTER, VP of Engineering, San Francisco Bay Area

On-boarding is very important. Provide training. Identify mentors. I try to get them to accomplish something small quickly. When you don't do this, I have seen even experienced people get into a bad pattern early. When you do, it makes the new employee feel good and it starts building their clout with the rest of the team.

—MARK HIMELSTEIN

*For me, the biggest challenge with new programmers
is to size them up and figure out what it will
take to make them effective contributors to the
organization. The big challenge I always found was
tight versus loose. For some programmers, you can
give them a big-picture idea, they develop their own
spec, you manage by objective; breathing over their
shoulder will make them less effective. For others,
you have to keep them on a shorter (or short) leash,
monitoring a series of short-term deliverables. In
particular, many programmers will argue they can
be managed hands-off, but some of them are not
telling the truth.*

> —JOEL WEST, Professor, Innovation & Entrepreneurship,
> Keck Graduate Institute of Applied Life Sciences,
> The Claremont Colleges; Former Programmer, Manager,
> and Entrepreneur in the software industry, California

*The most important factor in attacking complexity
is not the tools and techniques that programmers
use but rather the quality of the programmers
themselves.*

> —ROBERT L. GLASS, Software Practitioner,
> Pioneer, and Author[23]

*For every 10-percent increase in problem complexity,
there is a 100-percent increase in the software
solution's complexity. That's not a condition to
try to change (even though reducing complexity is
always desirable); that's just the way it is.*

> —ROBERT L. GLASS[24]

Robert is the editor of Elsevier's *Journal of Systems and Software* and the publisher and editor of *The Software Practitioner* newsletter.

---

23. Glass, "Frequently Forgotten Fundamental Facts about Software Engineering."
24. Ibid.

Keep track of everything you sign or approve.

—M. W. MANTLE

Something I have done for many years is to log everything I sign or approve into a simple spreadsheet so that I can go back and find the entry if there is ever a question about it. I've often felt this is overkill, because my HR and finance departments also keep track of these things. However, the number of times I've been able to go back and prove to HR and Finance that I actually did sign something has convinced me that observing this rule of thumb has made me a much better and more respected manager. This also leads to something that I have found is all too seldom true in the business world. Few people actually read over what they are asked to sign. Logging it forces you to read it over, at least enough to log the information. I've found many errors by following this rule of thumb that would otherwise go unnoticed.

The only line items you have to manage in budgets
for software development organizations are salaries,
capital expense, and training and travel. Everything
else is mouse nuts.

—RON LICHTY

The coauthor of one of my books, friend and first corporate boss David Eyes, was, at Apple, the first to use the technical term *mouse nuts* to refer to budget numbers that, while they might seem significant to an individual, are nothing more than noise in a corporate departmental budget. But it wasn't until after managing budgets through several more organizations and arriving at Schwab that I had a financial analyst who advised me not only what to ignore but what little I needed to truly focus on. Yes, look for anything else that's out of line significantly and ask why. But when the numbers are totaled, only salaries (including contractors and consultants), capital expense, and training and travel are big enough to cut when times are tough and expand when times are flush and make any difference in the departmental bottom line.

A verbal contract isn't worth the paper it's printed on.

> —SAM GOLDWYN'S LAW

Requirements engineering is primarily a communication activity, and it takes surprisingly little geographic separation to impede effective communication.

> —KARL E. WIEGERS, Principal Consultant, Process Impact[25]

He goes on to talk about the missed day-to-day interactions that clarify and refine requirements issues and, lacking them, "leads to more guessing on the part of the offshore developers, potentially slower development, and extensive rework."

With greater distance, you need to put more ceremony into communicating requirements.

> —MARTIN FOWLER, Guru in Software Development,
> Agile, UML, and Patterns[26]

The more distance between teammates, the more you have to formalize communication and make it explicit.

> —TED YOUNG, Development Manager/Agile Coach,
> GuideWire[27]

It's a good habit to start conference calls with chitchat on local news. Recent odd bits of local color—politics, sport, weather—help each side get a sense of the broader life context on the other side of the wire.

> —MARTIN FOWLER[28]

---

25. *Dr. Dobb's Journal*, September 2007, p. 20.
26. Martin Fowler, "Using an Agile Software Process with Offshore Development," in Cohn, *Succeeding with Agile*, p. 373.
27. Shared at Agile Open Space, February 26, 2010.
28. Martin Fowler, "Using an Agile Software Process with Offshore Development," in Cohn, *Succeeding with Agile,* p. 376.

Never underestimate the value of proximity.

—M. W. MANTLE

Dave Evans, the founder of Evans & Sutherland, told me once that "interpersonal communication is the inverse square of the distance domestically, and the inverse cube of the distance internationally." I've found that rule of thumb to be true. I have seen too many communication breakdowns just because someone is not sitting nearby. The farther the people are apart (down the hall, in the next building, in the next time zone, halfway around the world), the more difficult the problem. And when distances become international, the communication is often further impeded by time, language, and cultural barriers.

There's no substitute for face-to-face communication, particularly at pivotal points in the project.

—ADE MILLER, Principal Program Manager, Microsoft's Patterns & Practices Group[29]

I've managed programming teams from all over the world and have invested heavily in videoconferencing and telephone conferencing equipment and services. I still stand by my basic rule of thumb that until two people sit across the table and converse eye to eye, there are barriers to communication. I insist that the main people working with my offshore teams go visit them and spend some time with them in their facility. The sooner the better. It will never be easy, but thereafter things will become easier!

A collocated team will always outperform the equivalent distributed team.

—MIKE COHN, Agile and Scrum Thought Leader[30]

---

29. Ade Miller, "Distributed Agile Development at Microsoft Patterns & Practices," in Cohn, *Succeeding with Agile*, p. 368.

30. Cohn, *Succeeding with Agile*, p. 355, summarizing results from Narayan Ramasubbu and Rajesh Krishna Balan, "Globally Distributed Software Development Project Performance: An Empirical Analysis," *Proceedings of the 6th Joint Meeting of the European Software Engineering Conference and the ACM SIGSOFT Symposium on the Foundations of Software Engineering*, pp. 125–34.

Virtual teams yield significantly lower performance, lower satisfaction, and a lower results-to-effort ratio. Virtual teams appear to excel only at lower commitment, morale, and performance.

> —EMMELINE DE PILLIS and KIMBERLY FURUMO,
> Professors in Management, University of Hawaii[31]

Scrum can actually help geographically distributed teams perform at near-collocated levels.

> —MIKE COHN[32]

Mike cites the benefits Scrum provides to outsourcing that include "increased visibility from seeing demonstrable progress at the end of every sprint, the ability to adjust priorities after each sprint, more frequent communication, an emphasis on quality and test automation, and improved knowledge transfer, especially between developers doing pair programming."

Air travel from site to site is a costly yet necessary part of global teams.

> —ERRAN CARMEL, Professor, American University,
> studying the globalization of technology work[33]

An increased travel budget should be part of any distributed project.

> —MIKE COHN[34]

Unless you are big enough to put boots on the ground in the country where you will hire people, don't go offshore!

> —MIKE WESTERFIELD, Founder of Byte Works, maker of
> personal computer and mobile development tools, New Mexico

31. Emmeline de Pillis and Kimberly Furumo, "Counting the Cost of Virtual Teams," *Communications of the ACM*, December 2007, pp. 93–95, quoted in Cohn, *Succeeding with Agile*, p. 387.

32. Cohn, *Succeeding with Agile*, p. 355,

33. Erran Carmel, *Global Software Teams* (Prentice Hall, 1998), p. 157, quoted in Cohn, *Succeeding with Agile*, p. 368.

34. Cohn, *Succeeding with Agile*, p. 368.

....

Best practices for global development.

We have observed a number of practices that have been quite effective in improving communication. Among them are practices about:

- *establishing trust across sites by being even more responsive to remote colleagues than to local ones*
- *setting up liaisons at each site to facilitate cross-site communication*
- *establishing etiquette for answering e-mail and voice mail messages in a timely way*
- *planning for travel early in the relationship between sites—everything will work better after people have met.*

—DAVID ATKINS, MARK HANDEL, JAMES HERBSLEB, AUDRIS
MOCKUS, DEWAYNE PERRY, and GRAHAM WILLS[35]

....

In the U.S.A. it is "The squeaky wheel gets the grease," but in Japan (due to cultural differences) it is "The nail that sticks out gets pounded down!"

—M. W. MANTLE

This explains a lot about the difficulties of Americans working with the Japanese.

---

35. Atkins et al., "Global Software Development: The Bell Labs Collaboratory," www.cs.uoregon.edu/~datkins/papers/icse-collab.pdf.

Managing People

Trust your feelings, young Luke. The Force will be with you.

—OBI-WAN KENOBI, *Jedi Master in* Star Wars

We counsel many managers and programmers to listen to their intuition carefully; it's usually right. The older I get, the more I regret those times when I don't listen to my intuition. Programmers usually know the right things to do—if they allow themselves to trust their feelings.

Accountability is not micromanagement.

—MARK HIMELSTEIN

The author of *100 Questions to Ask Your Software Organization*,[1] speaking to the Best Practices SIG of the East Bay Innovation Group in 2006. We've always hated being micromanaged and thus have avoided being managers who micromanage. The challenge is to realize the line between micromanaging and holding your people accountable. Giving up micromanagement is not giving up expecting accountability.

---

1. Mark I. Himelstein, *100 Questions to Ask Your Software Organization* (Infinity Publishing, 2005).

Trust but verify.

—*RONALD REAGAN*

President Reagan was referring to the Soviets during the Cold War with his frequent use of this translation of a Russian proverb that had been equally frequently quoted by Soviet founding father Vladimir Lenin. Perhaps it was because of that context that I didn't pay attention until I heard another VP of Engineering use the expression in describing how he managed his team—and realized that it described my goal-state management style: my goal is absolutely no micromanagement, but enough checking to know that the delegation I'd done was appropriate.

One of the surest sources of delay and confusion is to allow any superior to be directly responsible for the control of too many subordinates.

—*V. A. GRAICUNAS*

Graicunas was an early-twentieth-century management consultant and the first to mathematically analyze the complexity of increasing management responsibility. Graicunas showed that as span of control increases, the number of interactions among managers and their reports—and thus the amount of time managers must spend supervising—increases geometrically. His formula takes into account manager-to-report, report-to-report, and manager-to-all-combinations-of-reports interactions, and he posits that supervision time increases proportionately with interactions. He showed that by adding a fifth report, while the potential for accomplishing more work may increase by 20 percent, the number of potential interactions increases from 44 to 100—by 127 percent! Eight reports increases to 1,080 potential interactions and 12 reports to 24,564 to track and manage! Graicunas recommended that managers have a maximum of five reports, ideally four.

Managers who use one-on-one meetings consistently find them one of the most effective and productive uses of their management time.

—*JOHANNA ROTHMAN and ESTHER DERBY*[2]

The statement is a match for our own experience.

One-on-ones: The single most effective management tool.

—*MARK HORSTMAN AND MICHAEL AUZENNE,*
Cofounders of Manager Tools LLC, a management
consulting firm[3]

A manager's task is to make the strengths of people effective and their weakness irrelevant—and that applies fully as much to the manager's boss as it applies to the manager's subordinates.

—*PETER DRUCKER*[4]

An apprentice carpenter may want only a hammer and saw, but a master craftsman employs many precision tools. Computer programming likewise requires sophisticated tools to cope with the complexity of real applications, and only practice with these tools will build skill in their use.

—*ROBERT L. KRUSE*[5]

Malcom Gladwell in his essay "Outliers: The Story of Success" reports on a study by K. Anders Ericsson, Ralf Th. Krampe, and Clemens Tesch-Romer that concluded that mastery of anything— whether it's music or programming or art or golf—takes at least 10,000 hours of deliberate practice.

---

2. Johanna Rothman and Esther Derby, *Behind Closed Doors: Secrets of Great Management* (Pragmatic Bookshelf, 2005).

3. www.manager-tools.com/2005/07/the-single-most-effective-management-tool-part-1?page=1.

4. Peter Drucker, *Managing for the Future: The 1990s and Beyond* (Penguin Books, 1992).

5. Robert L. Kruse, *Data Structures and Program Design, Second Edition* (Prentice Hall, 1987).

The team needs to choose the tools they use.

—*LISA CRISPIN, COAUTHOR OF* Agile Testing[6]

Lisa insists that managers should not be selecting and imposing tools. She made that point again in March 2011 speaking to the Bay Area Agile Leadership Network (BayALN).

A programmer is most productive with a quiet private office, a great computer, unlimited beverages, an ambient temperature between 68 and 72 degrees (F), no glare on the screen, a chair that's so comfortable you don't feel it, an administrator that brings them their mail and orders manuals and books, a system administrator who makes the Internet as available as oxygen, a tester to find the bugs they just can't see, a graphic designer to make their screens beautiful, a team of marketing people to make the masses want their products, a team of sales people to make sure the masses can get these products, some patient tech support saints who help customers get the product working and help the programmers understand what problems are generating the tech support calls, and about a dozen other support and administrative functions which, in a typical company, add up to about 80% of the payroll.

—*JOEL SPOLSKY*[7]

Joel Spolsky is cofounder of Fog Creek Software,"a New York company that proves that you can treat programmers well and still be highly profitable."He also writes the renowned *Joel on Software* blog.

---

6. Lisa Crispin and Janet Gregory, *Agile Testing: A Practical Guide for Testers and Agile Teams* (Addison-Wesley, 2009).

7. www.joelonsoftware.com/articles/DevelopmentAbstraction.html.

*A good programmer is someone who looks both
ways before crossing a one-way street.*

—DOUG LINDER

The best programmers are all musicians.

—PATRICK HANRATTY

Related during a visit in the early 1980s. Pat, creator of the
CAD program Anvil, kept an upright piano in his office.

*If you wrote your first program in college, you
probably don't have the passion.*

—ANONYMOUS

*A computer science education cannot make anybody
an expert programmer any more than studying
brushes and pigment can make somebody an
expert painter.*

—ERIC S. RAYMOND, Internet Developer and Author,
The Cathedral & the Bazaar: Musings on Linux
and Open Source[8]

*All programmers are optimists. Perhaps this modern
sorcery especially attracts those who believe in
happy endings and fairy godmothers. Perhaps the
hundreds of nitty frustrations drive away all but
those who habitually focus on the end goal. Perhaps
it is merely that computers are young, programmers
are younger, and the young are always optimists.
But however the selection process works, the result
is indisputable: "This time it will surely run" or
"I just found the last bug."*

—FREDERICK P. BROOKS JR.[9]

8. www.junauza.com/2010/12/top-50-programming-quotes-of-all-time.html.
9. www.softwarequotes.com/.

The trouble with programmers is that you can never tell what a programmer is doing until it's too late.

—SEYMOUR CRAY, *Founder of Cray Research and Designer of the Cray Supercomputers*[10]

Being married to a programmer is like having a cat. You talk to it but you're never really sure if it hears you, much less comprehends what you say.

—ANONYMOUS

Does a good farmer neglect a crop he has planted?

Does a good teacher overlook even the most humble student?

Does a good father allow a single child to starve?

Does a good programmer refuse to maintain his code?

—GEOFFREY JAMES[11]

When it comes to depicting the nerd mind-set, no one tops Stephenson. His predecessors in the cyberpunk science-fiction movement (writers like William Gibson and Bruce Sterling) depicted hackers as moody James Deans in leather. Stephenson lays out the way they really think and act—awkward, chatty mensches whose insistence on logic makes them borderline nut cases.

—STEVEN LEVY[12]

If you give someone a program, you will frustrate them for a day; if you teach them how to program, you will frustrate them for a lifetime.

—ROEDY GREEN, *Canadian Programmer/Consultant*

---

10. Ibid.

11. James, *The Tao of Programming*, p. 83.

12. Steven Levy' review of Neal Stephenson's *Cryptonomicon* in *Newsweek*, May 10, 1999.

Roedy Green is best known for maintaining the Java Glossary and for the tongue-in-cheek essay "How to Write Unmaintainable Code" that is said to have been required reading for some college courses.

. . . .

Humans have an attraction for complexity, and programmers especially so.

> —RUSS DANIELS, VP of Engineering, HP

Russ shared this with me at a dinner for executives that Rational Software threw in 2001. It struck me as so fundamentally true that I made note.

. . . .

Weinberg's Second Law: If engineers built buildings the way programmers wrote programs, the first woodpecker to come along would destroy civilization.

> —GERALD M. WEINBERG

Pioneer of computer programmer psychology, noted author, and software consultant, Gerald Weinberg wrote *Computer Information Systems* and *Secrets of Consulting*.

. . . .

Know the difference between an introverted programmer and an extroverted programmer?

When you're talking, the extroverted programmer looks at your shoes.

> —DAVID POLLAK, Founder of the Open Source Lift
> Framework for Scala[13]

It's a joke we'd both heard before.

. . . .

Real programmers don't work from 9 to 5. If any real programmers are around at 9 A.M. it's because they were up all night.

> —TOM VAN VLECK, Programmer since the 1960s

---

13. Speaking to the Best Practices SIG of the East Bay Innovation Group in 2008.

*[Late nights are just] the least stressful time. . . .
I'm so much more relaxed. . . . During the day,
there's always something coming up. . . . At night I
feel like this is my time and I'm stealing this time
because everyone else is sleeping. There's no noise
and no interruptions.*

—BRAD FITZPATRICK[14]

*The computer programmer is a creator of universes
for which he alone is responsible. Universes of
virtually unlimited complexity can be created in the
form of computer programs.*

—JOSEPH WEIZENBAUM

Joseph Weizenbaum became a computer science professor at MIT
after working on analog computers starting in 1952. He is most
famous for creating the 1966 program ELIZA, which, driven by
a script named DOCTOR and written in a language of his own
invention, SLIP (for Symmetric List Processor), engaged users in
a conversation that caused many to think they were actually talking to an empathic psychologist. Weizenbaum based its conversa-
tional style on the open-ended questions Carl Rogers employed
to encourage patient-therapist communication. The program used
natural language and pattern matching to figure out its replies.
When microcomputers were introduced in the late 1970s, ELIZA
was ported to become one of the earliest and most common programs on those platforms as well.

Managing senior programmers is like herding cats.

—DAVE PLATT, Programmer

*Everyone can be taught to sculpt: Michelangelo
would have had to be taught not to. So it is with
great programmers.*

—ALAN J. PERLIS, Yale University[15]

---

14. Quoted in Seibel, *Coders at Work*, pp. 74–75.

15. Alan J. Perlis, "Epigrams in Programming," *ACM SIGPLAN*, September 1982, Epigram #35.

Good programmers are up to 30 times better than mediocre programmers, according to "individual differences" research. Given that their pay is never commensurate, they are the biggest bargains in the software field.

—*ROBERT L. GLASS*[16]

Robert is the editor of the *Journal of Systems and Software* and the publisher and editor of *The Software Practitioner* newsletter.

Programmers prefer to stand on the toes of others, not on their shoulders.

—*UNKNOWN*

I heard this somewhere in the last ten years and it resonated.

Bill Joy is one of the leading programmers of his generation; he wrote much of the free Berkeley version of Unix, devised some of the critical underpinnings of the early Internet, and helped create Java. After leaving Sun Microsystems, which he had co-founded, he attempted to write a book. But in 2003 he told the **New York Times** *that he was putting the project aside. It was one thing to write for the compiler to interpret or the computer to execute; writing for other people was simply too hard. "With code," he said, "the computer tells you if it understands what you write. It's much harder to write prose. That is, if you want to be understood."*

—*SCOTT ROSENBERG*[17]

---

16. Glass, "Frequently Forgotten Fundamental Facts about Software Engineering."
17. Scott Rosenberg, *Dreaming in Code* (Crown, 2007), p. 299.

The process of preparing programs for a digital computer is especially attractive, not only because it can be economically and scientifically rewarding, but also because it can be an aesthetic experience much like composing poetry or music.

—DONALD KNUTH[18]

Knuth, the acclaimed author of *The Art of Computer Programming,* more than once referred to the aesthetic appeal of programming. It was a pull I felt, coming from writing and graphic design to programming—and was the source of a heated argument with my literary agent in the early eighties, who vehemently did not want my experience to be true.

Most good programmers do programming not because they expect to get paid or get adulation by the public, but because it is fun to program.

—LINUS TORVALDS, *Creator of Linux*[19]

Computer programming is tremendous fun. Like music, it is a skill that derives from an unknown blend of innate talent and constant practice. Like drawing, it can be shaped to a variety of ends— commercial, artistic, and pure entertainment. Programmers have a well-deserved reputation for working long hours but are rarely credited with being driven by creative fevers. Programmers talk about software development on weekends, vacations, and over meals not because they lack imagination, but because their imagination reveals worlds that others cannot see.

—LARRY O'BRIEN and BRUCE ECKEL[20]

---

18. Donald Knuth, *The Art of Computer Programming* (Addison-Wesley, 1968), vol. 1, p. v.

19. www.junauza.com/2010/12/top-50-programming-quotes-of-all-time.html.

20. Larry O'Brien and Bruce Eckel, *Thinking in C#* (Prentice Hall, 2002).

Being a contractor is kind of like being a houseguest in a dysfunctional family. You get a chance to leave when it's over.

> —*JOHN ANDERSON*[21]

John was OSAF's system architect (Mitch Kapor's Open Source Applications Foundation). Scott Rosenberg prefaced John's quote with this note, "Most recently he had become a highly regarded independent consultant, parachuting into companies with particularly thorny technical problems."

Never hesitate to dismiss a contractor who is not working out.

> —*RON LICHTY*

You have a contractor who is not delivering what you want and expect. With an employee, your tendency is (and probably should be) to coach, mentor, reset expectations, encourage, call to task, or otherwise try to fix the issue. But your contracts for contractors should give you freedom to dismiss them at any time with at most two weeks' additional cost (and ideally none). That's a major reason for using contractors instead of employees in certain situations and roles. The conundrum is often that the contractor is delivering part of what you need—do you eke it out, or start over? I have seldom found a time when it's not better to send the wrong developer home and to start over with the right one.

We have two ears and one mouth. Use them in this ratio.

> —*KIMBERLY WIEFLING*

That's who I heard it from, although a couple of millennia earlier, Epictetus, Roman (Greek-born) slave and Stoic philosopher (55–135 A.D.), said, "We have two ears and one mouth so we may listen more and talk the less."

---

21. Quoted in Rosenberg, *Dreaming in Code,* p. 63.

Keep it simple—don't overly complicate things.

Listen well, ask lots of questions.

Maintain a sense of pride in what you do.

Keep everything in perspective.

Communicate repeatedly—the biggest culprit across organizations is lack of communication.

Collaborate.

Learn how to debate effectively—not winners or losers—engage each other intellectually, discover the right paths.

> —DAVID DIBBLE

Dibble explained to Schwab's architects and developers, through the pages of a 2002 issue of the internal *Charles Schwab Architecture* newsletter, his rules of thumb for software architects in his organization.

People drift away from project goals quickly if left alone. Good project leaders talk to people almost every day. "What did you do? Why? Did it work?"

> —DAVE WILSON

Be a damper to the noise.

> —JOE KLEINSCHMIDT, CTO and Cofounder,
> Leverage Software

Keeping a team focused in the midst of the chaos that most product development environments represent requires a good engineering manager to pass along information while filtering out the chaos.

Would you bet your job on it?

> —CLAUDIA BRENNER, Product Manager and Designer

A critical question that Claudia Brenner reports she learned to ask when she was at IBM: "Here's how to divine whether a programmer actually believes what (s)he just told you."

Any code of your own that you haven't looked at for six or more months might as well have been written by someone else.

> —EAGLESON'S LAW

Document, document, document!

Documentation is like sex: When it is good, it is very, very good; and when it is bad, it is better than nothing.

> —DICK BRANDON

Test as you go.

> —ANONYMOUS

It's OK not to follow standards provided (1) you know why, and (2) you can articulate it.

> —ROBERT MARSHALL, VP, Schwab.com,
> as recounted by one of his development managers,
> Andrew Armstrong

Standards are important to establish, but it's equally important to recognize that few standards deserve to be hard-and-fast, unbreakable rules. But how do you establish the exceptions? In a Fortune 500 company like Schwab, there is likely a governance committee that will want to set exception policy—after the fact, if not before—which bears out what should be policy whether there's formal governance or not—that developers and teams that want to break the rules need to show they know the rules and understand them well enough to articulate why they should not apply to any specific case.

You know you've achieved perfection in design, not when you have nothing more to add, but when you have nothing more to take away.

— *ANTOINE DE SAINT-EXUPÉRY*[22]

Software architecture is the set of design decisions which, if made incorrectly, may cause your project to be cancelled.

— *EOIN WOODS*

Eoin is a software architect and coauthor of *Software Systems Architecture: Working with Stakeholders Using Viewpoints and Perspectives.*

Design first, code second.

— *ANONYMOUS*

You can't program in isolation.

— *ALLEN HOLUB, Programmer, Author, Educator, and Consultant*

This is one of Allen's rules of thumb in his book, *Enough Rope to Shoot Yourself in the Foot*[23] A variant of Jim McCarthy's warning— "Rule #31" in his book *Dynamics of Software Development*[24]— "Beware of a guy in a room."

---

22. Antoine de Saint-Exupéry, *Wind, Sand and Stars (1939).*

23. Allen I. Holub, *Enough Rope to Shoot Yourself in the Foot* (Computing McGraw-Hill, 1995), p. 14.

24. Jim McCarthy and Denis Gilbert, *Dynamics of Software Development* (Microsoft Press, 1995), p. 106.

Conway's Law: If you have four groups working on a compiler, you'll get a 4-pass compiler.

> —NAMED AFTER MELVIN CONWAY, Early (1950s!)
> Programmer and (2000s) Computer Science Educator

Conway, in 1968, observed that systems architected by multiple designers tend to reflect the organizations within which they were designed and particularly how the designers in the organization deign to communicate with each other. The software's structure tends to reflect the organization's social structure. Wikipedia calls the above version of Conway's Law "Raymond's version," since it was so restated by Eric S. Raymond, cofounder of the Open Source Initiative. The entry calls out "James Coplien and Neil Harrison's version" for taking a slightly different tack, "Make sure the organization is compatible with the product architecture."

If you're trying to ship a cross-platform product, history really shows. . . . If you want it to really be cross-platform, you have to do them simultaneously. The porting thing results in a crappy product on the second platform.

> —JAMIE ZAWINSKI, Early Netscape Lead Developer[25]

Beware of Lunde's Law: Any time the senior developers on a project are replaced by a new team, the new team will eventually find a compelling reason for a total rewrite. And that new team is wrong.

> —LUKE HOHMANN

Luke Hohmann, author of *Journey of the Software Professional, Beyond Software Architecture*, and *Innovation Games* and founder of The Innovation Games Company, warns of the dangers of bringing in "new blood."

---

25. Quoted in Seibel, *Coders at Work*, p. 20.

*Software expresses the team that created it.
Anything you need to know about the team can
be discovered by examining the software, and vice
versa. I highlight this idea because in my view it's
the basis of software development management.
The words and behavior of the team are really too
confusing at any given moment to diagnose, but the
software doesn't lie. The software will inevitably
express every weakness and strength, every gift
and curse, every unconscious ailment and top-of-
mind brilliance the team possesses. When in doubt,
turn to the software. You do have to be a bit facile
with interpretation, in understanding how symbols
emerge from groups of people. But if you are diligent
in your study of the product, you don't even need to
know the team to know what's wrong with it. . . .
The basic principle is, if you are having a hard time
understanding something about the team, you can
look to the software. If the team and the software
both tell you the same thing, you can act on it with
some degree of confidence.*

> —JIM MCCARTHY, *Coauthor,* Dynamics of Software
> Development [26]

*Flon's axiom: There does not now, nor will there
ever, exist a programming language in which it is
the least bit hard to write bad programs.*

> —LAWRENCE FLON

Flon, then at CMU, published an article "On Research in Structured Programming" in *SIGPLAN Notices*, October 1975, that
included his now-famous axiom.

AND
Work smart ~~not~~ ^ hard.

> —BOB HOWARD-ANDERSON, *as recounted by Jane
> Divinski, Consulting VP of Engineering*

---

26. McCarthy and Gilbert, *Dynamics of Software Development*, p. 50.

There's been so much made of working smart, not hard, which is what caught my attention when Jane told me Bob's revision of the rule. He's right. Smart-not-hard is almost never enough. We're constantly called on to work both smart and hard.

I think an hour of code reading is worth two weeks of QA. It's just a really effective way of removing errors. . . . I now believe that code reading should be happening all the time throughout the life of the project . . . once you get into the rhythm of it, it feels extremely natural."

　　　　　—*DOUGLAS CROCKFORD*

Crockford, inventor of JavaScript data interchange format JSON and former Director of Technology at Lucasfilm/LucasArts, was talking with Peter Seibel for Peter's 2009 book *Coders at Work.* Crockford noted regarding code reading, "For one thing it makes it easier to track the project, because we can actually see what progress people are making. And we can see much sooner if they're going off the rails or not. I've managed projects where we're up against a deadline and we had people saying, 'Yeah, I'm almost done,' and then you get the code, and there's nothing there, or it's crap, or whatever, and they're nowhere close to done. In management, those are the experiences you hate the most and I think code reading is the best way of not getting trapped like that."

I judge performance as the delta between the positive my folks contribute and the negative.

　　　　　—*JANE DIVINSKI*

Jane explained, "Several times I had problem employees who wrote copious amounts of decent-quality code but made bad design decisions or behaved in such a way that they adversely affected the overall group productivity. So those negatives are factored into my assessment. (Seems like a simple concept to me but you would not believe how some managers would insist on focusing only on the positive aspects of their employees' contributions.)"

The biggest bug and performance surprises are almost always where the coder least expects them. Corollary: There are almost always bug and performance surprises.

—RON LICHTY

It was one of my transformative steps from being a rookie programmer to being experienced—the realization that not only was I not as perfect as I wanted to think I was, but that my lack of perfection tended to crop up where I least expected it (or, to state that differently, in the parts of the code I was most certain were bug-free). What eventually made me managerial material was the realization that most of my peers were just like me.

I'll cancel the status meeting if you give me a status report by noon.

—BILL HOFMANN

Then Senior Director, Product Development, Advanced Technology Group, Sonic Solutions, Bill shared this clever approach to ensuring that he got status reports on time with the Best Practices SIG of the East Bay Innovation Group in 2007.

A meeting without notes is a meeting that never happened.

—NATALIE DEJARLAIS, Director of Applications
Development, San Francisco Bay Area

"People come away from meetings with differing views of what just happened," said Natalie, "which notes can clarify or give someone a chance to correct. People tend to forget tasks or deadlines they've agreed to, especially when they're not fun. And notes create a record that anyone can go back to and review what was supposed to have happened, or why an idea was discarded, or to whom a task was given. In my experience, when there are no notes, you tend to have the meeting/discussion all over again, because of memory lapses."

For every man-hour spent in project status meetings,
three man-hours of productive time are lost.

— GREG MCKINNEY

McKinney, a Senior IT Manager at Schwab and at Blue Shield of California, notes that "some managers tend to schedule more frequent project status meetings whenever a project falls behind schedule. I know one manager who scheduled twice-a-day status meetings. Then he kept wondering why there was very little progress made between meetings."

Measuring software productivity by lines of code is
like measuring progress on an airplane by how much
it weighs.

— BILL GATES

Scott Rosenberg, in *Dreaming in Code,* recounts an Apple 1980s anecdote about legendary coder Bill Atkinson, creator of Quick-Draw and HyperCard for the Macintosh and, even earlier, QuickDraw as the Lisa computer's graphic interface. The story, told by Atkinson's protégé Andy Hertzfeld, was that the Lisa team's managers had asked engineers to report, each week, how many lines of code they'd written, much to Atkinson's displeasure. The first week, Atkinson, having turned his attention to making QuickDraw faster and more efficient, had made the new version 2,000 lines of code *shorter* than it had been the previous week. He duly reported that he'd written minus-2,000 lines of code for the week.

One great irony inherent in the management of
software projects is that despite the digital precision
of the materials programmers work with, the
enterprise of writing software is uniquely resistant
to measurement.

— SCOTT ROSENBERG[27]

27. Rosenberg, *Dreaming in Code*, pp. 126.

There is no reliable relationship between the volume of code produced and the state of completion of a program, its quality, or its ultimate value to a user.

—SCOTT ROSENBERG[28]

The value we produce is measured based on "code" times the "frequency that the code is executed."

—MARILSON CAMPOS, VP of Engineering,
San Francisco Bay Area

If that's not clear enough, Marilson adds,"Don't write code that nobody is going to run."

Most software tool and technique improvements account for about a 5- to 30-percent increase in productivity and quality. But at one time or another, most of these improvements have been claimed by someone to have "order of magnitude" (factor of 10) benefits. Hype is the plague on the house of software.

—ROBERT L. GLASS[29]

Learning a new tool or technique actually lowers programmer productivity and product quality initially. You achieve the eventual benefit only after overcoming this learning curve.

—ROBERT L. GLASS[30]

---

28. Rosenberg, *Dreaming in Code*, pp. 127.
29. Glass, "Frequently Forgotten Fundamental Facts about Software Engineering."
30. Ibid.

This is one reason the whiteboard is such an iconic presence in any space where software is labored over; it provides a canvas for laying out the abstract processes of a complex program in ways that allow people to point to what they're talking about.

—*SCOTT ROSENBERG*[31]

I consider whiteboards so essential that when I started managing at one new company, I went home elated my first day that my new office had not one but two enormous whiteboards. If I had parenting to do over, the one change I'd make would be a whiteboard on the dining room wall to share visual thinking, not just conversation, with our kids.

When it comes to getting things done, we need fewer architects and more bricklayers.

—*COLLEEN C. BARRETT, President and Corporate Secretary of Southwest Airlines*

That's not a particularly software-oriented commentary, but it applies. In IT in Fortune 500 companies, there's room for architects who don't code, but scarcely anywhere else. Too many technologists, when they assume the title "architect," believe they just moved on from coding. In down economies, it's the non-coders who are in oversupply such that managers don't advertise for architects but for a "developer/designer" with "architecture smell" or "design smell" combined with a job description that makes it clear that lots of code is expected.

Testing is not a phase.

—*ELISABETH HENDRICKSON, Author of TestObsessed.com and Former Director of the Agile Alliance, 2007–2008*

If you're doing Agile and testing is a phase, you're not doing Agile.

---

31. Rosenberg, *Dreaming in Code*, p. 195.

QA must be part of the requirements process. Testers drive "done."

—TED YOUNG[32]

A team practicing collective ownership will write cleaner code (and presumably therefore have fewer bugs).

—MIKE COHN[33]

He added, "For proof of this look no further than your guest bathroom. Which do you keep cleaner: the bathroom only you use or the one that visitors are likely to see?"

I've had companies where there was an antagonism between the development teams and the testing teams. . . . It worked much better when we put the two teams together and made the testers responsible for helping the developers to make their programs better.

—DOUGLAS CROCKFORD[34]

There is evidence that doing TDD takes about 15% longer than not doing TDD (George and Williams, 2003). But there is also evidence that TDD leads to fewer defects. (Two studies at Microsoft found that the number of bugs found went down by 24% and 38% with the use of TDD (Sanchez, Williams, and Maximilien 2007, 6).)

—MIKE COHN[35]

---

32. Shared at Agile Open Space, February 26, 2010.

33. Cohn, *Succeeding with Agile*, p. 161.

34. Quoted in Seibel, *Coders at Work*, p. 123.

35. Cohn, *Succeeding with Agile*, p. 158.

....

Even if 100-percent test coverage were possible, that criteria would be insufficient for testing. Roughly 35 percent of software defects emerge from missing logic paths, and another 40 percent are from the execution of a unique combination of logic paths. They will not be caught by 100-percent coverage (100-percent coverage can, therefore, potentially detect only about 25 percent of the errors!).

—ROBERT L. GLASS[36]

....

Software that a typical programmer believes to be thoroughly tested has often had only about 55 to 60 percent of its logic paths executed. Automated support, such as coverage analyzers, can raise that to roughly 85 to 90 percent. Testing at the 100-percent level is nearly impossible.

—ROBERT L. GLASS[37]

....

QA is fundamentally different from development. Thinking about how to make something work and how to break it are different.

—JOHN STEELE, Director, Quality, Kaiser Permanente[38]

....

You can't have great software without a great team, and most software teams behave like dysfunctional families.

—JIM MCCARTHY[39]

He made this statement after directing Microsoft's Visual C++ program management team.

---

36. Glass, "Frequently Forgotten Fundamental Facts about Software Engineering."

37. Ibid.

38. Presentation to the Software Architecture and Modeling SIG of SDForum, March 2007.

39. www.junauza.com/2010/12/top-50-programming-quotes-of-all-time.html.

There is no "I" in "TEAM."

—*UNKNOWN*

Though this is a trite saying that seems to have originated with team sports, it applies to programming teams as well. I've used it several times to defuse discussions where programmers are becoming entrenched in their positions without giving fair hearing to others' view points. It always seems to work.

Gettin' good players is easy. Gettin' 'em to play together is the hard part.

—*CASEY STENGEL*

I recently answered the question "What is a ScrumMaster?" with an answer I've also used regarding a good software development manager: You first have to know the basics: how teams work and how to put process in place. But that's only the foundation. The essence is much more. Virtuoso orchestra conductors know the rules of music well—so well that they can rise above them to deliver something truly great. Great conductors know that it's not getting each of their musicians to play well but to get them all to rise above playing well separately to create something magical together. So it is with great ScrumMasters and great programming managers.

Most people really want to do a good job in their work. If they're not doing a good job, it's usually a management issue.

—*M. W. MANTLE*

In all my years of managing programmers I've really met only one who didn't want to do good work. Those who are not doing good work are usually hampered by lack of equipment, lack of clear direction, or some other issue or roadblock that could be removed by a good manager. I've found nearly all programmers really do want to exceed expectations, if they can.

Every programmer's motivation is different.

Understanding what motivates each one is the key to managing programmers effectively.

Contrary to what we usually believe . . . the best moments in our lives are not the passive, receptive, relaxing times—although such experiences can also be enjoyable, if we have worked hard to attain them. The best moments usually occur when a person's body or mind is stretched to the limits in a voluntary effort to accomplish something difficult and worthwhile.

—MIHALY CSIKSZENTMIHALYI, Psychologist[40]

We often also refer to "flow" as "in the zone"—that state in which we are fully absorbed by the challenge of the present and time evaporates away.

Promotions are generally not rewards for past performance. Instead, management uses promotions to advance those who display the potential to tackle the next level of bigger, tougher problems.

—RAY WEISS[41]

It's not my job to motivate players. They bring extraordinary motivation to our program. It's my job not to demotivate them.

—LOU HOLTZ, Former Notre Dame Football Coach[42]

We feel this way about programmers and programming managers.

---

40. Mihaly Csikszentmihalyi, *Flow: The Psychology of Optimal Experience* (Harper Perennial, 1990).

41. Ray Weiss, *The Technical Career Navigator* (Prentice Hall, 1994).

42. Quoted by Tom Peters in the *San Jose Mercury News*, September 24, 1994.

*If you want to build a ship, don't drum up people
together to collect wood and don't assign them
tasks and work, but rather teach them to long for
the endless immensity of the sea.*

—*ANTOINE DE SAINT-EXUPÉRY*[43]

It's all about motivating your team, communicating where you're
going, creating a vision of the destination that "swims" in front of
their eyes and becomes a common vision for them all.

*"You're saying, people do what I want because they
like me?"*

*"It's not because they like you. It's because you like
them."*

"Huh?"

*"You like and respect the people who work for you.
You care about them. Their problems are your problems; their concerns are yours. You have a heart as
big as a train and it shows. You give trust before a
person has really demonstrated trustworthiness. You
make us all feel like you've adopted us into your
family. That's why we follow you."*

—*TOM DEMARCO, Author and Guru of Software
Development Methods and Management*[44]

When I joined Apple, there were cassettes floating around of a
talk DeMarco had recently given there. "You have to listen," I was
told. They were right. Uncommonly good advice on software development. His most well-known books are probably *Peopleware*
and *Slack*, but all his stuff that I've read has been well worth it.

*Everyone on my team is learning. Everyone on my
team is treated like an adult. Engineers really like
working for me.*

—*BILL GROSSO, VP of Engineering, Engage*

---

43. Antoine de Saint-Exupéry, *The Little Prince* (1943).

44. Tom DeMarco, *The Deadline: A Novel about Project Management* (Dorset House, 1997), p. 166.

It's only a failure if we fail to get the learning.

—SCOTT COOK

Intuit Chairman Scott Cook made the observation after presenting an onstage award to a failed Intuit marketing team that used
a retrospective process to document its learnings. The team had
created a 2005 product, RockYourRefund.com, which tried to use
hip-hop to make doing taxes cool. Cook was quoted in "How
Failure Breeds Success," *Business Week* Online, July 10, 2006, a
story of how CEOs encourage their organizations to take risks.

*The thing about Google—and any large company
focused on skilled employees—is that everyone there
knows that people will spend time off work thinking
about work. It's inevitable. You're lying in bed and
your brain wanders onto a problem you're having at
work and in half an hour you've solved it. If you're
spending time away from work doing work stuff,
why would people object to the converse? We're
all adults here—we don't have to, or want to, be
micromanaged to death.*

—ZORBATHUT *(Google engineer nickname)*[45]

*At Novell, we just added a new title: distinguished
engineer. To become a distinguished engineer, you
have to get elected by your peers. That requirement
is a much tougher standard than being chosen by
a group of executives. It's also a standard that
encourages tech people to be good members of the
tech community. It acts to reinforce good behavior
on everyone's part.*

—ERIC SCHMIDT[46]

---

45. Commenting in The Awful Forums, http://forums.somethingawful.com/showthread.php?s
=cdce26da8f96c00ab821bccc0adb2461&threadid=1892424&perpage=40&page
number=5, excerpted at http://blog.outer-court.com/archive/2006-06-15-n22.html.

46. Interviewed by Russ Mitchell in "How to Manage Geeks," *Fast Company* magazine, May 1999.

If you don't want to lose your geeks, you have to find a way to give them promotions without turning them into managers. Most of them are not going to make very good executives—and, in fact, most of them would probably turn out to be terrible managers. But you need to give them a forward path, you need to give them recognition, and you need to give them more money.

—ERIC SCHMIDT, then CEO of Novell (later CEO of Google)[47]

Schmidt was calling out his involvement in establishing a parallel technical career ladder 20 years before—parallel to the traditional management career ladder.

Publicly reward or acknowledge engineers who act in a way that supports the culture that you want to create.

—JUANITA MAH, Engineering Manager, IBM and VMware

"For example," she illustrates, "if an engineer went out of his or her way to help resolve a customer issue, I might mention it in department highlight reports. If someone developed an innovative tool that significantly improved productivity, I might send that individual to an internal technical conference."

Involve people in goal-setting.

—DANIEL PINK[48]

Pink points out, "A considerable body of research shows that individuals are far more engaged when they're pursuing goals they had a hand in creating. So bring employees into the process. They could surprise you: People often have higher aims than the ones you assign them."

---

47. Ibid.

48. Pink, Drive: *The Surprising Truth about What Motivates Us.*

*No great programmer is sitting there saying, "I'm
going to make a bunch of money," or "I'm going to
sell a hundred thousand copies." Because that kind
of thought gives you no guidance about the problems.*

—BILL GATES[49]

Gates's thoughts, early in his career, on what motivates programmers.

*In the "real" corporate world, especially the East
Coast world dominated by Wall Street, those who
are at the top, or are rising toward the top, are
almost exclusively interested in enriching themselves
at the expense of their employees, customers,
shareholders, and any other unwary parties that
can be exploited.*

—STEVE BURBECK

He adds, "You have an obligation to yourself and to those you
hire and manage to know which side of the teeter-totter you are
on and which side the developers you manage are expected to
be on. Techies tend to be on the exploited side and, worse, to be
unaware that there are two sides."

*The single worst thing for an engineer is not to see
their work delivered.*

—RON LICHTY

I learned this early in managing—in my first director role,
actually—when the company, Berkeley Systems, had chartered
a team to do a new version of its core entertainment product,
After Dark, but failed to think through how much it could actually ship. When it finally set a limit, engineers who had been
working overtime for months saw a third of their efforts thrown
overboard—never shipped. Not only was the company's money
wasted, but the engineering staff was disheartened.

---

49. Quoted in Bernard Girard, *The Google Way* (No Starch Press, 2009), p. 64.

*People don't leave their companies. They leave
their managers.*

> —AN OLD HR NUGGET OF WISDOM, *shared by*
> REBECCA DAVIS, HR Manager/Consultant

*It's important to remember that the pressure of the
death march project team is felt by the spouse
and/or family members of the death march staffers.
. . . A thoughtful project manager might check to see
whether the spouse needs a taxi service to pick up
or drop off a child from school, or whether someone
from the office could pick up some groceries on the
way home to help the spouse who is stuck at home
with sick children.*

> —ED YOURDON[50]

*Regardless of whether or not the team members
are being compensated for their overtime work, the
worst mistake is not recording the overtime, on
the theory that since the team members aren't being
paid for it, it's "free." While this may be an accurate
perception on the part of the accounting department,
overtime is* **not** *free from the project manager's
perspective.*

> —ED YOURDON[51]

*One of the dangers that the project manager must
watch for is excessive* **voluntary** *overtime on the
part of enthusiastic young software engineers.*

> —ED YOURDON[52]

---

50. Ed Yourdon, *Death March: The Complete Software Developer's Guide to Surviving "Mission Impossible" Projects* (Prentice Hall, 1997), pp. 108–9.

51. Ibid., p. 111.

52. Ibid., p. 112.

Managing Teams to Deliver Successfully

> **Software is hard.**
>
> *—DONALD KNUTH*

Knuth is the acclaimed author of *The Art of Computer Programming*. Here, he was quoted speaking to an audience of 350 people at the Technische Universitat Munchen.[1]

> **Software isn't released, it's allowed to escape.**
>
> *—PROJECT MANAGEMENT LAY WISDOM*

> **. . . you're not here to write code; you're here to ship products.**
>
> *—JAMIE ZAWINSKI*[2]

> **Hofstadter's Law: It always takes longer than you expect, even when you take Hofstadter's Law into account.**
>
> *—DOUGLAS HOFSTADTER*[3]

---

1. Knuth's comment was captured in the widely shared PDF, *All Questions Answered*.
2. Quoted in Seibel, *Coders at Work*, p. 22.
3. Douglas Hofstadter, *Gödel, Escher, Bach: An Eternal Golden Braid*, 20th Anniversary Edition (Basic Books, 1999).

Always take redundancy over reliability.

—VLADIMIR BOGDANOV

Too much data could be worse than no data at all.

—VLADIMIR BOGDANOV

The secret of software development has always been good people and lots of Chinese food.

—JEFF KENTON, *Consulting Developer and Development Manager*[4]

Lots of Chinese food or pizza. Critical projects or milestones often require extraordinary effort to be exerted by the programming team. It's a simple thing that should be obvious: Programmers under schedule pressure will work long hours unless they are interrupted. Bringing in meals—Chinese food, pizza, or even meals from a great restaurant—keeps the programming team going. If you allow them to go out for food, their will to continue will erode and the extra effort will diminish.

Projects should be run like marathons. You have to set a healthy pace that can win the race and expect to sprint for the finish line.

—ED CATMULL, CTO, *Pixar Animation Studios*

At Pixar, Ed Catmull, its cofounder, president, and CTO, encouraged me to manage my projects this way, and I've used this as a rule of thumb ever since. When interviewing new candidates, I make sure I find a way to bring this up so that I set the expectation that there will be times when the programmer will need to work *very* hard and sprint for the finish line and project completion, but also to set the expectation that I don't expect them to "sprint" all the time.

---

4. www.embedded.com/shared/printableArticle.jhtml?articleID=166400761.

Programmers will always be able to justify any individual act of axe-sharpening . . . as "actually necessary." Some of them certainly are. It is the hard lot of the software manager to decide at what point the axe-sharpening . . . has lost touch with a project's original goal and to summon the programmers back from their happy tool-tending side-tracks to the primary task.

—SCOTT ROSENBERG[5]

My rules of thumb come in the form of questions.

The first and most important one: "Why are we doing this?" This reminds me to always check that my team is working only on things that align with strategic or tactical priorities for the product or organization. Too often we spend the scarce engineering time on things that aren't essential.

The second one is: "What problem are we trying to solve?" This reminds me to look past cool bells and whistles that Marketing often wants to see if there is an actual customer problem worth solving and only then look for a solution.

Both of these seem obvious and they should be, but all too often they are forgotten.

—TANYA BEREZIN, Senior Project Manager, Intuit

Half of projects don't go wrong; they start wrong. Get the first six weeks right.

—PRADEEP ANANTHAPADMANABHAN,
VP of Engineering, Razorfish

If you miss the market window, the business value is zero.

—POLLYANNA PIXTON[6]

---

5. Rosenberg, *Dreaming in Code*, p. 144.
6. Speaking to BayALN, the Bay Area chapter, January 2007.

Two-thirds of the innovation in the U.S.A. is the
result of trade shows.

—NOLAN BUSHNELL (paraphrased)

Nolan Bushnell, the founder of Atari, was genius in his comments
about non-movable milestones. Trade shows are scheduled far
in advance; they don't slip. So people work crazy hard to make
things happen for trade shows. Other non-movable milestones
can have a similar effect. A demo scheduled with the CEO or
board of directors, the end of a quarter or fiscal year, even a
holiday that marks the start of a three-day weekend can be used
to great effect.

When you end up making a tactical solution,
make sure that the strategic one is already
planned and approved.

—NASOS TOPAKAS

Topakas shared this observation about his tenure as Schwab's VP
of mobile trading systems development and continued, "Many,
many times I found myself supporting an ugly tactical solution
without support to replace it with the right one. My learning was
to always make a deal when I offer a quick and dirty solution so
I don't end up maintaining a mess."

Crisis builds consensus. Jump on it!

—KIMBERLY WIEFLING

Don't miss the opportunity to make progress that crisis offers.

The perfect project plan is possible if one first
documents a list of all the unknowns.

—BILL LANGLEY[7]

7. http://kurthaeusler.wordpress.com/2009/05/09/quotes/.

Every task must have one and only one Designated
Responsible Individual—a DRI. Two DRIs and
there's no one who is responsible. It's no better than
not assigning anyone. A project manager's job is
to make sure DRIs are assigned, not to do tasks.
Identify tasks, ensure a DRI is assigned, move on.
And check back regularly with three questions:
"Do you know your goal? Do you know your task's
contribution to the goal? What's standing in your
way of achieving your part of the goal?"

—RON LAFLEUR, *Management Consultant to the Apple*
software organization in the early nineties

Among the bad side effects of pathology: it becomes
unsafe to have a leanly staffed project.

—TOM DEMARCO[8]

This has been a particularly hard lesson to learn. I grew up on
a farm. I optimize for everything. I look for how to interlace the
work so that everyone does the most, learns the most (and has
the most fun). But do that in a pathological organization that
expects waste and yanks resources arbitrarily and you'll find, as
I did, that the finely honed organization you painstakingly crafted
gets whiplash and shrivels and projects become impossible to
deliver as key people are snatched away. In pathological organizations, you have to build slack to anticipate the slack-removal
forces that periodically sweep through.

Complexity kills. It sucks the life out of developers,
it makes products difficult to plan, build and test, it
introduces security challenges and it causes end-user
and administrator frustration.

—RAY OZZIE, *Creator of Lotus Notes; Founder,*
Groove; and CTO, Microsoft[9]

---

8. DeMarco, *The Deadline*, p. 132.

9. http://kurthaeusler.wordpress.com/2009/05/09/quotes/.

Rosenberg's Law: Software is easy to make, except when you want it to do something new.

Corollary: The only software that's worth making is software that does something new.

—SCOTT ROSENBERG[10]

Q: Do you have any advice for people starting to undertake large open source projects?

Linus Torvalds: Nobody should start to undertake a large project. You start with a small trivial project, and you should never expect it to get large. If you do, you'll just overdesign and generally think it is more important than it likely is at that stage. Or, worse, you might be scared away by the sheer size of the work you envision. So start small and think about the details. Don't think about some big picture and fancy design. If it doesn't solve some fairly immediate need, it's almost certainly overdesigned.

—LINUS TORVALDS[11]

The hardest single part of building a software system is deciding precisely what to build.

—FREDERICK P. BROOKS JR.[12]

The second-hardest single part might be communicating precisely what to build well enough to successfully achieve common understanding across the entire team. Only by listening carefully do you know you've been successful, which illustrates why listening is so much more important than speaking.

---

10. Rosenberg, *Dreaming in Code*, p. 268.

11. Interviewed in *Linux Times*, 2004.

12. Brooks, "No Silver Bullet—Essence and Accident," in *The Mythical Man-Month*.

It doesn't matter what software methodology you plan to use; you always need to know the requirements of what you're trying to engineer.

—*NASOS TOPAKAS*

He remarked,"This is something I've been saying to my business partners as they wanted to move to an Agile methodology so we can cut requirements documentation. They've been trying all kinds of methodologies so product managers can sit next to engineers and never document requirements—the result of which makes every project painful and long."

Without requirements or design, programming is the art of adding bugs to an empty text file.

—*LOUIS SRYGLEY*[13]

Walking on water and developing software from a specification are easy if both are frozen.

—*EDWARD V. BERARD, Object-Oriented Programming Pioneer and Guru*[14]

The Team Room is Agile's substitute for requirements.

—*ADE MILLER*

Miller said this in 2010, to the San Francisco Agile Meetup group, pointing out that the phone is a poor substitute for a Team Room. (That is, distributed teams don't work nearly as well.)

---

13. http://kurthaeusler.wordpress.com/2009/05/09/quotes/.
14. Edward V. Berard, "Life-Cycle Approaches," www.itmweb.com/essay552.htm.

*[On software requirements:] We have been
conditioned by conventional wisdom to accept
that people know what they want, even though our
experience is more like "people don't know what
they want, but they know what they don't want
when they see it."*

> —KURT BITTNER, *Software Development
> Solutions Strategist, IBM*[15]

*Iteration is critical: Customers don't know what
they want until they see it.*

> —RON MAK, *Middleware Architect of the NASA* Mars
> Rover *Mission's Collaborative Information Portal
> and Contributor to* Beautiful Code: Leading
> Programmers Explain How They Think[16]

Mak was speaking on NASA best practices to the Best Practices
SIG of the East Bay Innovation Group.

*Ambiguity in a specification is a sign of unresolved
conflict among the various system stakeholders.*

> —TOM DEMARCO[17]

*The hardest part of the software task is arriving at
a complete and consistent specification, and much
of the essence of building a program is in fact the
debugging of the specification.*

> —FREDERICK P. BROOKS JR.[18]

15. Kurt Bittner, IBM blog, "Managing Software Development," www.ibm.com/
    developerworks/forums/thread.jspa?threadID=51892.

16. Andy Oram and Greg Wilson, eds., *Beautiful Code: Leading Programmers Explain How They
    Think* (O'Reilly, 2007), Chapter 20.

17. DeMarco, *The Deadline,* p. 216.

18. Brooks, *The Mythical Man-Month.*

*In the software world, most of the choices that
arise boil down to one particularly heartbreaking
three-way trade-off. Optimists call it the quality
triangle. . . . I first heard this principle from a veteran
software developer and author named Dan Shafer who
. . . would lean back in his chair, rub his buddha belly,
and say, "There's an old saying: I can make it for you
fast, cheap, or good. Pick any two." You can't labor
long in any engineering realm without encountering
this painful formula . . . like all bad news in business,
it invites pushback from managers determined to prove
that their organizations can be the exception to the
rule. . . . In practice, what managers face is more like
a mixing board with linked sliders. . . . But a manager
gets to sit down at that console and move those sliders
around only if a project is organized enough to respond
predictably to decisions about cost and schedule and
features or quality.*

—SCOTT ROSENBERG[19]

*Customers will grade you more harshly on poor
quality than on missing features.*

—MARK CALOMENI, *VP of Engineering,
Accept Software, and Director of Engineering,
HighWire Press*

"Quality is my number-one priority," says Calomeni, who has
repeatedly put in place lightweight design processes and code
inspections, noting, "In hardware you have to do design—you
can't just sit down and start soldering components onto a board.
Unfortunately in software, you can."

*Customers can fire everybody in the company from
the chairman on down, simply by spending their
money somewhere else.*

—SAM WALTON, *Founder of Walmart*

---

19. Rosenberg, *Dreaming in Code*, pp. 118–20.

In the beginning, everyone will talk about scope, and budget, and schedule, but in the end, nobody really cares about any of those things. The only thing they care about is this: People will love your software, or they won't. So that's the only criterion to which you should truly manage.

—JOSEPH KLEINSCHMIDT

Do lots of user testing: Users are the best testers. (Developers are the worst testers!)

—RON MAK[20]

Software is a lot like sausage: Enjoy the end product but you really don't want to know what goes into it.

—ANONYMOUS

Project management lay wisdom. I first heard this from Harry Wilker, the SVP of Product Development at Brøderbund, who used this phrase to describe software projects. Since that time I've used this simile when I've found my executive team trying to micromanage milestones on projects and products. There is so much that can never be scheduled that goes on, like testing new compilers or OS versions, that trying to track *everything* is hopeless. It's better to just allocate a large chunk of unscheduled time to capture these other tasks. This is a good way to remind people of that fact.

As technical debt goes up, customer responsiveness goes down.

—JIM HIGHSMITH[21]

---

20. Speaking on NASA best practices to the Best Practices SIG of the East Bay Innovation Group.

21. Speaking on February 16, 2010, to BayALN.

Never underestimate the reality of bit rot.

Bit rot[22] is a colloquial computing term used to facetiously describe the spontaneous degradation of a software program over time. The term implies that software can literally wear out or rust like a physical tool. Many times, although there is no obvious change in the program's operating environment, a subtle difference has occurred that triggers a latent software error or incompatibility.

In practice, [Fred] Brooks found, nearly all software projects require only one-sixth of their time for the writing of code and fully half their schedule for testing and fixing bugs.

—SCOTT ROSENBERG[23]

A great developer spends two hours testing for every hour coding.

—BRUCE ROSENBLUM

Testing by itself does not improve software quality. Test results are an indicator of quality, but in and of themselves, they don't improve it. Trying to improve software quality by increasing the amount of testing is like trying to lose weight by weighing yourself more often. What you eat before you step onto the scale determines how much you will weigh, and the software development techniques you use determine how many errors testing will find. If you want to lose weight, don't buy a new scale; change your diet. If you want to improve your software, don't test more; develop better.

—STEVE MCCONNELL[24]

---

22. See http://en.wikipedia.org/wiki/Bit_rot.

23. Summary of one of Frederick Brooks's observations in Rosenberg, *Dreaming in Code*, p. 17. Brooks: "My rule of thumb is $\frac{1}{3}$ of the schedule for design, $\frac{1}{6}$ for coding, $\frac{1}{4}$ for component testing, and $\frac{1}{4}$ for system testing." Brooks, *The Mythical Man-Month*, p. 231.

24. Steve McConnell, *Code Complete* (Microsoft Press, 1993).

Do as little QA as possible and no less.

—*JOHN STEELE*

John said this in a March 2007 presentation to the Software Architecture and Modeling SIG I cochaired for SDForum.

Always hire people who are smarter than you. But never ship something you don't understand.

—*JOSEPH KLEINSCHMIDT*

Plan to throw one away; you will anyhow.

—*FREDERICK P. BROOKS JR.*[25]

Brooks notes, "In most projects, the first system built is barely usable. . . . The management question, therefore, is not *whether* to build a pilot system and throw it away. You *will* do that. The only question is whether to plan in advance to build a throwaway. . . .

If it doesn't work on my machine, it doesn't work.

—*JOSEPH KLEINSCHMIDT*

Good test automation is expensive.

—*BRUCE ROSENBLUM*

No test automation costs ten times more.

—*BRUCE ROSENBLUM*

Just about any process is better than no process. You can take baby steps at first, and see gains—as long as the team believes the process won't get dropped in favor of something else the next time a crisis erupts (as it will).

—*MARK GINNEBAUGH, Microsoft Certified Partner and President, DesignMind*

---

25. Brooks, *The Mythical Man-Month*, p. 116.

Do as little process as possible and no less.

—RON LICHTY

Paraphrased from John Steele's rule of thumb that he shared with the Software Architecture and Modeling SIG I cochaired for SDForum. Given that John is a Chief QA Architect, he applied it to QA. But I thought it a succinct rule of thumb applicable to process in general. I have for years been an advocate and implementer of what I've termed just-in-time and just-enough process. I liked John's way of phrasing it.

If your process requires no mistakes, it will fail.

—ROB MYERS, Agile Coach, Northern California

Brilliant process management is our strategy. We get brilliant results from average people managing brilliant processes. We observe that our competitors often get average (or worse) results from brilliant people managing broken processes.

—A SENIOR TOYOTA EXECUTIVE[26]

There is no such thing as a short-term fix in our business. There is never a way to improve productivity in the short term. . . . The only real variable you have to play with is the proportion of work hours that are effective. . . . You have to focus entirely on avoiding wasted time.

—TOM DEMARCO[27]

In an emergent process, there's no such thing as a best practice.

—TOBIAS MAYER, Certified Scrum Trainer

Tobias makes the claim that "there are good practices but no best practices. Organizations are unique."

---

26. http://kurthaeusler.wordpress.com/2009/05/09/quotes/.
27. DeMarco, *The Deadline*, p. 79.

CMM5 guarantees absolutely it will be done the same way twice. It does not speak to whether that's the right thing to do.

—JOHN STEELE[28]

When you want a project in the worst way, that is often how you get it.

—WATTS HUMPHREY, *Fellow of the Association for Computing Machinery (ACM) and Father of Software Quality*

It's dangerous to fall in love with prototypes. Prototypes = only 10 percent of making the product usable.

—JASON FEINSMITH, *CEO/Cofounder, Accomplice[29]*

The first 90 percent of the code accounts for the first 90 percent of the development time. The remaining 10 percent of the code accounts for the other 90 percent of the development time.

—TOM CARGILL, *then at Bell Labs, more recently a C++ and Java Consulting Programmer*

Titled "The Rule of Credibility" and also known as the "Ninety-Ninety Rule," Tom Cargill's aphorism was popularized by Jon Bentley in his column "Programming Pearls," *Communications of the ACM*, September 1985.

Never trade a bad date for an equally bad date.

—JIM MCCARTHY[30]

---

28. March 2007 presentation to the Software Architecture and Modeling SIG for SDForum.

29. From a talk to SDForum's Software Engineering Management SIG titled "Lessons Learned from a Software Startup," April 19, 2007.

30. McCarthy and Gilbert, *Dynamics of Software Development*, p. 141.

Define "done." It's hard to celebrate a job well done when your team doesn't agree on a definition of "done." What does it mean when someone on your software team says that their feature is complete? Does it mean:

- *It works on their machine?*
- *It has been checked in to source control?*
- *It has a full set of acceptance tests?*
- *The tests are all passing?*
- *Fully documented?*
- *Peer reviewed?*

Take the time to work out what your team really means by "done" and create a checklist. This will help you reliably deliver software and enjoy a shared sense of accomplishment.

—*CHRIS SIMS, Founder, Agile Learning Labs and before it, the Technical Management Institute*

In the software field, we are expected to accurately estimate the time it will take to do a job that requires creative thought, that usually requires the team members to learn new concepts, and that pushes team members to provide undivided attention for long periods of time.

—*CAROL L. HOOVER, MEL ROSSO-LLOPART, and GIL TARAN*[31]

Underpromise, overdeliver.

—*ANONYMOUS*

It beats any other approach we know. On the other hand, you can't underpromise by very much or you'll be labeled a piker.

---

31. Carol L. Hoover, Mel Rosso-Llopart, and Gil Taran, *Evaluating Project Decisions: Case Studies in Software Engineering* (Addison-Wesley, 2010).

> *If you don't have time to calculate value, we don't have time to calculate cost.*
>
> —JIM HIGHSMITH

Speaking to BayALN on February 16, 2010, he shared this mantra to product owners who demand schedule estimates but won't prioritize features or provide value estimates.

> *In applications with high technical debt, estimating is nearly impossible.*
>
> —JIM HIGHSMITH[32]

> *Estimate Early and Often.*
>
> —CAROL L. HOOVER, MEL ROSSO-LLOPART, and GIL TARAN[33]

The authors note, "Estimates are snapshots in time. As soon as we know more information, we should consider updating the estimates we have. Even global positioning systems (GPS) acquire information on a regular basis to update their estimates. With his famous 'cone of uncertainty,' McConnell explained that the only way to increase 'certainty' in estimation is to move in time toward the solution. As McConnell suggested, you cannot improve the estimate by staying with your current knowledge. Likewise, Cohn stated that trying harder at the same point may actually reduce the value of your estimate. Therefore, we propose that you estimate early and often."

> *Trying to get a better estimate, at any point, may actually reduce the value of your estimate.*
>
> —MIKE COHN[34]

---

32. Speaking to BayALN on February 16, 2010.
33. Hoover, Rosso-Llopart, and Taran, *Evaluating Project Decisions.*
34. Mike Cohn, *Agile Estimating and Planning* (Prentice Hall, 2006).

> *When a task cannot be partitioned because of
> sequential constraints, the application of more
> effort has no effect on the schedule. The bearing
> of a child takes nine months, no matter how many
> women are assigned. Many software tasks have
> this characteristic because of the sequential nature
> of debugging.*
>
> —FREDERICK P. BROOKS JR.[35]

> *A good organization learns to separate estimating
> from committing.*
>
> —MIKE COHN[36]

He notes the value of estimating and then lays out methods
for translating an estimate into a commitment.

> *The way it works within Google . . . To check in
> you need three conditions met: You need someone
> to review it and say it looks good. You need to
> be certified in the language—basically you've
> proven you know the style of this language—
> called "readability." And then you also need the
> approval above from somebody in the owner's
> file in that directory.*
>
> —BRAD FITZPATRICK[37]

> *If you're the ScrumMaster and everyone is looking
> at you, you're doing it wrong.*
>
> —MARILSON CAMPOS

The team should be looking at each other!

---

35. Brooks, *The Mythical Man-Month,* p. 17.
36. Cohn, *Succeeding with Agile,* p. 297.
37. Quoted in Seibel, *Coders at Work,* pp.73–74.

....

Once upon a time, there was a poor shoemaker living with his wife in a little house. They did not have much, not a table, not a sofa, and not even a fridge. Their cupboard was empty of goods. Our shoemaker was hungry, and he wanted the delicious donuts he saw in Dunkin Donuts on his way home. "My dear, what do you say about preparing some donuts this evening?"' he asked his wife. "With pleasure, my husband, but we have no ingredients to do it." "No matter, honey, take these twopence and bring us the ingredients." After some time, his wife returned back home. "I bought some flour to prepare the donuts." "So hurry please, I'm hungry," said the husband. "But I could not buy sugar," said the wife. "No matter, we will do without the sugar." "I could neither buy oil." "Let's make do then without oil, less cholesterol." "I could not buy eggs," said the wife, "they were too expensive." "So what, you are able to prepare them without eggs too." The poor woman mixed the flour with water, formed a couple of donuts, and then put them to cook. After five minutes she called her husband to the table and brought him the donut-like meal. He tasted them and said, "These donuts are not so tasty. I do not understand what everyone finds so good about donuts!"

—HAIM DEUTSCH, Israeli Programmer, R&D Manager,
ScrumMaster, and Certified Scrum Coach[38]

If you've ever got a boss who tells you to use Agile, then tells you you can't have a ScrumMaster or test-driven development, you can't use points, you need to estimate before you know anything, and that holding meetings every day, even just for 15 minutes, is a waste of everyone's time . . . The folks who designed the various Agile frameworks thought a lot about what practices would make software development successful; removing them may rob you of success.

---

38. From the January 19, 2011, ScrumAlliance newsletter, www.scrumalliance.org/articles/329-soft-measures-in-scrum-implementation.

Not all developers are suited to Agile.

> —TED YOUNG[39]

He noted that not all developers want to pitch in, collaborate, contribute, and participate.

When a team fails to complete estimated tasks in the time period for which they were estimated, shorten the next time period.

> —TOBIAS MAYER

Tobias says, "Don't give people more time, give them less (and less, until they begin finishing in estimated times)," in the Certified ScrumMaster training he delivers.

A symptom of continuing to hand off work in overly large chunks will be a tendency for no product backlog items to be finished until the last few days of the sprint. Testers on teams that work this way often complain that they are given nothing to test until two days before the end of a sprint and are expected to test everything that quickly. The best way to expose this problem is to create a chart of the number of product backlog items finished as of each day in the sprint.

> —MIKE COHN[40]

He notes that hanging the chart in the team area is often enough to enable team members to figure out the problem the chart exposes, find ways to finish product backlog items sooner, and create a smoother flow through the sprint.

---

39. Shared at Agile Open Space, February 26, 2010.
40. Cohn, *Succeeding with Agile*, p. 207.

....

Teams benefit from a regular cadence.

—MIKE COHN[41]

He cites it as one of the benefits of fixed sprint lengths.

....

If you plan for less than your capacity, you get less done than you could have. If you plan for more than your capacity, you get less done than you could have.

—KENT BECK, *Creator of Extreme Programming (XP),*
Test-Driven Development (TDD), and JUnit[42]

....

Why does the effect of pressure on programmers max out after only 6% productivity gain?

My answer: People under pressure don't think faster.

—TOM DEMARCO[43]

....

We're not here to bake the brownies in this meeting.

—DAVID HORTON, *Director, eCommerce Systems &*
Development, Williams-Sonoma

It's a phrase he uses when Agile stand-ups begin to get mired in detail.

....

Let's just do an experiment.

—KIMBERLY WIEFLING

It's an expression (and a course of action) she uses when an organization seems stuck in a rut, unable to decide on a course of action.

---

41. Ibid., p. 276.

42. Quoted at www.infoq.com/news/2009/05/Good-Velocity.

43. DeMarco, *The Deadline*, p. 195.

Setting up a team is like baking a cake: You stick in the wrong combination of flavors and you won't like the taste of it, but get it right and it will be real sweet!

—NEIL MARTIN, Development Manager at Elateral, UK[44]

You have to be a casting director.

—MARK HIMELSTEIN[45]

I don't want people who want to dance; I want people who have to dance.

—GEORGE BALANCHINE[46]

Don't take chances on team jell if you don't have to: Seek out and use preformed teams.

Keep good teams together (when they're willing) to help your successors avoid problems of slow-jelling or non-jelling teams.

Think of a jelled team—ready and willing to take on a new effort—as one of the project deliverables.

—TOM DEMARCO[47]

The quality of code you demand during the first week of a project is the quality of code you'll get every week thereafter.

—JOSEPH KLEINSCHMIDT

---

44. In response to Q&A in the Agile Alliance group on LinkedIn.

45. Speaking to the Best Practices SIG of the East Bay IT Group, June 2006, in response to a question about balancing different types of programmers on a team.

46. Quoted by product visionary Clark Dodsworth in his keynote address to the Entertainment Computing Conference on May 10, 2003.

47. DeMarco, *The Deadline*, p. 93.

*The only reasonable schedule estimate for testing
is based not on people but on defect density.*

—*JIM HIGHSMITH*[48]

*. . . the designer of a new system must not only be
the implementer and the first large-scale user; the
designer should also write the first user manual. . . .
If I had not participated fully in all these activities,
literally hundreds of improvements would never
have been made, because I would never have thought
of them or perceived why they were important.*

—*DONALD KNUTH*[49]

Knuth is the acclaimed author of *The Art of Computer Programming.*

*Learning to program has no more to do with
designing interactive software than learning to
touch type has to do with writing poetry.*

—*TED NELSON*[50]

Ted Nelson, a pioneer in user interface design across big data
sets, founded and spent much of his working life exploring and
expanding on Project Xanadu, the first hypertext project. It was
Nelson who, in 1963, coined the terms *hypertext* and *hypermedia*.

*Always code as if the guy who ends up maintaining
your code will be a violent psychopath who knows
where you live.*

—*Variously attributed to MARTIN GOLDING and to
JOHN F. WOODS*

---

48. Speaking to BayALN, February 16, 2010.

49. Knuth, *The Art of Computer Programming.*

50. Ted Nelson, "The Right Way to Think about Software Design," *The Art of Human-Computer Interface Design,* ed. Brenda Laurel (Addison-Wesley, 1990), p. 243.

Write your code like you will have to debug it when you are low on sleep, drunk, or hungover—because you probably will.

—ANONYMOUS[51]

Good design adds value faster than it adds cost.

—THOMAS C. GALE, Chrysler Chief of Automotive
Design and Product Development[52]

*Small teams are more productive than large teams. . . .
A 5- to 7-person team will complete an equivalently
sized project in the shortest amount of time.*

—MIKE COHN[53]

He quotes a study by Doug Putnam of QSM. Putnam studied
491 projects between 2003 and 2005 with team sizes from 1 to
20 people. QSM maintains the software development industry's
most thorough metrics database. Putnam found that the smaller
the team size, the more productive each team member was.
However, the difference between teams sized from 1.5 to
7 people was very small. Smaller teams took slightly longer
than teams of 5 to 7. Larger teams took much longer.

*Large teams (29 people) create around six times as
many defects as small teams (3 people) and obviously
burn through a lot more money. Yet, the large team
appears to produce about the same amount of output
in only an average of 12 days less time. This is a
truly astonishing finding, though it fits with my
personal experience on projects over 35 years.*

—PHILLIP ARMOUR, Longtime Industry Veteran[54]

---

51. www.junauza.com/2010/12/top-50-programming-quotes-of-all-time.html.

52. Ibid.

53. Cohn, *Succeeding with Agile*, p. 181.

54. From "Software: Hard Data," *Communications of the ACM*, September 2006, p. 16, quoted
    in Cohn, *Succeeding with Agile*, p. 181.

....

*The long-term impact of changing the size of a team
isn't apparent until the third sprint after the change.*

—MIKE COHN[55]

....

*. . . each new delay introduced the temptation to hire
more bodies, yet the new hires never seemed to speed
the schedule along.*

—SCOTT ROSENBERG[56]

....

*Brooks's Law: Adding manpower to a late software
project makes it later.*

—FREDERICK P. BROOKS JR.[57]

55. Cohn, *Succeeding with Agile*, p. 303.

56. Rosenberg, *Dreaming in Code*, p. 19.

57. Brooks, *The Mythical Man-Month*, p. 25.

6

Becoming an Effective Programming Manager: Managing Up, Out, and Yourself

THE PREVIOUS CHAPTER DISCUSSED THE FIRST AND MOST IMPORTANT PART of your job—managing down. This chapter addresses those other parts of your job that you must also do to be a truly effective programming manager:

- Managing up
- Managing out
- Managing yourself

These topics deal with managing your boss(es), managing your peers and others inside or outside of your organization, and managing yourself. Your boss and colleagues are not your direct reports; they have their own agendas that may conflict with yours, they may not respect you or even know who you are, and they cannot be managed in the same way you manage your team. Managing yourself is a 24/7 job that you need to embrace and can always improve on.

Managing Up

Managing up is how you effectively manage your boss and those to whom he reports. You also need to figure out the reporting, the communicating, and the other actions you can take to ensure that you are viewed as an effective and successful programming manager.

It may seem strange to think about managing your boss, but as it turns out, it may be more important to manage your boss successfully—at least to you personally—than to manage your staff. That's because success is not just about what you do but how you are perceived: Perception is almost universally treated as reality.

The single most important leader in an organization is your immediate supervisor.

—*JIM KOUZES, Leadership Speaker and Coauthor,* The Leadership Challenge[1]

You can safely assume all perceptions are real, at least to those who own them.

—*JOE FOLKMAN, PhD, Author on Psychometrics, Leadership, and Change*[2]

Understand Your Boss

Managing up starts with understanding your boss(es) and what kind of person(s) they are: Are they technical? Sales and marketing types? Financial types? Some other type? Are they big-picture or detail-oriented? What are their hot buttons?

How you manage up depends on correctly understanding this about not only your boss, but also others to whom you may indirectly or implicitly report. If you report to the VP of Engineering, your communications and reporting will likely be quite technical in nature. If you report to the CEO or VP of Products, you may need to make your reporting less technical and more informational and perhaps more product-related. Furthermore, the

---

1. James M. Kouzes and Barry Z. Posner, *The Leadership Challenge, Fourth Edition* (Jossey-Bass, 2007).

2. Joe Folkman, PhD, *Turning Feedback into Change!* (Novations Group, 1996), p. 7.

more senior your boss, the more concise and big-picture your communication must be: fewer details, more breadth; fewer words, more bullets.

It is critical that you consciously assess how to communicate effectively with your bosses. Even if you ask them what they want, you may deliver the wrong kind or level of information to them; their self-assessment may fall short of what it is they actually want. So you can and should always keep iterating and adjusting how much you communicate. Certain events may call for more, or less, information to be communicated.

Mickey recalls, "At Brøderbund, for many years I reported to one of the cofounders of the company, the original technical guy who had become the CEO. As such he was very interested in the technical initiatives that were going on and personally tested each product before it was released. You can imagine that my communications to him via reports and e-mail were quite technical in nature. Later on, he was replaced by an executive brought in from Kraft Foods who was a brand management specialist. You can imagine how little the new guy was interested in the technical details or even how the technology development was progressing. My change in reporting and reporting style was dramatic."

....

You don't have to like or admire your boss, nor do you have to hate him. You do have to manage him, however, so that he becomes your resource for achievement, accomplishment and personal success.

—PETER DRUCKER, Management Guru[3]

Does your manager want a regular one-on-one meeting with you? Or perhaps more importantly, will he be receptive to your proposing a regular one-on-one to ensure that regular communication takes place? Some managers will insist on having one-on-ones to review current status and issues while others will avoid them. It's best to assess for yourself what is appropriate with your boss.

What are the initiatives your boss is responsible for? Think about how you can contribute to their success or even drive one or more of them on behalf of your boss—perhaps without being asked or by volunteering to take on the tough stuff.

Another important thing to assess is your boss's ego. Though this can be a touchy subject, understanding how much ego your boss has can help

---

3. Peter Drucker, *The Practice of Management* (Harper & Row, 1954).

dictate how you pursue certain things. For example, certain bosses want to be the public voice for the organization (Ron and Mickey have known many CTOs and CEOs who fit that mold). If you find yourself in that situation, you should avoid public speaking opportunities unless your boss delegates them to you. You can increase the probability by volunteering to help with a presentation or two, but let your boss determine that you are OK to be sent to do the presentation or you may find yourself at odds on seemingly trivial matters. When you understand how ego impacts your boss's actions, you can more carefully pick and choose areas to pursue or avoid.

Package Your Communications

Just as your programming team needs to know you are taking care of stuff without distracting them, likewise your boss needs to know you are taking care of stuff without distracting him. That means he needs to know the kinds of things you regularly handle without his direction or involvement, but not the details of those things. You can always provide more details upon request. Over time, you and whomever you report to will develop an understanding of what you will do and the boundaries of your authority. Then you will likely report less about standard actions or activities you take care of on an ongoing basis and more about nonstandard actions or issues you are having. Initially, you should report on everything.

> *Deliver prompt, clear, proactive communication. The people above you in the org chart are trying to run a business. They need accurate, up-to-date information in order to do that efficiently. This is especially critical when problems are creeping in—deadlines/features/quality may be at risk while your VP/CEO/marketing rep/etc. is telling customers/investors/media how great everything is going. Speaking up in a timely manner when things aren't going well is as difficult as it is important.*
>
> —TIM SWIHART, Engineering Director, Apple Computer

Keep your reports to one or two pages, with addenda if necessary to include more detailed information. Report regularly, without exception. Do the report ahead of time, or delegate it to one of your staff if you are out of the office or unable to complete it. There is nothing like regular reporting to gain your manager's confidence.

Be mindful of who else may view what you communicate. Always make sure your reports are professional in nature, and avoid any negative comments that may find their way to those you would not like to hear them. At times, oral communication is better than written reports. In today's world of "discoverable e-mail" it is often better to just pick up the phone or step into the office to discuss negative topics with someone than to commit them to e-mail or written documents.

Another important part of communication is the ability to create and deliver good presentations. Master the art of making good presentations. An effective manager must be able to communicate effectively; making good presentations is today a necessity. However, make sure you invest the appropriate amount of time creating an effective presentation. The more people who will see the presentation—or the more influential the people—the more time you should spend to make it effective.

There are many classes on effective public speaking and communication. Take a class if necessary; it will probably be well worth the time you spend if it helps you communicate more effectively. Do not just read PowerPoint slides. Slides should summarize your comments, not present them. Slides should drive home your verbal points.

....

The amount of time spent on a presentation should be proportional to who may view it directly—and indirectly.

Understand Your Boss's Boss

To be successful, it is not just what and how you do your job that counts. It is also how you help your boss succeed. While you could ignore this section and still be successful, embracing the ideas in this section may help you be more successful. It is human nature to reward those who help us do our jobs. So understanding how you can help your boss be successful may provide opportunities for you to conspicuously, or inconspicuously, help him do his job better. Understand what your boss is being judged on by his boss. What makes him successful? What can you do to help make him successful?

Usually these issues will be less tactical and more strategic in nature. So understand whether your manager's objectives are about

- Improving quality
- On-time delivery

- Innovation
- Something else about products
- Issues reporting
- Collaboration and partnering
- Revenue and/or expenses

When you can identify the kinds of things that are important to him, proactively try to contribute to one or more of them. Ask how you can help, or take your own action and wait for further encouragement before continuing. You will usually get some feedback that will dictate your next step. Be careful not to go overboard without direct encouragement, or your actions could be interpreted negatively and backfire on you. The last thing you want to do is give your boss the impression that you are bucking for his job.

Timing

When does your boss want to hear from you? When does he want successes to arrive? Providing timely information to your boss before his weekly staff meetings could be very important. Providing it a day later could be too late.

Similarly, providing timely feedback before budget cycles could be a tremendous help to make your boss's (and your) life easier for the coming year (or budget cycle). Provide it too late, and you and he could run into serious issues.

Think consciously about timing. Good timing is almost as important as good luck. Remember, movie studios release movies at certain times for good reasons. The timing of a movie release can make or break its chances for an Academy Award. Similarly, be mindful of good timing for communicating or completing projects, prototypes, or demos. Know when important company meetings take place or decisions are made. Having a demo ready for an important board meeting could be critical for you and your team. If you miss that opportunity, it may be another six months before the next opportunity presents itself.

Be a Model Employee

In today's busy workplace, doing our job well is often our sole focus. However, there is more to being a model employee than just doing your job well. Here are some tips for becoming a model employee, at least in the eyes of the person to whom you report.

Be "low maintenance"; that is, don't bring every problem to your boss for solution. Pick your battles carefully, and take only really important issues to your boss for resolution. Better yet, solve the problem without his help if possible. Also, avoid simply taking a problem to your boss; rather, bring several potential solutions along with the problem. Even if you don't believe they are good solutions (or that you have the best solution), having a list of possible solutions shows you've done your homework and are seeking his counsel, not throwing the problem into his lap.

Nothing stops a witch hunt faster than owning up to being the culprit.

> —TIM SWIHART

Volunteer to help solve his problems. There are times when certain issues will be nagging your boss, so if you can help, offer to take one or more of them off his plate. For example, at Charles Schwab, when he saw his boss agonizing over having gone through three QA managers in less than a year, Ron volunteered to manage the QA department in addition to his own department for six months while they figured how to organize and manage the department in the long term.

Learn how to amaze and delight. Learn what makes your boss really sit up and take notice, and find ways to overdeliver and delight by providing more than what he expects. Sometimes it doesn't take all that much.

Underpromise, overdeliver.

Bottom Line

Managing up effectively is probably of more consequence to a manager's career and career development than any other activity. You can do a great job of managing your team(s) and delivering projects, but if your boss is not your champion, your career will suffer. It might not be apparent to you, but as a result of closed-door executive meetings or private decision making by your boss your salary, bonus, stock options, perks, and opportunities will be less than they might otherwise have been.

So be proactive: Manage up and you will likely reap career rewards. You have everything to gain and nothing to lose but time and energy.

Managing up can also be rewarding in its own right since you will implicitly cement closer ties and relationships up the chain of command as you make the effort to communicate more. You might make, of one of those bosses, a friend who will be in your corner for the rest of your career.

Managing Out

Managing out is how you effectively manage relationships with your peers and others in departments in the organization outside of yours. Managing out can also refer to managing relationships outside your organization—with technology providers, vendors, partners, competitors, and important influencers. Managing out is important for those interested in managing their career. Moving beyond your comfort zone and engaging others inside and outside of your company will do as much to accelerate your career as doing a spectacular job of managing programmers and delivering projects successfully—maybe more.

Collaborating within Your Department

It is critical that you collaborate within your department. If you cannot collaborate with your closest coworkers, how can you be successful collaborating across the organization?

Collaborating locally has the direct effect that it will make your own boss's work easier, since you will be solving problems among yourselves that he might otherwise need to be involved in resolving. Local collaboration will also expedite projects, since problems and issues will be resolved more quickly without undue attention. Collaborating within your department will also bring you and your peers closer together, since you'll be sharing problems and solutions, commiserating together, and encouraging each other directly.

This collaboration can also take the form of trading favors to provide above-and-beyond-the-norm assistance with problems that may arise, sharing resources and training, and watching each other's backs. When people can look to their closest peers as their primary support system, they find themselves willingly assisting each other and helping to make each other successful. If you stay in an organization for any reasonable length of time, some of your peers will likely end up as your closest friends. These relationships are to be savored and nurtured.

Understand Other Departments

It is important that you understand what other departments do, and that you value them and their contributions. All too often, the programming and product development staffs undervalue the contributions of the finance and marketing departments. Instead, always make sure you really appreciate the contributions of other departments, which are every bit as important as yours.

As you are hired or are promoted into a programming manager position, study the org chart carefully. Then seek out the department heads of the various functional departments and make sure you get to know them or your organizational peers within those departments. Ask them to go to lunch or just stop by to chat occasionally. Build bridges across departments before the bridges are necessary. Then, when you need something from them, submitting a request or asking a favor will be easier both for you and for them.

The bridges you need to build are not just to help you; they can also be important avenues to fostering bidirectional collaboration between your teams. For example, after Socialtext sent a much-too-generic marketing piece to attendees at a technical conference, Ron invited the marketing director to lunch. Ron not only showed him the opportunity that getting technical people on board with the product could provide but also how they might work together to help achieve marketing goals and avoid repeating the mistake of sending mistargeted marketing materials to other technical conferences.

The following departments are ones where getting to know the department heads, or at least a peer at your level, in the following departments, will be helpful in most organizations. In parentheses are the areas and issues over which you may want to engage.

- Finance (invoices, payments, and payroll)
- Purchasing (purchase requests, vendor qualification, and expediting purchases)
- Legal (contracts, intellectual property, mergers and acquisitions)
- Human Resources (hiring, firing, performance reviews, internal and external salary equity, internships, and recruiting staff and contractors)
- Marketing (market research, trade shows, corporate communications, press releases, collateral, and spiffs)
- Sales (customer feedback, customer issues, customer connections, and the customer pipeline)

- Technical support (critical customer issues, customer feedback, trends, and outstanding issues)

As implied above, it is important to build relationships before you need them. Find ways and even go out of your way to do so. Besides directly seeking them out, try to get to know these people informally in participatory activities:

- Cross-functional training (training together can forge strong bonds)
- Organizational social activities (company meetings, company parties, softball and bowling leagues, beer bashes, drinks at the local pub, and the like)
- Informal lunches
- Friday afternoon bashes

Informal connecting has become more difficult since the weekly Friday afternoon beer bash has fallen out of favor at so many places. Ron recalls of his years at Apple, "The Friday afternoon beer bashes provided a way to touch base broadly in a short amount of time. I found I could be behind by a week trying to connect with people only to catch up in just a couple of hours at the beer bash!"

Likewise, Mickey remembers fondly the Brøderbund Friday afternoon beer bashes where "everyone got together at 4:30 for chips, veggies, dips, and a keg of beer. By 5:30 the keg would be gone, and also most of the staff. But it provided a very informal way to talk to almost everyone in the company and to learn more about them, their lives, and what they did."

The Friday beer bashes have fallen out of favor because of increased scrutiny of company-supported activities that could lead to drinking and driving, combined with dramatically tightened budgets. Unfortunately, the good was thrown out with the bad when companies became more risk-averse and eliminated this important socializing activity.

If you can, find ways to re-create the spirit of these Friday afternoon beer bashes for your team. Hold departmental "happy hours" occasionally to celebrate major milestones or releases; be an instigator to meet at the local watering hole for drinks after work on Fridays or special days; buy a round for your team at a special place; bring in a caterer to serve chocolate fondue if you have team members in from out of town; and most importantly extend the invitation to attend such events to others outside your department to try to inspire that important cross-departmental communication. Seek out others in your organization to be "co-conspirators" and share the burden of instigating these events.

Make an effort to know everyone's name. In small companies or organizations it is easy, but as companies start to grow past 100 it becomes challenging. Institute welcome rituals that will make everyone know each person's name; go out of your way to know who they are and welcome them warmly. This small amount of energy on your part will be returned many times over. As the company reaches 250, keep trying to know everyone. There will come a point where you cannot keep up, but try to be the one person who knows more people than anyone else.

Finally, whenever possible, be a leader, not a follower, in cross-functional activities. Your willing participation will raise your stature throughout the organization and help you succeed in more ways than are obvious. The time you spend in these activities will be abundantly rewarded in increased capacity to perform your job.

Leverage Important Support Functions

In addition to managing programmers, you'll likely be responsible for other management tasks on which your performance will also be judged and for which the organization provides support. These include

- Human resources actions
- Budgeting and managing expenses
- Bringing in legal oversight for contractual and licensing issues

As a manager, you must learn to leverage the support organizations that can help you accomplish these tasks: Human Resources (HR), Finance, and Legal. Many programmers view these departments skeptically. However, as a manager, you must learn to leverage them to further your own agendas.

Human Resources (HR)

As we noted with respect to creating and delivering solid performance reviews, you should make your HR department your ally and partner. In fact, a good HR department can be helpful in many other ways. We strongly recommend that you establish good relationships with the members of your HR staff so that you can feel comfortable talking to them about HR-related issues that may come up and strategizing about how to handle them. We have been in organizations with great HR departments and in organizations with poor, or even incompetent, HR staff. Regardless, having a strong relationship with HR has been an asset in helping us manage effectively.

Some HR departments are put in the position of enforcing rather rigid compensation and promotion guidelines. In that case, finding out how to work with the HR staff to maximize what compensation you can award your staff is imperative. Even the most rigid guidelines can have flexibility when necessary. Involving your HR staff in strategizing your personnel moves can help you effect good outcomes from negative situations.

HR can be a sounding board and a place to seek counsel regarding cases of extreme performance problems, harassment, interpersonal issues, and other staff problems. They may also help you arrange (and sometimes fund) team-building exercises or activities.

A good HR department is interested in the overall mood of the organization and in each individual feeling appreciated and/or rewarded appropriately for their contributions. They can be a source for, or at least an ally in, helping you obtain bonuses and non-cash rewards or incentives and find other creative ways to reward, thank, and appreciate individuals and teams.

Mickey recalls, "At Brøderbund, we had a fantastic HR vice president who was the best HR person I ever worked with. She helped formalize the process of annually reviewing all staff compensation and established a system for making sure inequities across the organization were addressed. The executive management of the company met to debate the pros and cons of what positions were equal to other positions within the company, and everyone had a chance to argue for their point of view. This process[4] made crystal clear to me the ongoing need to make allies within other departments and within HR."

HR can also be a great help in forecasting your people and space needs. Though explicit requests for people and space often flow up through your manager, an HR department is often responsible for helping to project growth to management. Making sure HR is aware of your current needs or "forecast" for people or space can often make acquiring those resources easier. If you do not use every avenue available to acquire the resources you need, your efforts will more likely be rebuffed.

Go out of your way to get to know the key members of the HR department. They can be of incredible help to you in difficult times as well as in your own personal advancement. As a former programmer yourself,

---

4. Brøderbund HR called this process the "card game," since all the positions were written on 3-by-5 index cards and laid out on a table where changes in ranking could be made visibly and tangibly. The process was very efficient and mostly fair, though Mickey didn't always get what he wanted.

you will likely feel strange about this since you probably viewed the HR department with much skepticism. But just as Dilbert has given programming managers a bad image, the caricatured Ratbert "evil HR director" has done the same for HR. They want to shed the "evil HR director" stigma in the same way you want to shed the "Pointy-Haired Boss" stigma. You will find that you can play this card to enlist them to help you further your plans and goals.

Finance and Managing Budgets

Most finance departments are charged with monitoring budgets and tracking expenses. In fact, though, they actually do many more things that are not nearly as apparent to the technical staff, such as paying bills, collecting payments due, tracking revenue, and running payroll.

Finance is the responsibility most technical managers dislike most. However, many technical managers are allocated a budget, explicitly or implicitly, and to be successful they must manage it. Even in the most cash-rich companies where profits and budget dollars seem to flow freely, knowing how to manage a technical budget is important.

....

In the beginning, everyone will talk about scope, and budget, and schedule, but in the end, nobody really cares about any of those things. The only thing they care about is this: People will love your software, or they won't. So that's the only criterion to which you should truly manage.

—*JOSEPH KLEINSCHMIDT, CTO and Cofounder,*
Leverage Software

Most managers, when they get budgetary control for the first time, don't realize that in programming departments only a very few budget line items are consequential. Almost all other budget items are insignificant. Don't spend time or energy on the petty stuff.

The following are budget items that most technical managers need to pay attention to.

HEADCOUNT. About 90 percent of a typical programming department's budget is in its headcount and allocated overhead (i.e., the cost of benefits, office space, IT, and the like that each salary is "burdened" with). Always make sure you budget adequately for the staff you anticipate needing, and that you base your numbers on market-rate salaries and anticipate any likely salary inflation. (Remember, if you hire the right people, the rest of your job will be a lot easier.) Delaying one hire by four to six weeks will have a dramatic budgetary effect on even a medium-size department. Our experience shows that hiring the right candidates almost always takes longer than you planned, which has the effect of freeing up dollars that can be allocated to cover other budget problem areas. That's about all the control you, as a manager, have over salaries and overhead.

CONSULTANTS AND CONTRACTORS   Make sure you have a consulting budget, and use it to make up for openings for which you can't hire the right people, or to get you through crisis situations. Mickey has always used budget from positions he hasn't filled to hire consultants and contractors to help out on small projects he would not otherwise get done.

EQUIPMENT AND TOOLS   Many development managers don't worry about equipment budgets; capitalizing the cost of desktops makes equipment costs inconsequential compared to salary costs. And there's a mapping: A new hire requires both salary and equipment. For those reasons, some managers are taught to think of equipment as allocated overhead. But if your organization is picky about making equipment cost "actuals" match "projected," make sure when you budget that you allocate dollars to turn over your equipment every two to three years. As a best practice when equipment dollars are tight, Mickey and Ron give their newest and best equipment to the programmers who are producing the best results.

Learn the rules for capitalizing equipment and accounting for subsequent depreciation. Most companies capitalize all but the cheapest equipment (that is, they write it down over a period of years, minimizing its impact on any given year, by removing the cost from the balance sheet and substituting a depreciation item—the fraction of the cost applicable to this year). Some companies are also permitted by complex tax and accounting rules to capitalize certain development costs.

Your finance department should be making the decisions regarding whether and how to capitalize equipment and development costs. With your finance department as an ally, this trick alone may allow you to manage within your budget yet effectively have more dollars to spend on staff or contractors.

Conversely, cash-rich companies often expense as much as possible, taking the expense off of the balance sheet as quickly as possible and driving every new dollar received to revenue. If you're in one of these companies, ignore all the preceding discussion about capitalization. You're in a great position to ask for, and receive, almost anything you need that will improve productivity and/or promise to reduce development time for new projects or products.

TRAVEL AND TRAINING   If you need to budget for travel, try to budget conservatively, but at least in traditional companies don't worry too much about this line. Most programming organizations travel infrequently.

For virtual organizations, however, budgeting travel requires much more scrutiny and planning. At Socialtext, for example, where development was scattered across three continents, $1,000 per programmer per quarter was budgeted so that each programmer could attend quarterly meetings to get face-to-face interaction—much more than would be budgeted for programmer travel in traditional organizations. Similarly, ensuring outsourcing success requires flying teams to work face-to-face periodically, as well as flying managers to assess and coordinate the multiple teams.

The other line items in the budget are of little or no consequence for most engineering managers.

In general, the bigger the department, the more important budgeting and tracking budgets become. Most budgets are tracked on a month-by-month basis but rolled up and reviewed quarterly. In most organizations, small variances (over or under budget amounts) are ignored each month, provided the variances at the end of the quarter are all positive or near zero.

As you may have inferred, we like to get agreement for overall expenses for our programming organizations, then have the flexibility to move funds between line items—for example, to lighten up on FTEs and bring in more contractors, or spend less on travel to fund more training. That works in some organizations, but others are more rigid about transferring money between budget lines.

In many (but far from all) organizations, if you have a positive variance (you spend less than you budgeted), you can carry it forward into the next quarter to spend the budgeted amount appropriately. Likewise, negative variances may be carried forward as well, with the expectation that you will spend less to cover the negative variance from the previous quarter.

The end of the fiscal year, however, usually calls for a forecast of budgets for the next fiscal year and a closeout of all budgeted items that all too often results in a "use it or lose it" mentality and inappropriate spending. We advise you never to spend just to deplete a budget, though the temptation will be very strong since the following year's budget may be reduced by the amount not spent. In those companies that deal with quarterly budgeting in the same way—that is, use it or lose it—the same advice applies.

Learning to speak the jargon of the finance world (it's not unlike the tech world, with tons of acronyms and rules that apply in certain situations) can help you interact with Finance appropriately. Mickey once attended a two-day mini MBA course that was tremendously effective at dispelling much of the mystery that had previously clouded his dealings with the finance department, and he recommends that you find such a course yourself. But neither of us recommends pursuing an actual MBA degree if your career plan is to remain a technical manager.[5]

Legal

Your contact with Legal is likely to be rare, but even in small companies where there is no in-house legal counsel, legal issues may arise that are important to understand and deal with. Most companies have new hires sign an intellectual property agreement that (basically) signs over the rights to all intellectual property developed on the job to the company, as well as a nondisclosure agreement (NDA) that requires employees to keep confidential a broad range of information from ideas to code. If questions or issues arise, they may motivate your first contact with your legal department, but as an effective manager you'll want to be proactive in getting to know Legal and reaching out to them for advice, direction, and approval. With a solid connection, you may find them reaching out to you for advice, as well. Areas that need particular attention include

- Contracts and licenses
- Open source software licenses
- Patents and other intellectual property (IP) issues

Managing Outside the Company

Most programming managers are focused on managing their programming team or teams. But there may be relationships outside your company to manage, in addition to any external technical staff you may have. These include

---

5. While our recommendation against getting an MBA degree may seem harsh, we've never seen where having an MBA actually helped a career in technical management. At Brøderbund when a candidate arrived with an MBA degree on his résumé, he would often be told that it "would not be held against him"—by the business side of the company!

- Customers
- Technology providers
- Technology innovators and work disruptors
- Tools vendors and suppliers
- Government, trade, and international standards organizations
- Industry consortiums
- Professional organizations
- University educators
- Local connections

As a programming manager, you may not need to actively manage some or most of these relationships; most would be managed at a higher level of your company or organization and many by other departments. But even if they don't fall to you, you should be aware of them and actively manage some of them, especially the ones that can directly impact you and your teams.

Customers

Meeting your company's customers is one of the most important things you can do. Go out of your way to meet with interesting customers and get to know their key technical contributors and decision makers. It will be good for your company and good for you.

Customers can fire everybody in the company from the chairman on down, simply by spending their money somewhere else.

—SAM WALTON, *Founder of Walmart*

The relationships we established working with customers have had a lasting impact on our lives. One of Mickey's E&S customers later hired him. Another of those customers recruited him when they founded Pixar. Others of our customers have become close friends—important parts of our personal lives for decades.

Technology Providers

We think almost every development manager needs to pay attention to key technologies and track when new versions are being released. The best example of a technology provider most of us should be aware of is Microsoft; its Windows platform shapes much of the world of software development today. Apple's OS X and iOS, Google's Android, Java, Adobe AIR, and similar platforms, technologies, and frameworks clearly fit into this category as well. So do compilers and IDEs.

What you do with that knowledge varies. If you must support a platform's emerging versions in your products, you must actively manage your relationship with that technology provider to be successful. Be aggressive at tracking their roadmaps and planning your development schedules to align. You may need to have developers or code at the ready in order to participate in early beta tests, for example.

On the other hand, an emerging platform may represent a distraction for your team. Perhaps what you need is little more than assurance of forward and backward compatibility until such time as others have proved the technology or it has become pervasive across your customer base. In that case, time spent evaluating the versions when they're new and identifying their impact on your products or organization too early is wasteful and disruptive. Your goal in tracking these technologies is to be aware of the siren song and keep your programmers from succumbing.

Mickey selects new technologies for evaluation carefully and calls up the image of Obi-Wan Kenobi to help explain why some technologies are not necessary to evaluate. "Beware the dark side of the force," he often says about new technologies that will suck time and resources with no obvious contribution other than some vendor's desire to find new customers. He used the saying with both his engineers and his CEO, all of whom were attracted to bright, glittery things.

If a technology is truly important, you will know soon enough if you need to adopt it. The rest will simply fade away without your expending any of your precious resources evaluating them.

....

Never change compilers, or upgrade to a new version, at the last stage of a sprint or product release.

Technology Innovators and Work Disruptors

Innovators with key technologies can greatly influence your development. A new generation of chips from Intel may dictate work you must eventually undertake. New rich Internet application (RIA) technologies have been disruptive to the work of teams developing highly interactive Web-based applications, putting them on the hot seat to embrace one or another of Flash, Flex, AIR, AJAX, JavaFX, Silverlight, Curl, HTML5, or some other approach. Mobile has meant picking platforms to support from a long list of possibilities.

Such decisions cannot be made lightly and should be part of a more strategic company roadmap process rather than a decision made by individual engineering managers. That said, having experience with a new technology (whether directly, or by having members of your staff evaluate it for you) can get you a seat at the table for these strategic discussions, which can be a good career move.

Be sure that decisions to embrace new technologies are always conscious ones; don't let your staff make them for you since they can have a far-reaching impact on your company or organization.

Bottom line: Be prepared to actively embrace or deflect technology innovators and work disruptors.

....

"Change equals opportunity" and "Beware of change" are the yin and yang of innovation and work disruptors.

Tools Vendors and Suppliers

As a programming manager, you are probably most impacted by the development tools your teams use, such as source control systems, compilers, IDEs, and project management tools. You should be constantly on the lookout for new tools you can make or buy that can help you and your teams work more effectively. Nurture relationships with the vendors of these tools; they will provide assistance, expertise, and even free products to encourage your use. They can also become a source of good networking opportunities and even friendships.

As an example, Mickey embraced a static code analyzer (sort of a super-lint) that he brought in to help him deliver better-quality products. "This tool helped us identify hundreds of potential bugs in our embedded software. The tool was not spotted by anyone on my technical staff, which disappointed me since they are the ones who should be ferreting out new tools that can help their teams work more effectively. Instead, I spotted it as I wandered a trade show floor looking for new products and services that could help us do our work better."

Locating this tool, and then having one of his directors evaluate and recommend it, was what it took to acquire this relatively costly tool for the teams that would use and benefit from it. The vendor provided lots of help and assistance, which was crucial in completing the evaluation with minimal impact to Mickey's staff. The relationship gave Mickey the opportunity to get to know the vendor better and eventually even produced a case study for the vendor, which Mickey sponsored and helped author. Finally, Mickey's staff got a reminder of his technical expertise and, perhaps more important, his industry experience. And Mickey leveraged the visibility to give credit to the director he enlisted to evaluate and champion the tool.

Government, Trade, and International Standards Organizations

Participating in standards committees can increase your interpersonal, debating, and social skills; give you a certain industry stature; vastly expand your network; but also try your patience, distract you from your core responsibilities, and otherwise take a toll.

Standards can be very important in the adoption of new technologies. They are set by committees and working groups of individuals and representatives of organizations and companies that have interest and expertise in the technologies.

Usually committee meetings are moved from locale to locale, often attractive international venues, perhaps as a perk to encourage participation. Become a committee member and you will be required to attend, giving you the opportunity to see places you might otherwise never find the time or have the opportunity to visit. While the meetings may be grueling, they are often accompanied by working dinners and social outings with opportunities to meet interesting and sometimes influential people. This is networking at its best.

The work is challenging because it entails drafting, reviewing, discussing, debating, arguing, voting, and considerable personal effort by many individuals. Many people thrive in such settings; others detest them. Regardless of your inclination, participating in one of these committees is something you may want to consider at some point in your career.

Mickey was on an ANSI (American National Standards Institute) committee in the seventies and eighties where he met several people who remain good friends to this day. He detested the committee work but considered it worth his time given the benefits it provided.

Industry Consortiums

Industry consortiums are similar to standards organizations but are typically less formally structured and run, without the requirement that their work product be suitable for scrutiny and public comment. Furthermore, you may not be eligible. Depending on the industry, participation may not be open to technical staff, or you may need to lobby or campaign to participate. Don't be shy; becoming part of the right working group can be a life-changing event: You get many of the travel, socializing, and networking benefits without the grueling work required by standards committees.

Professional Organizations

There are any number of professional organizations available to software developers, including ACM (Association for Computing Machinery, the professional organization for programmers), IEEE (Institute of Electrical and Electronics Engineers), and IGDA (International Game Developers Association). All of these organizations have publications and meetings that are worthwhile.

To increase your participation beyond reading their publications or attending their conferences or meetings, volunteer to participate in the organizations. They all want and need volunteers, and like the standards committees and industry consortia they provide an opportunity for travel, to meet people you might otherwise never meet, and to create lifelong friendships from the bonding that can occur while working toward a common goal outside the day-to-day workplace.

At Pixar, the ACM computer graphics special-interest group SIGGRAPH and its annual conference provided a showcase for the company's technical prowess and products, as well as a key venue for recruiting and networking. Mickey recalls that "many members of the Pixar technical staff are SIGGRAPH volunteers, and others have been awarded distinguished honors by SIGGRAPH for their technical contributions. It is an important professional community to Pixar and its employees."

Mickey has attended the SIGGRAPH conference almost every year since 1978 and continues to attend regularly, even when his company's products were not directly focused on computer graphics. The opportunity to network and reestablish friendships at each SIGGRAPH conference continues to be an important part of his life.

Starting at Apple, Ron made a point to attend the conferences put on by SIGCHI, ACM's special-interest group focused on the computer-human interface, as well as monthly meetings of its Bay Area chapter. The focus on getting the user experience right led many Apple staff to both participate in and be a force within the CHI community.

We encourage you to investigate a professional organization that has topics of interest to you. Step beyond your boundaries. Attend and volunteer to help. You will likely find that you will expand your professional circle of friends, explore new horizons, and find unanticipated personal and professional rewards.

University Educators

Regardless of where you are located, there will be university researchers and educators near you. Meet them and form relationships whenever possible. Computer science and information technology educators can give you advice and consult with you. More importantly, they can recommend students to you (and you to their students), becoming an important source for recruiting raw talent and new employees. These relationships will likely require little more than an occasional e-mail or lunch (on you) to keep current but may lead to expanding your social network and friendships. This is an investment of time that can pay big rewards.

You can also establish more formal ties with local educators. Years ago Mickey pioneered a relationship with the University of California Berkeley International Diploma Program, which requires that each student complete a three- to four-month internship. The internships that Gracenote provided to a continuous flow of their students in turn provided Gracenote with local expertise from around the world to improve its music information. The interns were not only motivated and knowledgeable but went back to their home countries as evangelists for Gracenote and its products.

The opportunities for working with local educators are endless; take the time and you will likely find yourself rewarded many times over for the time you invest.

Local Connections

Take every opportunity to expand your connections with local technical talent. Do this by networking at local professional organization meetings, by attending trade shows, by reviewing interesting résumés and inviting the candidates to come talk to you even if you do not think you will be able to hire them (keep the résumés you review, grouped by type of person—for example, product managers, Web programmers, DSP programmers, etc.). Be a constant talent scout, looking for talent that you may someday be able to use.

> *Your power is almost directly proportional to the thickness of your Rolodex and the time you spend maintaining it. Put bluntly the most potent people I've known have been the best networkers—they "know everybody from everywhere" and have just been out to lunch with most of them.*
>
> —*TOM PETERS*[6]

A number of the important technical staff at Gracenote (including the current president) had their first contact from a phone call by Mickey to "chat" followed by an invitation to stop by, have lunch, and continue to talk. Often these people were hired a number of months later when the right opportunity for their talent opened up. At Brøderbund, Mickey hired one programmer more than two years after first chatting with him.

Ron's Best Practices SIG cochair, Mark Friedman, recently created a consulting organization seeded with talent that had emerged at their meetings (including, in one engagement with a start-up, bringing Ron in to consult with the engineering VP on the topics of this book, making his team more manageable and changing how they worked in a way that dramatically improved both results and morale).

The important thing to remember is never to pass up an opportunity to connect with people who appear technically interesting. Reach out, talk to them, meet with them, and keep them in mind. Save résumés in well-categorized folders. Keep a Rolodex of interesting contacts. Leverage LinkedIn. Use any tool that will help you meet, classify, and remember great technical talent.

In addition to cochairing Software Development Best Practices, Emerging Technology, and Software Architecture SIGs in the Bay Area, Ron regularly attends Agile, Engineering Leadership, Consulting, and software and product management SIGs and meetups, which not only keep him current

---

6. Tom Peters, *The Pursuit of Wow!* (Vintage Books, 1994), p. 36.

with emerging technologies and approaches but provide a rich network of colleagues to partner with and hire.

Bottom Line

Managing out is an important part of being a very effective manager; it's less about doing a good solid job of managing programmers and more about long-term career growth. The extra effort is not rewarded with direct deliverables from your staff but with a richer personal and professional network, both within your company and without, and with more effective hiring and recruiting, all of which can have a big impact on your staff and on the delivery of its projects and products.

Managing Yourself

The hardest person to manage is always you. Each one of us is well versed in denial—we overlook bad habits, poor practices, and questionable behavior we would not tolerate in others. To effectively manage yourself requires first realistically assessing your habits, practices, and behaviors; identifying those you want to change; and implementing plans that will lead to improvement. Areas to assess include

- Personal style
- Time and priority management
- Communications management
- Management practices
- Follow-up management
- Find a mentor

Personal Style

One important thing to look at is your personal style—that is, how you comport yourself overall. Style includes many things, from your appearance and dress, how hard you work, your punctuality, your behavior (personal and professional), your consistent interest in your staff as people and not just programmers, and other factors. We feel it is important that you choose a style that is basically you and then make small modifications, if necessary, to improve on that style. The following are some examples that have worked for us.

Appropriate Appearance

The old adage "You are what you wear" is a good one to think about. If you appear slovenly, you will have to do more to rise above negative perceptions of that appearance as you interact with your boss and other executive management. (Your team will likely not be as sensitive to this as your peers and upper management.)

The challenging side of this change is that if it results in your dressing significantly better than your staff (for example, wearing a coat and tie every day while your team is in T-shirts), it can be an artificial barrier to communicating with them.

We recommend that you strike a good balance between appearing like just one of your team and dressing to impress upper management. Mickey chose his style long ago, when he was in college: "I went to college in the late sixties/early seventies and like most wore 501 Levi's almost all the time, along with my rough-out cowboy boots. But I also was a professional guitar teacher with dozens of students every week. My compromise was to wear my 501s and cowboy boots with clean, pressed dress shirts. I adopted this attire as my 'uniform,' and it carried me through most of my career.

"There were times when I actually had to wear a tie and dress pants every day, but I didn't stay long in those places. It just wasn't me. Of course, there were times when I wore a suit and tie all the time (like on visits to Japan, where that attire is expected), but that was the exception. In my last job, as SVP of Development at Gracenote, I actually dressed in slacks and shoes rather than 501s and cowboy boots most of the time since I (unfortunately) spent as much time (or more) with my peers and boss as with my staff.

"Even then, I would often wear my 501s and cowboy boots whenever I was mostly with my staff, and I adopted a long-standing tradition of casual Fridays and Hawaiian shirts instead of button-down—but even my Hawaiian shirts were always clean and pressed!"

Mickey is convinced that this kind of "middle-of-the-road" approach helped him relate to both his peers and his staff effectively. It has worked for him for over 40 years.

Your style, of course, is dictated by where you work and what the work culture is at your company or organization. If you worked at IBM in the seventies and eighties, you wore a white shirt and tie. But in most high-tech start-ups and organizations in the United States today, attire is not dictated, so you have a chance to set your own style.

Cleanliness and good personal hygiene are givens; make no compromises there.

Work Ethic

Your work ethic is something you get to choose, but our experience shows that those with a good work ethic are most successful. Many managers and executives subscribe to the belief that "first one at work, last one to leave" is the best approach. In Japan, where the people are known for their over-the-top work ethic, that is the de facto behavior of all managers.

Mickey and Ron have also subscribed to this belief and spent their careers operating this way. But it actually is more than just being the first one in the office and the last one to leave; it is leading by example. That is the better approach to choosing a good work ethic, since it extends far beyond just being there for your team. It extends to never asking your team to do something that you yourself wouldn't do. To that end, Mickey never asked a team to spend a late night or weekend without also staying late or coming in on the weekend to work with them.

In today's day and age of 24/7 communication, you really never leave the office; you're (unfortunately) always at work, so leading by example is a much better way to operate. Make sure you always think about the example you set in all your actions, such as arriving for work early and leaving late and being available 24/7 if necessary, arriving on time for meetings, coming prepared for discussions, acting professionally at all times, saying "thank you" to your staff and teams, and every other way you telegraph your character.

....

Leading by example occurs whether you like it or not.

—*JATEEN PAREKH, Founder and CTO*
of Jelli Crowdsourced Radio

These are the actions that speak the loudest to your staff. There will be more on this topic in Chapter 7 where it is discussed in relation to motivating your staff.

Know Your Staff

There are two styles managers often choose between: being aloof and distant, or being one of the team. But in reality, neither choice works well if taken to the extreme.

We recommend that you steer a course that begins on the former path, since you cannot just be one of the team if you are to manage them successfully. However, you don't want to be so aloof and distant that you don't socialize with or get to know the team. You must be open and accessible, so your staff will be willing to come talk to you about problems or issues, regardless of whether they report directly or indirectly to you.

> *If a team member drops by at an awkward time and wants to chat, set aside what you're doing and pay attention. They may be building up the courage to tell you something big. I've noticed this to be especially true when the sudden chatter isn't from somebody who normally drops by for idle conversation. It might be as simple as being unable to get a piece of information needed to complete a task or might be as big as an impending divorce, the death of a loved one, or something equally devastating on a personal level to them . . . things that can throw a real monkey wrench into your carefully laid schedule. If they know you'll make them your top priority when they drop by, they're more likely to drop by sooner when things are about to go very wrong.*
>
> —TIM SWIHART

The best path here is to find opportunities to get to know your staff personally. Remember when they started at the company (their anniversary date); know where they are from and when they go back home for visits (you learn a lot about people by talking with them about their hometown); know the names of their spouses or partners and how many children they have (if any); know what kind of car they drive and what they would like to have; know where they like to go for vacation and what hobbies they have. These are the types of things you should find out to help you know your staff better. And the better you know them, the more they will feel open to talking with you about anything.

There will be more on this topic in Chapter 7 as it is discussed with regard to motivating your staff.

The important takeaway here is to consciously think about what style you have and what style you would like to cultivate. It takes work, but the payoff is important to your success as a programming manager.

Time and Priority Management

The most important commodity you have is your time. Be stingy with it, but at the same time give it freely to those who really need it. Find ways to manage it well, and your life will be better.

....

Don't let the day-to-day eat you up.

— *DAVID DIBBLE, EVP, Schwab Technical Services*

The key to effective time management is to keep an active and accurate calendar. Outlook and more recently Google Calendar and other group and personal calendars have made this easier, but at the same time they have made it more difficult. Mickey uses his Outlook calendar to control all the appointments, meetings, and activities in his life. He loads all work items, as well as personal items, into the calendar. However, he does not let his calendar control him. That is, he delegates control to people for viewing or rearranging his calendar, but he does not delegate the ability to accept meeting invitations. Some people do delegate their calendar completely to an assistant but, given that they are delegating control of their lives, do so usually only after finding an assistant truly attuned to their priorities.

By keeping an accurate calendar, viewable by others, you demonstrate your planning and management abilities on a daily basis. Make sure you are on time for meetings and appointments; make sure you end meetings on time; do not tolerate poor meeting etiquette in others.

To ensure that he is on time for meetings, Mickey keeps the clocks in his office and cars and his wristwatch seven minutes fast. Though he knows the clocks are seven minutes fast, this buffer keeps him (mostly) on time, even if the previous meeting has run over by a few minutes.

A critical time management tool is a priority list of items to do. Creating a "to do" list that gives you immediate visibility to what needs to be done is a great step toward better time management. Create a new "to do" list each day, either by reviewing your current list and striking items you have completed or creating a new list. Don't bother to try to create the list in any order. Make sure you add to this list during the day, as new things come up and you remember items you previously forgot to put on the list.

Then prioritize the list.

....

Every hour of planning saves about a day of wasted time and effort.

—STEVE MCCONNELL, *CEO and Chief Software Engineer, Construx Software, and Author,* Code Complete *and* Rapid Development[7]

One tool to help you prioritize your "to do" list is to recognize the difference between "urgent" and "important."

ur·gent—*adjective.* compelling or requiring immediate action or attention; imperative; pressing: *an urgent matter.*

im·por·tant—*adjective.* of much or great significance or consequence: *an important event in world history.*

We hope nearly everything on your priority list is either urgent, important, or both. The key to prioritizing is to identify those items that are neither urgent nor important and strike them from the list, and to find those items that are both urgent and important and do those first, working the urgent or important items next, choosing as best you can to prioritize them appropriately. Prioritizing the urgent and important items is key; too often we allow the urgent to prevent us from ever solving the important. Figure 6.1 shows this as a truth table where the urgent and important items are the "Do Now" category.

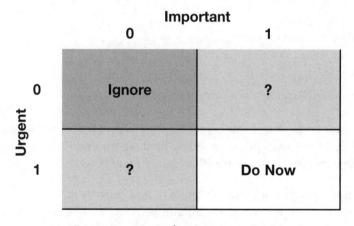

Figure 6.1   Urgent/Important truth table

---

7. Steve McConnell, *Code Complete, Second Edition* (Microsoft Press, 2007), and *Rapid Development: Taming Wild Software Schedules* (Microsoft Press, 1996).

Mickey often keeps his "to do" list in an Excel spreadsheet, so that he can print it out quickly and add or strike items easily. A priority column enables sorting the list from highest to lowest priority, making it easier to visualize the list and work on the top-priority projects first.

Most successful people keep lists of things to do. By making this an integral part of your life, you too will find the power and feeling of accomplishment from managing your "to do" list each day.

Communications Management

The advance of technology has created avenues for communication that far outstrip our ability to deal with them. E-mail, text messages, "always-on" smartphones, blogs, tweets, social networks, Skype, RSS feeds, and other technologies now permeate our lives in ways that would have been unimaginable only a few years ago. We have become slaves to this communication onslaught in ways that appear to have diminished the overall quality of our lives. Many, especially the younger generations who grew up with this "always-on" barrage of information, are addicted to it, as shown by the uproar and disruption when Twitter or Facebook goes down.

To be an effective manager you must establish control over the flood of information and manage it. You cannot let it rule you.

The biggest impediment to concentration is your computer's ecosystem of interruption technologies . . . leaving your IM running is like sitting down to work after hanging a giant DISTRACT ME *sign over your desk.*

—CORY DOCTOROW, *Science Fiction Writer*[8]

This is not an easy task, and we have no foolproof recommendations or we might well have written a best-selling book about that instead. However, a few things are clear in the context of managing effectively:

1. You must establish a workable practice and process for managing your work e-mail—much of the e-mail you receive must be responded to in a timely fashion—and you must establish methods and boundaries for managing your electronic calendar.

---

8. Cory Doctorow, *Context* (Tachyon Publications, 2011).

2. You cannot let the constant barrage of e-mail distract you from your important job of managing your staff and projects. The "ding" of a new e-mail message carries with it a sense of urgency, but it is likely not important. Keep focused on the important things.

There is never a way to improve productivity in the short term. . . . The only real variable you have to play with is the proportion of work hours that are effective. . . . You have to focus entirely on avoiding wasted time.

—TOM DEMARCO[9]

3. Just because someone calls or texts you, you do *not* have to answer or respond. This is especially true for callers who vie for your attention. Recruiters could take up an hour of more of your time each day if you let them. If you happen to take a call from someone you do not know and do not need to know, get rid of them quickly (hang up on them if necessary). It is OK; they are intruding on your time! It is important to learn as a first-time manager that you own your time.

4. While in meetings or in focused moments, do not allow your attention to be diverted by answering calls or text messages. We try to keep our cell phones on vibrate, so that we can subtly check to see if an urgent call is coming in without disrupting a meeting. We will rarely answer a call during a meeting, letting it fall over to voicemail for all but the most urgent calls or important callers. We also turn our phones off when in sessions (sometimes only with ourselves) where focus is required and disruptions would be very distracting.

5. Set communication boundaries and realistic expectations. In this day when people have expectations for a quick response to almost every inquiry, it is imperative that you set communications boundaries and make sure they are workable for the people you work with (and in your personal life). Mickey usually reads e-mail at the beginning and end of each day. He does not respond to every e-mail that comes along immediately, even if he could, so that expectations are not raised for an immediate response from him. He will, of course, monitor his in-box and respond to important messages during the day, but the bulk of the messages and meeting invitations go unanswered for hours.

---

9. DeMarco, *The Deadline*, p. 79.

6. Use assistants, if available and appropriate, to delegate meeting management. Outlook and other calendaring systems allow you to designate delegates who can access your calendar. These delegates can be assigned levels of access—for example, view only, or view and edit meetings. This will allow others to be able to change meeting times and move your schedule around appropriately. It is possible to shield personal items from your delegates, which we strongly encourage for confidentiality and to maintain control of your life. Don't delegate your life away.

7. Plan your time carefully to reduce demands and a flood of information. Review your calendar each week and each day, and make sure you block off time to do work you need to do. Open time on your calendar will often be sucked up by meetings, some of which you really don't need to attend. Pick and choose your attendance carefully and consciously. Don't just accept because you were invited. "Do I really need to be there?" is a question you should ask yourself and those who invite you to meetings. Mickey prints out his calendar each day for the current and following day (double-sided for easy reference) and uses it to control his time. Last-minute meetings will go unattended unless the inviter reaches out and contacts Mickey personally to confirm attendance. That seems like a problem, but it actually helps instill a respectful approach to meeting etiquette that is too often sorely lacking.

8. Establish, or help establish, appropriate e-mail etiquette. We are flooded with e-mail on a daily basis, some (if not much) of which could be avoided if proper e-mail etiquette were followed. Help educate others in the appropriate use of e-mail by working to establish and promote organization-wide e-mail etiquette to reduce this flood of e-mail. A set of suggested e-mail and meeting planning etiquette guidelines is included as a tool for this chapter. Figure 6.2 shows an example of some good e-mail etiquette guidelines.

There are many other techniques for managing the information barrage that is part of your daily life. The key is to consciously work at managing this flood of information effectively. You cannot let it control you—you must control it.

E-MAIL

Is e-mail the right vehicle?

- Phone or face-to-face may be more appropriate.

Be clear and to the point.

- Create a meaningful subject line. Use the best possible description of your topic and purpose in the subject line.
- Clearly indicate when an action or decision is needed, if comments are requested, or if the message is just an FYI.

Use To/CC/BCC appropriately.

- People on the To line should expect an action item; the CC line is for FYI only.
- Be very careful when using BCC. Forwarding a person a sent e-mail may be safer.

Avoid overusing Reply All.

- If the message was sent to a distribution list, consider whether everyone on the list really needs to see your reply.
- Reduce threads to just the appropriate people; distribution lists are not always appropriate.

Stay on topic.

- Make sure your comments are appropriate for the subject-line topic.
- Stick to one topic in a thread.
- If the topic changes, start a new thread with a new subject.

Reduce lengthy e-mail threads.

- If an e-mail thread goes back and forth more than three times, call or set up a meeting to discuss the topic.
- Be careful when forwarding threads to new or external people; there may be something in the thread you do not want everyone to see.

Figure 6.2   Sample e-mail etiquette

Management Practices

To manage effectively, you must establish management practices that work for you and your staff and make you successful. In our experience, this mostly means communicating effectively, one-on-one and in a team setting. The following are some management practices we have found effective and that work for us. Review this set, but think consciously about what will work for you and create your own list of practices that you use religiously.

To be an effective manager, you must be an effective communicator. The most effective communicators are good listeners. People in general and your staff in particular want to be heard. If you are not listening to them, they will not be happy. Period.

> *Wisdom is the reward you get for a lifetime of listening when you'd rather have been talking.*
>
> —*ARISTOTLE*

This means you need to develop and refine good listening skills. There are a variety of books, courses, and seminars on the topic, but the following points summarize some simple practices you can follow (in any conversation) to enhance your personal skills.

Pay Attention to the Person

It is surprising how few people actually follow this simple practice. Put down your phone or crackberry, stop doing e-mail, sit back, and look at the person doing the talking.

> *The single biggest problem in communication is the illusion that it has taken place.*
>
> —*GEORGE BERNARD SHAW*

Make eye contact and listen carefully to what the other person has to say (and process the information they're presenting). Note that information is not restricted to their words: Observe their posture and body language and their degree of passion or engagement. Take in everything. Often the nonverbal clues are the most telling.

Listen Reflectively

This means taking in what a person says and then playing back or paraphrasing what you think you heard to make sure you understood them correctly. This often starts with finding a break in their monologue and saying something like "So let me see if I understand; you're saying that widget x needs gadget y to operate correctly?"

Like many of you reading this book, we came up through the ranks as programmers ourselves; programmers are not known for our communications skills and are portrayed by jokes like this one: "What's the difference between an introverted and an extroverted programmer? An extroverted programmer looks at *your* shoes when you're talking."

Break Down Barriers to Communication

Having a conversation with someone from behind a desk—or really with anything between you and the other person—is off-putting. At times this is appropriate, such as if you are going to be "coming down" on someone or terminating them. But if you are trying to communicate with them, stand up from your desk, walk around it, and sit down next to them. Then turn your chair to face them (either directly, or at least more frontally). This does two things: It says, "I am giving you my complete attention and am here for you," and it symbolically removes any barriers to communication and suggests, "Let's work together" or "Let's solve the problem(s) together."

Both Mickey and Ron have followed this practice consistently. Mickey made sure he conducted all of his one-on-one meetings with his staff sitting side-by-side in his office. Similarly, he conducted all interviews with candidates sitting close together facing each other. One of the people who joined Gracenote told Mickey that a key factor in his decision to join the company was Mickey's walking around his desk to sit next to him during his initial interview. He related that the openness and congeniality he felt from that simple act were key factors in making him want to work at the company—a simple act with far-reaching impact.

Understand What Is Really Important

Many people view management as a top-down, authoritative position, that is, being on top of the pyramid—king of the hill. We would counsel, instead, that you consider yourself to be at the bottom of a pyramid, with your staff on top. They, and the work they do, are what are really important.

To lead the people, walk behind them.

—*LAO-TZU*

This view is what we call the "inverted pyramid," where the people who do the actual work are on top, and those who manage them are on the bottom. Those on the bottom are delegated problems to resolve that have stymied those on the top. Treating those on the top with respect and appreciation is natural, and understanding that they can delegate to you, not vice versa, empowers them and puts your job in true perspective.

If he works for you, you work for him.

—*OLD JAPANESE PROVERB*

The inverted pyramid, as shown in Figure 6.3, is a powerful image to convey to your staff; use it frequently in explaining your role—not just to your direct reports, but to all those who report indirectly to you as well.

Of course, acting appropriately on what is really important is hardly limited to your interactions with your staff. Make sure that you are truly

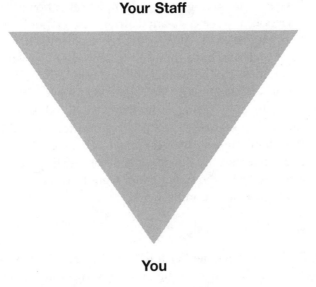

Figure 6.3   The inverted pyramid

working on important things that will make a major difference in the long run, not just the near term. Given the increased demands on your time today, this means you have to pick and choose what things you will address. Consciously choose the important ones, and let the unimportant ones slide.

An excellent example that even the most seasoned manager faces is hiring. If you have an open requisition to hire someone, it should be on the top of the list of things you need to get done. The more you delay, the longer it will be before you actually have help in place to get things done. What could be more important? Yet, in the day-to-day world of meetings, tasks assigned to you, reports to be completed, and other work, filling open positions can too easily take a back seat to those other activities. Make items like hiring a top priority and spend at least some time on them each day.

Make Progress Every Day

If at the end of every day you have accomplished only one important thing, at the end of a year you will have accomplished 365 important things (or 260 if you did just one a day for every workday in a year). Make a task list each day and knock off as many tasks as possible. Feel a sense of accomplishment for each task you complete. Relish the fact that the list has shrunk each time a task is completed or removed, even if it was removed because it was no longer necessary! Applaud yourself for your accomplishments each day. Make a toast over a glass of wine at night and savor the small victories of the day.

Be Part of the Solution, Not Part of the Problem

All too often we find ourselves caught up in situations that, for whatever reason, don't make sense. It may be that you were delegated a problem that has now become an albatross around your neck, or it may be that you find yourself contributing to the confusion around an issue, not the solution. When you find that happening, make sure you step back and reassess the situation. Determine if you need to let go of the problem or the direction in which you have been driving a solution. Often you can allow another solution to present itself without imposing your will.

However, sometimes being part of the problem is a good thing. For example, Mickey was constantly challenged by one of his CEOs to make projects meet their agreed-upon schedules. Yet schedules continued to slip on occasion. That is because Mickey has a firm belief that in most software development projects, the work will fill the time allotted to the tasks. Making less aggressive schedules will lead to a bigger problem, that of not getting key deliverables done.

Mickey tried to be part of the problem and not part of the solution, which he pointed out to his CEO from time to time. "I am part of the problem here by choosing to schedule aggressively, even if we may slip a few dates," Mickey told his CEO. "If I were to create a schedule we could be guaranteed to meet, you would not like the schedule. In my experience effort will fill the time allotted, so I schedule aggressive times knowing full well they will likely slip, but resulting in completing projects in about the shortest period possible."

Which is the bigger problem: projects that take too long across the board or schedules that occasionally slip but are closer to optimum? Mickey consciously chose the latter and defended his actions as being part of a good problem, not a bad solution. It usually disarmed the conversation.

The key here (and with most things) is making a conscious decision to be part of the problem, not an unconscious one! Generally you should be part of the solution, not part of the problem, so being part of the problem should be rare and done very consciously.

Follow-Up Management

As discussed in the section on time management, keeping a daily "to do" list is usually a key part of time management. However, follow-up management—that is, following up on the things you were supposed to get done—is as important as time management. Following up is usually way too much of your job as a manager. "Was this done? If not, why not? When will it be done?" These are obvious questions for those who report to you, but they are also important questions for yourself.

As we discussed earlier, not everything must be done. We discussed important versus urgent tasks, and how delaying some urgent but less important tasks may actually make them go away. That is a good tactic when you can use it. But regardless of the importance of a task, you need ways to ensure that things that need to get done actually get done.

There are three primary tactics we suggest you embrace to help ensure that you follow up on tasks and assignments.

Daily Task List

As discussed earlier, this is the primary tool that Ron and Mickey employ in their daily lives to make sure the important things get done. Prepare the list every morning and cross items off as you accomplish them during the day. Outlook and other calendar programs provide an electronic version of the task list that automatically carries forward from day to day and is effective for some. Ron keeps a simple TextEdit list. Regardless of the mechanism you employ, embrace one and use it daily.

The one thing that Mickey has done for the past 20-plus years that he finds especially effective is to start each day by spending 15 to 20 minutes in his hot tub contemplating the results from the previous day(s) and thinking about the important things he needs to accomplish that day. While these are not always work-related, often they are. This morning ritual has helped him retain his sanity over the years, and when it can't happen (for whatever reason—being out of town or having a very early morning meeting, for example), he misses it very much. Ron feels the same way about his morning shower. This contemplative effort usually surfaces two or three things he must accomplish that day and brings them to the front of his mind—which is good, since writing them down in the hot tub or shower is very difficult. So we couple our practices with a first-thing-in-the-office (or at home on the weekends) practice of reviewing yesterday's task list with today's "front of mind" items and making a combined new daily task list.

These daily rituals work for us, but you will need to find your own rituals that work for you.

We have run across a lot of technical people who like David Allen's *Getting Things Done*[10] (GTD) as a formalized methodology and tool set for personal productivity. It doesn't matter what tools you use, as long as you make them a daily ritual and make them work for you.

Action Items

Action items are similar to daily lists but are usually more formalized and part of a larger process. For example, at Gracenote most of the management and project meetings had a designated recorder who took notes of action items and distributed them afterward. When the meeting reconvened,

---

10. David Allen, *Getting Things Done* (Penguin Books, 2002), www.davidco.com.

the first act would be to review these action items and record the status, progress, or closure of each one.

....

A meeting without notes is a meeting that never happened.

—NATALIE DEJARLAIS, *Director of Applications Development, San Francisco Bay Area*

If people take them seriously, action item lists can be a great way to ensure follow-up on things that must get done. It usually takes management support and peer pressure to make them effective. Those who do not follow up on their action items should be coached to improve during their quarterly or annual reviews.

Reminders

Most calendar programs also provide an automatic reminder feature that will allow you to set a reminder for a later day, not only for you but for others. Some of Mickey's staff (those dealing directly with customers) used these frequently to make sure they got the follow-up from the programming staff (and Mickey directly) that was needed in a timely manner. Mickey relates, "The Professional Services folks at Gracenote managed our post-sales customer relationships and had a continual stream of questions and issues that needed to be followed up and resolved. They used many mechanisms, but one they employed for important and urgent items was to set a reminder for those from whom they expected a follow-up response. Since they reserved this for important and urgent items, when you saw one of these pop up for you, you knew that you must address it right away. They were used very effectively."

Find a Mentor

As part of your continued learning as a manager, find one or more mentors. If you were to poll a reasonable sample of very successful people, you would likely find that many of them would point to one or more mentors in their life who helped them in some significant ways to become the successful people they now are.

Books have been written on finding and building mentor relationships, but the essence is identifying an approachable person you respect and asking them to help guide your career development and navigate management's hard problems. Not everyone you contact will make themselves available, so you must be persistent in your quest until you have one or more people engaged with you on your journey.

You can do your asking in a very explicit fashion—or not. Many stories have been told of the junior person who has become a fast-rising star after having sought out a seasoned senior executive as a mentor, not unlike Luke Skywalker seeking out Obi-Wan Kenobi in his quest to master the Force and become a Jedi knight. Such relationships are powerful and are retold in myth and story.

However, implicit mentoring is much more common, though less legendary. Implicit mentoring often is a by-product of a work relationship or a chance encounter when the person looking for guidance follows up to make it something more. Over his career Ron has followed up with managers with whom he interviewed and felt immediate respect for and connection with, contacting them after his job search was complete to follow up, suggest an informal meal, and judge the mutual interest in a friendship or at least occasional get-together. In fact, this is how Ron and Mickey turned a one-time interview into a lasting friendship and this book.

The key ingredients to getting a mentor are being open to the opportunity and seizing the initiative.

Our advice to you is to look for those whom you respect and from whom you would welcome guidance in your life and career, then engage with them in some small or larger way.

Bottom Line

People too often think of themselves last. They pay themselves last by contributing to their savings only after everything else. They turn their attention to their own professional growth and personal discipline last, too.

Making time to manage yourself effectively will pay big dividends in your day-to-day work. The topics covered in this section are suggestions for ways to manage yourself more effectively, but it's you who needs to spend the time reflecting—and perhaps collecting feedback from your respected mentors—to identify what you really need.

Make the time to work on managing yourself; set aside an hour every week by blocking off an appointment with yourself and spend it proactively focused on improving your own style, your time and priority management, your communications, and your follow-up habits, or with a mentor.

It may be the best hour you spend every week.

Summary

This chapter is an important one for those managers who want to manage their careers. Few managers will rise through an organization merely on the strength of their skills in managing programmers alone, which are the focus of the other chapters in this book. But also managing up, out, and yourself will help set you apart; make you an even more effective manager of your team(s); and also help you create the visibility, relationships, and impact that can help turbopower your career.

Tools

We have prepared two tools to assist you in managing yourself. The Word documents provide examples that you can easily adapt for your organization. See the Tools section, after the chapters, for the link to the Tools Web site, from which you can download the following tools:

- Sample e-mail etiquette
- Sample meeting planning guide

7
Motivating Programmers

CHAPTER 5 DISCUSSED THE VARIOUS FACETS OF MANAGING PROGRAMMERS. One of them—being able to actually motivate them to accomplish great feats and deliver difficult projects—is so important to managing effectively that this chapter is devoted to this single topic. You can be good at this and passable at most of the rest of the topics in this book and still be a great software manager. If, however, you are not good at motivating your staff, you will not likely succeed as a software manager.

With that in mind, it is important that you relate the information presented in this chapter to your own experience and blend the two into a method and style that will work for you. We encourage you to seriously consider the manner in which you try to motivate each programmer and redouble your efforts armed with the knowledge presented here. It will benefit you and your organization.

Motivational Theories

Several motivational theories emerged during the twentieth century that have helped shape the thinking of businesses regarding motivation. Though a bit theoretical for this book, it is important to be aware of these theories since they periodically but inevitably come up during management discussions. Having a basic knowledge of these theories will help you speak more authoritatively regarding your motivational efforts and gain management support for them.

Though the literature is now rife with motivational theories, there are three primary ones that warrant brief review:

- Maslow's Hierarchy of Needs
- McGregor's X-Y Theory
- Herzberg's Motivation and Hygiene Factors

Maslow's Hierarchy of Needs[1]

Abraham Maslow developed the Hierarchy of Needs model in the middle of the last century. His book *Motivation and Personality,*[2] originally published in 1954, introduced the Hierarchy of Needs to the business world. Maslow maintained that human needs can be categorized into levels, from the most basic like food and shelter to the highest, reaching for self-betterment—and that we are not capable of being motivated by a level until our needs at all the underlying levels are fully satisfied.

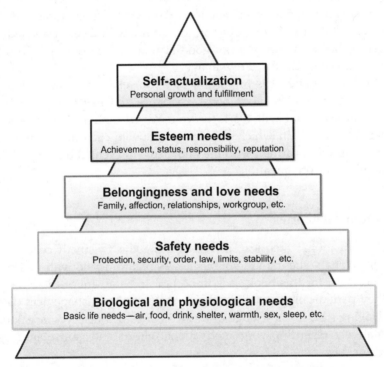

Figure 7.1   Maslow's Hierarchy of Needs

---

1. A. H. Maslow, "A Theory of Human Motivation," *Psychological Review* 50, no. 4 (1943): 370–96.

2. Abraham Maslow, *Motivation and Personality* (Harper, 1954).

The Hierarchy of Needs theory is considered as valid today as when Maslow devised it, and it is frequently introduced in management training for understanding human motivation and personal development. Indeed, Maslow's ideas surrounding the Hierarchy of Needs continue to challenge us today to provide workplace environments that encourage and enable employees to fulfill their own unique potential (self-actualization).

Mickey: "It is surprising how often Maslow's Hierarchy of Needs comes up during serious management discussions, though not always in the context of motivating staff. I have been in meetings regarding product features and marketing rollout plans where a reference to Maslow's Hierarchy will be thrown out to ensure that we are addressing the primary needs of our customers or prospects. It has also come up during staffing and planning discussions regarding compensation, space, and equipment."

You do not need to have a detailed grasp of all the levels of the hierarchy, but understanding that people are motivated in very similar ways based on physical, psychological, and emotional needs is important. Study Maslow's hierarchy and understand the various levels, and it will help you be a better manager and recognize and address these needs in those you manage.

McGregor's X-Y Theory

Douglas McGregor proposed his famous X-Y Theory in his 1960 book *The Human Side of Enterprise.*[3] Theory X and Theory Y are still commonly referred to in the field of management and motivation, and while more recent studies have questioned the rigidity of the model, McGregor's X-Y Theory remains a valid basic principle from which to develop a positive management style and techniques. McGregor's X-Y Theory remains central to organizational development and to improving organizational culture.

McGregor's X-Y Theory is a simple reminder to use common sense in managing people, which under the pressure of day-to-day business is all too easily forgotten.

McGregor maintained that there are two fundamental approaches to managing people. Some managers tend toward Theory X (authoritarian) and generally get poor results. Enlightened managers use Theory Y (empowering), which produces better performance and results and allows people to grow and develop (see Figure 7.2).

While Theory X is not widely used in software and high-tech companies in the United States, it is much more prevalent in some other cultures (Japan,

---

3. Douglas McGregor, *The Human Side of Enterprise* (McGraw-Hill, 1960).

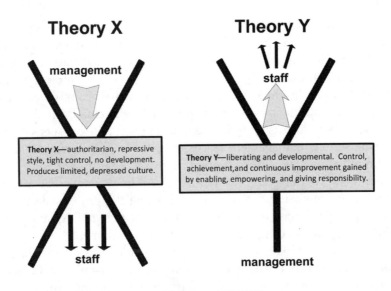

Figure 7.2   McGregor's X-Y Theory

Korea, China, and old-school India). In those cultures, a strong authoritarian approach is deeply ingrained in many companies and engineering practices. This is something to be aware of and may require that you deploy an alternate management approach when working with offshore teams or developers.

Theory X-Y provides a tool for discussing alternative management styles with your staff and those in cultures where the Theory X approach is common. Understanding that not everyone responds to management the same way will give you an upper hand in being more effective.

Herzberg's Motivation and Hygiene Factors

Frederick Herzberg, clinical psychologist and pioneer of "job enrichment," is regarded as one of the great original thinkers in management and motivational theory. His book *The Motivation to Work,*[4] written with research colleagues Mausner and Snyderman in 1959, first established his theories about motivation in the workplace. Herzberg expanded his motivation-hygiene theory in his subsequent books, and the absence of any serious challenge to Herzberg's theory continues to effectively validate it.

---

4. F. Herzberg, B. Mausner, and B. Snyderman, *The Motivation to Work* (Wiley, 1959).

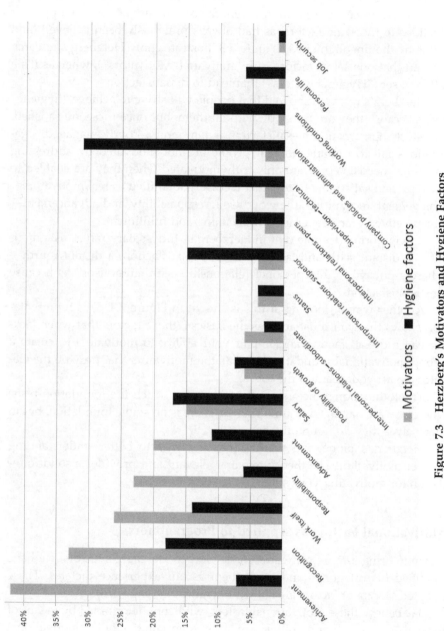

Figure 7.3   Herzberg's Motivators and Hygiene Factors

Herzberg was the first to show that satisfaction and dissatisfaction at work nearly always arise from different factors and are not simply opposing reactions to the same factors, as had always previously been believed (and still is by the unenlightened). Figure 7.3 illustrates how Herzberg's research showed that one set of factors truly motivate ("Motivators"), whereas it's a different set ("Hygiene Factors") that lead to dissatisfaction.

Herzberg's research showed that people will strive to achieve "hygiene" needs because they are unhappy without them, but once these are satisfied, the effect soon wears off—satisfaction is temporary. Poorly managed organizations fail to understand that people are not motivated by addressing "hygiene" needs. People are only truly motivated when they are enabled to reach for and satisfy the factors that Herzberg identified as real motivators— achievement, recognition, the work itself, responsibility, and advancement— which deliver a far deeper level of meaning and fulfillment.

It is important to note that in Herzberg's study, salary ranks, as a motivator, a distant sixth and, as a cause for dissatisfaction, a distant fourth— it barely outranks "interpersonal relationship with supervisor" as a cause for dissatisfaction.

Another way of looking at this is shown in Figure 7.4. This representation shows that you must address the basics ("those factors that when lacking cause dissatisfaction and impair your ability to motivate") to create a strong motivational foundation, but it's the motivators that provide the elevators to lift your team to the top.

The foundational factors are the pilings on which the foundation rests; when they are damaged or undermined, there is no stable foundation, but in themselves they do not motivate.

Herzberg's pioneering work paved the way to better understanding worker motivation. The theory remains relevant and provides a solid foundation for motivating your staff.

Motivational Factors as Applied to Programmers

To try to bring a more software-centric view to Herzberg's factors, we have modified his categories and rated them as our experience dictates. These adapted Herzberg factors are shown in Figure 7.5 (page 276).

We believe these motivational factors, while not determined by means of formalized research and polling, are more representative of the motivational

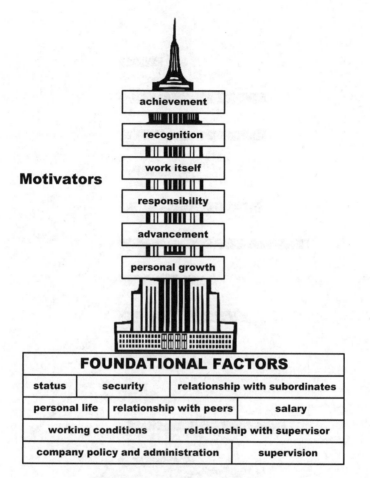

Figure 7.4   Herzberg's Motivators

factors that actually matter based upon our many years of managing and working with programmers. We believe the top motivational factors are

- Making a difference (in the world)
- Learning and growing
- Toys and technology
- Recognition and praise
- Having fun
- Upside

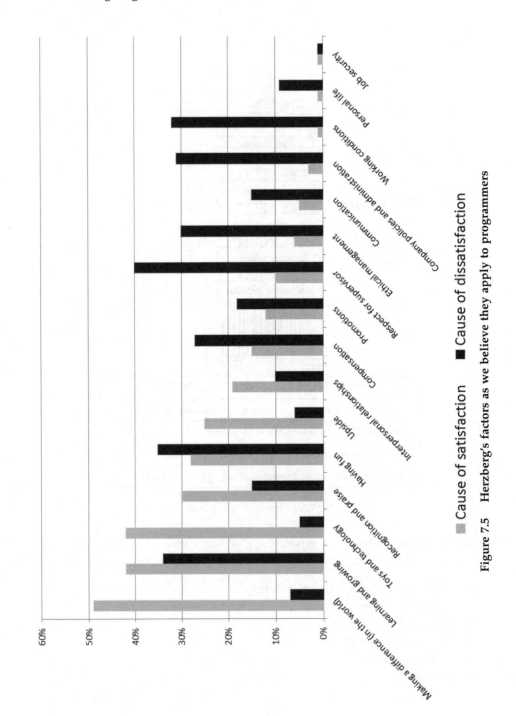

Figure 7.5   Herzberg's factors as we believe they apply to programmers

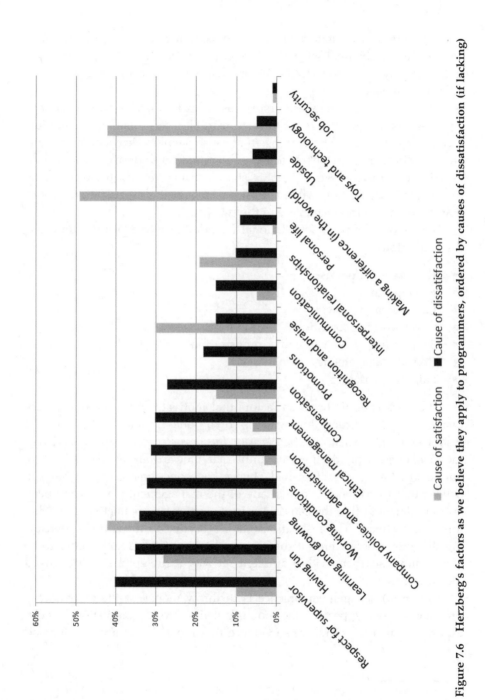

Figure 7.6 Herzberg's factors as we believe they apply to programmers, ordered by causes of dissatisfaction (if lacking)

We were also intrigued when we noticed, after debating the rankings and arriving at the final set shown in Figure 7.5, that these top motivational factors largely correspond to the factors that make up most successful start-up environments.

The "aha" when Herzberg first released his findings—and the continuing "aha" as new managers continue to read Herzberg—is that it is not just about motivators. In fact, the things that cause people to leave organizations are an entirely different set of factors—those that cause dissatisfaction.

Figure 7.6 is the same chart as shown in Figure 7.5, just ordered by causes of dissatisfaction when they're lacking in the organization. Notice how different the top factors are in the two charts.

We believe the basic foundational factors that when lacking can cause dissatisfaction are

- Respect for supervisor
- Having fun
- Learning and growing
- Good working conditions
- Sane company policies and administration
- Ethical management
- Fair compensation

The stark contrast between factors that motivate and those that demotivate was what struck Ron with his own "aha" moment when he first read Herzberg's article[5] in the *Harvard Business Review*. "Whenever I had sat in management meetings up until that time to talk about motivating our teams, the conversation had always been one-dimensional. I have to believe that I was the first one in any of the management teams I had been on to understand that the causes of dissatisfaction are distinct from the factors that motivate. The realization that we needed to focus first on ensuring that our people were satisfied with a basic set of factors in order to be able to motivate them with a different set was a true epiphany. It changed the conversation."

Common management practice is to throw money at the motivational problem by posting performance bonuses tied to project completion. But our experience matches Herzberg's evidence that money's not a motivator and

---

5. F. I. Herzberg, "One More Time: How Do You Motivate Employees?" *Harvard Business Review* 65, no. 5 (September–October 1987): 109–20.

risks being a demotivator. That conclusion was substantiated by Daniel Pink in his popular book *Drive: The Surprising Truth about What Motivates Us*.[6]

Pink draws on studies dating back 30 or more years to show that contingent rewards (if you do this, you get this) turn play into work and drain motivation. If money is so motivating, how do you explain contributors working for free on Wikipedia or open source software?

Pink cites repeated studies that show that, in fact, contingent rewards—for example, the promise of bonuses for finishing faster—for the most part cause projects to take longer than they would have without the promise of a reward. The studies show that rewards narrow focus, which is just fine for motivating piecework but counterproductive for creative work—the essence of our programming craft. Furthermore, rewards can become addictive ("I won't give extra effort unless you offer me a bonus") and can foster counterproductive short-term thinking ("Who cares how many bugs—I'm going for the bonus!").

"When people use rewards to motivate," Pink says, "that's when they're most demotivating."

He does not propose dropping salaries. On the contrary, he says, "One reason fair and adequate pay is so essential is that it takes the issue of money off the table so that [people] can focus on the work itself."

Nor does Pink argue against noncontingent awards (rewards devised after the fact), as long as they are not predictable enough to become expected. In our experience, unexpected rewards for outstanding performance after projects are complete serve to reinforce extra effort and excellence.

Pink goes on to propose what he terms "Motivation 3.0," based on what he calls out as the three key elements of intrinsic motivation: autonomy (or self-determination), mastery (achieving "flow"), and purpose (in the service of some greater objective). These match motivators we'll discuss in the rest of the chapter.

Pink concludes what we have seen many times over the years: "Intrinsically motivated people usually achieve more than their reward-seeking counterparts."

Putting Theory into Practice

Understanding the hierarchy of needs, seeing that an enlightened management style can be beneficial, and realizing that job satisfaction and

---

6. Pink, *Drive: The Surprising Truth about What Motivates Us*.

dissatisfaction come from different factors are important messages that set up the rest of this chapter. Putting theory into practice is always where the rubber hits the road.

....

In theory and practice, practice wins out.

—COMMON WISDOM

The rest of this chapter discusses the tactics we employ to address those causes of satisfaction and dissatisfaction that we, as programming managers, can impact. We start with the basic foundational factors that you need to get right before you can even begin to motivate your staff. These match closely to the top seven causes of dissatisfaction (when lacking), that we have adapted to programmers from Hertzberg's work:

- Respect for supervisor
- Having fun
- Learning and growing
- Good working conditions
- Sane company policies and administration
- Ethical management
- Fair compensation

We then continue with the most important motivating factors, which also match closely to the top six motivational factors that we adapted to programmers from Hertzberg's work:

- Making a difference in the world
- Learning and growing
- Toys and technology
- Recognition and praise
- Having fun with your staff
- Upside

Use all of these to help get you and your team working to peak productivity and motivated to make outstanding contributions.

Foundational Factors—Causes of Dissatisfaction (When Lacking)

Work hard to make sure you provide all of the foundational factors, or you will find your staff dissatisfied. While similar to motivational factors (in fact, some are the same, with different emphasis), foundational factors are essential to provide before you can begin to motivate your staff. As shown in Figure 7.4, the foundational factors are just that—they're the foundation you need to make sure is in place.

Respected as Supervisor

You earn the respect of your staff as their supervisor in many ways. The techniques that follow are ones that we have seen work for ourselves and others.

Gain Technical Respect

As discussed at length in Chapter 5, a big key to successfully managing and motivating programmers is to have the technical respect of those you manage and your peers. Without technical respect, every attempt to motivate your staff will be thwarted actively or passively. Nothing further will be forthcoming in this chapter to help you address this issue. However, we again point you to Chapter 5 to reinforce its importance in helping you succeed in motivating your staff.

Respect Others

An important way for you to earn the respect of your staff is to reciprocate by showing respect for them. The golden rule remains an important rule to follow: "Do unto others as you would have them do unto you." We all value and desire respect, and showing respect to each member of your staff will pay you large dividends. It isn't always easy to respect each person and often takes restraint and forethought. However, it is a key to managing people effectively, especially programmers and other technical people.

> *I have no right, by anything I do or say, to demean a human being in his own eyes. What matters is not what I think of him; it is what he thinks of himself. To undermine a man's self-respect is a sin.*
>
> —ANTOINE DE SAINT-EXUPÉRY

Respect is demonstrated in many ways. Here are some of the most important:

- Listen to other people and make sure they feel heard.
- Notice and pay attention.
- Know their names, greet them personally, and engage them in conversation.
- Know some things about them. Are they married? Do they have children? What is important to them? Notice things in their lives: a new car, new clothes, vacations, for example. Show personal interest in them.
- Ask their opinions about relevant technical issues.
- Never demean them.
- Praise publicly; reprimand privately.
- Say "thank you" (at least ten times every week).

By respecting each member of your staff, you will set the stage for them to respect you as well. And as we have discussed, having your technical staff respect you is important to being a successful manager.

It is easy to demonstrate respect for some because their track record and personality demand respect. Demonstrating respect for others, especially for less experienced or more problematic employees, can be more difficult. But even problem employees deserve respect, and it will make your job of interacting with them, disciplining them, or even dismissing them easier. Go out of your way to show proper respect to all your staff.

> *You like and respect the people who work for you. You care about them. Their problems are your problems; their concerns are yours. You have a heart as big as a train and it shows. You give trust before a person has really demonstrated trustworthiness. You make us all feel like you've adopted us into your family. That's why we follow you.*
>
> —TOM DEMARCO[7]

Establish Your Culture

Creating a successful programming culture is an important part of every manager's job. It is so important that we dedicate the next chapter to this topic.

---

7. DeMarco, *The Deadline*, p. 166.

Lead by Example

Most truly effective managers lead by example. That means conducting yourself as you would like your staff to act. It can be simple things like arriving at meetings on time, always acting courteously and professionally, and never asking your staff to do something you haven't done, or wouldn't do, yourself.

The most effective managers demonstrate an exceptional work ethic. They arrive early and leave after most of their staff. If their staff is expected to work on the weekend, they are there with them.

Leading by example also means protecting your staff, when necessary, and pushing them into the limelight while you watch from the shadows. Leading by example is easier to talk about than to actually do well. But paying attention to the little things that are part of leading by example will make a big difference in how well your staff performs.

Help Solve Technical Problems

When serious technical problems arise, stepping back and having a technical conversation with one or more of your staff is an important and often rewarding experience that allows you to accomplish several things simultaneously:

- Demonstrate your interest in and concern for your staff and their problems.
- Earn respect for your technical command.
- By being a sounding board, enable your staff to solve the problem just by talking it through out loud.
- Ensure that appropriate solutions are being investigated.

Engaging in brainstorming and deep-dive technical sessions is usually a very rewarding experience, even more so if doing so helps resolve the problem. It also gives you firsthand experience and insight into the technical capabilities of your staff. And it serves as a motivational tool since you are giving your full attention to them and their problems.

Be careful. Your goal here is to mentor and coach, not to micromanage or prove you are smarter than your staff. Do it well and your staff will come away feeling empowered and capable. This isn't about you; it is about them. In those cases when you come to the solution before them, ask yourself how you can help your staff discover the solution. It's not time to tell but to teach. Being smart as a manager is not about how quickly you can find the answer but about how effectively you can mentor your staff to do so.

Once a solution has been found, consider hosting a meeting with the broader team to review the issue and revisit the solution. Put your staff "onstage" to do the explaining whenever possible. This provides you with an opportunity to do coaching on how the problem was broken down, to explain the solution(s) that were investigated, and to share the final solution(s) that were implemented. These "lessons learned" sessions do not need to be big or formal meetings; they are best done in small, informal sessions. But the opportunity to engage directly with your staff, as broadly as you feel comfortable, presents an opportunity that you should take advantage of whenever possible.

Manage and Coach

The best managers act not just as managers but also as coaches. The difference between a coach and a manager is often not obvious.

....

Manager: a person who controls and manipulates resources and expenditures

....

Coach: a person who gives instruction or advice to others

Coaching requires that you extend yourself to the person you wish to coach. Coaching cannot be done from afar. It requires one-on-one communication and direction and an intimacy that is personal, and it provides close guidance and nurturing.

Mickey says, "Some of my most rewarding times with my staff have been those one-on-one sessions where I helped them understand things better: a session with a newly hired programmer explaining the background and context for one of their first assignments, or a one-on-one meeting with one of my directors where I acted as a sounding board for problems or issues they faced."

Often, the coaching is mostly listening and agreeing on directions or suggesting small changes to planned actions.

Coaching provides the opportunity to really connect one-on-one with your staff—not just those who report to you but also those individual contributors who may not report directly to you. Seek out such opportunities; they will help provide the personal communication channels that are so important when you need to ask for extra effort or extraordinary performance.

> *There's a trite, but true, saying in coaching: A friend*
> *loves you just the way you are. A coach loves you too*
> *much to let you stay that way.*
>
> —LYSSA ADKINS[8]

Focus on Your People

In the 1980s, Lee Iacocca, who as chairman of the Chrysler Corporation had rescued the company from bankruptcy, discussed his philosophy in his best-selling autobiography: "People, products, and profits. People come first."[9] Iacocca meant that your first priority should be your people. If you have great people and they are engaged and motivated, you can make great products. If you have great people and great products, the profits will follow. It all starts by focusing on hiring, retaining, and motivating the people—your staff.

> *If you're a people manager, your people are far more*
> *important than anything else you're working on.*
>
> —TIM SWIHART, *Engineering Director, Apple Computer*

This is a simple formula for success that has been proven by many. All too often, however, top management overlooks the people part and focuses on the products and profits. Your job is to always make them the first priority.

> *Your job as a manager is to* never *overlook your people*
> *and always make them the first priority.*

This can sometimes be difficult. What is best for employees may not always seem best for the company. For example, if you don't allow your staff to get burned out, they may not appear to be working as hard as they otherwise could. But they will have the will and reserves to "kick on the afterburners" when it is critical that they do so for a project.

Another example of this is when an employee has obtained a certain expertise that is unique or not easily replaced. If you act from a strict company perspective, you will try to keep this person in that job for as long as

---

8. Lyssa Adkins, "I Am a Scrum Coach and I Am Not Nice," September 25, 2010, www.coachingagileteams.com/2010/09/25/uncategorized/i-am-a-certified-scrum-coach-and-i-am-not-nice/.

9. Lee Iacocca with William Novak, *Iacocca* (Bantam Books, 1984), p. 176.

possible. However, that is probably not best for the person, who will probably eventually become unhappy and may leave the company. By instead moving that person into another role or giving them different responsibilities, even though your "backfill" will not be as good as the person they replace, you will win the loyalty of the original employee. Should the new employee have problems or even leave, you still have your expert for backup. In the end it is a win-win situation.

A more difficult challenge is an employee who really doesn't have a good growth path within the organization. You know all too well that over time the employee will become unmotivated and unhappy. Coaching the employee about their options, which might include helping them seek a position in another company, will bring you loyalty and friendship that will transcend job and company. Mickey still receives calls from former staff members who seek his advice when they are considering job changes. Such long-lasting connections pay dividends in recruiting and retaining staff, even in heated market conditions—many of Mickey's staff at Gracenote worked for him for years, and for years before that at Brøderbund—and prove the value of putting people first.

Having Fun

It is important to allow play into your workplace if you expect your staff to work hard. If you think of play as "unprofessional," rethink.

One example you should encourage is out-of-the-office play. Wednesdays from noon to 1:30 P.M. (or sometimes 2:00) were soccer days at Gracenote. Mickey encouraged this outlet for those on his staff who chose to participate.

This kind of play results in several positive outcomes:

- Camaraderie
- Informal communication among participants
- Better health

For years when he was at E&S, Mickey and several of his coworkers played basketball twice each week from noon to 1:30 P.M. at the local gym. The bonding that happened as a result of those play sessions formed close friendships that Mickey continues to maintain and value years later.

Except for times with the tightest budgets, taking your team for a fun off-site can deliver team-building effects far greater than the cost. Ron took Apple teams to ride the antique Big Trees steam train into Santa Cruz, where he bought them lunch and unlimited-ride tickets on the Boardwalk midway. He took Schwab teams to Angel Island in San Francisco Bay, accessible only by ferry, to picnic and bike. Mickey recounts the Nerf wars that happened on certain Fridays at Brøderbund, and the playful atmosphere that has permeated the environment at Pixar from its earliest days.

Other forms of play include the toys on your desk that bring people into your office for a mental break; group lunches marking completion of important milestones; catered or brown-bag lunches where members of the technical staff, or invited guests, share interesting topics; periodic company beer busts; and casual gatherings after work at the local watering hole where drinks are consumed, friendships deepened, and stories shared.

The higher in management you rise, the more and better toys you should keep on your desk.

—RON LICHTY

Another form of play is company parties to celebrate special occasions, such as company anniversaries or holidays. Mickey would throw occasional pizza parties at his house to which he would invite the entire department to join him to help make pizza and top it with their favorite toppings. He used these pizza parties as more than just departmental events, expanding the guest list to other companies and individuals working in the same area of technology. They were great events for helping to bond his staff and also make new friends. Many personal relationships, and even some marriages, resulted from introductions at these parties. Years later, people still ask him when he'll be holding his next pizza party and if he'll make sure they are invited.

All of these outlets are forms of play that help make the hard work worthwhile and possible. You cannot expect people to work hard all the time. Providing escape valves will pay big dividends. The key is to find ways to encourage your staff to work hard and play hard.

Learning and Growing

Because programmers are not primarily motivated by compensation (or "not coin-operated," as we have heard it said), providing an atmosphere of learning and opportunities to grow is exceedingly important. Strive to provide access to technical training (on- or off-site), presentations about new technical developments, new development technologies, and other learning opportunities. If you are budget challenged and cannot provide formal training to all of your staff, you should still bring in vendors and peers to present new products or industry developments. Getting a vendor to present a new development tool is free, and you may actually realize you have to have it!

Likewise, encourage your executive team to make a presentation on a company or technology they have experience with that may be of use or interest to your staff. Or get a member of your board of directors or board of advisers to make a presentation on a topic relevant to you and your staff.

Having ad hoc training sessions like these is not a substitute for more formal training programs, but it can go a long way. Likewise, just sending around notices of relevant software industry special-interest group meetings or forums can help your team see that you are interested in providing opportunities for them to learn and grow.

One other topic worth addressing here: What your staff learns from you will make a key difference in how long they stay with you and your company. If you cannot teach them anything new or positive, your chances of keeping your key staff members diminish. As Mickey relates, "Even as an executive, I've found that if I am not learning something from whomever I report to, I become dissatisfied (and eventually leave). Learning new things about my job and profession from my boss is as important to me as it is to my staff—if I'm not learning, my motivation decreases and my desire to find another situation where I can learn and grow increases." An oft-repeated refrain is that "nobody ever jumped ship who wasn't already standing by the rail." Helping your staff to keep learning and growing will move them farther away from the rail.

....

Everyone on my team is learning. Everyone on my team is treated like an adult. Programmers really like working for me.

—BILL GROSSO, *VP of Engineering, Engage*

We'll revisit this topic again in the Key Motivators section, but you must have foundational opportunities to learn and grow in place to have even a chance to motivate your staff.

Good Working Conditions

If your staff doesn't like being at work, they will likely find reasons and excuses for not being there!

Unfortunately, you have little control over the physical space you have; physical working conditions are mostly dictated by the company or organization you work for, and most companies try to standardize space so that certain teams or workers do not feel greatly advantaged or disadvantaged. You often have to do the best you can do with the physical space you have.

The good news is that if you allocate space fairly and appropriately, you'll avoid most problems. Luckily, providing good working conditions entails much more than just the physical aspects of your workspace.

Make the Workplace a Good Place to Work

Many things go into making a workplace a good place to work. Nearly all the ideas in this section will help you do that. However, it is also a good practice to step back occasionally and think about whether you're succeeding—and what you can do to make your staff's working conditions better. Without regular monitoring, compromises, shortcomings, and unintended consequences will slip by without your noticing that they are eroding your culture or your working conditions. Be vigilant. Address these issues when they come up. It is imperative that you provide an environment where you and your staff not only want to go to work each morning but eagerly look forward to it!

There are many things over which you do not have a lot of control. You usually don't get to pick where the office is located or, for those who work in it, how it is furnished or equipped. But you do have control over many smaller things, such as providing freedom for your staff to personalize their workspaces. You can also make sure there are plenty of whiteboards—the remake of conference rooms in a remodel at Gracenote included floor-to-ceiling whiteboards. And at design time, you can push for areas conducive to design and collaboration—that's how every pod of engineering offices (mostly offices, not cubes) came to be designed around comfortable internal common spaces when Apple built its campus on Infinite Loop in Cupertino.

....

If your current employees are happy, they will refer other great employees to you. So make your place a desirable place to work—including offices for programmers, good leadership, and perks.

—GREGORY CLOSE, *Manager, Project Manager, and Start-up Founder, San Francisco Bay Area*

We've rarely experienced situations where software managers couldn't get support for providing tools that promised to increase the productivity of their staff. That includes better computer equipment, the latest design and analysis tools, collaborative source- and bug-tracking systems, training (though the amount of training budgeted is always an issue), and even bringing in consultants to introduce new techniques or processes that will help your staff.

Constantly look for work/life-enhancing changes. Things that can enhance a workplace range from small rewards for milestones reached and T-shirts to kick off projects to stocking snacks in the break room, setting up brown-bag lunches and seminars on new and interesting (but relevant) topics, and making sure there are toys and other opportunities for fun around the office.

Make your workplace a hangout where you and your staff want to work. Make it your job to create a uniquely great place to work. In our experience, this will do more for overall staff retention than adding another 10 percent to the raise pool.

"No Jerks" Rule

One step you can take to ensure that your workplace remains a great place to be is to establish and enforce a "no jerks" rule. Do not tolerate jerks in your organization, regardless of where in the organization they might reside.[10]

A mildly entertaining book that popularized this rule is Robert Sutton's *The No Asshole Rule*.[11] The author uses this single rule to help guide you to build a better workplace. If you have jerks working for you, get rid of them. If you have cynics working for you, get rid of them. Do not tolerate behavior that will demoralize or impair your staff.

---

10. Of course, if your staff never encounters them, you shouldn't really care or spend any significant political capital trying to exorcise them from the organization. However, you should urge that jerks be restrained or terminated regardless.

11. Robert Sutton, *The No Asshole Rule: Building a Civilized Workplace and Surviving One That Isn't* (Business Plus, 2010).

If peers or others who interact with your staff are jerks, talk to them. Spur them to change their behavior. At the very least keep them away from your staff. If that doesn't work, take it up with your boss (and their boss if necessary), or talk to HR about it, or mount a campaign (subtle or otherwise) to get the issue addressed. Don't just accept it if it impacts your staff in any way!

Be Flexible

Flexibility is important to creative people. The thought of being cast into a cookie-cutter sea of cubicles is enough to drive many creative people away from the corporate world. To that end, if you are in a traditional corporate world, it is important to be flexible whenever and however you can about things like

- Working hours
- Dress
- Personal space
- Equipment and tools
- Compensation for extra effort
- Time off

Some of these examples are relevant only to the corporate environment; in the virtual world flexible working hours, dress, and personal space are mostly not observable.

Software companies are famous for their flexible working hours, yet it is surprising how often we have had to defend our staff to senior management (usually to the CFO, or chief bean counter) at companies where we have worked. In today's world of virtual teams, high-bandwidth VPN access to networks from home, 24/7 development via offshore team members, and compressed development schedules, you would think that this would not be an issue. Yet, "when people are in the office" remains a metric by which productivity is measured perceptually. Defend your ability to provide flexible working hours as a fundamental right to get things done. The simplest defense is the establishment of core office hours when all technical staff (in the same time zone) will be available for meetings or communication. This usually is sufficient to defuse the too-frequently-asked questions about "why the technical staff are not working hard."

The only dress code in today's software companies should be one of appropriateness. In companies in which developers don't have customer contact, the rule should be that what people wear not be offensive or inappropriate.

Space can be difficult to personalize in today's cubicle world. Encourage it when you can. At Pixar, the animators take great pride in customizing their workspaces, going so far as creating caves from fabric and erecting fake palm trees. At Gracenote, the functional groups were allowed to buy a couch of their choice to use as a central meeting space for hanging out, group discussions, and overall a more casual environment. Mickey populated the walls of his office with electric and acoustic guitars, as shown in Figure 7.7. Such things help set the tone for personalization and create an impression of casualness in an otherwise frenetic and pressure-filled environment.

In some settings you can allow your strong contributors to select their own computers and equipment. Make sure your best developers have the best equipment. It motivates them to raise their performance even further and encourages better performance across the organization.

In most organizations with salaried workers there is *no comp time*. That is, not only is there a policy that salaried workers are not paid overtime for

Figure 7.7   *Creative decor in Mickey's office*

work done past 40 hours per week, but it's also rare to give salaried workers hour-for-hour time off for extra time worked. That said, as a manager who puts your people first, you need to reward those who deliver extra effort with some downtime. Both of us have done that, in various companies, by telling programmers to take some extra time off "unofficially"—that is, the time is not reported as vacation time or paid time off. How much depends on the effort they put in and is a decision between manager and employee. However, it should never be one hour for each extra hour worked, which would lead to problems and issues that are just best to avoid.

Sending people on your staff off for a couple of days after finishing a milestone or a project does a few things: They will return more rested and ready to continue; it will show that you really care about them as people; and they will know that when you ask them to put in extra effort for something, you will recognize their effort appropriately. This can go a long way toward their viewing you as a great manager.

Feed Your Team

Depending on your staff, providing snacks and food will be a more or less effective motivator. The rule of thumb we found early in our careers is that providing after-hours meals and quality food helps get critical projects completed 30 to 50 percent faster. Almost without exception, if your staff leaves for dinner, they do not return to the office.

....

The secret of software development has always been good people and lots of Chinese food.

—*JEFF KENTON, Consulting Developer and Development Manager, Boston Area*[12]

We feel less certainty about the numbers than we did a few years ago. Today's low-cost home computers and high-bandwidth access anywhere mean that employees theoretically can work as effectively from home. But our experience tells us that it's more often the camaraderie that keeps teams focused during after-hours sprints and that attaining that from the isolation of programmers' homes is significantly less effective. Mickey has achieved considerable success on certain critical projects by catering dinners for his development teams.

---

12. Jeff Kenton, "Doing Everything Wrong," *Embedded Systems Programming*, August 2005.

Another approach is to set up an "after-hours refrigerator" stocked daily with fresh sodas, juices, sandwiches, entrées, salads, desserts, and other foods. When Mickey implemented one at Brøderbund, he observed that many important products were delivered on time only because the team could continue to work productively together past dinnertime. The cost for contracting the in-house deli to stock the fridge was several thousand dollars per month, but spread across a staff of hundreds, the "bang per buck" impact was priceless.

During the dot-com boom, several San Francisco catering companies began serving the high-tech community. Through the magic of corporate accounts, technical staffs could order in dinner and work into the night. This still occurs, though some of the larger, more notable firms now facilitate food via in-house catering. Google is well known for its free four-star, in-house food available for its technical staff throughout the day and into the night. This was apparently so successful that some of the Google in-house chefs have "spun out" and created a San Francisco company[13] that services Twitter and other companies with all-organic breakfasts, lunches, and dinners for their staffs.

In the virtual office world, where your staff may have continuous access to food and drinks in their home workspaces, your challenge becomes finding other tools that will help you achieve the camaraderie and team bonding that shared meals provide. We discussed in Chapter 5 the value of in-person visits by virtual team members. Building camaraderie during those visits through food and extracurricular activities can be as important as the meetings themselves.

Sane Company Policies and Administration

Unless you start a company and have full control over its policies and communications, you will never have an opportunity to ensure that all the policies and members of the administration are sane. However, here are things you can do to make the most of the policies and administration you do have.

---

13. Gastronaut LLC (www.gastronautsf.com) has built a devoted word-of-mouth following among techies and now delivers many hundreds of meals a day to companies including Twitter, Square, Yelp, Grockit, and Causes.

Communicate

Feeling connected motivates programmers—they want to feel part of the company and its mission and its vision. There is nothing like clear communication up and down the organization to achieve that goal. Yet effective communication seems widely lacking in many software organizations.

Communication takes various forms, such as

- Company vision and mission
- Annual company goals
- Company-approved product, project, or team goals
- Product or project requirements
- Agreed-upon project or team schedules
- Major schedule changes
- Weekly status of individuals and teams
- Individual objectives
- Vacation schedules
- Meeting announcements
- Good news

As you can see from this list, which is far from complete, many of these items are communicated down to the technical staff, while some of these items are communicated up to management. The key word here is *communication*, and if it's not flowing, it is your problem to solve.

It turns out that you have to work hard to make sure communication is actually consummated; too often things are said but no communication happens. It's not enough to tell things; you need to make sure that the recipients of the information actually get it and understand it.

In small organizations, you can share information personally so you know if communication happens. As organizations grow, you need to find ways to make sure that communication is flowing even if you have an intermediary doing it. This is true both "up" and "down" the organization. That often calls for written communication that people can study and read.

One thing both Ron and Mickey have done is to hold regular staff meetings with their direct reports where they share information from the executive staff meetings they attend. Many on their staffs who do not attend executive meetings are hungry for this information. They know it can help them anticipate new opportunities for the company and solve problems they may be facing in the future. At Brøderbund, Mickey made this a weekly lunch meeting; he and his staff would meet at one of the local restaurants to review the information. Because it was a less formal meeting, it was not as productive as it could have been, but it was always well attended. And it built a bond with his staff that has lasted long since he worked with them.

At Gracenote there was a quarterly "all hands" company meeting where the CEO presented general company news and the results of the previous quarter, along with accomplishments and news from various departments in the company. Additionally, Mickey often held a monthly departmental meeting, where anyone who directly or indirectly reported to him (or anyone who just wanted to attend) met to review company happenings over the previous month. This meeting tended to be less formal than the CEO's and gave individuals a chance to talk and ask questions of others.

....

Communicate repeatedly—the biggest culprit across organizations is lack of communication.

—*DAVID DIBBLE, EVP, Schwab Technology*

Meetings such as these are a good opportunity to review the company's goals and project progress, as well as project schedule changes, general holiday and vacation news, and company news in general. It doesn't require a monthly newsletter, but it does require setting up the meetings and holding them regularly so that people are not hungry for information in their absence.

In one department at Apple, Ron regularly opened his staff meetings with an invitation to share gossip. The company was big enough that rumors both good and bad would regularly fly about. Ron found that the rumors his staff shared were frequently the ones of most concern to them. Getting them into the open kept him in tune with his team's concerns, occasionally gave him early warning of impending changes that someone on his staff had heard before him, provided him with the opportunity to give "sense of the staff" feedback to more senior management, and supplied him with the latest rumors to check for truth.

Protect Your Staff from Organizational Distraction

A good manager knows how to communicate with his staff, but he also knows how to protect them from being buffeted, whether from the winds of rumors about organizational shake-ups and project priority changes or, in smaller companies, the continual influx of conflicting requests and dramatic changes in direction coming from the sales organization. Protecting your staff from organizational whiplash of these kinds is necessary so that they can remain focused and productive.

....

Be a damper to the noise.

> —JOE KLEINSCHMIDT, CTO and Cofounder,
> Leverage Software

Of course, at times there will be legitimate changes to project priorities or direction, and in those cases you must inform your staff of any impact on them. But you can proactively ensure that changes are as unobtrusive as possible by taking actions like waiting until a milestone is reached before allowing the new information and priority change to be disseminated to your staff.

You can think of communication as offense and protecting your staff from too much information as defense. Winning a game usually requires excellent offense and defense. Likewise in software development—you must practice both skills to be an effective manager.

Protect Your Staff from Bad Organization Communication and Policies

Few things are as disruptive to a well-functioning programming team as "off-the-wall" communiqués or policies handed down from management. The canonical example is a memo that announces that all employees must adhere to standard office working hours. Other examples run the gamut of folly and senselessness. We believe it is imperative to insulate your team from such communiqués or policies whenever possible.

The next chapter, "Establishing a Successful Programming Culture," covers this topic in detail, so we won't elaborate on it further here. However, you should recognize that protecting your team from these kinds of issues is imperative. They can be one of the biggest demotivators you face. Do all you can to head these issues off before they infect your team.

Ethical Management

Be Ethical and Professional at All Times

If you expect great things from your staff, you must set an example. One of the most important examples to set is that of a professional and ethical person. A manager who is ethical is forthright and honest in dealing with his staff and others. He can be trusted to keep confidences and stand up for his staff against anyone in the company. A professional shows up on time to work and to meetings without being reminded. A professional does not use abusive or profane language and projects an aura of being in control of a situation without undue attention. A professional has high expectations of himself and others and demonstrates an aura of cool and calm under fire. A professional tells the truth and does not try to manipulate facts or people.

One definition of being a professional includes five key traits:[14]

1. *Character*
   Demonstrating integrity and trust, honesty, truthfulness, forthright-ness, trustworthiness, being responsible and accountable, being diligent, doing what is right, and projecting a professional image

2. *Attitude*
   Requires adopting a serving mentality, seeking responsibility, determination, and being a team player

3. *Excellence*
   Always pressing for excellence, continual improvement, being attentive, and following instructions

4. *Competency*
   Demonstrating expertise, performance, personal effectiveness, and being a good communicator

5. *Conduct*
   Showing professional maturity, that manners matter, loyalty, respect, confidences and confidentiality, and a touch of class

We ourselves choose a broad definition of *professional* to include characteristics that we both aspire to and wish to see in those we report to. They include publicly recognizing and praising your staff for their accomplishments, taking responsibility for failures, and not "throwing any of your staff under the bus" of management opinion.

They also include fairness. People will accept the negative and the uncomfortable—as well as the uneven distribution of rewards—if the good and the bad are perceived as being fairly distributed. We do not define "fairly distributed" as "equally distributed" but rather given to those most

---

14. James, R. Ball, *Professionalism Is for Everyone* (The Goal Institute, 2008).

deserving. Salary increases, bonuses, and stock options are not equally distributed in most companies but are given based upon performance. Those who perform best should receive the most. Similarly, should a cutback need to take place, targeting those who are contributing least will be perceived as fair. What doesn't work is favoritism: Whether rewards or reductions, never dole them out based upon personal biases rather than performance.

If you are a manager who is ethical, fair, and not self-promoting, you will be a long way down the road to having your staff think you are a great manager.

If you, as a manager, must ask your staff to take on difficult tasks and meet demanding schedules, it will be much easier to do this if your manner and behavior are professional. Explain the situation calmly, and tell the truth unfailingly. Our experience shows that people respond to such requests and will, in fact, move mountains if you ask them to do so and explain clearly why the mountain must be moved. Most programmers respond to this much better than to demands from management to meet this milestone "or else."

> *Management is getting people to do what needs to be done. Leadership is getting people to want to do what needs to be done.*
>
> —WARREN BENNIS, *Professor of Business Administration, USC*[15]

Be Fair

Our experience shows that a manager who can be fair to his staff can become a great manager. While being fair extends to assignments, equipment, collaboration, and all aspects of management, it begins with compensation.

It is important to recognize that being fair does not mean treating everyone the same. It means rewarding staff in such a way that it is consistent and understandable to all. No one will be upset if the best programmers on your staff are paid the best. What your staff will perceive as unfair is if you treat the best and the worst the same. Fair compensation includes compensating your staff at the level they could reasonably expect to receive at other companies located near you and promoting appropriately.

---

15. Warren Bennis, *Managing the Dream: Reflections on Leadership and Change* (Basic Books, 2000), p. 27.

COMPENSATE FAIRLY. Compensation is usually a demotivator and not a motivator. This is the insight that runs so counter to common wisdom that it formed the core of Ron's "aha" when he first read Herzberg, whose work we summarized at the beginning of this chapter.

If someone feels underpaid (rightly or wrongly), they will likely be less motivated to put in extra hours or make extraordinary efforts. Contrary to common wisdom, your compensation thinking should be focused on finding and meeting that baseline that lets all of your staff feel fairly compensated, not attempting to motivate staff to do more by paying more. What Herzberg (and many others) demonstrated is that once people feel justly compensated, they will likely not be out to prove they are worth their compensation—that is, more pay mostly doesn't motivate more work. Rather, once people feel justly compensated, they will be focused on doing a good job and not worrying about their compensation.

For this reason, making sure your staff is fairly compensated is extremely important. The challenge is to identify "fair." Certainly, all your employees should not be paid near the top of their salary range for similar skilled technical staff. Our own approach is to use market rates as a baseline, to make sure staff is paid at, or above, those rates for their level of experience and skill, and then to work proactively to ensure that pay for those who consistently deliver outstanding performance pushes toward the top of their range.

If possible, make sure your HR department is using an industry standard salary survey service such as Radford Surveys. This will help you determine if you are paying competitive market rates for your staff and provide the ammunition you may need to help convince your management that market adjustments may be necessary. Never take HR-provided information at face value. HR may have a different agenda from you. And too often HR does not understand the nuances and complexities of the technical job market that make fairly compensating your staff a challenge. Always listen to the marketplace, the candidates you are talking to, and the anecdotal information you gather regarding current salary levels in your locale.

Using data like this, and anything else you can think of, can give you confidence to look your staff in the eyes and tell them you are convinced you have done every creative thing in your power to make their compensation fair and even aggressive. This assurance should also be convincing to your technical staff. They will be largely satisfied with their compensation—that is, until someone tries to lure them away with a bigger compensation package. If that happens, use such example(s)—the fact that you have lost

employees or candidates to others willing to compensate them more—
to lobby for additional compensation for your staff. Use a problem as
an opportunity.

From Mickey: "I always told people that I tried to manage so that I could
post the salaries of my staff outside my door and no one would be surprised
at those who were the most highly compensated. I would have hated to do
that—there were always inequities that I was struggling to overcome. But
nonetheless, it is a useful exercise to understand how close you are to being
able to post the salaries of your technical staff. It helped me manage better and work hard to overcome the inequities that I inherited or needed to
introduce on occasion."

Paying fairly will help keep your staff from becoming demotivated.
But you must do more to motivate them. You must demand excellence and
reward outstanding performance. Make sure you give the biggest raises,
the best equipment, the choicest assignments, and the most praise to those
who consistently perform in an outstanding manner. Also, work hard to get
permission to dole out "spot bonuses" to individuals and teams that go to
extraordinary lengths to meet committed dates or reach major milestones,
whether they're money, Amazon coupons, or gift certificates for dinner out
on the town. Such recognition is guaranteed to make a star performer or
team feel appreciated.

You need to think about one other form of compensation. Stock options,
equity, ownership—there are lots of ways to talk about it, but this upside
has been the fuel that has powered the success of many start-ups in Silicon
Valley and around the world for the past 40 years. A later section will talk
about using this as a motivator. The relevance for this section is that you
should make sure that if stock options or their equivalent[16] are available,
they are granted to your staff equitably. You (and your manager or HR, if
you need some assistance) should help your staff understand the potential
value of stock options. All too often, especially in start-up companies, this
is (unfortunately) not the case, which can cause more severe demotivation
issues than salary inequities. Lobby hard for additional equity for your staff,
especially the outstanding performers.

---

16. Often in today's world, stock options have been replaced by restricted stock warrants
(RSWs). RSWs are actually better than stock options because they are outright grants of stock
to employees. The face value of the stock is incurred as income, but the ability to redeem the
stock warrants is restricted until the vesting dates have been met (typically some percentage
of the stock warrants vest per year over a four-year period). For purposes of management,
you can think of stock options and RSWs as essentially the same type of compensation.

PROMOTE APPROPRIATELY   You must manage promotions carefully. Promotions are a reward to those who have demonstrated that they meet or exceed the criteria established for a job. All too often there are not agreed-upon objective criteria, so the decision whether to promote someone becomes problematic. Without objective criteria, the decision is subjective, which makes it open to debate not only with your manager and HR but also with the employee. This is all the more reason to make sure that you have established job descriptions that formalize the criteria for each job, as we discussed in Chapter 2.

Even with clear job descriptions, the evaluation of an employee's readiness for a promotion can still be debatable. One school of thought is that a person should perform the job you are expecting them to be promoted into before you promote them. This is especially true the higher in the organization you rise. Mickey recalls that his CEO at Gracenote would never consider someone for a promotion to a director or VP position without the person clearly performing at that level already. One of Ron's VPs at Schwab called out the reason: Companies do not want to promote people only to have to give them failing grades on their first reviews in the new position or put them at risk in the first downturn.

For individual contributor positions, the requirement for serving in a position before being promoted to it is not as clear. We have both promoted programmers into more senior positions as much to motivate them as to reward them for their past efforts. Some individuals are not wired to function outside their job description, making it a reasonable strategy to promote them into a "bigger" position and make it clear you expect them to meet or exceed the "bigger" position's expectations.

Sometimes the promotion is intended to restore balance to an inequity within your organization. Inequities often occur when you hire someone new with a title and/or salary that are inflated from your current staff comparables. We try hard to avoid such situations, but they inevitably occur. When they do, we then work hard to correct them. This is one of the hardest lessons to learn as a manager: that is, how to turn a negative (creating inequities) into a positive (by using it as an excuse to reward your strong performers).

One other situation to be aware of is that a promotion for one employee may demotivate others who believe they deserve promotions that have not been forthcoming. This issue is often not directly related to the promotion you just announced! That is, the people who harbor these "persecution" feelings don't really want that job; they just want a promotion. Usually, these individuals are in denial about how they are actually performing and resentful that someone else is getting a promotion. Be on the lookout for these types of people because they can become a morale problem for your entire staff. Take action quickly when you spot these chronic complainers and clarify any performance issues that may be blocking their progress. Don't let these sorts of problems fester in your organization.

That said, all too often people are passed over for promotions who do deserve them. Loyal, talented, and hardworking employees who do not actively campaign for promotions all too often are not promoted as often as the loyal, talented, hardworking employees who do. We recommend that you review all your staff when you determine that it is time to promote someone. Use this as an opportunity to make sure you're not overlooking "less-squeaky wheels" who are as deserving of a promotion if not more so. This is hard to do, but your staff will know and appreciate you when you are fair and work proactively to address such issues.

Key Motivating Factors

If you provide the foundational factors, you will have provided the foundation. Now you can more readily motivate your staff by applying the motivating factors. This does not mean that your staff cannot be motivated without first shoring up the foundational factors, but your job will be easier if there are no causes of dissatisfaction to dilute their motivation.

There are no "silver bullets" for creating a motivated staff, but those motivating factors listed below are a good place to begin. As shown in Figure 7.4, once you've got the foundational factors in place, the motivational factors lift the team to top performance.

Making a Difference in the World

It is the rare individual who does not want to make a difference in the world. Many if not most of us chose to program at least in part for the opportunity to positively impact the world we live in. If your organization is building or providing something that can be pitched as making a contribution—improving the world in some way—you will have an easier time recruiting and motivating your staff. People are always willing to work harder and longer when they feel their efforts matter.

....

Never doubt that a small group of thoughtful, committed
citizens can change the world. Indeed, it is the only thing
that ever has.

—*MARGARET MEAD (1901–78), U.S. Anthropologist*
and Popularizer of Anthropology

Steve Jobs was the master of high-tech evangelism. His famous challenge
that recruited John Scully out of Pepsi to run Apple in its early years was "Do
you want to sell sugar water or change the world?" Steve's Apple employees
have been fanatical about being part of Apple's mission to change the world.

Ron joined Apple "between Jobs"—after Steve had left, before his
return—but Steve's fervor remained. Even in those years, everyone felt the
intensity of the vision. One of Ron's colleagues once described getting to
work at Apple as being like being invited onstage to play with the Beatles.

You don't have to be Steve Jobs or Apple to be able to appeal to this universal inner need to make a difference. Mickey has personally both felt that
same inner impetus and appealed to it at Pixar, Brøderbund, and Gracenote.
At Pixar, Steve Jobs (of course) painted the vision of dramatically changing
the antiquated world of animation and bringing "insanely great" animated
movies to the masses; Brøderbund painted its vision as making "great
educational products that will make children learn better from a younger
age using computers"; Gracenote was "fueling the fires of the digital music
revolution" that helped bring about the iPod, digital music downloads, and
a personal music transformation for the world.

At Berkeley Systems, Ron and his colleagues felt lucky to be able to create engines of delight, their screen saver lines then being the most widely
enjoyed entertainment products in the world. At Schwab, Ron collected and
retold apocryphal stories of Chuck Schwab's empathy for average Joes who
had reached retirement with no savings to pull them through, and of the dramatic examples of customer service Schwabbies had delivered over the years.

These "world-changing goals" vary in how they inspire, compared
to Steve's pitch at Apple, but they all helped fire up and fuel the staff at
these companies to work harder and reach higher. Harness this if you can.
It doesn't take a Steve Jobs to pitch this kind of vision (though being an
"insanely great" communicator with a "reality distortion field" certainly
doesn't hurt). Look for and find how your company is helping to change the
world and point it out in your recruiting pitches, in your regular communications to your staff, and especially when you're calling upon people to dig
deeper and work harder for some milestone. It will make a difference!

Learning and Growing

Few can be successful in the software industry without continually learning and growing professionally. Technology changes so rapidly that new college grads would likely be obsolete within only a few years if they didn't continue to learn. This does not mean you do not continue to use what you learned in college, but it is often augmented by new techniques and tools and approaches and frameworks in the ever-changing world of software development.

....

If you don't like change, you're going to like irrelevance even less.

> —GENERAL ERIC SHINSEKI, *Chief of Staff,*
> *U.S. Army*

Change means the best programmers are lifelong learners who are excited by learning new tools, techniques, and technologies and being challenged by new problems to solve.

One of the easiest things you can do to help foster a great learning environment is to establish an ongoing series of technical presentations to your staff. Technical presentations can come from outsiders (the fruits of your networking efforts), interviewees (an interesting project they have been part of), your current staff (an overview of an interesting project they are working on), customers (how they are using your product in a unique or exciting fashion), authors (talking about their latest books), consultants (making a pitch for their special skills), vendors (talking about their latest products), product managers (talking about their latest customer visits and interesting tidbits they picked up from the customers), or even yourself talking about something new you learned (an opportunity to help reinforce your technical learning and encourage technical respect from your staff).

With so many possible things to choose from, the hardest thing to do is to set up the sessions and coordinate the presentations. We suggest that you give yourself a break and delegate this to one or more of your team members who would like to take it on as a special project. Doing so will accomplish two things: It will help free you from the ongoing task of making the arrangements for these presentations; and it will provide an opportunity for others to network, coordinate, and participate in a low-pressure environment. This will be good for certain members of your staff, so rely on them to take on this special project.

If your organization provides aid for further education, encourage your top performers to take advantage of that, if necessary pointing out classes you think they would benefit from to encourage them.

If you're not learning while you're earning, you're cheating yourself of the better portion of your just compensation.

—NAPOLEON HILL[17]

Another great learning opportunity comes from trade shows and technical conferences that cater to software development or your specific industry. Encourage your top performers to attend the sessions and keynotes—the passes are generally quite pricey—while encouraging all your key staff members to sign up for a free or low-cost "expo" pass to walk the show floor, take in the sights, see and hear about new products, and listen in on the conversations. Our experience is that all too few take advantage of these opportunities to foster industry awareness, even those who live in Silicon Valley or a major city where the only cost is a day of their time.

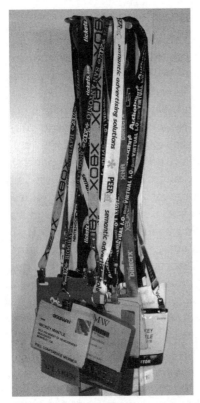

Figure 7.8
Mickey's collection of conference and trade show badges

Collect the badges from the conferences and trade shows you attend and hang them in your office. This shows two things explicitly: You are active outside of the company, learning and networking; and you encourage attendance at such events. It also shows something else, but more implicitly: namely, that you are committed to being in the middle of technical conferences and trade shows and to spending the time and energy necessary to attend these events. Figure 7.8 shows a collection of badges from conferences and trade shows that Mickey has collected over the years.

17. Napoleon Hill, *Think and Grow Rich* (Tribeca Books, 2012; originally published in 1937).

Toys and Technology

One of the simplest ways to reward and motivate programmers is to equip them with a top-of-the-line development machine and environment. Though this was even more true in the past, when the difference between generations of machines was starker (e.g., 300MHz versus 1GHz processor speed), it remains true today primarily because of this rule of thumb:

Software gets slower faster than hardware gets faster.

—*NIKLAUS WIRTH, Inventor of Pascal*

It seems ridiculous that even with many-GHz processors, fast buses, and megabyte cache memories, it remains all too true: Software is still slow! So providing your best programmers with the best equipment will help make them even more productive and also help motivate them to be the very best. Given the multiyear amortization of capital equipment, it may not even be a budget item that gets much attention.

Make sure you provide your team with all the tech toys you can afford or find: dual-screen, 25-inch monitors; color printers; and even high-end stereo equipment. Don't forget about company-sponsored "cool" mobile phones, tablets (great incentive gifts!), and even Internet-connected consumer electronics devices.

Mickey relates, "I bought everyone on one of my teams at Gracenote a Sony Blu-ray disc player so they could experience the Gracenote technology embedded into the device firsthand at home. It provided a great excuse to reward everyone on the team, help them build pride in what they had developed, and motivate them to find and fix any issues they might notice when using the device. The team was jazzed, and with the cost of great consumer electronics devices today it didn't really cost that much."

Finding ways to use toys to reward individuals or teams will win you points with your staff and help motivate them. This is one of the simplest "win-win" things you can do!

Recognition and Praise

An important part of your role as a manager is to make sure that the appropriate people receive recognition and praise for exemplary work. It baffles us that so few managers do this regularly; it costs nothing and takes no more than a few seconds of time, yet it makes such a significant difference in the attitude, work ethic, and overall accomplishments of all technical staff.

If anything goes bad, I did it. If anything goes semi-good,
we did it. If anything goes real good, you did it. That's
all it takes to get people to win football games.

—PAUL "BEAR" BRYANT (1913–83), Longtime
University of Alabama Head Football Coach

Everyone wants to be praised. From the time we are born, we learn that smiles and praise go hand in hand and make us smile and feel good in turn. Praise from someone whom you respect and work for is tremendously rewarding and makes you want to exceed their expectations and gain additional praise.

However, you must never deliver praise halfheartedly or falsely. Save praise for those occasions when praise is deserved. Your staff will detect lack of sincerity and it will erode the effect of praise truly deserved.

If you make your praise specific, you'll also make it feel more sincere and authentic. Not just "good job," but also "The user interface changes you made improved the ease of use enormously. When I brought up the screen, my eye zeroed in on the exact thing I first needed to do. I'm thinking customers will experience it the same as I did; really nice." By being specific, you communicate that there really is a reason for the praise—and you're also calling out behavior or achievement that is worth repeating.

Praise is appropriate whether given privately or done in a public setting where others may hear your comments. Find time to praise your top performers as often as it makes sense. If your top performers are like those we have managed, you can find opportunities nearly every day to commend them for their work and efforts.

Likewise with recognition directed to individuals, groups, and teams. Recognition can be for a task completed, for a project completed, for a job well done, for a milestone achieved, for anything that is worthy of recognition. It can be delivered verbally, in e-mail, in video, in a meeting, in the hallway, over lunch, on the way out to the car on the way home, and in fact anywhere. Never pass up an opportunity to say, "Thank you and a job well done!"

I praise loudly; I blame softly.

—CATHERINE THE GREAT OF RUSSIA

Mickey worked for one CEO who had a hard time saying thanks and recognizing effort. Rather he would focus on what did not meet his expectations and all too often chastise an individual or team for not meeting his expectations even if they actually accomplished the task that they had set out to accomplish. "We called that 'moving the goalposts'; the team would work tirelessly to meet a prescribed milestone only to go into a meeting, be rebuked for not doing enough, and then be sent back to 'finish the job appropriately,' typically with an unrealistic schedule. Many were the times that I would seek out those individuals afterward to praise them for their efforts and apologize for the CEO not having recognized the effort that they had put in. I tried to coach my CEO to acknowledge the effort they put in, praise them for what they had accomplished, and then urge them to meet his expectations. If he had done this, the team would not have been demoralized by these meetings and would have accepted his higher expectations and new tasks enthusiastically. As it was, meetings with the CEO were dreaded by the technical staff."

Find creative ways to recognize and praise; Amazon or Starbucks gift cards are now favorites among techies, but our experience shows that a simple "thank you" is easier and does 95 percent of the same job as small gifts or token gestures. That said, tokens of appreciation, especially unexpected bonuses for outstanding performance, are always welcome!

Having Fun with Your Staff

Previously in this chapter we listed "having fun" as one of the foundational factors for a successful programming manager. It's also a motivating factor because there is another dimension to having fun that, if you can achieve it, will make your job as a manager much easier. That is the ability to loosen up and enjoy working with your staff.

You don't have to have fun every day, but if you can't sit down and laugh with individuals or members of your staff about events of the day, or the random things that happen, or just a chance joke, you and they are likely not having fun!

....

Celebrate your success and find humor in your failures. Don't take yourself so seriously. Loosen up and everyone around you will loosen up. Have fun and always show enthusiasm.

—SAM WALTON, *Founder of Walmart*

Laughter is the best medicine for handling problems and breaking the ice at tension-filled times. We have found that the ability to laugh with your staff is a key factor in making a workplace fun and you a great manager.

Upside

Upside has always been an important ingredient in personal performance. From ancient times, individuals have been driven to be successful by the promise of multifold return on their investment of hard work and results. In the high-tech software world this has traditionally been in the form of

- Higher salary
- Significant bonus
- Stock options (or equivalent)
- Strong company growth
- Increased perks

The past half-century is rife with stories of company founders being rewarded with stock options resulting in net worth in the millions and billions of dollars.

For a company that is pre-IPO on the way to a public offering, the ability to offer stock options that have the potential of 10 times, 100 times, or even higher return is a powerful incentive.

Mickey has experienced this several times, not always with the outcome he had hoped. "At Evans & Sutherland, which went public in 1977, I did not have any pre-IPO stock options. But one of the fellows in my office did, and the day E&S went public was the day I realized what I had missed out on. He had actually not received the options directly but bought them from one of the original E&S employees so that guy could buy a couch. My colleague's $500 in stock options were worth $125,000 when they went public! I finally figured out what the pre-IPO game was all about." Thereafter, Mickey always placed significant value on any *upside* that was part of his own total compensation package. "Since that time, I've never been satisfied working strictly for salary. Whenever the upside of my compensation disappeared (for whatever reason), I found myself less incented, and I eventually moved on to another position with real upside."

If you have the ability to offer stock options as part of the total compensation package, you have a tool you can use to incent your staff and teams to deliver on unrealistic schedules. "Regardless of what the reality of the upside actually is, I have seen teams dig deep and deliver amazing results in ridiculous times," says Mickey. "Since the reality of the upside is really unknown, the power of the incentive is actually greater—and greater yet for programmers, who by their nature are optimists!"

The actual form of the upside is irrelevant except to the individual. The key is to have some sort of upside you can use to incent higher performance from your staff. Without some sort of upside, you must motivate your staff with the other four incentives (which are more tangible, but have less upside potential):

- Higher salary
- Significant bonus
- Strong company growth
- Increased perks

Higher salaries and the potential for significant bonuses are good motivators, but both are usually contingent upon personal performance objectives. Also, the lower in the organization you and your team reside, usually the smaller the bonus potential. These factors make them much less of an extra incentive and usually are more likely viewed as just part of the job.

Strong company growth may not have the same upside, but don't dismiss it; it has upside nonetheless. That's true in part because growing companies tend to be well funded and offer healthy, positive morale—it's just way more fun to work in a booming company. It's also true in part because strong company growth portends opportunities for increased responsibility, which means that your ability to rise in the organization is greater (an IPO actually tends to create a vacuum of people at the top, which provides its own set of opportunities).

Increased perks are probably the most difficult to apply universally. You have to understand what's truly important to each individual on your team to know which perk to offer more of (if there are perks that are even of interest). But these are often what motivate your staff the most, as we discussed in the Toys and Technology section. This is an area where you likely have the most latitude and the most direct impact on individuals on your staff. Dispense these perks appropriately and you can accelerate projects and specific tasks greatly.

Use any form of upside as a tool; relish it and use it creatively as best you can!

Personal Commitment

Though this is not one of the foundational factors or key motivators, we have found that for motivating staff, the ability to seek out and obtain personal commitments for key deliverables is an important ingredient that defines an outstanding software manager. A key to obtaining personal commitments at critical times is casual engagement all the time. That is, while it is important and necessary to schedule one-on-one (1:1) meetings with your staff, it is of equal importance to get out of your office and wander around and talk to people. None of us managers ever do this enough. It is all too easy to go to meetings and let people come to you. But by wandering around and talking to people, you accomplish two important things:

- You let people know that you are interested in them and what they do.
- You learn what people are actually doing.

In the glory days of HP, when both Bob Hewlett and David Packard were still operationally involved, they institutionalized the concept of "management by walking around (MBWA)" and made it part of each manager's objectives. Many attribute MBWA to HP's early success.

By wandering over, stopping by someone's desk, and chatting with them for a minute or two, you get a chance to know much more about them than you would during a 1:1 meeting in your office. You can see firsthand how they work, observe the pictures of their family on their desk or wall, find out what problems they might be having (even small problems should be of interest, because they would never bring small problems to you), and generally just get to know them better.

By engaging them in light conversation, you also get to see what they are actually working on, and you can learn more about the design and development practices of your staff. You can also help spot roadblocks they might be encountering, such as design or debugging issues, QA bottlenecks, or the need for faster machines for compiling or data processing. If you pay attention to the small things, you can learn a lot.

But you can't be too obvious about this wandering around. If you systematically stop at each person's desk one after the other, your folks will quickly be "on to you" and the benefits will be diluted.

Mickey always made it a common practice to wander around near the end of the day and talk to his staff. He passed up those who looked very engrossed, and he didn't stop at each desk. "I didn't follow any set pattern but tried to wander around and talk to people at least a couple of times each week, commonly at the end of the day, though not always. We talked about all kinds of things, but there was usually a thread of business or projects or programming or debugging or just 'thanks' to most of my stops. I didn't limit it to just my staff. I talked to lots of people and was sure I was the only one in my company who actually knew almost everyone's name. I think this made me more approachable to most of the staff, and I'm sure I knew more of what was going on than I would otherwise."

....

People drift away from project goals quickly if left alone.
Good project leaders talk to people almost every day.
"What did you do? Why? Did it work?"

　　　　　　　—DAVE WILSON, *Software Architect,*
　　　　　　　San Francisco Bay Area

Another good idea is to bring your boss with you when you go wandering around, or encourage your boss to do it alone. You can introduce him to people (if necessary) or at the very least tell him about the projects the various people you talk to are working on. It demonstrates your command of the details of what people do, makes them feel even more special, and helps your manager become more approachable as well.

Of course, MBWA should never be used for probing discussions or critique of any individual. That is best done 1:1 and behind a closed door.

By wandering around and talking to your staff, you set the stage for an important part of motivating programmers, that is, seeking a personal commitment from them. If you barely know their names and seldom talk to them, it will be more difficult for you to seek them out to ask for their help when you need it. But sooner or later, that is what you will need to do.

When important projects or milestones are looming, the best way to ensure peak performance by your staff is to seek a personal commitment from those key contributors who are most capable of producing success. In a private setting (or as private as possible, without dragging them off to your office or a conference room), approach them and discuss the looming project or milestone. Discuss with them their part of the project. After it is clear to both of you what their contribution will be, reiterate why the project or milestone is important and ask them if they will "move heaven and earth" to make sure the milestone or project is completed on time or successfully.

Most technical people are not motivated by fear or rewards, but rather by personal pride and wanting to perform well for their peers or manager(s).

By securing a promise as a personal commitment, you will find that people work harder than you might expect from almost any reward you could offer. Make sure you acknowledge their efforts and spend at least as much time afterward discussing the project's or milestone's completion as you did when originally soliciting the commitment.

Keep in mind that you cannot seek this kind of commitment too often or it will lose its motivational effect. Save it for truly important projects or milestones.

The reverse of wandering around is being accessible in your office. Always encourage people to come talk to you when they have a problem or issues. This should include all of your direct reports, of course. But if you have indirect reports, you need to go out of your way to encourage them to talk to you as well. If people feel like the only time you are going to talk to them in your office is when there is a problem, it will be a dreaded occasion if you call them in to talk about something. But if they wander into your office and you can chat with them informally there, it will help ensure that you are perceived as approachable—which is an important reputation to have.

Mickey relates, "I often will go out of my way to mention to one of the technical staff that I would love to have them stop by to chat when they have a chance, either when I see them in the hall or by sending them an e-mail, a quick phone call, a text message, or IM. This encourages them to come and talk to me and helps open the informal communication channels that are so important to establish."

Technology Offense and Defense

You and your staff are continually inundated with announcements of new technologies. Some of them are obviously important, and you must play good offense and investigate, anticipate, and plan for their adoption. One of the biggest motivators for most programmers is the chance to investigate innovation and learn new things. Rewarding staff who are doing excellent work by sending them to a technical conference to report on a new area of technology or assigning them to investigate a new release of software or survey a breakthrough that you need to consider adopting are great motivators. They will use these brief breaks from their usual tasks to recharge themselves and feel fulfilled. You must ensure that your key contributors have time in their schedules so that you can give them these kinds of rewards. Consider this an important "offensive play" in your management playbook.

However, this sometimes requires a judgment call on your part. All too often many of the new technologies inundating you and your staff are half-baked, unimportant, and will never see commercial success. Any time spent investigating these is time wasted and lost! For such technologies, play strong defense by ensuring that your staff is not seduced by the allure of new "shiny things."

You may even have to put an edict out to keep your team from exploring a particular new thing. Mickey recalls how he used to monitor the Microsoft and Apple technology announcements closely when at Brøderbund. "I recall walking over to a particular programmer's desk and picking up the latest package from Apple that introduced a new functional programming methodology for beta testing. I took it back to my office and locked it away in my file drawer so no one would see it or try to pursue it. I didn't want anyone wasting their precious time on a new programming methodology (which, by the way, subsequently never made it out of its beta test)."

In other cases, your team may be committed to a specific version of a foundational technology, making newer versions a distraction. At Schwab, Ron found his teams bombarded by the WebSphere and WebLogic sales teams wanting to "share" their latest advances—while the versions that he needed his teams to focus were the ones that had already been vetted and accepted by Schwab's data center operations team. He typically gave two or three lead programmers passes to IBM's and BEA's most exclusive conferences while doing everything in his power to keep the rest of the team from having their thinking tainted by "the latest."

At Gracenote, Mickey was pleased by the approach to upgrading Oracle releases taken by his database team and DBAs. "Rather than jump on each new release that came out (e.g., Oracle 10i, Oracle 11g, etc.), the team always waited at least a year before upgrading to a new major release from Oracle. It is usually much better to let others act as guinea pigs for Oracle development and wait until at least two point releases have come out before even beginning the evaluation of the new release. With mature software products it seldom pays to upgrade immediately, since there is seldom major functionality you've been waiting for that is a must-have for your team."

Ron became enamored of Agile methodologies early on and particularly Scrum for how it solves the need programmers have for stability, constancy, and "flow," even as it recognizes and solves for the dramatic fluctuations and frequent changes that software requirements tend to take during a project. By breaking large projects into sprints, delivering working functionality at the end of every sprint, virtually barring mid-sprint change so developers can go heads-down, but enabling between-sprint change of any magnitude, all while focusing on delivering the highest customer value possible, Scrum delivers both yin and yang, the calm at the eye of the storm, stability inside total change. He thinks of choosing Scrum as both offense and defense.

Understanding Your Programmers' Motivations Begins on Day One

As Herzberg's research showed, there are many factors that contribute to job satisfaction and dissatisfaction. But how these factors rank and how important they are to anyone specifically will vary. More than most, programmers are individualists, so it only stands to reason that what motivates each programmer will vary from person to person. One of the first things you should do is try to understand what motivates each one of them.

The best time to do this is before you hire them. That is a time when you have a chance to explore what really does motivate them, since the topics of work, benefits, working environment, whom they report to, and compensation are all on the table for discussion. We relish those introductory discussions since it gives us a chance to understand what really makes the candidates tick. We are often directly part of the hiring process, even though we are not the hiring manager. This also gives us a chance while interviewing the candidates to validate the assumptions we made looking at their résumés. These deeper assumptions we mentally, or actually, file away for later use.

However, it is not often that you have the chance to hire all your staff. Many will be inherited from the previous manager, who most likely will not pass on many managing tips to you regarding how to motive the staff you are inheriting. It is then important to you to begin to determine what makes each programmer "tick." This can be done in a one-on-one discussion with the person, which takes the place of the hiring interview to build assumptions about what motivates them.

Unlike at the hiring interview, not all of the topics will be on the table, and you most likely will not want to dig into and surface issues that might otherwise not be a problem. For example, we usually stay away from asking about compensation or departmental inequities, since rarely will a new manager be able to address these issues immediately. Rather, the one-on-one discussion will likely be used to understand the programmer's education, background, job experience, length of time with the current organization, current responsibilities, future career goals and plans, current problems and issues, and other things they would like to talk about. If they bring up compensation and departmental inequities, we listen carefully but never promise to address the problems. Depending on the person and the circumstances, we may say that we'll look into them but promise nothing definite about actions or changes.

Following on these one-on-one discussions, we review the personnel files of each individual to gain insight from past reviews or other information that may be in those files. We then discuss them with our peers and our boss to try to glean tidbits of information related to each person. The opinions of our peers or boss will likely be impressions that are not necessarily accurate, so we give them less weight. Nonetheless, by this time we probably will have developed a mental model of what makes each person tick. And using that information, we can build on our assumptions and assess for ourselves whether our assumptions are valid.

The mental model we build for each person is mostly a prioritization of the topics in this chapter. By mentally ranking these items for each individual, we can begin to make sure that those most important to each individual are reinforced when they perform in an excellent or outstanding fashion. We think that all these are important, but when you have the opportunity to reward outstanding performance, make sure to address those that will have the most impact on the individual.

Summary

There is no magic silver bullet that will allow you to motivate your programming staff. Setting realistic milestones and making sure everyone is working toward these milestones is a good starting place. But it takes continual efforts and personalized attention to make sure your staff is motivated to work hard and meet demanding milestones. The information presented in this chapter can get you thinking about how best to motivate your staff, but in the end you must think about this over and over and continually work to make sure your staff is motivated every day, week, month, quarter, and year. The age-old adage of getting "all the oars in the water at the same time" is a good one to help you visualize how your motivated technical staff can and should work together as one.

Tools

There are no tools associated with this chapter.

8

Establishing a Successful Programming Culture

ONE OF THE QUESTIONS WE ASKED BACK IN CHAPTER 1 WAS "What is a great programmer?"

But a question more relevant to you is "What is a great manager of programmers?" An essential and significant element of your role as a great manager is to create and nurture a successful programming culture. For most of us, that's a culture that supports and encourages the delivery of quality software on time and within budget by a team that developers feel proud and gratified to be part of for a long time.

You were hired to manage, right? But even if you follow all of our earlier advice, it's not easy. Your programmers don't always act rationally or predictably. Some have chaotic personal lives. They don't always get along. They can be blunt, reclusive, irritable, manic, silent, impatient, petulant, abrasive . . .

Your organization may not care much about them (unless their irrational behavior spews beyond your department, of course). But your organization cares a lot about your ability to produce and deploy software that meets organizational goals and customer needs.

Almost any group of programmers, no matter how dysfunctional, will care, too. They care about being productive and building successful products and services.

As for you, you care even more. In addition to wanting what your developers want, and wanting to meet your organization's expectations, you want to be a high-performing software development manager who can stretch beyond the ordinary to achieve the remarkable.

You need help. You somehow need to create internal and external expectations for greatness. You need to instill confidence that you and your team(s) can deliver. You need a culture that supports your goals and objectives. And you need to create an environment of excellence that attracts and retains top talent and motivates stellar work.

Powerful cultures drive high-performance work in ways that no amount of personal motivation alone can achieve.

Under the right conditions, the problems of commitment, alignment, motivation, and change largely melt away.

—*JIM COLLINS*[1]

Defining "Successful"

OK, so it may not be greatness you need to deliver. For some projects it may be functional but frequent delivery. For others your stakeholders may expect their product to be "flawless." Some teams are formed to help visionaries conceptualize products. Other teams are formed to keep products running as the environments they're built within change.

You may find you have organizational goals as well, goals such as developing and retaining quality programmers, perhaps.

It is essential to creating and nurturing a successful programming culture that you understand what "successful" means for your company, your organization, your project, and your team—and how to measure it.

The Programming Culture

Unless you lucked out and inherited it, you have to create your own successful programming culture. To maintain it, even if you inherited it, you need to nurture it. These are truisms whether you and your team are developing packaged software, software as a service, embedded software, B2B software components and services, or internal applications for the firm's employees. They are true whether you're part of a tiny start-up, a large corporation, a nonprofit, or government. Your mission is to deliver value. And that requires managing the people and the culture.

---

1. Jim Collins, *Good to Great* (HarperCollins, 2001), p. 11.

Creating a powerful programming culture requires establishing

- A work setting that is conducive to developing outstanding quality software and values on-time creation and delivery of on-target, customer-focused software
- An atmosphere of respect and fairness that keeps your staff at their most productive
- An environment in which commitment and motivation are easily nurtured and grown
- Metrics for your products, projects, and deliverables so your team can measure its efforts and improve its results

The challenge is: How do you do that?

Company Culture

All organizations—large and small, companies, governments, and nonprofits alike—have a corporate culture already. It's important to understand your organization's culture in order to create the culture you desire.

If it's a strong, positive culture, it may provide you with a platform you can leverage to create the right environment for your own team. Or it may be one that is so corrosive that you need to wall it off entirely to give your team an insular environment in which it can accomplish good work undistracted.

To figure out the corporate culture, listen to the CEO. Steve Jobs in a video conversation in 2007 (with Bill Gates), for example, said he wanted employees at Apple to feel like they were doing the best work of their careers. Chuck Schwab used those same words in the mid-nineties when the brokerage was moving stock trading online.

In most large companies, it's easy to identify the culture and values the company espouses. You'll find well-phrased statements of vision and values, sometimes referred to as purpose and principles, printed on posters and plaques, T-shirts and coffee cups, the company Web site and laminated wallet cards.

That said, view what you hear and see with some skepticism. What companies espouse is not always how they behave. Look deeper than the words. Enron claimed to stand "on the foundation of its Vision and Values," trumpeting values that included "Respect, Integrity and Communication." Regarding respect, its Web site expounded that "ruthlessness, callousness and arrogance don't belong here." That hardly seems consistent with the directive CEO Jeffrey Skilling is said to have given his management team to "cut jobs ruthlessly by 50 percent."

Even where values have been forsaken, smart development managers recognize that the company's values, with words painted everywhere, can be leveraged. A good development manager at Enron would have forged a programming culture around "respect, integrity, and communication," regardless of their absence in the milieu around them.

For organizations less than 30 or 40 years old, our experience is that the culture almost without fail reflects the personal standards and core values of the company's founder(s). Listen to stories from the earliest employees about how the founder established and grew the company. The stories at Apple of Steve Jobs leading the Mac team—virtually living together, working day and night, printing T-shirts with "Working 90 hours a week and loving it," raising a pirate flag in fierce pride and defiance—without question forged intense esprit de corps. But this environment also created interdepartmental rivalries and frustrated cross-company collaboration. In fact, Apple was long an aggregation of teams more than an integrated company.

Ultimately, culture derives not from the words that are espoused, but from the lessons that are communicated through action. Look for how employees, shareholders, and customers are perceived and treated—and the stories employees tell—regardless of the culture your organization claims to live by.

Leveraging the Complexity of Your Company's Culture

At Charles Schwab, Ron created a small department of 25 to lead a three-year initiative to move all of Schwab's application development to Java. "More than any other company I've seen, Schwab's values were applied equally to employees, customers, and shareholders alike. Daily interactions more often than not mirrored its published values. Schwab's espoused principles— *Fairness, Empathy, Responsiveness, Striving, Teamwork, Trustworthiness*—were modeled by founder Chuck Schwab. Whether seen from inside the company or out, Chuck Schwab is a man who is both extraordinarily entrepreneurial and at the same time one of the most caring and ethical heads of any company anywhere. Where *Teamwork* in most companies refers to *your* team, there was a sense at Schwab that teamwork meant everyone."

But even in the best of companies, the best of values can be a mixed blessing. Ron's Java initiative, at its core, was about building and sharing best practices, about finding and sharing common ways to do things. A slam dunk in an organization with *Teamwork* as a core value, right? Getting teams to share best practices, approaches, patterns, and even code should be easy.

But look at the values again. *Striving* plus *Responsiveness* can be translated, in practice, into relentless delivery of customer value. Developers driven to deliver relentlessly will tend to focus single-mindedly on their own work and neither learn from those around them nor, at the end of a project, find time to share.

To make his Java initiative successful Ron had to leverage and emphasize the *Teamwork* value while deflecting the countermanding pull of the *Striving* and *Responsiveness* values. "I found I could get the attention of teams by posing the challenge in terms of results. 'We have a choice: hundreds of one-off projects that take too long and all repeat the same mistakes endlessly; or cultivating a culture of sharing, reaping savings from a pattern of reuse and shared best practices.'"

Company values can be a blessing and a bane, even in great companies. Once you've assessed what you have to work with, you can decide which parts you can leverage and which parts you need to shield your team from.

Walling Off Your Company's Culture

In a later section we will discuss programming cultures and the values you may want to emphasize. But it should be obvious by now that you may have to wall off some or all of your company's culture.

You know that achieving long-term success requires that you strengthen your architecture, refactor your code regularly, develop regression tests, improve your processes, upgrade your hardware and software platforms, and do the myriad other things that reduce technical debt and keep you in the game. Mickey often uses the metaphor of oil changes to drive the point home: "Making products is kind of like driving a car. You have to occasionally, but regularly, change the oil."

Yet in some companies, senior management may give short shrift to all but customer-driven projects and ask the question "Why is anyone working on anything that's not an obvious customer feature?"

....

As a rule of thumb, one MBA can neutralize the efforts
of five good engineers.

> —GUY KAWASAKI, *Early Apple Evangelist and*
> *Founder, Garage Technology Ventures*

To be successful in the face of customer-value-only senior management, you need to protect programmers working on under-the-hood efficiencies from organizational disrespect. They need encouragement, nurture, and praise that will come only from within your organization.

They need you to wall off the company's culture, substituting one of your own creation.

Mickey recalls the need to do that as Brøderbund's culture changed. Brøderbund's original culture emanated from its founding CEO, Doug Carlston. His vision drove programmers, artists, animators, sound designers, QA staff, producers, and even its technical support staff to make great products that had aesthetic style that usually far exceeded that of competing products. But after going public, Doug spent less time at the company and eventually ceded responsibility to someone who was hired as the new CEO.

This new CEO was not from the software industry and was brought in at a time when content was king and licensed content and brands (e.g., Dr. Seuss) were becoming increasingly important. In fact, he came from a premier consumer brand company, Kraft Foods, where he made his mark managing Kraft Velveeta Cheese. "I began walling off my teams from this new CEO after he told me that 'making software is a lot like making cheese' on more than one occasion. I never really understood how making software was anything like making cheese, but I did understand I needed to insulate my teams from inane comments from the new CEO and adhere to its original culture of making great products."

Other elements of corporate cultures can be even more toxic to software team success. As one example, you'll need not only to wall off but figure out ways to circumvent cultures that encourage extreme competition and noncooperation among employees.

What Part Does Technology Play in Your Company?

Aside from whether your organization's corporate values are strong or weak, positive or not so positive, you need to also consider the relative importance of your software development organization within the corporate ecosystem. While you may, over time, be able to affect how senior management views your organization, you first need to understand how they perceive you now.

A firm may view its technology organization as the road to its future profitability, the core of its current value proposition, a cost center to be endlessly squeezed, or an organizational annoyance. To create an environment of excellence and high-performance teams, the culture you devise will necessarily be different for each of these cases.

While a financial services firm may recognize technology as core to its business, a raw materials company may never see IT as more than a cost center—unless some smart technology leader identifies (and shows, sells, and convinces senior management) how technology can differentiate the company's offering from its competition.

The Apple II was the cash cow that enabled Apple to build the Lisa and Macintosh businesses, but the engineers who got the glory within Apple were those working on the future platforms: the Apple III, the Lisa, and the Macintosh. Apple II engineers had to be motivated not by glory, which they would never again get, but by serving the then-largest personal computer customer base in the world, by having a fondness for a platform many of them had grown up with, and by finding ways to show the "glory teams" just what the "inferior" platform could do—making the old horse dance.

How companies perceive their development organizations may change over time, often in step with business cycles. The 1990s boom cycle, in which online activity drove fundamental growth, led to a frenzy of development and developer hiring. On the other hand, the bust cycle that followed in the early part of the next decade was typically focused on cost reduction, with companies slashing their technology organizations' roles to little more than core operations. Notice, in the following descriptions we wrote of the two drastically different economic climates, how the results, which we've italicized, were so similar:

> In the midst of the technology boom, when Web applications couldn't be developed fast enough, development managers working on Web functionality at Schwab joked that just trying to get the vision from their business partners was "like dogs chasing cars trying to read the hubcaps." Developers were seen as the drivers of the company's success, but were nonetheless *frustrated because there were too few programmers for the number of projects,* matched up against the relentless pace, *which resulted in having delivery expectations that were unreasonable with too little time to design and execute.*

> In the bust, development projects were cut back, but layoffs made even deeper cuts in the number of developers, leaving those remaining feeling unappreciated given the new economic reality and *frustrated because there were too few programmers for the number of projects, which resulted in having delivery expectations that were unreasonable with too little time to design and execute.*

It's almost funny how the frustration can be the same in climates so radically different, but as similar as the words are, the emotional and psychological components of culture building required to protect and support your team are very different. In the first case, everyone from senior management to customers to the marketplace was savoring and honoring Schwab teams' products; the managers' challenge was to help overtaxed engineers feel valued as individuals. In the wake of layoffs, the remaining engineers often felt valued as individuals (they were the ones who still had jobs!) but weren't at all sure anyone truly cared about their work.

What Drives Your Company?

The final element of organizational culture to understand for your culture-building efforts is: Which function is in the driver seat? Is yours an engineering-driven, a marketing-driven, or a sales-driven company? Is your nonprofit driven by its fundraising or by its mission?

What drives the organization often defines tech's role within it.

Ultimately, the essential balancing act that drives decisions in programming organizations is between being innovative on the one hand and being responsive to customers and markets on the other.

This is a fulcrum of programming culture, but every organization sets it differently. If you get it right for your organization, it will be easier to succeed. If you can't understand where the organization's fulcrum is set, you clearly don't belong. The fundamental question becomes whether you're trying to serve customer needs or developing technology for technology's sake—technology because it's cool.

In the mid-seventies, Evans & Sutherland found itself with a line of systems that were modestly successful and certainly innovative but that suffered one complaint: They cost too much. A new product team was charged with developing a compatible, lower-cost, next-generation product. Mickey recalls, "The team made the mistake of responding to a secondary customer complaint—that the system stole too many cycles from customer computers. The team innovated brilliantly, adding a 68000 into the box to offload some of the CPU processing. But in doing so, the team diverged from its prime directive. With the programming paradigm changed, the system was no longer compatible with the previous system. Customers experienced chaos. Worse, the change failed the original objective to be cheaper. Technology obsession to do something new and cool, while it had the veneer of doing something for the customer, fundamentally opened the door for competitor Silicon Graphics to do a cheaper, tightly coupled graphics system—computer, software, and display—and walk away with the marketplace."

Start-ups early on are often technology-driven or vision-driven. But at some point, many if not most companies switch to being customer-focused.

The games and screen savers that Brøderbund and Berkeley Systems built demanded lots of innovation, but that innovation was focused almost laserlike on supporting the entertainment value of their games.

Focus on customers is critical for most organizations. When Mickey hears the word *framework* from a programmer on his team—advocating that the team should build one—his antennae go up. "It's all too often a sign of innovation for innovation's sake," he says.

> . . . it comes back to worse is better. If you spend the time to build the perfect framework . . . well guess what: release 1.0 is going to take you three years to ship and your competitor is going to ship their 1.0 in six months and now you're out of the game. You never shipped your 1.0 because someone else ate your lunch. Your competitor's six-month 1.0 has crap code and they're going to have to rewrite it in two years but, guess what: they can rewrite it because you don't have a job anymore.
>
> —JAMIE ZAWINSKI, *Early Netscape Lead Developer*[2]

Beware of technology for technology's sake. Apple's system software group repeatedly lost its way. Instead of solving problems that customers like Mickey's Brøderbund team struggled with, Apple rolled some of its most talented engineers into the "pink" group, then spun them out into Taligent, an Apple/IBM joint venture legendary for its inability to ship the operating system it had been charged with creating. It was a mistake that cost Apple dearly.

> My rules of thumb come in the form of questions.
>
> The first and most important one: "Why are we doing this?" This reminds me to always check that my team is working only on things that align with strategic or

---

2. Quoted in Seibel, *Coders at Work,* pp. 22–23.

tactical priorities for the product or organization. Too often we spend the scarce engineering time on things that aren't essential.

The second one is "What problem are we trying to solve?" This reminds me to look past cool bells and whistles that Marketing often wants to see if there is an actual customer problem worth solving and only then look for a solution.

Both of these seem obvious and they should be, but all too often they are forgotten.

—*TANYA BEREZIN, Senior Project Manager, Intuit*

It is similarly the case that too many programmers are eager to implement from scratch rather than leveraging already written and debugged code. It has oft been said that "programmers are the only people who prefer to stand on the toes of others rather than on their shoulders."

Characteristics of a Successful Programming Culture

In the end, whether you inherit a positive programming culture or create your own, developing it and keeping it positive requires you to make conscious, intentional decisions over and over.

Celebrate what you want to see more of.

—*TOM PETERS*

Furthermore, it means modeling the culture you're trying to create. Your team looks to you as a model of the behavior you expect and want to see. There may be no stronger illustration of the adages "It's not what you say, it's what you do" and "Actions speak louder than words."

Both of us have known managers who set up programming teams to compete against each other, contending that it is scrapping that motivates programmers to do their best work. We think those managers don't belong in an engineering organization. Some of them came from sales. Sales is an individual sport. It's competitive, with salespeople competing against both quotas and each other.

The reward for being a top-performing engineer, on the other hand, is seldom a trip to Hawaii, or golf with senior management. In fact, rewarding competitive performance, whether with those kinds of grand rewards or subtler ones, is almost always inappropriate and counterproductive. Software engineering is a team sport. Smart engineering managers make sure their top performers are happy but reserve the big rewards for entire teams, sending them off on team trips and off-sites, for example, as welcome breaks from arduous development marches.

....

The complete team succeeds or the whole team fails.

—AGILE ADAGE

Ron helped turn around a start-up inside Fujitsu that was months late delivering its product. The effort had been based around a culture dominated by a few senior programmers willing to be heroes but expecting to be treated as such. Ron built teamwork out of discord by setting expectations that the work and the rewards would be shared. The team would have to together meet corporate's new aggressive deadline or no one would benefit. "When I arrived, it was a team that had not once met a deadline. But working together, they not only met but beat this one."

In programming, leading teams to their highest levels of performance requires creating cultures that encourage mutual respect, innovation, following standards, expectation of delivery and of excellence, high levels of communication, fairness, empowerment, professionalism, teamwork, passion, customer focus, and technical excellence.

Mutual Respect

Probably the foremost characteristic of successful programming cultures is respect. When team members respect each other, they listen to each other and give consideration to each other's input, insights, and ideas. Your team members don't have to like each other, and they don't have to want to socialize with each other. But members of a highly functioning team listen to each other and work collaboratively.

We discussed in Chapter 5 needing your team's respect and in Chapter 7 giving your team your respect. Neither is enough. Creating a culture in which every member of the team respects every other team member should be your goal.

To get it, exemplify and set a culture of courtesy, respect, and regard.

Innovation

It's a rare programming organization that doesn't thrive on and require a culture of innovation. Even when the focus seems directed entirely on delivery, programming is a creative effort. Furthermore, for most projects these days, outside technologies need to be explored, evaluated, and incorporated—from routines to components, from packages to open source.

It's easy to see that it's counterproductive to force a creative group like a programming team to work within constrictive bounds. While product management and your customers may determine the "what," your programmers determine the "how," and it takes a great deal of thought and creativity to pick the best "how."

No matter how good a programmer you were, your team will soon be as good and almost certainly better. They're in the code every day. They understand it. They know how to accomplish what needs to be done better than you can tell them. The best among them will "see" how to implement features that deliver peak performance, or premier reusability, or optimal maintainability. What they need to know from you is which of those is most important, and how to balance them against delivery dates.

Setting no bounds at all can be very dangerous. Beware of the dark side of innovation: There are reasons to set and enforce standards and best practices. It's a rare programming team that doesn't propose to write code that could better be purchased, borrowed, or reused. Writing code is a siren song; there is constant temptation to write what should be borrowed.

Similarly, technology organizations are attracted to new technologies, but unless your team is charged with research, new unproven technologies can be ratholes. Mickey has a rule to "never use a Microsoft product whose version is less than 3.1." There's a parallel rule for most technologies and most vendors.

....

Innovation is hard to schedule.

> *—DAN FYLSTRA, Cofounder of VisiCorp, distributor*
> *of the first spreadsheet program, VisiCalc*[3]

Be intentional in establishing the right balance between innovation and being market- and customer-driven.

---

3. Dan Fylstra is widely attributed on the Web as having said this.

What projects you take on, how you do them, and your expectations all communicate your culture with regard to innovation, technical excellence, and business and customer focus.

The right level of innovation is a fine line. Your job is to find that line and to communicate and monitor it. If you do a good job defining it and making your definition part of your culture, your organization will mostly monitor itself.

- To encourage innovation, you must encourage risk.
- To encourage risk, you must tolerate failures.
- To tolerate failures, you must be patient.
- To communicate your encouragement of innovation, you must reward dedication, not success.

While neither reckless risk taking nor failing to learn from one's mistakes should be acceptable, you need to create room for "noble failures"—projects that, despite purposeful effort and dedication to success, fail anyway. You know you're encouraging risk appropriately when noble failure brings no disgrace even as the effort and dedication are lauded and acknowledged. By encouraging and creating a culture of "smart" risk taking, you will give your developers permission to create and deliver amazing solutions.

Standards

Among expectations, you should expect your team to follow standards.

Cars have brakes so that they can go faster, not so that they can go slower!

—DAN KELLER, SVP, Schwab Technology

Standards can't be arbitrary; they must be meaningful. You should adopt or develop standards and set them for design, documentation, testing, and process that match the needs of your organization and your customers—and expect them to be adhered to.

Other standards can apply to

- Requirements
- Coding
- Code quality

- Use of automated document generation
- Development process
- Build process
- Test case tracking
- Traceability
- Check-ins (e.g., code review before check-in)
- Source control
- Open source use
- Intellectual property (IP)

....

It's OK not to follow standards provided (1) you know why, and (2) you can articulate it.

—ROBERT MARSHALL, VP, Schwab.com

Delivery

Virtually every programming organization needs a culture of delivery. Whether it's shipping or going live, on-time completion needs to be explicitly valued.

Most organizations translate development into a series of delivery dates. If the dates are unrealistic—if everyone knows they won't be met—the schedule is moot; there is no delivery goal against which individuals and the team can be measured. Not only will you need to figure out how to rein in your project(s) and set dates that are believable, but you'll have to change your team's thinking to believe that dates are meaningful, realistic, achievable, and worth striving to meet.

....

If you plan for less than your capacity, you get less done than you could have.

If you plan for more than your capacity, you get less done than you could have.

—KENT BECK, Creator of eXtreme Programming (XP), Test-Driven Development (TDD), and JUnit

On the other hand, we've walked into organizations where goals, dates, and even assignments are unclear, and where no one knows what "done" looks like. Here, too, you have your work cut out for you, first to define the product you're building, and then to build a believable project plan that your team can sign up for.

A culture of delivery is not just about setting goals and dates, but also about clearly defining your project and leading your team to crisply execute a development process that achieves it with minimum pain for everyone.

Communication

It is only through stellar communication that you can ensure that every member of your team is moving in the right direction. That means you must make it your job to foster communication, to make sure it occurs, and to include everyone by bringing in and encouraging the most reticent members of your team.

....

The trouble with programmers is that you can never tell what a programmer is doing until it's too late.

—SEYMOUR CRAY, *Founder of Cray Research and Designer of the Cray Supercomputers*[4]

The culture you must create encourages communication at every level. It says, through both your words and your nonverbal cues, that the team can come to you at any time with any problem or issue. Your culture must encourage and reward them to do so earlier rather than later. By encouraging your programmers to bring you issues earlier, even though they may not be sure the issues are or will become problems, you will have the most complete information, the longest advance notice, and the widest resource options to help resolve them.

At Brøderbund, Mickey adopted the mantra "I hate surprises" and preached it to his teams often. He went so far as to put a sign on the wall of his office that said, "I'm the kind of guy who hates surprises" that his direct reports would have to look at when they met with him one-on-one. That is not to say he didn't get surprised (he did all too often), but the message did encourage his staff to communicate new information as soon as it was available.

---

4. www.junauza.com/2010/12/top-50-programming-quotes-of-all-time.html.

So first and foremost, develop a culture that encourages developers to talk with you early and often. Listen carefully. Reserve emotion for the problem, not the messenger. Focus not on fault but on solution.

....

Fix the problem, not the blame.

        —OLD JAPANESE PROVERB

Your culture also needs to encourage developers to talk with each other, both formally and informally. Communication is rarely a programmer's strongest skill, so your culture has much to overcome. Ensuring communication among teammates is the central reason that Agile methodologies stress daily stand-up meetings.

Too little communication can quickly result in "versionitis": Two programmers start working on puzzle pieces designed to fit together but that in remarkably short order diverge, the pieces taking different directions, the API between them badly broken. Too little communication can result in productivity plunges, as one developer waits for a dependency to be delivered that its developer doesn't realize has become critical—or sometimes even that a teammate is dependent upon it. You and your programmers must also discuss and agree on who will do what, or you'll inevitably get redundant code.

When the need for communication extends across teams, typically on larger code bases, the roadblocks can get even worse. In Chapter 9 we'll discuss the successful delivery of software and solving the challenges of inter-team communication. But with regard to culture, you want it to support and encourage dialog at all levels.

In fact, your culture needs to encourage developers to feel free to talk with anyone in the organization to get the information they need to do their jobs. A manager's job is not to bottleneck communication or to be its gatekeeper but to encourage, enable, and reward communication at every level that increases knowledge about the work.

Communication is one of the issues that makes managing "virtual" or geographically dispersed teams so hard. The ambient communication among colocated teammates enables collaboration naturally. Informal conversations that occur while wandering the hallways or running into each other over snacks result in increased team awareness, knowledge, and sharing that we tend to take for granted.

Programmers who are colocated experience each other's rhythms, chat casually outside their offices about their progress, and catch the eye of colleagues to ask for help with a design issue or debugging.

These subtle interactions don't exist for geographically dispersed teams.

Communication Among Virtual Teams

While we've seen research into tools that support these kinds of nuances at a distance, and we've thought about setting up monitors and cameras to give remote employees more "presence," we know of no virtual mechanisms that deliver even semblances of effective, nuanced, in-person interactions.

Virtual teams must be committed to communicate at levels beyond colocated teams: more communication, more e-mails, more sharing in the team wikis, better documentation, more voice and instant-messaging channels. You need to monitor the chat circuits and make certain your people are communicating.

....

The more distance between teammates, the more you have to formalize communication and make it explicit.

*—TED YOUNG, Development Manager and
Agile Coach, GuideWire*

A useful practice in virtual team management is to have each team member specify in prioritized order the best methods to contact and communicate with them. For example, I might specify that my teammates will get the fastest response time from me (perhaps maximum 30 minutes) if they call or leave voicemail on my most useful phone number. And they'll get the second-fastest response time from me, within 2 hours, if they use method B, which is e-mail or IM.

What everyone must recognize is that inevitably, dispersed programmers will be repeatedly interrupted when they're in "the zone." The interrupter simply can't see when they're heads-down. There are far fewer clues to identifying when a remote teammate is available.

Similarly, while it's all too easy for programmers on colocated teams to get stuck without your knowing it—thrashing and beating their heads against hard problems while giving no indication they've made no progress—it's an order of magnitude likelier on virtual teams. Too, programmers on virtual teams are more likely to be charging ahead, churning out code—but going down the wrong path—without your knowing it. Only a culture of robust communication will give you a shot at intercepting and resolving issues before they're out of control.

At Gracenote, one of the database programmers was interested in the Japanese culture—so interested that he volunteered to move to Tokyo for a period of time. Mickey jumped at the chance to have someone working on the ground in Japan who knew the database development practices of the team in the United States. "He moved to Japan and quickly was able to be productive implementing needed enhancements for the Japanese market that could never have been communicated or prioritized for the team in the U.S.A. However, it did not accomplish one of the goals of the posting; this particular developer was not able or willing to communicate with the team back in the U.S.A. frequently or often enough. Though his contributions remained outstanding and critical to serving our customers in Japan, his lack of communication skills combined with the distance and eight-hour time difference did not greatly expand the communications between the two organizations. Though his stay in Tokyo was successful, a better communicator would have made a much bigger impact on bringing the two organizations together."

Mickey has often thought about finding or developing tools that would make virtual team members more present virtually/physically with their teams. He considered having developers install tools that tracked their computer activities (keystrokes, mouse clicks, windows opened, etc.) but realized his programmers might view such measures as draconian and invasive. He considered setting up a virtual office for remote staff—a monitor and a camera—not always watching, but like an office behind frosted glass, where you can't see in but you get a sense of availability and presence. He hoped that providing blurred images only (not clear ones) and some sort of "at my desk" or "away from my desk" system of messaging, displayed on a monitor in the middle of the team, would give local team members a sense of connection with virtual team members. But when his plan to provide virtual presence was met with disinterest by local and virtual team members alike, he never pursued it.

This is a need felt by many, and in fact companies[5] that spent years developing systems that promised to monitor the activities of remote developers effectively have come and gone. Though intrigued, Mickey never found the time or the right project to try them. But sooner or later advanced

---

5. For example, 6th Sense Analytics, Inc. Sadly, the company was not successful. But you can still check out their demo from 2007 at www.youtube.com/watch?v=J1UmQXsZsLM.

tools may provide the functionality we have been longing to find that supports distributed team building without feeling prying or heavy-handed.

Fairness

A culture of fairness lets your staff work with the trust and assurance of knowing that rewards (and critique) will be delivered fairly, not arbitrarily.

There's something about the perception of unfairness that drives human beings to distraction so, if only for averting consternation, you want to avoid it.

Easier said than done. One of the baselines of fairness is pay. While American companies go to great lengths to discourage employees from sharing their salary and bonus numbers, don't count on secrecy: No matter what you do, programmers in many if not most organizations seem to know what their colleagues—at least some of them—make. If your salaries are out of whack, your team knows.

And it's almost impossible for them not to be. Market rates for programmer salaries seem constantly in flux. There's almost no point in time where the salary of a recent hire or a transfer into the group doesn't skew what's fair. Mickey says, "My breakthrough moment as a manager came when I realized that I could not always be fair—*but I could always make sure that a steeper slope of the curve for their salary changes would eventually solve the problem.* At Evans & Sutherland in the early eighties, I had a young programmer who was a rock star, yet he made less than half the salary of a more seasoned programmer who couldn't carry the new guy's lunch box. It was the realization that I could fix situations like that over time, even if I couldn't fix them all at once, that let me live with the short-term inequities. Over time, I ensured that my groups' salaries were stack-ranked by performance."

If at all times you strive for fairness, people will be OK that at any point in time there may be inequities. A fair culture is one where you're moving toward fairness at all times.

While salaries may be stack-ranked by performance, they can't possibly reflect the order-of-magnitude differences between people's productivity. Perks help. We believe in giving out perks based on performance. Think about what it is you're rewarding, and reward what you value. Then gravitate perks—new machines, conference attendance, better office space—to the top performers at all times. That's fairness as well.

Empowerment

While new programmers (and even seasoned ones thrown into new situations) need direction, nothing encourages productivity as much as empowerment. When people know that the difference they can make is directly proportional to the effort they put in, and when they have some say in the effort they make, the resulting productivity can be dramatic. Apple was a big company at the point Ron arrived there. But with a mission to change the world and empowerment to make it so, every contributor in R&D poured their heart and soul into making a difference.

Conversely, there's little that will kill productivity more than micromanagement, the need of some managers to tell their teams not only what needs doing but how, down to the smallest details. Programming is a job that ought to be fun. Give programmers a job to do that challenges them to step up, think through, stretch their mental models, and craft effective solutions, and you give them the opportunity to exceed your expectations. Tell them detail by detail how to go about their tasks—or show a lack of trust through nagging follow-ups and incessant checking—and you will squelch every ounce of inspiration and creativity right out of them. It's one of the reasons that most successful programming managers are former programmers: They can quickly grasp whether a developer is on track through the most informal of conversations, without having to ferret out that assessment through long strings of questions that can feel pestering.

....

Never tell people "how" to do things. Tell them "what" to do and they will surprise you with their ingenuity.

—*GENERAL GEORGE S. PATTON*

Empowerment, like many other aspects of management, requires balance. Assigning a programmer whose capabilities you don't know to code a critical module and then not checking back to assess progress is an invitation for disaster.

....

I inspect what I expect.

—*ALAN LEFKOF, President and CEO, Netopia[6]*

---

6. Alan noted, "I learned this from Lou Gerstner at McKinsey."

....

Trust but verify.

    —*RONALD REAGAN*

....

Accountability is not micromanagement.

    —*MARK HIMELSTEIN, Interim VP of*
    Engineering, San Francisco Bay Area

Professionalism

A programming culture that encourages professionalism is one that nurtures integrity, promotes continued learning, rewards the pursuit of certifications, applauds membership in professional organizations and communities, makes professionalism part of the path to technical leadership, and overall develops team members' abilities to be outstanding in representing themselves and their organization, both internally and externally.

Little is more representative of being professional as a programmer, a manager, or almost any other role in your organization than integrity—doing what you say you'll do. One of Ron's earliest coaching experiences as a manager was with a young product manager just out of college who believed that responding with "yes" to every request from the engineering managers with whom he interacted was what professionalism was about—regardless of whether he had any hope of delivering on those promises. Ron's young charge was making a mess of the team's relationships. *Yes* is a word that others love to hear, but only when there is follow-through and delivery.

The ability to be insightful—to synthesize and to reflect—is a skill worth valuing and nurturing. In part, it comes from reading widely in the field. The ability to appropriately contribute one's insights to the team is commonly part of the transformation of a team member into a technical leader.

We think you should encourage programmers to join ACM, IEEE, and other professional organizations and communities. Both membership and conference attendance put members in contact with like-minded professionals, plus they encourage and nurture your folks to step up to a higher plane of responsibility and understanding.

Certification has long been valued in other disciplines such as medicine, law, and various branches of engineering. While Microsoft seems to use certification as a lock-in, keeping its developers focused on its own technologies, Microsoft has nonetheless managed to attach value and recognition to certification.

Developing a culture that honors and rewards looking, acting, and being professional lends credibility to your team members and your team. There is good value in encouraging professionalism.

No Jerks and Bozos

One of the worst mistakes a manager can make is to tolerate unacceptable behavior that threatens the productivity of the team. Managers find taking action with respect to behavioral problems difficult, and as a result, they too often delay. That just lets problems fester.

....

It's not what you do; it's what you don't do!

—*PHAC LE TUAN, VP of Engineering and*
CEO, San Francisco Bay Area[7]

Managers worry that their team will see them as arbitrary, unfair, punitive, and retributive or mean. In fact, just the opposite is more often the case. By the time you realize a behavioral problem is impacting team productivity, the rest of your team has known about it in excruciating detail for considerable time—and is wondering why you haven't addressed it. Since you've created a culture committed to productivity and delivery, they will not abide excuses to tolerate less.

You must address the problem, and you can't delay. Yes, use process, don't be arbitrary in the consequences, and be caring and empathetic. In fact, the first inkling you have of a problem is the time to leverage those relationships you've been building with HR to get some coaching in handling situations like this. But don't delay addressing the problem. As we described in Chapter 5, you should be timely in giving honest, direct feedback to the employee, expect change against a plan you create together, and clearly state the consequences of not delivering on that plan.

Don't tolerate cynicism in your organization, either. Private cynicism is acceptable, perhaps even necessary; you should be open to cynicism being brought to you with the expectation to work it out. But public cynicism is a disease that can hobble your team and your company. Left unchecked, it spreads. Exorcise it.

---

7. He was commenting on the challenges of managing at Apple.

View dealing with bozos, cynicism, and jerks as opportunities to model a culture of communication, productivity, empowerment, fairness, and professionalism—the culture that you want your entire organization to aspire to.

Excellence

Have you ever paid attention to sports teams? Some of them win despite themselves. They make errors. They don't seem that good. But they expect to win. And they do.

Then there are teams that have never won, a fact that seems to be the very thing preventing them from doing so.

Magic doesn't come to those who don't expect it.

—DIANA VREELAND[8]

There have been studies that show that the same kids will, if told they're smart, deliver excellence—and if told they're dumb, deliver failure.

A culture that honors, demands, and expects excellence is orders-of-magnitude more likely to get it.

Look at a man the way that he is, he only becomes worse.
But look at him as if he were what he could be, and then
he becomes what he should be.

—JOHANN WOLFGANG VON GOETHE

Expect buy-in to your team's and the company's goals. And expect commitment to making your projects successful. Expect excellence.

Programming Excellence

On the flip side of not tolerating bozos, make it easy and rewarding to be a top performer. Listen to your top performers for what blocks them from delivering their best work and fix those things. Encourage and reward programming excellence.

---

8. Quoted in *The Week,* January 2006.

Teamwork and Collaboration

Your culture should be based around creating high-performance teams.

Valuing teamwork has been embedded in our comments on mutual respect, fairness, communication, and not tolerating bozos.

But it bears stating explicitly, especially having just told you to nurture great programmers: *What you should avoid at all costs is a culture that overly rewards heroes.* At first glance it seems reasonable and fair to reward the cavalry for riding in to save your late, bug-ridden projects. Certainly the programmer who stays up all night to work out the last bugs, get the product deployed, or get the system back online after an outage should be gratefully acknowledged.

But your goal should be to have a culture of teamwork and delivery in which everyone has pitched in. You should see results that require no one to pull an all-nighter, with the application going live a day ahead of schedule, and reliability better than forecast.

Create the right balance between rewarding teams and rewarding heroes, and you'll have many team members willing to save the day, but few times when you need them to do so.

Passion

As we've noted before, programmers tend to be motivated, above all else, to make a positive difference in the world. Not every company and product makes a positive contribution to humankind, but for those that do, it is a small step from motivation to passion.

Passion is an emotion that comes from the heart—from the core of one's being. Passion comes from knowing who you are and what matters to you, and seeing the direct connection to what you do.

Help your team members understand themselves and their core values—and the connection between their core values and their work—and you'll trigger passion in your folks that will make getting up in the morning, coming in to work, and their every moment in the office a source of pleasure and deep personal satisfaction.

Customer Focus: "It's the Customer Experience, Stupid!"

One of the things development organizations have the toughest time shaking is arrogance that they know what's best for the customer—better than the customers themselves know.

Virtually every software development organization should be customer-focused and customer-experience-centered. Gaining a customer perspective is critical. We've known development managers who had their software teams also take on a support role for a period of time. This helped change those teams' perspectives on the customer usage of their products and their pain points. The teams' ability to create usable products improved dramatically and was reflected in the products they later built.

In Mickey's first major project out of college, he had an experience that molded the rest of his career. "I was a team member, and later the technical lead for a major project for the U.S. Navy in my first professional job with Kenway Engineering. After the project was installed for the customer, I was the software side of the on-site technical support team (one software, one hardware) for a six-acre aircraft rework facility that our system had automated. Having to be on-site, working directly with the customer's staff every day, while also being distant from the corporate headquarters, dramatically impacted how I came to appreciate the needs of the customer and their daily input and also how difficult it can be to be located remotely from the development team at corporate headquarters. Both lessons have made me a better manager who listens to and is motivated to fix customer issues and also to support any remote technical support staff as best I can."

With respect to customer empathy, the fact is, as proclaimed on a button distributed at ACM's Computer-Human Interface Conference a few years ago, "We are not the customer." We know too much. We know how the code is written. We know what the software is supposed to do. We know how it works. We know how to make it work. Compared to us, the customer is almost blind.

....

Do lots of user testing: Users are the best testers.
(Developers are the worst testers!)

> —RON MAK, *Middleware Architect of the NASA*
> Mars Rover *Mission's Collaborative Information Portal*

You don't find out whether your software truly works from your developers or QA team; you find out by putting customers in front of it and watching them try to use it. At this stage, metaphorically blind customers stubbing their toes where the programmers know better than to step are the best drivers of improvement.

As Mickey recalls, "Among the first programmers hired at Gracenote was a developer who had been using the original CDDB service to create a media player as a freeware project. He became the in-house developer who provided feedback directly to the programmers developing the client SDK and the online service. He had great insight into what our customers' developers would want to see for their interfaces. He became our in-house alpha application developer who helped make every aspect of our initial offerings better. We did not follow up and hire or train other application developers for the additional products or services we created, due to budget constraints. In retrospect, this was shortsighted since it likely would have ensured that those additional products and services worked better and were more customer-focused. This is a key lesson that unfortunately is learned time and again by many companies."

Most programs would be improved by making developers "eat their own dog food"—use the software they make. And it's a bad omen when an organization that could be using its own software is instead using someone else's.

The ultimate metric that I would like to propose for user friendliness is quite simple: If this system were a person, how long would it take before you punched it in the nose?

> —TOM CAREY

Learning

Programming organizations should be learning organizations.

There is no such thing as writing a piece of code perfectly. Code is never finished. Programmers have to learn when to let it go. Conversely, Ron recalls the head of the art department at Fujitsu telling him that some programmers didn't know what "done-ness" was: They would say something was done when the core internal function was demoable, not when it had a smooth UI and met the actual requirements.

There are nights that I go out and play a piece perfectly.
Then, the next night, I go out and play it better. . . .
Perfection is the first stage of obsolescence.

—*JEAN-PIERRE RAMPAL*[9]

Programmers must continuously learn to code better programs and deliver better products.

Go out of your way to make sure your developers get some learning during the year. Give someone a book, send them to a conference, challenge them in one-on-ones. Encourage them to learn and to keep learning. Set up brown-bag lunches where they can share with each other. Even code and design reviews provide a place where programmers are learning.

Make learning an integral part of your culture.

Environment

Too many software development organizations are penny wise and pound foolish: You would think that, after spending serious money to hire programmers, organizations would maximize their investment by providing the fastest workstations made, along with all the hardware and software tools their developers request.

But all too often we see organizations in which the CEO has a more powerful workstation than the developers; developers have to fight to justify every tool purchase, sometimes including their development environment itself; and they spend days doing hand work to substitute for a few hundred dollars' worth of tools that would accomplish the task in minutes.

If you find yourself in such a culture, you're not going to change it overnight. But you should make it your goal to get your programmers what they need to be their most productive. You can state that while your culture is not yet about providing the hardware and the tools needed to be most productive, it's a culture whose leader—you—uses every opportunity to pitch and procure them.

A programmer is most productive with a quiet private
office, a great computer, unlimited beverages, an ambient
temperature between 68 and 72 degrees (F), no glare on

---

9. Perhaps the world's best flute player, quoted in Dale Dauten, *The Max Strategy* (William Morrow, 1996).

*the screen, a chair that's so comfortable you don't feel it,
an administrator that brings them their mail and orders
manuals and books, a system administrator who makes
the Internet as available as oxygen, a tester to find the
bugs they just can't see, a graphic designer to make their
screens beautiful, a team of marketing people to make
the masses want their products, a team of sales people to
make sure the masses can get these products, some patient
tech support saints who help customers get the product
working and help the programmers understand what
problems are generating the tech support calls, and about
a dozen other support and administrative functions which,
in a typical company, add up to about 80% of
the payroll."*

—*JOEL SPOLSKY, Blog Author,* Joel on Software[10]

One way to help convince your management about the value of tools is to use a woodworking or automotive repair analogy. Almost everyone has done some woodworking or auto repair at some time in their lives and in the process has discovered how important it is to have the right tool for the task. In woodworking, not having a plane available to shave off a fraction of an inch from a board will lead you to sand or file the board to remove the increment of wood. A task that would have taken a couple of minutes will turn into tens of minutes—perhaps hours. Likewise, if you have the wrong wrench while repairing a car (even changing a tire), you can spend hours trying to get a simple job done.

Getting the right tools for your programmers will save them hours of development and debugging time. Tools like static code analysis or advanced debuggers will reduce your overall development time and likely improve the overall quality of the code.

Second, if yours is a culture of long hours in the office, it should support what it promotes—providing food (snacks, quick meals, even complete meals), fun (Ping-Pong tables, posters in the hallways, music out front), beer busts and jam sessions, and subtle environmental things.

---

10. Joel Spolsky, "The Development Abstraction Layer," *Joel on Software*, April 11, 2006, www.joelonsoftware.com/articles/DevelopmentAbstraction.html.

In the midst of the stress of building the System 7 Finder, Apple bought the team Nerf guns to fight stress overload. Developers welcomed those afternoons when one of their teammates brought in his two-year-old (who picked up the Nerf weapons with glee) as moments that reassured them of their humanity—moments that got them through.

Many a pressure-cooker programming organization has been successful by providing a less corporate feel with subtle shifts that lighten the intensity.

Summary

Being a great manager of programmers starts with nurturing a successful programming culture, a culture that sets expectations for mutual respect and fairness, project delivery, innovation as well as compliance with standards and best practices, empowerment paired with professionalism, rock-solid communication, passion and customer focus, unrelenting learning, and high-performance teamwork and collaboration. If those elements are not consistent with the company's culture, you'll have to wall off your programming culture and impede offending values from permeating your milieu. To the extent that they're in sync, you'll want to leverage those positive elements of the company's culture to support and enable your environment of excellence, attract and retain top talent, and motivate stellar work.

As we said at the beginning of this chapter, powerful cultures drive high-performance work in ways that no amount of personal motivation alone can achieve.

Tools

We think the characteristics we've listed for a programming organization are so important to its success that we've created a separate list of them for you to refer to frequently. See the Tools section, after the chapters, for the link to the Tools Web site, from which you can download the following:

Characteristics of a successful programming culture

9

Managing Successful Software Delivery

EVERYTHING THAT HAS BEEN PRESENTED IN THIS BOOK SO FAR has only set the stage for the ultimate objective: managing programmers to successfully deliver software—corralling their creativity, harnessing their meticulousness, and directing their efforts.

It should come as no surprise that most programming managers find that they are judged and rewarded first and foremost on successful execution: their ability to serve up, on schedule and within budget, features and function that match their customers' wants and needs. But for the need to deploy or deliver software that does useful stuff, most organizations would never hire programmers, let alone tolerate the unpredictable, often socially unsophisticated, and sometimes downright antisocial behavior that tends to show up somewhere in most programming organizations.

It's a rare programming manager who does not have this delivery responsibility. At the same time, it's common for most of us to share responsibility for delivery with a project manager (or at least have their help with the details). If you don't, be prepared to learn all the project management routines as well as the development management ones. We'll leave the particulars of project management to the hundreds of project management books that examine every aspect of scheduling and tracking projects using the scores of regimens and methodologies available.

We will focus here on the part programming managers play in successfully developing and delivering software.

Figure 9.1, which was passed hand to hand through engineering and software development organizations long before there was e-mail or even

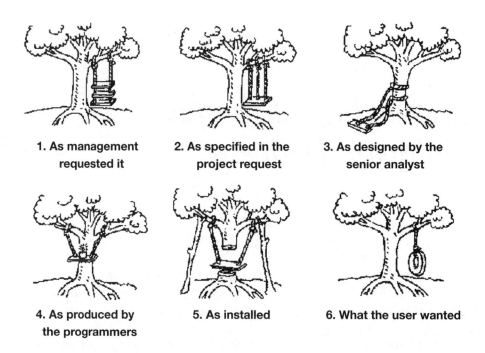

1. As management
requested it

2. As specified in the
project request

3. As designed by the
senior analyst

4. As produced by
the programmers

5. As installed

6. What the user wanted

Figure 9.1   The apocryphal software development lifecycle gone awry[1]

fax machines, aptly spotlights how many points in the development process a project can go awry. It reminds us to beware of any project that does not accurately capture the customer's requirements; getting the requirements wrong is a sure recipe for failure.

Defining the Project

Projects begin with a vision but are delivered by way of requirements, assumptions, expectations, risks, milestones, and deliverables.

Nothing epitomizes the difficulty of building software so much as how hard it is for product managers to tell you clearly, in writing, what it is your team should build. "They don't know yet what it is they want us to build, but they *have* given us a deadline that they want it by." It's painful how

---

1. Robelle, "The SMUG Book," www.robelle.com/library/smugbook/quality.html. Original source unknown.

often we hear that from programming managers and programmers. It happens all the time.

The most recent variation was this one: "The business loves Agile. They think it means that if they sit close to us so they can answer our questions about the requirements, they don't actually have to give us any!"

It's awfully hard to be successful delivering what customers want when you have to make it up as you go along. Guessing has never been a good foundation for knowing what to build.

Studies have repeatedly shown that building to ambiguous requirements—or to the wrong requirements—is among the costliest errors in software development and among the top causes of project failure.[2] Failed, incomplete, and ambiguous communication of requirements between business people and programming teams is at the crux of the problem. And the further into the project lifecycle the error is propagated, the more costly it is to correct.

Ensure That Requirements and Assumptions Are Clear

Your job from the beginning of a project is to ensure that there is clear, crisp communication about requirements, assumptions, expectations, risks, milestones, and deliverables. It's not that you'll do all the communicating yourself, but you have to make sure someone does. And groups that must be in the loop include product management, programmers, and QA.

Programming managers long held out for having requirements be complete before deploying their troops to execute code, but the Waterfall model—in which each phase (requirements, design, coding, testing, etc.) must be completed before the next begins—was long ago shown to be an inadequate match for the reality of how software needs are understood and specified. In both of our careers, of the hundreds of projects we have worked on, each of us has seen just one project that was fully and completely described before coding began. Both cases were over 20 years ago. It virtually never happens.

On the one hand, we have frequently encountered projects where requirements were inadequate. Too often, poor communication of requirements is tolerated by organizational cultures, often for lack of understanding of the consequences. When Ron arrived at one company, he discovered

---

2. Dean Leffingwell, "Calculating Your Return on Investment from More Effective Requirements Management," www-128.ibm.com/developerworks/rational/library/347.html.

product managers collaring programmers in the hallways and directly charging them with new deliverables orally, without consideration for previous assignments and commitments, or for the likelihood of miscommunication and misunderstanding. "I had been hired to make development predictable. The company had recently released a new version of its premier product after taking 18 months instead of the six expected and assigning almost three times the programmers budgeted. I soon learned the reason: The product description had been 'Just like the previous version only better.' Not one of the basic requirements had been worked out (let alone communicated) beforehand. It was a time when consumer products were delivered on floppy disks, but no one had worked out how many floppy disks this new version would ship on. When that decision had been finally made, 14 months into development (and eight months after the original delivery goal!), fully a third of the new functionality had to be jettisoned to make the product fit.

"I'm not given to edicts, but in this case I issued one: No development would commence until a minimum set of requirements was delivered in writing.

"To make it more palatable, I offered to sit at the keyboard and take producers' dictation (I never had to). Regardless, development had to know how many floppies, what computer systems it would run on, which versions of operating systems would be the minimum supported platform, what countries (and thus what languages) we needed to be able to localize to, and what we were trying to accomplish. Once we did that, the division delivered every subsequent project on time for the length of my tenure there."

On the other hand, we have seen product management teams churn out product requirements documents (PRDs) so long and complex they're unreadable. Mickey describes a company where the lead product manager's PRDs, always written in long prose, had grown longer and longer until programmers just couldn't figure out what to build. "There was too much there. We couldn't figure out how to distill all those words into a design document. So we instituted a new PRD style.

"We were at a point where everyone was ready to revolt against the long prose form, so everyone on the team helped drive the change. Just by setting a standard for requirements that every feature had to have a number and a priority, our ability to execute improved at least two times, and possibly much more. Individual requirements became traceable from PRD through development to QA. Programmers no longer had to wade through documents. QA finally had features they could tag tests against. And product managers, once they had the form, found requirements much easier to write."

However, the desire for clear requirements presumes that business people can fully envision what it is they and your customers want. Nowhere is that more difficult than with highly interactive user interface design. UI development, possibly more than any other single factor, has led to the popularity of Agile programming and specifically the practice of developing in short iterative cycles (sprints) with customer delivery at the end of each one. By delivering working code early and often, you get frequent checkpoints to validate your understanding of the requirements.

....

Iteration is critical: Customers don't know what they want until they see it.

—RON MAK, NASA Middleware Architect

Scrum formalizes the role of Product Owner as having responsibility for delivering requirements as stories, one per 3-by-5 card, prioritized not only initially but before every subsequent sprint. Low-priority stories don't have to be fleshed out by the Product Owner or estimated by the team until they rise to become candidates for the next sprint. At that point, though, they must be as thoroughly described as requirements in any other system.

Regardless of methodology, programming managers need to be especially vigilant for requirements under development that are ambiguous. What tends to happen when programmers encounter an unclear path in program logic is that they forge ahead, filling in the logic they think fits. When that happens, programmers are in effect defining the requirements. But it's a rare case in defining requirements (generally only when the target market is other programmers) that programmers understand the product as well as product managers, whose job is (or should be) devoted to understanding customers.

There are several solutions for ambiguous and incomplete requirements. One is tooling. There are now commercial tools on the market that read use case requirements and use natural language understanding to identify and highlight ambiguity. They enable product managers to ferret out and fix requirements ambiguities before ever delivering them to the programming team.

Another solution is to strengthen, enhance, and augment communication between requirements providers and programmers, which is why most Agile methodologies include a practice for colocating programmers with product managers and even customers; then when ambiguities come up, there is a product owner right there to clarify.

If neither is possible, programming managers need to step in to provide liaison between requirements providers and programmers, raising their own communications at both ends, to increase the likelihood that programmers know what is being asked for and are not making it up as they go along but rather asking for the clarifications they need.

Limit Requirements to "What," Not "How"

Programming managers need to be vigilant that requirements not specify implementation.

Good requirements describe the solutions customers need and the value they will provide customers, the "what." Requirements that also choose technologies and implementation paths—that tell you not only what to make but also how to make it—fail miserably at leveraging the knowledge, research and analysis skills, and creativity that a good programming team can contribute to delivering not just an adequate solution but a stellar one.

Your challenge is to push back against requirements that specify the "how."

If you find yourself getting requirements that specify the "how," it may be because your business partners don't trust you or your team or the larger technology organization to make good implementation decisions. Your best defense is to become transparent in your technology decision making—to share your thinking at every stage of the design process so that over time you build their confidence in you and your team.

On the other hand, you may be getting requirements filled with "how" because your business partner saw a demo from one of your competitors at a conference. Or it may be that requirements are easier to write that way: It's easier to tell you to use XYZ technology than to actually spell out what the software should accomplish. Sometimes projects were formulated when product managers became inspired by reading about underlying technologies, but rather than specifying the vision and relying on their technology partners to see if there are even stronger technologies to build it from, they write the requirements as though the one they heard about is the only choice. Mickey: "When product managers are quite technical, they often cannot resist the temptation to detail exactly how a particular feature in a require-ment should work. I've seen cases where the actual algorithm for producing a particular result is specified (including flowcharts and inputs/outputs for specific functions). While the level of detail is appreciated on one level, I've seen programmers' attempts to implement such detailed functionality result in spaghetti code. Instead, I would much rather my programmers distill the requirements and find ways to solve the particular requirement in a more general fashion that can be used for other 'requirements' that are also speci-fied. Unfortunately, it takes a great programmer to know when to step back from such detailed requirements and generalize the solution(s).

"Allowing more junior programmers to implement such detailed requirements is usually a problem waiting to happen. Be on guard for such occasions and work to bring more experienced programmers to bear on these kinds of requirements. The results will likely exceed the expectations of the product manager who could see only one way to do the implementa-tion or devise the algorithm."

You need to talk through the requirements with your business partners and help them get to both an understanding of, and an ability to commu-nicate, what it is they really want in the form of requirements that give you the freedom to deliver their vision.

You also need to be prepared for the possibility that your business part-ners have a strategic purpose in mind: Their solution may be based on there being a partner company that is strategic in some way other than having the best solution, or a provider that your company plans to merge with or absorb. In this case, it's important that if there are serious drawbacks to embracing the partner solution, you lay out the pros and cons as clearly and nonjudgmentally as you can. Sometimes the answer is to go ahead anyway. But other times, after weighing the impact, the better solution will trump partnership. The choice is seldom yours to make but often yours to provide the measure of.

Seek to Delight Customers

What differentiates an excellent programming manager from a merely competent one is the determination not just to accept the handoff of requirements—that is, not just to develop and deliver what is asked for—but to truly understand what it is your business partner is trying to accomplish—to deliver what is desired. The ability to delight customers makes exceptional software managers and their teams stand out.

In part, that means listening and reading not just for what is said but for what is meant. It means asking questions until you fully understand what the customer/product owner/product manager/business partner truly wants and in some cases helping them broaden their understanding of what might be possible.

A canonical example is the windowed interface. When user interfaces were limited to a command line, what customer would have made the leap to ask for icons to represent files, windows to reveal file system directories, and a mouse to visually move and copy files? But Xerox's programmers, and later Apple's, designed just such visual interfaces in a quest to enable nontechnical customers to work more quickly, easily, and intuitively.

A similar example is the now-prevalent iPad tablet. Tablet computers had been created for years before the emergence of the iPad. Mickey still has a functioning ThinkPad X61 tablet laptop computer that he bought several years ago when Microsoft announced the "year of the tablet computer." It is essentially a laptop computer whose keyboard folds under the screen to allow a stylus (one comes with each unit) to be used instead of the mouse to select icons and touch type on a "soft keyboard." Though it was a novelty when it first appeared, he quickly lost interest in using it as a tablet for any but the simplest activities. But then the iPad appeared, and the world went wild over the intuitive use of the touch screen and the gestures that make all manner of interaction easier. All of this could have been implemented on the ThinkPad tablet, but it wasn't. It had all the basic capabilities (sufficient horsepower, touch screen, form factor, etc.) but the vision wasn't there. It was merely a stylus-enabled laptop computer. As Apple proved, customers couldn't request what they couldn't imagine; no one thought they needed an iPad. And now Mickey can't live without his.

You will seldom have an opportunity to so dramatically deliver what your customers want—as opposed to what they know to ask for. On the other hand, there's hardly a project for which you can't deliver subtleties and nuances that will give your customers what they really want but didn't know to ask for.

Quickly Ballpark the Magnitude of Effort Required

It's a rare project that begins without a sense of the cost. There is almost always a budget.

It's not based on much. Until your programming team digs into each feature and each and every area of risk, you can't know the cost. That's like expecting your dentist to know how much it will cost to fix your teeth before you've opened your mouth to give him a look—without benefit of probing, X-rays, or giving you your choice of amalgam or gold. Your dentist can only describe what he's seen in other mouths and the costs for various courses of treatment other patients have required.

If you've made progress toward getting clear requirements, you have about as much information as your dentist, who knows little more than that you want strong, white, cavity-free teeth. Clear requirements settle the amalgam-or-gold question, but you still don't know how much of either you will have to have, or whether you'll need a root canal first.

Your challenge is to do some back-of-the-envelope numbers that estimate the order of magnitude of the effort required.

With respect to cost, whether budget or time, success as a programming manager will often be judged by underpromising and overdelivering.

Nothing is worse than to leave your business partners—and too often, as a result, customers—with unrealistic expectations with respect to the date, the feature set, or both. On the other hand, it's a fine line to walk between over- and underpromising: Overpromising will put your team on a death march, but serious underpromising will mar your credibility and possibly the opportunity to even take on the project.

It's helpful to begin a conversation with your business partners to educate them about the unpredictability of software development. Almost without exception, whatever it is you're building has never been built before—not in this way, not with these tools, not for this platform, not with the peculiar experience your team brings. Part of your job is to introduce practices that make software development more predictable. But it's the nature of the beast that it's just not reliably predictable.

Many managers are tempted to agonize over estimating. It's in our nature to be analytical and exacting. But the fact is that, for most projects, no amount of study can make early estimates better, and getting down in the details at this stage can sometimes make estimates worse. More often than not, what's called for, what's needed, and what is most appreciated are ballpark numbers—order-of-magnitude estimates—that are more rapidly supplied than analysis would ever allow.

Recognize Nonnegotiable Dates

You may well get one more requirement along with the product description, and that is a date. "Every time we got in trouble, it was because of a company- or customer-imposed date," says Mickey.

While sometimes, in the statement "We want this then," the "then" can be negotiated, development can't always be a party to setting the date. Sometimes dates represent opportunities that can be realized only by meeting hard deadlines:

- The space shuttle launch date is set months and sometimes years in advance.
- There's an industry conference that is make-or-break for your product.
- Retail products must arrive at distributors by May and September to make critical selling seasons.
- The U.S. tax deadline of April 15 demands that tax software be ready by January 31 when W-2s are issued.
- Few companies will change out their accounting, payroll, and benefits systems except at year-end.
- Voting machines must be ready, certified, and delivered before Election Day.

....

If you miss the market window, the business value is zero.

—*POLLYANNA PIXTON, Cofounder, Agile Leadership Network (ALN)*

In cases such as these, where the "then" is nonnegotiable, it is important to quickly figure out what "this" really is, how negotiable those features might be, and how to prioritize those features. Recognizing that the date can't slip makes getting the features prioritized correctly a critical part of building your plan.

Ultimately, the overriding axiom of requirements is "Do whatever you can to get the requirements right and to understand what customers really want and need, and the rest will be a lot easier."

Inspire the Team

Understanding and agreeing on what your team is building, and by when, is a good start but not enough. You need to focus your team on the goal and motivate them to "give it their all," "go for the goal line," "win one for the Gipper," "go with all they've got," or even "push the envelope."

....

If you want to build a ship, don't drum up people together to collect wood and don't assign them tasks and work, but rather teach them to long for the endless immensity of the sea.

—ANTOINE DE SAINT-EXUPÉRY[3]

People too often undervalue a good project name and T-shirt. There was a joke at Apple about the key phases of project management. The first phase was "Give it a project name" and the second, "Create the T-shirt." Only then would you be ready for the third, "Write the project plan." Project names and T-shirts were so important because Apple learned early on that they help bring teams together, form cohesion, and give focus.

Many teams use project names for focus and inspiration. The Macintosh Finder, being the core user interface every Mac user sees, was code that everyone at Apple had ideas for. It was hard to say no. Ron's team named one of its Finder projects the "Bungee Finder" to stay focused on that release's goal to enable malleable extensions for graphics, networking, and scripting. When the Mac changed processors from Motorola to PowerPC, the first system software release to deliver native support was labeled "Truth"— a spare proof that the OS could be rewritten—to be followed by "Beauty"— only then would enhancements and improvement be allowed.

When Ron took on an initiative at Schwab to move its thousand-person application organization from any-language-goes to a single object-oriented programming platform company-wide, "I named our team 'Java Object Services' and we created the tagline 'Java Object Services: The Object Is Service.' Mousepads and T-shirts reminded my team to focus on service. And we were sending a message to our customers: Embrace Java, and you can expect help that's dedicated to your success."

Even with a good project name and a T-shirt, a project's vision often becomes lost in technical myopia. It's easy for programmers to get focused on algorithms, building blocks, and code and lose sight of customers, their wants and needs, and their hopes and dreams. Good programming

---

3. Saint-Exupéry, *The Little Prince.*

managers inspire their teams to stay focused on customers and to deliver on project goals.

While project incentives are typically given out after projects ship, it is during the planning phase—and at key inflection points—when programming managers can negotiate unusual incentives for mission-critical projects, carrots like trips to theme parks and special bonuses.

Key inflection points occur throughout the project. Mickey realized for a June deliverable that the team had to reach interim milestones it was not on track to meet. He knew he'd have to ask them to turn on the afterburners—a level of commitment and effort that would deserve reward. Before going to the team, he talked to his CFO. "Here's what I'm going to do. If they pull this project in, they're going to deserve some special bonuses." His CFO nodded an OK—an OK that might well not have been as apparent or as easy to get after the work was done. Mickey exhorted the team, they did turn on the afterburners to meet the Memorial Day milestone, then met the June deliverable that had seemed impossible just two months before. There was no issue when Mickey went back to get the special performance bonuses he'd queued up beforehand.

When Ron worked with his Fujitsu executive team to reshape a hopelessly behind project to meet a go-live-or-shut-the-doors 75-day deadline, he right then also got agreement all around: If the schedule was met, there would be a reward that would be memorable. In fact, the team took the scaled-back project live in 74 days, with a day to spare. On the 75th day, the entire team took the day off together—an hour's flight south to Disneyland.

Whether you control a budget or your manager does, early is the time to allocate chunks of budget to reward people whom you'll ask for all-out effort to deliver more than anyone expected.

Finally, don't underestimate the value of asking your team for their input. Team meetings where you seek input from members, combined with valuing that input by adopting the best of it, cannot be underestimated for their value to inspire the team to greatness. Additionally, the camaraderie of engaging the team in sharing in and valuing the mission can contribute to great team spirit.

Planning the Work

Of all the people involved with a product—and we hope you have highly skilled project and product managers to work with who do their part—the programming manager is the person most likely to organize the features, identify the tasks required to accomplish them, and then figure out what needs to be done—and set realistic expectations of how much can be done by when.

You'll repeatedly be under pressure to do this planning. There are axioms, techniques, and tools that you can master that will make you better at it.

Break the Project into Features, and Prioritize Them

Job one is to make sure that the project is

- Broken down into features (both customer-facing features and the foundational elements your team needs to code to support them)
- Prioritized based on *two* criteria: customer value and risk

You should expect a good product manager, sometimes working with a project manager and even with the development team, to do the feature breakdown and a good product manager to bring customer understanding to feature prioritization. These days, you're sooner or later likely to run across the concept of "Minimum Marketable Features,"[4] often abbreviated MMFs.

Ensuring that risk assessment is part of prioritization, on the other hand, requires your involvement: It takes programming talent to effectively assess risk and all too frequently considerable programming management experience to explain why it is important.

Prioritization is critical to project success. If features aren't prioritized, development will likely proceed with programmers picking features to work on based on their being easiest, most fun to develop, or just "shiny"—cool, new, or interesting. Faced with a complex and daunting effort, programmers may simply start with what's known, hoping it will lead them to understand the unknown by the time they get to it.

Prioritizing features by product priority is obvious: Starting with the features that your business partners, your customers, and the market are clamoring for the loudest—and the features that will best differentiate you from your competition, ones that are market- and customer-focused—will ensure that they are ready when it comes time to ship.

---

4. Minimum Marketable Features (MMFs) were posited as units of marketable value by Mark Denne and Jane Cleland-Huang in their 2003 product management classic, Software by Numbers, a book capable of thrilling a programming manager's soul for finally bringing analytic rigor to product management to match the project management rigor that programming managers have always been expected to deliver. More detail about MMFs later in this chapter.

That's why Agile methodologies are based on this principle: frequent deliveries (a delivery every sprint) of the then-highest customer value features, followed by a reprioritization of the remaining work. Regardless of methodology, delivering high-value features first often reveals that the remaining feature list isn't prioritized as correctly as originally thought, and it often exposes a whole other set of features that were never on the list but are clearly higher in priority than those that everyone thought would be next.

Most seasoned managers will agree that identifying risks to the project and giving priority to activities that minimize and eliminate them are of equal importance to delivering the highest customer priorities—so much so that it has become a rule of thumb:

....

Do risk-first development.

The challenge can be that too many product managers are not classically taught to recognize the import of risk and to honor it as a component of prioritization, let alone one equal to customer priorities. On the other hand, there are few product managers who do not value quality and who do not understand that getting a solid foundation in place is critical to quality. Your job is to communicate the essential role played by the foundations you need your team to construct for the features that your product manager considers critical to deliver.

The fact is that the majority of risks and the hardest bugs often lurk in the most complex and least understood parts of the design. Furthermore, these are the very areas that require the most flexibility and creativity to solve. If you put them off, since options and design flexibility decrease as more and more of the surrounding code is completed, you paint yourself into a corner. Only by tackling them first can you reduce unknowns adequately to predict completion time with any level of certainty and to know how to build out the surrounding code.

Pay attention to what's nagging at you. In the earliest days of Java, Ron was managing a team developing financial tools for at-home investors, many of whom used modems to access the Web. While his team had worked through many of the risks of developing highly interactive applications, there was not a lot of Web wisdom yet regarding how to package applets to download them quickly to consumers' PCs. "To my peril, I left the applet-packaging question nagging in the background—until one day my business partners asked a critical question: How long would customers wait for the functionality to download? It was only reasonable to expect an acceptable answer as the 'price of admission' to keep the project rolling. But not having a ready answer left my business partners distrustful, so much so that it required fire drills just to get the team a week to experiment with various solutions.

"Escalation went to levels of management that should not have been summoned except to congratulate the team later on their groundbreaking achievement. Management in fact did eventually laud the team, and the product received industry awards soon after it was launched, but only after it was almost canceled for lack of an answer to a legitimate and foreseeable risk."

Break Features into Tasks and Sub-Tasks

Once you have identified and prioritized features, they need to be broken into tasks.

It is generally the project manager's role to ask programmers to break their features down into tasks. It is likely your role to work with your programmers to do so. It's almost certainly your role to sanity-check the results. You need to ensure that

- They've thought through the features and identified everything that needs doing
- They're not trying to "boil the ocean"—to take on more than they can, or should try to, accomplish
- The task breakdown makes sense
- The granularity of the tasks is appropriate both for setting milestones and for estimating times required

Tasks are the building blocks of estimating. While many Agile projects break features into tasks as short as a half-day, a good rule of thumb for non-Agile estimation purposes is to estimate no task to be less than two days or more than a week. Tasks shorter than two days tend to get padded, resulting in project estimates that are too large. Conversely, a task longer than a week is a red flag that the task is not fully understood, and tasks that are not understood tend to be seriously underestimated. You can and should break long tasks down into sub-tasks.

When breaking down features into tasks for project estimation, tasks should be big enough to require at least two days but small enough to require no more than a week of development.

Engage Your Team in a Bottom-Up Estimate

While you can do little more than a top-down, back-of-the-envelope estimate when you first get a project, once you get detailed requirements your project manager will quickly need to engage your team to build a real estimate—bottom-up numbers from your programmers that together represent a more realistic estimate of the work. You will guide the project manager in divvying up tasks to members of your team to estimate. The project manager will use a project-scheduling tool or at least a spreadsheet to assemble them into threads of work.

As you sanity-check the results, keep in mind that no two programmers, for a given set of tasks, will give you the same answers for how long each will take. Some programmers are underestimaters, some overestimaters, some inconsistent, and only a very, very few remarkably accurate. Furthermore, each has different knowledge, skills, and experience that could bring accuracy to estimating one task while being wildly optimistic or pessimistic about another. You need to get to know your team and their strengths and their estimation abilities as quickly and as soon as you can. Your project leads may be the programmers who are best at making those estimations, and who best understand the validity of their teammates' estimates.

Experience will lead you to develop multipliers from programmer to programmer, as you learn how accurate each is at estimating. You'll need to work with the project manager to adjust estimates, as they come back, to take into account each programmer's estimation accuracy.

Assemble Task Estimates into a Project Estimate

One of the challenges of estimation is that features often turn out to be more complicated than they appeared at first glance.

....

The first 90 percent of the code accounts for the first
90 percent of the development time. The remaining
10 percent of the code accounts for the other 90 percent
of the development time.

—TOM CARGILL, then at Bell Labs, more recently
a C++ and Java Consulting Programmer[5]

Another is that a five-day task is typically a task that takes five days of development—but in few organizations do programmers actually do five days of development in five calendar days.

Programmers are called into meetings, whether one-on-ones with you, team meetings, design meetings, QA meetings, bug meetings, meetings regarding maintenance of previous versions and previous products, code reviews, or meetings for lots of other good and useful and legitimate purposes—as well as a few (and unfortunately in some organizations more than a few) that are wasteful. And no one takes into account that four half-hours tucked between five hour-long meetings do not represent two hours of work—and may, in fact, represent no work at all, given that it takes programmers time to find where they left off, to reestablish the contexts of logic and program and data flow, and find their way back into the "zone." One partial solution we've used is to establish one or two days a week as "no-meeting" days. Such days can be very productive for a team, though it takes discipline and persistence to make it through a day without allowing a "critical" meeting to be called that would likely involve your programmers.

Nor do programmers or their managers adequately factor in the time sink that e-mail represents. Nor can anyone estimate the effect of unforeseen technical emergencies or fire drills.

In estimating, programmers also seldom factor in time they need away from actual work. Programmers overestimate how hard and long they can sustainably work.

One very conservative industry rule of thumb is that programmers typically spend no more than 55 percent of their time coding. If true for your team, it means that an 11-day task will take 20 calendar days to accomplish! As a result, you cannot get a project estimate by dividing total estimated programming time by the number of programmers. After you add up all

---

5. Titled "The Rule of Credibility" and also known as the "Ninety-Ninety Rule," Tom Cargill's aphorism was popularized by Jon Bentley in his column "Programming Pearls," *Communications of the ACM*, September 1985.

the weeks of tasks, you need to multiply by the inverse of the percentage of time programmers spend actually coding in your organization (multiply by one over 55 percent, or by 100/55, in this example) to get actual calendar weeks you can expect the project to require. Only then can you divide by the number of programmers available.

The actual percentage can be widely debated, but it is nowhere near 100 percent. We tend to use 60 to 70 percent.

Agile, as frequently practiced, has a mechanism called velocity that pegs actual against estimated times, and then uses the result to hone a team-wide multiplier. Over time, velocity enables a team whose members do not change to achieve better and better estimates. When teams first adopt Agile processes, smart Agile coaches frequently start by assuming a velocity factor of three; that is, programmer time available is actually just one-third of their combined 40-hour weeks. In subsequent cycles or sprints, they adjust the multiplier to achieve increasingly accurate schedule predictions.

One additional "gotcha" to watch for is to be sure you have specialized skill sets available when they're required. If you have 10 weeks for the project and 30 calendar weeks of database development, having lots of Web and applications developers to choose from does you no good—you need three database programmers.

Your project plan must also take into account more than coding. Project estimates need to incorporate design and QA appropriate to your technology and your domain, integration in large complex environments, and the documentation required for best practices purposes. Both these tasks and the productivity multipliers for each vary widely from company to company, from domain to domain, and, as we noted earlier, from programmer to programmer. What is critical is that your project manager takes them into account when estimating.

Look for the Limitations on Estimation

Everywhere along the way, you need to switch on your "red flag detector." Also commonly referred to as your "gut" or intuition, this is what Malcolm Gladwell writes about in his book *Blink*.[6] You're going to get estimates from programmers for how long things take, but your gut already has an idea of how long things should take. When you get estimates that are seriously

---

6. Malcolm Gladwell, *Blink: The Power of Thinking without Thinking* (Little Brown and Company, 2007).

at variance, raise a red flag—ask questions until you understand, whether it's that the task has risks your gut hadn't been taking into consideration, or the programmer is padding estimates (or underestimating them) because the tasks are ones he's never done. If someone on your team has done it, get their estimate, and either have that programmer design and code it, or have him mentor the programmer responsible for it.

....

In the software field, we are expected to accurately estimate the time it will take to do a job that requires creative thought, that usually requires the team members to learn new concepts, and that pushes team members to provide undivided attention for long periods of time.

—*CAROL L. HOOVER, MEL ROSSO-LLOPART,* and *GIL TARAN*[7]

Even if you're using Agile methods, there is no substitute for a manager or project manager who knows each programmer's estimation ability—and who has a good red-flag detector to recognize aberrations. A compiler change that might seem to be a small change can in fact require tweaks through such a broad swath of the code that even tripling estimates for debugging won't be enough time to reestablish code stability. It's the kind of thing that should stand out like a sore thumb to a seasoned manager. "Yes, we need to upgrade compilers, but tell me about the experience other companies have had. What makes you think it will be seamless for us?"

Before you actually assign tasks to a programmer, go through the estimation process with him individually, and come up with a date he is OK with committing to.

Finally, remember the rules of thumb first popularized by Fred Brooks's *The Mythical Man-Month*, which essentially say that hiring more programmers will, in the short run, slow you down. It's only on the project after this one where you'll get value from new hires you make now. Don't make the mistake of thinking you can assign new programmers tasks without taking into account that they will perform at a slower rate and require a mentor.

---

7. Hoover, Rosso-Llopart, and Taran, *Evaluating Project Decisions.*

As Brooks[8] said so well:

··

Men and months are interchangeable commodities only when a task can be partitioned among many workers with no communication among them. This is true of reaping wheat or picking cotton; it is not even approximately true of systems programming.

And

When a task cannot be partitioned because of sequential constraints, the application of more effort has no effect on the schedule. The bearing of a child takes nine months, no matter how many women are assigned.

And

Brooks's Law: Adding manpower to a late software project makes it later.

Get Agreement Around the Risks, Not Just the Schedule

If the project is of any significance, even if you've covered all the preceding issues, you're still not ready to commit to a feature set and hard date. Rather, it's time to assign levels of confidence to your estimates. You should already have ordered the feature set in such a way that the critical features will be undertaken first. That will give you a reasonably high level of confidence that they'll be ready to be part of the final product. As you might expect, your level of confidence will fall off for features scheduled later.

It's worth repeating that mitigating risks must be given priority as well. You need to factor in risk based on how much you know about the project. New leading-edge technologies that your team has no experience with (not to mention bleeding-edge technologies that almost no one in the world has experience with) have risks that are sky high; everyone involved needs to be wary. You can (and should) accompany your risk assessment with a plan: Outline all the approaches your team will take to mitigate those risks.

---

8. Brooks, *The Mythical Man-Month*, pp. 16, 17, 25.

Mitigation almost always starts with giving focus to risks from the very beginning: getting them known, resolved, and out of the way as early as possible.

In addition, your team (and the company) needs you to

Stand your ground if the risk is too high.

It benefits no one to acquiesce to your business partners and commit to deliver functionality that you don't yet understand. On the other hand, you should be able to offer a roadmap that shows how your understanding of the solution will emerge, risks will be mitigated, and a point will come when you can pledge with some certainty what your team can deliver.

You will find yourself, at times, in negotiation over moving up the date or adding functionality. The rule to fall back on is this:

Development is a triangle: good, fast, cheap—pick any two!

Fundamentally, if you're going to add features, you either have to remove features of a similar size to meet the same date, deliver with reduced assurance of quality, move the date to give your team more time, or apply more resources.

It's a dance to negotiate features, quality, time, and resources. To avoid being seen as stubborn or blocking, follow the rule of thumb that one of Ron's bosses once coached him to use: Present the reality and then

Always present three options—three alternatives to choose among.

She suggested that while you may think there are only two options, in fact there are always at least three; it's your failure to think deeply or broadly enough that prevents you from coming up with at least three. In Ron's experience, offering two alternatives tends toward "either/or" arguments. Things look black and white, even though they seldom are. But offering three alternatives tends to lead to open discussion of the issues, engaging all involved in looking for a best solution. It works much of the time.

Allocate Sufficient Time for Unit and Project Testing

Make sure sufficient time has been allocated for testing, enough time for

- Programmers to test their work—unit testing
- The cycles required once programmers' work is integrated into builds and tested as a whole—integration testing
- Even more iterations when the work is handed off to business owners for user acceptance testing and everyone realizes in how many places either the team failed to fully understand what users wanted or to describe it clearly and unambiguously enough to deliver it

Scheduling time for testing means adequately estimating how long an iteration takes as well as forecasting how much iteration will be required.

....

In practice, [Fred] Brooks found, nearly all software projects require only one-sixth of their time for the writing of code and fully half their schedule for testing and fixing bugs.

—*SCOTT ROSENBERG*[9]

Estimation Is a Unique Challenge Every Time

It's important to note, in summing up this planning and estimation section, that there are no one-size-fits-all answers. They vary dramatically by

- Programming paradigm (as one example, it's often said that the change from procedural to object-oriented was the change from 20 percent design/80 percent development to 50/50)
- Methodology (Agile approaches using test-driven development—so that unit testing is accomplished concurrently with development—result in lower QA overhead for the remaining automated regression testing, exploratory testing, system testing, user acceptance testing, etc.)
- Size of project (a Waterfall method on a two-year project must dedicate long stretches of time to requirements, design, and QA phases)

---

9. Rosenberg, *Dreaming in Code.*

- Target platform and delivery mechanism (Web applications that can be updated on a moment's notice require less design and QA than shrink-wrapped products, even those that can be updated online)

Which is to say, there is no rule of thumb for estimating either design or QA.

When you find yourself challenged to schedule a project with a company, team, paradigm, methodology, or product domain that is new to you, we suggest two approaches:

1. A team experienced in the programming paradigm, methodology, project size, and target platform will have, in its more senior members, the expertise to tell its manager what they need.
2. Lacking that, these days we might leverage our LinkedIn networks by posing a question that generally states the setup and the parameters—platform, project size, paradigm, methodology, purpose of the change, goals you're trying to achieve, and so on. It's a way of reaching out for the particular mix of expertise that will give you good insight despite the uniqueness of your problem.

Determine the Pace of the Project

Managing the pace of the project generally falls to the project manager, who typically creates the project schedule and then drives it. But an experienced programming manager will ensure that his team is presented with a realistic schedule.

Mickey counseled his managers with this rule of thumb:

....

Major projects must be run like a marathon. Set a good
pace and be prepared to sprint for the finish line.

You can ask people to sprint from time to time, and you can ask them to run their hearts out for the finish, but you can't ask them to sprint for the entire length of long projects.

An unrealistic schedule—expecting people to work ten or more hours a day and/or weekends for protracted periods of time—sets them up for burnout and you and your team for failure.

So your job is to review, scrub, scrutinize, edit, improve, hone, adjust, and tweak the schedule into one you and your team understand, accept, believe in, and can live with.

....

Hofstadter's Law: It always takes longer than you expect, even when you take into account Hofstadter's Law.

—DOUGLAS R. HOFSTADTER[10]

Kicking Off the Plan

Kicking off projects deserves a discussion of its own. Here is your opportunity to transition from planning to momentum, from a few people thinking about the effort to engaging the entire team in the vision.

Participate in a Project Kickoff

The project kickoff is the prime opportunity for you and your business partners to paint a vision of the goal—how the product will turn out, what it will achieve, where it fits in the larger context—and to excite and motivate your team with the import of what they're about to embark on, the opportunity it represents for them, and the contribution it will make to the company, the community, and your customers.

The kickoff sometimes occurs before the planning we've just described, sometimes after. But always, you and your business partners want to take the opportunity to set the right tone. You wouldn't be undertaking even the most minor projects if they didn't have importance to some extent, and this is your chance to tell that story.

Crystallize the requirements. Try to describe the project in one sentence—give it an "elevator pitch";[11] ensure that every team member is crystal clear about what you're all building.

---

10. Hofstadter, *Gödel, Escher, Bach.*

11. An elevator pitch is the condensation of your idea into a statement that is concise, pithy, and short enough to deliver during the average elevator ride, something on the order of 30 seconds or less.

Define "Done"

The project kickoff is often the right time to get agreement around the question "When is a feature, task, or sprint done? What constitutes 'done'?"

Defining "done" is a joint exercise with the business, the development team, project management, QA, and sometimes others to define when each feature can be declared done. In addition to being coded, will it need

- Design review
- Peer review (or pair programming)
- Code review
- Unit testing
- Check-in to source control
- Commenting in source control
- Performance testing
- Refactoring
- Any changes required to build it communicated to the buildmeister
- Online help written and integrated
- Built out of source control
- Unit tests passed on the source control build
- Automated regression tests for the integrated application passed on the new source control build
- Bugs fixed
- Installation scripts written
- Tested on multiple platforms, browsers, configurations, etc.
- Story or use case test plan updated
- Documentation written
- Product managers', product owner's, and/or customers' acceptance that it meets expectations
- Task hours recorded
- Tasks closed out

It's important for the team to agree to the elements of "done" and agree to deliver them. It's infrequent that two teams agree on the same definition of done. The definition might even change (with team agreement) from iteration to iteration, from task to task, from sprint to sprint.

Define "Success"

It's critical to get stakeholders to agree around and provide the answer to the question "What will constitute project success?" The product owner ultimately owns the definition of acceptance, and thus of success.

The project kickoff is the time for the product owner to deliver their consensus answer to the team.

One of the things programmers hate most is working their hearts out, only to have their work received poorly because it's too late, not what was asked for, or what was asked for but not what was wanted.

Make clear the expectations, whether they're for speed, features, quality, time to market, certain specific features, integration, ease of use, or other factors; lay out what matters most. Define the key metrics that will determine when they have occurred.

Ron's area of Schwab had stakeholders create a weighted scorecard for each project, spreading 100 points across time to market, quality, and cost. One project's scorecard looked like this:

45% Time to market
35% Quality
20% Cost

Scorecards were shared broadly, so everyone on the team always knew to focus first on making or beating deadlines, while delivering pretty solid quality (though some bug fixes might be left to after completion), even if more resources had to be brought in to succeed.

What that formula left out was scope. Ron, in his talks around the Bay Area, frequently asks programmers and project managers how many have been given 400-page requirements documents. Typically, most hands go up. He then asks, "What percentage of the requirements in those documents get delivered in the final product?" Outside of the occasional space program project, the typical answers range from 25 to 50 percent. It's not infrequent to get answers as low as 15 percent.

As programming managers we need to get, from our business partners, clarity for the entire team around feature prioritization. To be successful, we'd sure better deliver the right 15 percent—the most important 15 percent, the 15 percent of features that provide the highest customer value!

Scrum processes formalize prioritization into iterative cycles. What the team really needs is to know what provides the most value to be candidates for the first sprint, pretty good prioritization of the next most important features, with prioritization getting rougher and more general as the current perceived value of backlog features decreases. Product owners repeat the same prioritization when the next sprint's features need to be agreed on, ensuring that the team is always working on the highest-value work.

Establish a Project Workbook

As the programming manager, it likely falls to you to keep on top of the details of a project. Mickey devised a solution to this challenge early on, in his first management role when he became the project leader of the project he was working on, by creating a project notebook. It became the prototype for subsequent ones.

In recent years, he reworked the paper format into a spreadsheet, which we have generalized for your use in the Tools section. There are tabs for requirements, use cases, action items, notes from team meetings, and links to design, development, QA, and release documents.

At Gracenote, the process was formalized to benefit all team members by having the program management team maintain workbooks for all priority projects. These workbooks became a key management tool for managing priority projects at Gracenote. A project workbook, such as that shown in Figure 9.2 and 9.3, provides a standardized and centralized communication vehicle for projects, allowing team members to quickly ramp up to speed when they come onto a project, the team members to report progress in a consistent fashion, and governance of projects to be done consistently.

Maintaining a project workbook may seem like a lot of work, and it can be to keep it up-to-date and correct. Regardless of format, our experience shows that keeping a formalized central clearing place for project tracking will make everyone's life easier.

Wikis have become increasingly popular as a central clearinghouse for all project information, including technical details and team status reports. For some projects, it may make sense to gravitate all project workbook information to the wiki, but we think the discipline of maintaining a common project workbook format for all your projects makes it worth keeping the project workbook as a separate document linked to the wiki.

Details of your project workbook may differ, since it should reflect the product development lifecycle (PLC) you should have established. The example project workbook supplied as a tool for this chapter assumes a formalized PLC and has checklists for each phase of the PLC, as shown in Figure 9.3.

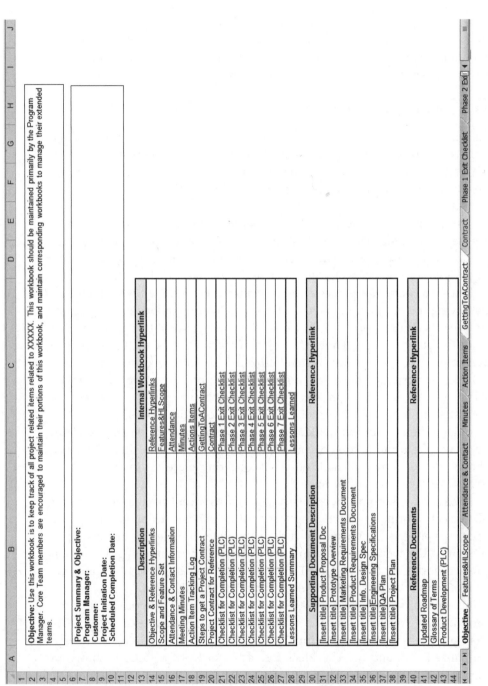

Figure 9.2   Example project workbook

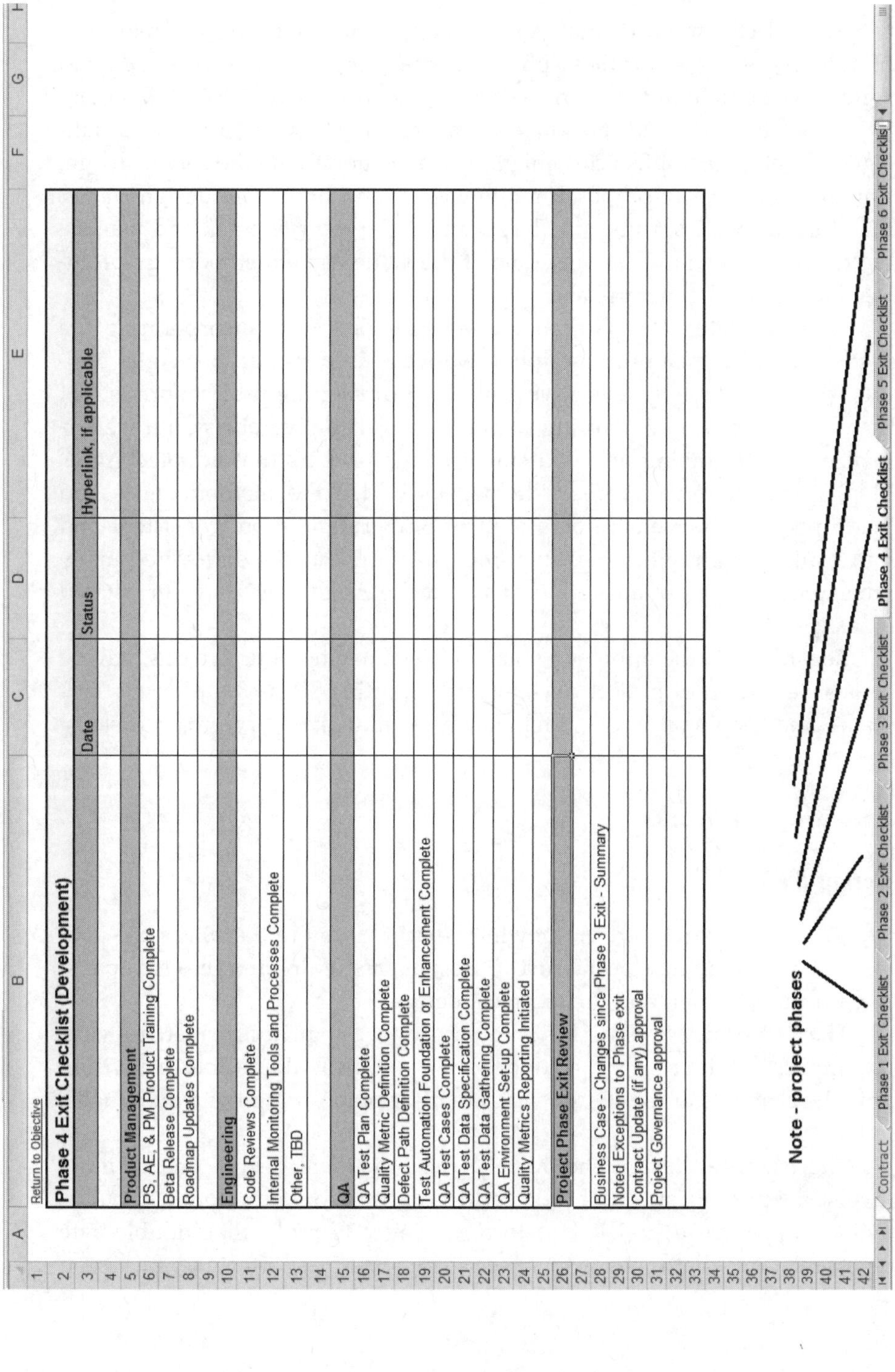

Return to Objective

Phase 4 Exit Checklist (Development)

	Date	Status	Hyperlink, if applicable
Product Management			
PS, AE, & PM Product Training Complete			
Beta Release Complete			
Roadmap Updates Complete			
Engineering			
Code Reviews Complete			
Internal Monitoring Tools and Processes Complete			
Other, TBD			
QA			
QA Test Plan Complete			
Quality Metric Definition Complete			
Defect Path Definition Complete			
Test Automation Foundation or Enhancement Complete			
QA Test Cases Complete			
QA Test Data Specification Complete			
QA Test Data Gathering Complete			
QA Environment Set-up Complete			
Quality Metrics Reporting Initiated			
Project Phase Exit Review			
Business Case - Changes since Phase 3 Exit - Summary			
Noted Exceptions to Phase exit			
Contract Update (if any) approval			
Project Governance approval			

Note - project phases

Contract | Phase 1 Exit Checklist | Phase 2 Exit Checklist | Phase 3 Exit Checklist | **Phase 4 Exit Checklist** | Phase 5 Exit Checklist | Phase 6 Exit Checklist

Figure 9.3   Project workbook details

As projects embrace Agile methodology, many question the relevance of adopting it across all these phases. Some companies that have adopted Agile development practices in the development phase use Waterfall methodology in the early and late stages of a project. These "hybrid" Waterfall-Agile development lifecycles might use a Waterfall methodology to get started in the project proposal, requirements, and high-level design stages, then turn to Agile sprints, stand-ups, and Agile tools to track and manage the sprints, hoping to leverage some of the value Agile methodology promises for the development phase.

Mickey relates, "At Gracenote, we struggled with incorporating the Waterfall project planning discipline we were used to into our Agile projects. We liked the way teams were working during the project sprints, but there was resistance to agreeing to overall project deliverables until we formalized the beginning and end stages of the projects that adopted Agile. This 'Wagile' hybrid approach helped us bridge the methodologies and made project management across all of our projects more consistent and our results more predictable, an approach to Agile that I discovered many other programming managers trying to make Agile work have gravitated to, as well."

Regardless of the approach you take to managing your projects, having a consistent form of project tracking and reporting such as a project workbook—and keeping it updated religiously—will make every project easier.

Executing the Work

Design the Work

Design is an integral part of knowing what it is you're building—the plan for how you're going to construct it. Design can be divided into two parts: the functional design and the technical design.

The first principle of design is to ensure that your design matches your requirements. With a good functional design, you should be able to envision how the elements of the design will, point for point, bring the requirements to life.

The technical design should take the functional design one or more levels deeper. First, it should address the non-functional requirements. If you've ever tried to force-fit Unicode and other double-byte representations onto character and string routines after the fact, you know that internationalization and localization are best designed in before coding begins.

The technical design will also almost certainly chart the flow of control and data through the program, often visually with diagrams. And it should specify or address protocols, APIs, security measures, timing, threads, interprocess communication, and scalability.

The opportunity to specify everything can itself be a danger. Traditional software development often resulted in no development until design that addressed every requirement was complete. But ask programmers what percentage of requirements are actually delivered and you will likely hear numbers as low as 15 percent. Priorities change, projects are scaled back, early partial deliveries are deemed "enough"—whatever the reason, all too often 75 to 80 percent of the effort of both detailing requirements and designing for all of them not only turns out to be waste but results in delay.

....

The perfect is the enemy of the good.

      —VOLTAIRE

Agile methodologies were, in part, a reaction to overdesign, in alignment with Voltaire's rule of thumb. Some claim that Agile methodologies like Scrum and Extreme Programming (XP) would have programmers skip design entirely. But in our experience, what Agile coaches tend to argue heatedly are the timing, granularity, and depth of design, not whether there's any at all.

The cost of traditional development also led Mark Denne and Jane Cleland-Huang to devise a product development approach that breaks down proposed products into "Minimum Marketable Features" (MMFs) and then shows how to apply rigor to devise the minimum marketable product that will provide the best ROI. The minimum marketable product gives designers a target. Designing for anything more delays getting the minimum marketable product to its customers. Given that design is inherently unpredictable—design is often little more than an approach or a theory about how the actual design will emerge—and given that subsequent features may be canceled or customer feedback may morph them beyond recognition, refactoring the design for subsequent development is more often than not both cheaper and more cost-effective than attempting to design for every possible feature up front.

On the other hand, most programmers, given their druthers, would launch into coding with no attempt to design whatsoever. Letting your team take a ready-fire-aim order of things can be costly. So it's as important to do an adequate level of design up front as it is to avoid design for design's sake.

Good design adds value faster than it adds cost.

—THOMAS C. GALE, Chrysler Chief of Automotive Design and Product Development

The most ubiquitous tool of design is the whiteboard. If you have any say in designing your offices, put whiteboards everywhere—in the offices, in the hallways, in the break rooms. Ron laughs when he remembers an office he moved into after managing for 15 years. "It was more spacious than any office I'd had up to that time. There was room to hold meetings of not only two or three but five or six people without having to reserve one of the conference rooms. On top of that, there was a great view of San Francisco's hills. But what I raved about to my family was not its size or its view but that it had two enormous whiteboards. I was in design heaven."

Drawing the design on a whiteboard is a good start, but it's not enough. Our rule of thumb is simple:

Require a design document.

Make someone write it down in a document. The act of committing design to a document, even if it was previously shared on a whiteboard, forces design to crystallize. And a design document enables other team members to wrap their brains around the design to embrace it, and forces them to critique it. Note, don't let someone try to pass off a Powerpoint presentation as a Design Document—bullet points are not a design!

The right elements of design can speed understanding and simplify coding. In a networked application, what's required may be "swim lanes" that represent the communications architecture—a diagram that shows the communication round trips between components. With such a diagram in front of you, you can easily see what communications protocols you need to employ and what security steps you need to take to protect data in the stream and at the endpoints.

Similarly, for user applications, use case diagrams and activity diagrams may help identify ambiguities in the requirements and simplify coding the stories your application is implementing.

Once you've required a design document, it really comes down to identifying how much design is enough to proceed. This is one of those places where having been a programmer can guide you. Most programmers have experienced projects at both extremes, some with more design than was necessary, and others with so little design that if you were lucky enough to get away with it in the short run, it probably left you with headaches in the long run.

An application intended only for brief use may require little design, perhaps as little as a page of notes. But we've learned to be wary. There are scads of programs now in daily use for decades that have version numbers marking them as prototypes or proofs of concept. They started life with their teams believing them to be single-use executables, but along the way they took on lives of their own. The cost to support and maintain half-baked applications can be enormous.

There are no absolutes as to how much time design should take. As with planning and estimation, appropriate design varies dramatically by programming paradigm, methodology, size of project, and target platform and delivery mechanism. Managers who spent their programming years coding procedural applications have found themselves confused and anxious managing object-oriented programming projects in which the percentage of project time devoted to design doubled or tripled what they'd been used to, only to discover that good design made coding itself take proportionately less.

The rule you can be sure of is this:

....

If design is one percent of project time it's almost certainly too little; if it's more than half of project time, it's almost certainly too much.

Hold a Design Review

You want your designers to present their designs to their peers to flush out design flaws, identify missed complexities, uncover unexpected interactions, and show other limitations that are seldom found by means other than increasing the number of eyes studying it.

The less obvious benefit to design reviews is to make your entire team better designers. Design reviews are an opportunity to teach design—both principles and process—to your junior people, as well as to establish design as a best practice within your team and to repeatedly raise the level of design quality.

By establishing an expectation of design reviews, you can assign component designs to junior or midlevel programmers with the confidence that you're providing them, you, and your organization with a safety net that will ensure that they don't fail. That will give your senior people the time they need both to lend their experience across many components and to take responsibility for the overall design itself, the critical place where you rely on their extensive experience to achieve success.

And while you may sprinkle senior people sparingly into the technical talent in component design reviews, you should expect all of your senior designers to review overall project designs.

Complete a Prototype to Inform the Design

If the application you are proposing to create represents a new approach, a new look, a new feel, or leads you into uncharted territory in some other way, you'd be well served to assign a programmer to create a proof of concept or a prototype.

Proofs of concept, or PoCs, help your designers and programmers assure themselves that they understand how to solve the problem and may additionally convince your business partners or clients that you and your team know what you're doing.

On the other hand, if you don't know what you're doing, proofs of concept help you flush out the risks early on and identify what you need to do to be successful.

If you're not sure you know what you're building, both proofs of concept and prototypes are exceedingly useful for asking the question "Is this what you had in mind?" As we have said before, requirements are seldom complete, seldom unambiguous, and seldom fully thought out. Proofs of concept and prototypes can enable you and your team to participate and collaborate with your business partners in homing in on exactly what needs to be built.

The danger of prototypes is that they can look too good, too complete, too ready. And that can be dangerous for two reasons.

First, the more polished a prototype looks, the less willing partners and customers are to criticize it and suggest changes. Study after study has shown that polished UI prototypes fail to get the critical customer feedback that designers desire and that has led to a surge in paper prototyping, hand-rendered wireframes, and use of tools like Balsamiq Mockups[12]—walking customers through rough sketches instead of finished screens looking for feedback. Scott McCloud's *Understanding Comics*[13] introduced the concept to Mickey that "less is more"; that is, the less information provided during the prototype stage, the more the user (i.e., the customer) has to think about the function of the interface rather than the form. Ever since, "I have encouraged prototypes that focus on function to be as basic as possible, and it has proven to me that better, more polished graphics would have inhibited the feedback, not enhanced it."

Second, a polished interface can mask the twine and baling wire and general lack of application logic beneath the surface. Many a programming manager has had the experience of presenting a prototype with high production values to a partner or customer only to be asked to make a few tweaks and deliver the finished product next week. It looks too good, the customer thinks, so it must be done. Here again, using iconic rather than finished artwork can help establish the preliminary nature of the prototype you're showing your partners and customers.

Set Agreed-Upon Milestones

You can pace the project by setting interim milestones. The traditional milestones are

- Prototype or Proof of Concept (PoC)
- Alpha
- Beta or EA (Early Availability)
- Final or RC (Release Candidate) or GM (Golden Master)
- GA (General Availability) or Production or Live when the software is widely available to the public

Agile methodologies may not name interim milestones, since, by Agile definition, the product is releasable at the end of every iteration or sprint, making each iteration or sprint a milestone.

Regardless of the methodology and the milestones you use, though, you need to ensure that everyone agrees on what the milestones mean. That's

---

12. Balsamiq Mockups are easy to iterate, have the look of low-fi hand-drawn sketches, come with scads of predrawn UI components, and can be linked to produce clickable prototypes for demos and usability testing. www.balsamiq.com/products/mockups.

13. Scott McCloud, *Understanding Comics: The Invisible Art* (William Morrow Paperbacks, 1994).

a challenge in many organizations. In some companies, Alpha software is feature complete; Beta is software stable enough to be given to users outside the development group for real-world testing and feedback, its internals stable enough for outside programmers to develop to and rely on its APIs. In other companies, Alpha and Beta software may not be feature complete at all, only stable enough to ask users for feedback. In yet other companies, Beta is software that is ready for product managers to demo, but don't let customers touch it until there's a Preview or Early Access release!

Regardless of what you call them, just make sure everyone agrees on what your milestones mean.

Once the methodology and milestones are set, ensure that they're clear and clearly communicated so that they help you know the state the project is in.

By scheduling your team to demo its milestones to a senior manager, the more senior the better, you can use milestones for motivation. Mickey notes that at Brøderbund he differentiated new projects from revisions. "Unlike revisions, where we knew where we were going already, new projects are hard." To motivate achieving new-project milestones, he would arrange to have them demoed to an executive producer, a senior consultant, a board member, or whenever possible the CEO. Even early milestones. "People would work their butts off as the milestone approached because they didn't want to look bad in front of the CEO—and no one wanted to move the date. We would always invite our CEO to review Alphas and Betas. People really tried to shine. The CEO showed up less than half the time, but our people loved the guy. Knowing he might be there was a terrific motivational tool."

Confirm That Regular Check-In Meetings Have Been Set

Once work begins, milestones aren't enough to ensure that your team is on track, working hard, and focused on highest priorities by working down and checking off tasks and features.

Using the methodology your team or your company has chosen may lead to using tools like story cards, burn-down charts, use cases, punch lists, function points, or feature deliveries to measure progress. It may lead project managers to visit programmers individually or to hold progress meetings weekly or stand-up meetings every day.

Project managers will run the project plan. You need to partner with them. Ensure they're able to collaborate with your people to gather project progress information and identify concerns and impediments. Provide them with a sanity check that what they're hearing and the conclusions they're drawing match reality.

Keep in mind that regular check-in meetings may be as valuable for the team to exchange information about what they're working on as they are for the project manager to chart progress. This in part accounts for the growing popularity of daily Agile-style stand-up meetings. Programmers who don't talk with each other all too often run roughshod through code, taking too little care and wreaking havoc, whereas programmers who regularly share their plans, tasks, and steps with each other get feedback from their peers. They tell each other about demons lurking in the code, particularly brittle areas where it's easy to inadvertently break things, hidden secrets that never got documented, and how things really work.

These days, everyone should be given access to the most recent project updates. Scrum prescribes "information radiators"—typically task boards covered with prioritized stories and tasks, their states indicated by position or notation, located in a team room where everyone can see status at any time. Geographically dispersed teams replicate task boards using software tools that are similarly updated and shared in real time. Project managers keep their plans on wikis or in shared spreadsheets or using other collaborative project tools that provide similar transparency.

Often your inter-team collaboration systems can provide you with insights into project progress as well. You'll find you can keep track of your team and their contributions to projects by monitoring or reviewing check-ins. It will give you a sense of who is exceptionally productive, who is struggling, what should be fixed, and what is working.

Ron's Fujitsu programmers were expected, upon every check-in, to e-mail the team a description of the changes incorporated therein. Another team, on every check-in, filled in an e-mail form with date, change, programmer, code reviewer, description, bug numbers fixed, code branch in the source system, lists of files and databases changed, and notes to other programmers, testers, and the documentation and build teams. The system automatically mailed these submission documents to internal listserv subscribers (other programmers, plus managers, QA, build team members, writers, and others), as well as archiving them into a searchable database.

Another way to get a sense of activity and productivity is to regularly dip into the source code and bug management systems yourself.

Actively Drive Development

Participate in stand-ups or regular status meetings, even if you don't have to. New managers too often revert to the meeting avoidance behaviors they had as programmers. But status meetings are how you make sure the project is going well. You may discover that some teams are truly self-managing and you're not needed, but that will be much more the exception than the rule.

More often than not, status meetings reveal opportunities for insight and action: to facilitate conversations among programmers you know should be talking, observe a participant who has become disengaged, see who is going above and beyond and is due for reward, anticipate problems, spot impediments, identify dependencies, and recognize when you need to marshal resources (whether equipment or contributors) for your team to be successful. In the end game, when it's common for teams to get mired in details, we have often found ourselves the only voice in the room who can still identify the priorities and drive the release home.

> *Programmers will always be able to justify any*
> *individual act of axe-sharpening . . . as "actually*
> *necessary." Some of them certainly are. It is the hard*
> *lot of the software manager to decide at what point*
> *the axe-sharpening . . . has lost touch with a project's*
> *original goal and to summon the programmers back*
> *from their happy tool-tending side-tracks to the*
> *primary task.*
>
> —*SCOTT ROSENBERG*[14]

You have a crucial responsibility, stated or not, to keep clear on the vision. The very qualities that make programmers exceptional—ability to tend to detail and to balance multiple thoughts and threads simultaneously—can also let them get easily lost in the details. You play a crucial role keeping conversations out of ratholes and projects out of the weeds.

If your developers are working in Scrum, each sprint represents a new opportunity to rally the team, to repeat (or revise or refocus) the vision, to apply it to the specifics of the sprint objectives, to explain why the features

---

14. Rosenberg, *Dreaming in Code*.

and the release are important, to remind everyone of the delivery date, and to firmly affix a sense of urgency in everyone's mind. Many companies hire project managers, program managers and scrum masters for their ability to make and run the plan, not rally the team. You'll frequently find that task left to you.

You'll also find that you frequently need to renegotiate the feature/quality/time trade-offs. Requirements change; Sales gets input from customers; what was unimportant last month becomes a requirement for next month; understanding develops as the UI reveals how product features should emerge. But development's limits remain the same: There are only so many hours before you burn out your team. Unless lower quality is a possibility, or releasing as Beta instead of Final by the date, or moving the date, you need to ask, "If we implement this, what in the previous list of features can Sales or Marketing give up so you can still make the date?"

The job of a first-line manager is to know the context daily, if not hourly or even up to the minute—what's important, what's critical, what's needed, what's expected, when, and what's late.

You need to be prepared to shoot off a flare when you see that the team needs help. Sometimes you'll need more people. Sometimes you need to borrow already trained resources from peer groups or bring in a short-term contractor or consultant. But beware the Mythical Man-Month principle: Adding people frequently does not decrease but rather increases delivery times.

You need to ward off distractions to your programmers. There is no end to distractions in corporate environments, whether from other managers and project managers who are wandering through or executives tin-cupping for pet projects, or because of emergencies and issues. Be the shield that protects your people from unwanted outside distractions.

But don't forget to introduce a few distractions. If your team hasn't already done so, find things that let them play together, have fun, take breaks, relieve tension. It was not infrequent at Apple to see a foam Frisbee floating over a cube wall as an indication that one programmer or another was taking a needed break.

Talking with the members of your team is important; it lets them know you care what they're doing. As managers, we've learned to put out toys—not for ourselves, but to engage and encourage members of our teams to drop in. Managers' toys are a way to connect with individuals, to get people talking.

Desktop toys should be intriguing, unusual, fun. Ron first realized that while playing with the magnetically floating disk his own Apple manager strategically placed on the visitor side of his desk. Getting the thing spinning let his visitors momentarily distract themselves. Magical things happen in the subconscious during moments of distraction.

Toys can relieve the tension, but in the end it's all about the software, and you need to do one last thing to actively manage it. Unless it is downright unfeasible, run the software yourself. Nothing better communicates your own commitment to the product and its importance than your using it. Updating to every new build will give you a sense of the feature development and quality of the product that no amount of explaining can.

When Ron was at Apple, the head of Apple II development was notorious for flushing out bugs in minutes that weeks of QA testing hadn't found. Steve Jobs long set the bar on managerial engagement: Running his teams' software, he drilled down on every detail he deemed important to Apple's customers.

Ensure That Agreed-Upon Standards and Requirements Are Met

To release your code, you need to meet a level of quality your customers demand or at least can live with. As a programming manager, you will be held accountable not only for meeting the date but for delivering a quality product. You may have a QA organization to test your product. But don't be misled. Quality is owned by development. It's your job. QA's role is to help you measure how successful you've been.

....

Customers will grade you more harshly on poor quality than on missing features.

—MARK CALOMENI, *VP of Engineering, Accept Software*

What level of quality can your customers live with? We somehow simultaneously hold two opposing thoughts about bugs: that code should be bug-free, and that the programs our teams write will never be free of bugs. There are applications such as space missions where bugs are not tolerated. NASA programmers talk about layer upon layer of process that helps them prevent as well as detect bugs (though even at NASA bugs still seep through, as the

Mars Climate Orbiter debacle illustrated[15]). Early in his career when he was still a programmer, Ron wrote code for a measurement instrument used in both nuclear reactors and cancer treatment; it can be very sobering to go to work every day knowing that software failure could cost human life.

Web applications, on the other hand, are often deployed with minimal testing. Not only does finding the wrong search result seldom have serious consequences, but a good recovery strategy leveraging easy and quick software back-out or change-out can update bad software in a matter of hours and sometimes minutes.

Ultimately, you need to balance the rigor of your testing against the risk of shipping your program with known or unknown bugs. As a programming manager, you may have little say over how many people in QA test your product for how long. But you can set standards for how code is designed, written, and reviewed that decrease the likelihood of bugs.

Sooner or later, you will manage programmers who will repeatedly argue that various defects that negatively affect customers (or will likely do so when the product is released) aren't really defects because they meet the specs the programmers were given. Beware of engaging in this argument.

In most cases, your job is to get your team to step out of the notion that they are order takers—rote implementers, automatons—and get them to realize that they are, can, and should be collaborators in the joint effort to *make customers happy*. A perfect implementation of a bad spec does not deserve a badge of honor. Encourage them to transcend the spec. Steer your team to be empathetic to your customers and to question and propose improvements to specs that seem to miss the mark.

....

You need to "listen deeply"—listen past what people say they want—to hear what they need.

> —JON MEADS, *Principal Consultant and*
> *Founder, Usability Architects, Inc., Portland, OR*

Second, you want your response to real bugs not to be punitive but to focus on how to avoid similar problems in the future. Your mission should

---

15. Noel Henners of Lockheed Martin Astronautics, the prime contractor for the *Mars Climate Orbiter* craft, said at a 1999 news conference that his company's programmers "were responsible for ensuring that the metric data used in one computer program were compatible with the English measures used by another program. The simple conversion check was not done. It was overlooked."

be not to find fault, but to improve process: better smoke tests, a better test framework, a continuous build process, ensuring live code branches don't go unbuildable or unrunnable, timely design and code reviews by the right reviewers, just enough coding guidelines (and a process for honoring and enforcing them), a robust source control system, tools that support your process, training in coding best practices and debugging best practices, timely QA feedback, mentoring by your best coders and debuggers of your newest, least experienced programmers . . .

Entire books are devoted to the topic of increasing code quality, so we'll discuss just a few of our favorite techniques here.

Leverage Test-Driven Development

Ron is currently enamored with test-driven development (TDD), where before a single line of program code is written, one or more tests are written to prove the code works. Since the code doesn't exist, the test fails, proving the test. Then when the code is written (and written correctly), the test passes, proving the code (and again proving the test). The test is typically then added to a suite of regression tests that can reprove the code should it be refactored later.

The change is a subtle one, thinking about the test first. But it has the added advantage of providing absolute certainty that you understand the requirements. As a programmer, you may be able to write code when requirements are ambiguous, but writing tests that prove requirements that are ambiguous is almost impossible.

So the coding/testing cycle becomes a testing/coding one, and once it is ingrained, you should see no development-time cost to TDD, only better quality. But to Ron's thinking, the genius of TDD comes when you want to refactor your code—to improve the code to, say, be more efficient but do exactly the same thing. Ron and Mickey, like most programming managers, have had to support aging, brittle code that has a propensity to fail far from the site where changes are made with no indication at the time of coding that anything is awry. By automating the body of tests generated by the test/code cycle, you should be able to change any part of the code and within minutes run your hundreds or thousands of regression tests in automation, and know that your code works exactly the same—that you have introduced no unexpected side effects.

> *There is evidence that doing TDD takes about 15% longer*
> *than not doing TDD (George and Williams, 2003). But*
> *there is also evidence that TDD leads to fewer defects.*
> *(Two studies at Microsoft found that the number of bugs*
> *found went down by 24% and 38% with the use of*
> *TDD [Sanchez, Williams, and Maximilien, 2007, 6].)*
>
> —MIKE COHN[16]

Sometimes teams are so far from owning quality that interim steps are necessary. Ron likes one that a colleague used requiring that, during check-in, programmers write a description, as little as a paragraph or two, of how they will test their code, which begins to build a mentality of quality ownership.

At Pixar, a key part of the RenderMan project was the creation of a regression suite. Mickey: "The regression suite for RenderMan processed innumerable files to generate images from the detailed 3-D scene description that could be compared, pixel by pixel, with images generated previously. Every time a bug was found, the scene that surfaced the bug was added to the RenderMan regression suite; so it was with the ballroom scene in Disney's *Beauty and the Beast* movie after one bug in that scene took days to identify and resolve. I wish creating and maintaining regression suites was as simple for other applications."

Hold Stand-Up Meetings

Ron is a fan of the quality aspects of the stand-up meetings enforced by many Agile methodologies. In Scrum, for example, stories that need implementing are publicly claimed by programmers in a way that another member of the team who knows the code or the routines around it can voice concerns and "gotchas" to watch out for.

Insist on Code Reviews

Finally, we have both been ardent proponents for all of our careers of requiring code reviews. Knowing that others will review their code leads programmers to be more painstaking so they won't be caught having made silly mistakes. The act of explaining their work has long been shown to help

---

16. Cohn, *Succeeding with Agile*, p. 158.

programmers spot errors they would not otherwise have seen. And all the studies show it is much more cost-effective to fix problems when code is fresh in its programmer's mind than later when caught by QA or users and it's stale. Furthermore, code reviews can serve as a way to mentor junior programmers to code better. Fundamentally, second and third sets of eyes see problems the initial coder would not, which leads us to require code reviews of every check-in, and frequently even double reviews of check-ins as we increase vigilance approaching a code freeze.

It can be challenging to get a practice of code reviews started. Programmers may be reluctant to submit their code, fearing criticism. You can overcome their reluctance by recruiting your most senior programmers to lead. You can overcome your own reluctance to distract your team by limiting the number of reviewers to two to four, but requiring participation from invitees.

Have the code owner fill out a template or ideally a wiki page describing the sections that need reviewing along with a due date giving reviewers about a week. You may want to use both template and wiki page, since some programmers, particularly junior ones, may be reluctant to publicly ask what might be dumb questions. There should be a table for reviewers to enter their observations, specifying the line of code each comment refers to and whether the reviewer feels a recommended change is required or just should be considered. If code to be reviewed is a bug fix, a review request should also include diffs, whether generated by hand, from source control, or using a tool like CodeCollaborator.

When the comments are all in, the owner organizes them, separating them into two lists, the first being changes the owner agrees with and will implement. Those changes should be reviewed as part of your lightweight check-in/bug-fix review process. A second list, which becomes the basis of the review meeting, features, in a final column in the table, the owner's questions and concerns for each of the items he doesn't understand, disagrees with, or rejects. No disagreements, no second list, no meeting. Unless the current design fails to meet requirements, shunt design issues—how it could or should be done better—off to a different meeting.

Once you have a culture of reviewing code, you may also want to set up a cycle of senior programmers reviewing the work of a peer or more junior programmer by pulling and reading diffs for that programmer over some previous number of days.

Running the End Game

The end game is the final sprint to the finish line. Shipment, Golden Master, Release, Live, Done—whatever you call completion, finishing software can be hard. No other part of the development cycle requires more attention, more focus, more tenacity.

Even if you are not a believer in daily stand-up meetings at any other time in the development cycle, this is when you most want to use them. You need your team talking to one another about the little changes they're making. You need the wisdom of your crowd to nip wrong moves quickly—ideally before they're even made—and to share experience about how to safely overcome critical issues. You need your team sharing the little details they need from each other.

No New Features

This is a time when you've got to be done adding features; what you're doing now is iterating for quality. In your role as manager, you will be called on to remove roadblocks, to triage changes, to surface those that matter and to fight for not fixing (and not risking the release for) things that don't matter. You'll almost certainly have fixes that are compelling, yet not enough so to risk breaking the release. In many organizations, you may need to repeat the mantra "no more features" regularly. Taking stands will inevitably make you unpopular, sometimes with your team, other times with QA or product managers. But it's your job.

....

A couple of weeks before release, get a Go-No/Go from each team member. This gives the team a chance to rate their work and show some confidence or lack of it.

—KINNAR VORA, *Engineering Director*

The first end game he ran at Check Point, Ron asked that check-ins be severely limited to just those critical to the release—and that they be reviewed by not just one reviewer, as was the norm throughout Check Point projects, but by two. By getting one more set of eyes on code changes, Ron hoped to detect problems earlier.

"There were not always good second reviewers, so I issued a few exceptions, but for the most part we followed this protocol," he says. "It was a shock. 'We've never required this before,' my programmers told me.

When I realized the first few to check in changes were taking it personally, I rephrased my request: 'It is our fervent hope that today's check-ins will be the absolute last to this Release Candidate. Is there a reason, even after you have had two teammates review your code, that you're willing to risk it be *you* who prevented us from releasing? If you think it's worth taking the risk of breaking the RC, talk to me. But don't touch the code base unless you have. Thank you for your support.'

"Phrased that way, no one took it personally. And it dramatically reduced the number of check-ins and improved their quality."

Run the Product

Even if you haven't run your product's daily builds to this point, unless it's unfeasible for an ordinary programming manager, you want to run it now. You'll be a help to QA, if only as another set of eyes, and you'll contribute to polishing your product's fit and finish.

Perhaps equally important, running the product gives you the opportunity to interact with team members in product-specific ways. Your team will respond to you differently, and with more respect, when they realize you're running what they're writing. Your running their work communicates that you care, which is exceptionally important for morale. They may blow off QA, but they'll go out of their way to make sure they don't introduce problems you might find.

Finally, you'll get a sense of the quality so far. There will come a moment when you need to argue that your product is good enough—that it's time to ship it.

Be Prepared to Declare Success and Start on the Point Release

There are always more features than time to implement them. There are always more defects than time to fix them. There is a temptation, whether you're building a shrink-wrapped product, embedded software, or a Web application, to hold off until it's "done." It never will be. There are always bugs. There is always work to do to make it better.

....

Software is never done.

The challenge is to know when you can let it go, when it's "good enough." Mickey has made the statement that it comes down to having to pry the code from your programmers' hands: "Sometimes you have to shoot the programmer to ship the product." It's up to you (or perhaps the product manager or senior management) to make the call that it's sufficiently done.

All the QA reports in the world won't tell you when that is. It's a judgment call. You need to take into account the QA reports, Beta reports from customers, and every other bit of data you have. But when you make the case to ship, it helps to be able to say, as Ron did recently, "I've been running this product on my main machine for over two months without a single major problem. We have a great QA organization, and I know we can stress the product in unusual ways or take it out to edge cases and make it fail. But they haven't found a truly serious new problem in two weeks. Let's ship this puppy!"

You also need to be prepared to redefine success—sometimes dramatically—to get product in users' hands sooner. When Ron arrived at Fujitsu, the development team had been promising its consumer product "next month" for almost a year. When he discovered the team was still nearly a year from completion, and executive management in Japan threatening to shut the project down if something wasn't shipped within 75 days, Ron took deep dives: with his development team to identify what was working, what could be made to work quickly, and what would provide impact; and with the management team to envision a dramatically scaled-back product that would nonetheless deliver an entertainment experience that would wow expectant customers. (Development then delivered that product in 74 days—with a day to spare.)

In best cases, you'll find yourself with a product that is ready to ship when predicted. More frequently, you'll believe yourself on track only to discover issues: a flurry of previously undiscovered bugs, user testing that shows you've stumped customers, or a Beta program that reveals users had something slightly different in mind.

Any of these may send you back to the drawing board—or not. Your ability to differentiate what is important from what's not—always useful—becomes critical in identifying the criteria that will let you "declare success."

Web delivery may let you release early. After all, you can update Web content daily if necessary. When Ron's investor tools team later tackled trading for Schwab's most demanding customers, active traders, they first released core functionality, then proceeded to issue nine releases of new features (and two maintenance releases) over the next eight months.

Even spacecraft software is designed to be updatable externally these days.

At the other extreme, one of Mickey's teams at Gracenote delivered software embedded in newly manufactured automobiles. Such software must be right or risk an expensive recall to swap out firmware.

Know When to Cut Your Losses

Someday you're going to find yourself with a project that is just not deliverable. You, or more likely senior management, will determine it is unfeasible to continue the project. It may be because market conditions have changed. Or because you're too far out in front of the technology and it's taking too long and costing too much. Sometimes it's because the team made commitments based on staffing that later was not forthcoming and you are just too underresourced to get the job done. Other times it's because your team made wildly optimistic but unrealistic schedule commitments that you are not able to meet.

After Ron's first team at Schwab met an aggressive schedule to code and deliver an online Asset Allocation Advisor Web client in 1997—one of the first full-blown commercial Java applications on the Web—the team confidently proposed a follow-on portfolio-tracking project that would aggressively deliver not only the client but also port the server to the then-new Java language. To be so early with so much—application servers did not yet exist in 1997—the team would have to architect fundamental building blocks ahead of industry standards.

"It may be that management never quite believed it would take the resource requirements the team had estimated," Ron remembers. "The project was certainly caught in the crosshairs when budgeting conditions changed. While the first project had focused on delivery regardless of cost, this time the response was different. Schwab didn't easily tolerate projects that couldn't be delivered within a quarter. The project was abruptly abandoned by direction of senior management.

"Senior management made a careful point not to blame the team and its leaders. Key people were pulled in for one-on-ones with the business unit's most senior managers, where they were lauded and thanked for the progress they'd made. The architecture was clearly valued; a core group remained assigned to nurture it. But even with all that, the part of the team that was reassigned was devastated."

To try to reestablish equilibrium, Ron took everyone off-site to share camaraderie and talk through what they'd accomplished. "Despite everything, much of the team was dispirited for months," Ron recalls. "One of the two best project managers I have ever worked with was fed up and promptly left, despite my giving her a promotion and a raise. Having the rug pulled out was very hard for the team to swallow."

Ironically, the core group that was charged with finding some way to leverage the architecture did so. Over the next 18 months, industry tools caught up. This time leveraging the new commercial platforms, the team built a trading application that for years to come would continue to satisfy Schwab's most demanding customers, in part because it was as flexible and scalable as the earlier team had predicted.

On the other hand, in a somewhat parallel experience, Mickey was able to hold on to a Brøderbund team after killing their project. Mickey had commissioned a project to develop a framework built on Macromedia Director, the preeminent multimedia authoring tool at the time. After an investment of many calendar months, it became apparent that the effort was not leading to success. "I gently reassigned the lead programmer and closed the project down. With careful messaging to motivate team members in their reassignments, we were able to keep the team from leaving.

"We had begun the project to satisfy demand from senior management for a nonproprietary solution they expected would be cheaper than building from scratch. They weren't happy either. It took lots of explanation about the lessons we had learned, but we were ultimately able to deploy a team with deeper skills able to craft a ground-up proprietary framework that was dramatically better."

There may be times when keeping the team isn't what's important. Another Brøderbund project was as problematic, but shutting it down was easier. PrintShop Publisher was assigned to an offshore team. When it turned out they were unable to deliver, the project was killed, then resurrected using a different team and a different model. "Killing the project didn't remove the need for the product. But when the offshore team couldn't deliver, we didn't need them to stick around. We deployed a different team in California on different technology to deliver the product we needed, a product that is still shipping today, years later."

Regardless of the reasons, there will come a time when a project must be halted. Unless handled carefully, canceling a project can lead to severe morale and esteem issues for the team and for you and can cause good people to leave. Think carefully about the ramifications before you proceed. Ensure that your management is bought in and supports the action, recognizes the consequences, and is on board with communicating it sensitively.

OEM *and International Versions*

You're not off the hook when you deliver if you have OEM and international versions, or any other adjunct or derivative releases. Too many teams run their hearts out to finish the core release, only to find their energy too depleted to get the important ancillary releases out to their markets, too.

You need to employ all the tricks in your arsenal to keep your team motivated through completion of *all* releases.

Delivering the Software

While project managers still have delivery details to pay attention to, your job as a programming manager is mostly done. But there are five more things to think about.

Celebrate

Celebrate in some tangible fashion as soon after a project is declared successful as possible. Here is the opportunity to let go of all the stress of delivery and just celebrate together.

One of Mickey's most memorable celebrations came after one of his teams at Pixar had been charged with creating its first consumer software product, Mac RenderMan. The project was aggressively scheduled (four to five months), was completed from inception to shrink-wrapped product delivery on time, and was deemed an unqualified success, from bits to packaging. It was made more special by the fact that it had sponsorship from Pixar CEO Steve Jobs and represented Steve's first return to Mac software after leaving Apple and founding NeXT.

What made the celebration truly memorable was that it honored all of the bits-to-packaging product team and involved all of senior management at Pixar at the time, from Steve to the Pixar cofounders, Ed Catmull and Alvy Ray Smith. Over dinner in a cozy private room at one of the Bay Area's renowned restaurants located in a repurposed brick kiln, the team was toasted and feted in a way none of them will likely ever forget.

Gifts were frequently a part of celebrating releases at Apple. No matter the project, a project T-shirt or polo was de rigueur; if you hadn't ordered them by the time anyone heard about the project, you'd be considered highly overdue. For a project named after the popular sit-com *WKRP in Cincinnati*,

everyone who had contributed was rewarded with a radio in the form of an antique studio microphone from the early days of radio.

We've both handed out plenty of certificates over team dinners, with cameras clicking to record the camaraderie. For consumer software delivered as shrink-wrap, a copy of the packaged result is prized.

Ron has taken teams on ferry excursions to picnic and bike ride on Angel Island, the Ellis Island of the West Coast. He has arranged for lunch on the wine train in the Napa Valley. His teams have ridden the Roaring Camp Railroad from the shade of the redwoods in Felton to the beach at Santa Cruz, where he bought everyone a day pass to the roller coasters, Ferris wheels, and the rest of the rides on its boardwalk, plus lunch in a restaurant out on the pier.

The memorable reward that Ron had promised his Fujitsu team was not originally Disneyland. That suggestion came from one of the team's leads, who suggested a trip to Disneyland could be had for the price of an expensive meal in San Francisco. Ron challenged her to prove it, with the result that she came back with budget-beating prices not only for flights and admissions but dinner with Mickey Mouse. It wasn't just the 75-day march the team was celebrating but the effort that had been under way for 18 months before it as well, a project that had been an enormous challenge and had been accomplished at last.

Completing quarter-long projects may not justify more than dinner, although don't forget there are plenty of team activities you can think of that cost very little (and you may have to think of them during lean times). It may sound corny, but a team event at a bowling alley where everybody participates is one of the more bonding experiences that can still be had at little cost. You may have to coax some of the more skeptical that they'll have fun, but without exception bowling events and their ilk are always enjoyable and bring teams together.

If you're delivering product to the marketplace, you may feel the need to celebrate when the first set of bits are done. Just don't lose focus on the follow-on versions; as we noted earlier, you need to keep people motivated to deliver all versions. Celebrate, but keep taking care of business.

Retrospect

You'll want to give yourself a brief time after delivery for everyone on your team to breathe. But before everyone gets busy on their next project, you'll want to hold a retrospective or lessons-learned meeting (long

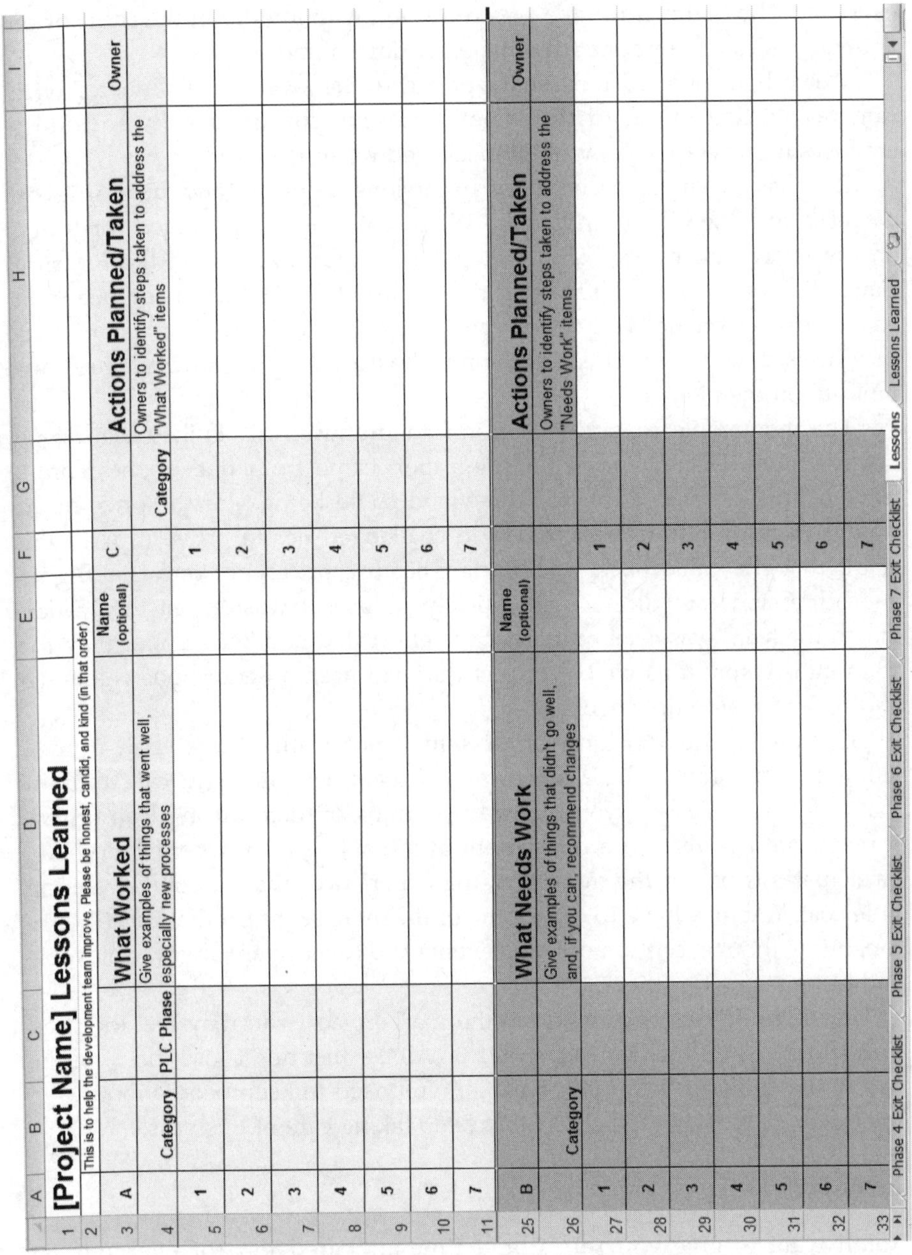

[Project Name] Lessons Learned								
This is to help the development team improve. Please be honest, candid, and kind (in that order)								
A			What Worked	Name (optional)	C		Actions Planned/Taken	Owner
	Category	PLC Phase	Give examples of things that went well, especially new processes			Category	Owners to identify steps taken to address the "What Worked" items	
1					1			
2					2			
3					3			
4					4			
5					5			
6					6			
7					7			
B			What Needs Work	Name (optional)			Actions Planned/Taken	Owner
	Category		Give examples of things that didn't go well, and, if you can, recommend changes				Owners to identify steps taken to address the "Needs Work" items	
1					1			
2					2			
3					3			
4					4			
5					5			
6					6			
7					7			

Phase 4 Exit Checklist / Phase 5 Exit Checklist / Phase 6 Exit Checklist / Phase 7 Exit Checklist / Lessons / Lessons Learned

Figure 9.4 Lessons learned for a particular phase from the project workbook

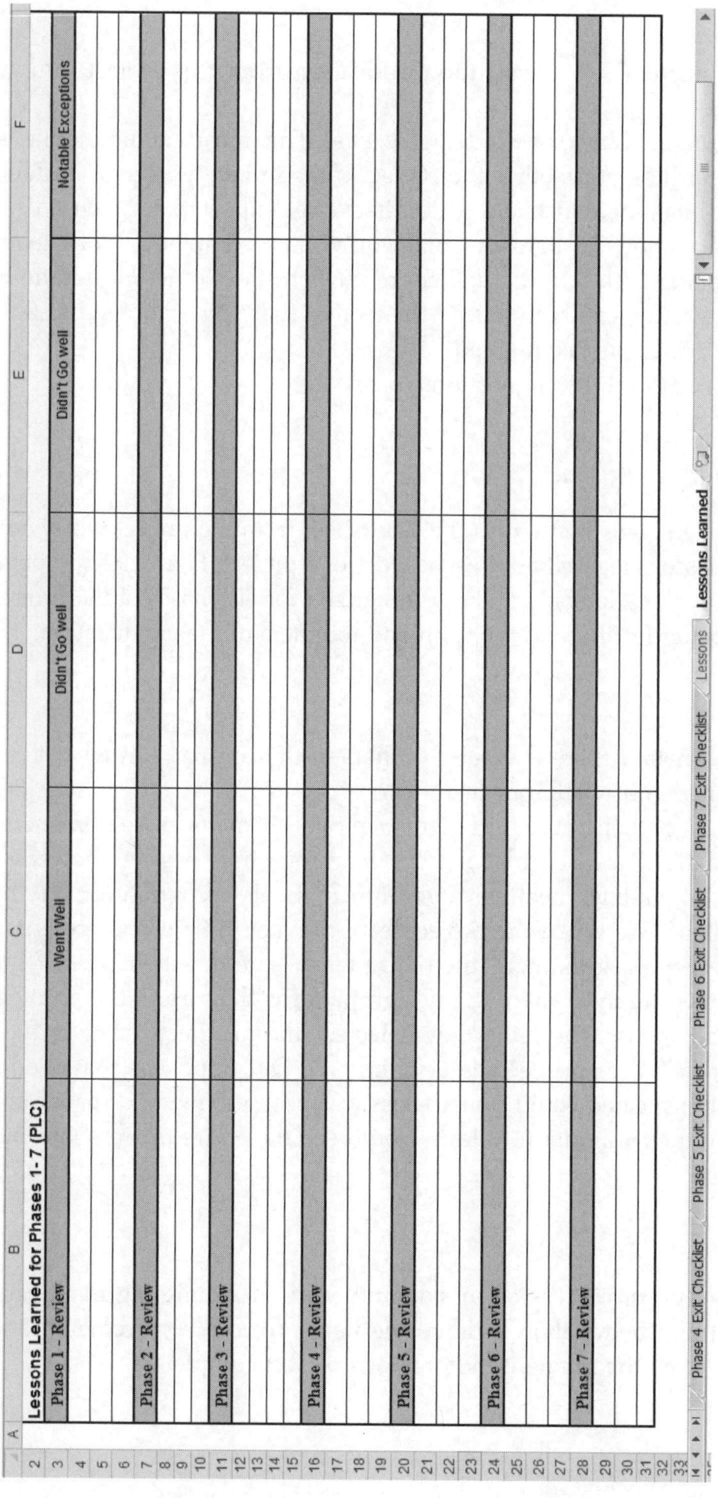

Lessons Learned for Phases 1- 7 (PLC)					
		Went Well	Didn't Go well	Didn't Go well	Notable Exceptions
Phase 1 - Review					
Phase 2 - Review					
Phase 3 - Review					
Phase 4 - Review					
Phase 5 - Review					
Phase 6 - Review					
Phase 7 - Review					

Phase 4 Exit Checklist   Phase 5 Exit Checklist   Phase 6 Exit Checklist   Phase 7 Exit Checklist   Lessons   **Lessons Learned**

Figure 9.5   Lessons learned summarizing all phases from the project workbook

called a postmortem) to reflect upon and learn from the project you've just completed.

Your goals should be to avoid defensiveness. That means avoiding blame at all cost, regardless of whether the project came in late, was over budget, shipped with bugs, or had to be scaled back. Set expectations focused on the next project—how, in light of what you've just completed, your team can imagine being better, faster, and more efficient next time. Expectations focused on the future can help relieve the feeling that you're looking to find fault with the project just completed.

The important high-level questions to ask are

- What did we do well?
- What could we do better?

Figure 9.4 (on page 398) shows the worksheet from the project workbook for recording lessons learned after each phase of a project. Figure 9.5 (on page 399) shows how these lessons can be summarized for all phases of the project to give even better feedback to the team and to others in the organization.

Share

Ask yourself whether there is value to others in the company in what your team contributed and what your team learned.

When Ron led Schwab's initiative to move all of its development to Java, he formalized the sharing of team learnings into project showcases delivered at brown-bag meetings over lunch. Every programmer in the firm was invited. "We urged the project team not just to field one presenter, but to have every programmer—the entire team—present their part of the story. We wanted them to share the design patterns they used, the application server they chose, the IDEs they selected, the architectural tiers they devised, their delivery approach, everything. . . . Our hope was that even a team more sophisticated could nonetheless learn something, and that teams just beginning their migration to Java would see the entire process laid out before them."

Refactor

The time between projects is often slack time. As programming managers, we'd like nothing better than to have the next project's requirements and kickoff ready to go the moment the previous project completes.

But in reality, it's a time when product managers are overwhelmed with work. They have their hands full with the release just completed, getting it out the door, into the hands of distributors and customers, and messaged correctly, delivering press tours, and visiting analysts.

It seems inevitable that with all that, they give short shrift to readiness for the next effort.

Not having a next project ready, though, doesn't mean your team should languish. Downtime is often a perfect time for your programmers to refactor the gnarliest areas of code, create and update documentation, and otherwise draw down the technical debt that built up as the team rushed to finish.

At Berkeley Systems, VP Jack Eastman instituted a system that assigned screen saver teams to contribute to the engine and libraries during these times. The product teams took pride in pushing the boundaries of what could be accomplished in a screen saver. To leverage their innovations most effectively, that code needed to be generalized and moved into the core common code—the engine and libraries.

The brief reassignments served not only to refresh the platform with the latest stuff but to reenervate the engine and libraries team with fresh blood straight from the front lines. It helped keep the core team from becoming an "ivory tower"—as some core teams tend to do—but rather helped them stay in touch with their customers by means of customer-team programmers joining them frequently.

Point Releases

It's easy to think you're done when you deliver software, but in most cases the key task of the post-release phase is to listen to customer feedback.

While you may have applied your best efforts at testing, you may nonetheless have missed critical bugs or performance issues that you need to quickly address and hurry out the door in a point release—the 1.1 or 1.0.1 version, depending on your version-numbering scheme.

Summary

You're managing a team of programmers for the express purpose of delivery, and that means collaborating with product managers and project managers from start to finish—from ensuring you're getting good requirements and understanding what's important and what's nonnegotiable (often iteratively), to defining what "success" and "done" will look like, planning and estimating the work, kicking it off, and driving it to completion.

Along the way, you'll want to inspire your team and make sure they understand the big picture and their role in it; ensure that risks are identified and addressed up front; help your programmers find their pace; identify the right level of design needed; implement processes to boost the likelihood of quality; check in with your team and make sure there are mechanisms for your programmers to check in with each other; run interference with distractions; test the result yourself; and celebrate when it's done (while making sure the ancillary releases get as much attention as the core release you're celebrating).

Tools

We have prepared a number of tools to assist you in getting your software defined, planned, designed, developed, and delivered. The project workbook contains many tools in the form of Excel spreadsheets that you may find useful. There are also Microsoft Word documents that provide full examples that you can easily adapt for your organization. See the Tools section, after the chapters, for the link to the Tools Web site, from which you can download the following tools:

- Developing and delivering software checklist
- Requirements definition
- Functional design
- Technical design
- Test-build plan
- Project workbook
- Check-in meeting
- Code review meeting

Tools

THIS SECTION CONTAINS A LIST OF THE TOOLS referenced in the chapters of this book and a link to where they can be downloaded from the Web.

We have developed or collected these tools and have used them to assist in managing numerous programmers, programming teams, departments, and organizations. We encourage you to personalize the tools and adapt them to help you manage your programmers more effectively.

The tools listed here are organized by the chapter with which each is associated. These tools, which consist of Microsoft Word and Excel files, may be accessed via the Web site

managingtheunmanageable.net/tools

Please follow the directions on this Web site to obtain access to the tools.

Chapter 1: Why Programmers Seem Unmanageable

There are no tools for this chapter.

Chapter 2: Understanding Programmers

Programmer Levels.xls

Job Descriptions

Client Programmers.doc

Server Programmers.doc

Database Programmers.doc

Independent Contractor Agreement.doc

Roles and Ranking System.xls

Chapter 3: Finding and Hiring Great Programmers

Job Description for Principal Software Engineer.doc

Resume-Reading Checklist.xls

Candidate-Screening Spreadsheet.xls

Interview Schedule.xls

Interview Questions.doc

Interview Summary.xls

Reference Checklist.xls

Hiring Checklist.xls

Chapter 4: Getting New Programmers Started Off Right

Hiring Follow-up Checklist.xls

Need to Meet Checklist.xls

Sample Contacts Checklist.xls

New Hire's First-Day Buddy Checklist.xls

New Hire's Career Mentor Checklist.xls

First-Day Checklist.xls

First-Day Agenda.xls

Sample Welcome Message.doc

Developer Skills Census and Inventory.xls

Skill Sets and Capabilities Dashboard.xls

Chapter 5: Becoming an Effective Programming Manager: Managing Down

Performance Management Tools

Review Templates

Self-Review Form.doc

Programming Review Form.doc

Nontechnical Review Form.doc

Performance Review Summary.xls

Performance Review Matrix Spreadsheet.xls

Quarterly Objectives Workbook.xls

Termination and Exit Checklist.xls

Managing Tools

Sample Status Report.doc

Training Log.xls

Chapter 6: Becoming an Effective Programming Manager: Managing Up, Out, and Yourself

E-mail Etiquette.doc

Meeting Planning.xls

Chapter 7: Motivating Programmers

There are no tools for this chapter.

Chapter 8: Establishing a Successful Programming Culture

Characteristics of a Successful Programming Culture.xls

Chapter 9: Managing Successful Software Delivery

Developing and Delivering Software Checklist.xls

Basic Document Templates

Requirements Definition.doc

Functional Design.doc

Technical Design.doc

Test-Build Plan.doc

Project Workbook.xls

Meeting Templates

Check-in Meeting.xls

Code Review Meeting.xls

Index